THE MILITARY

THE MILITARY

The Theory of Land Warfare as Behavioral Science

By

HARRY HOLBERT TURNEY—HIGH

*Professor Emeritus of Anthropology
University of South Carolina
Visiting Lecturer in Psychiatry and
Behavioral Science, Medical
University of South Carolina*

THE CHRISTOPHER PUBLISHING HOUSE
WEST HANOVER, MASSACHUSETTS
02339

COPYRIGHT © 1981
BY HARRY HOLBERT TURNEY-HIGH
Library of Congress Catalog Card Number 80—70839
ISBN: 0—8158—0403—2

First Edition

PRINTED IN
THE UNITED STATES OF AMERICA

In Memory of the Partisan Soldier
JOHN COLUMBUS HIGH
of
McNeil's Rangers

PREFACE

This work is a companion to *Primitive War: Its Practice and Concepts* first published in 1949 and, again, in 1971. The world was deep in war fatigue at the first publication, and many anthropological reviewers viewed this work with a dim eye. It was suggested that I thought war was good fun; that I was disloyal to the spirit of anthropology which is "dedicated to civilian values." Anthropology, as anthropology, is dedicated to no values at all. If it is, it loses its objectivity. One man said that I had "a distinguished military record," which was a surprise both to the Pentagon and myself. Well, this war fatigue is largely dissipated today.

The readers of both books will note that while the first is replete with footnotes to the original source, the second is not. This is because I want the reader to digest all the works in the brief bibliography. There are no new factual data here. They are all in the cited books. The novelty lies in the holistic approach and a devotion to general systems theory.

The present work was planned to describe truly military operations, or civilized, or political warfare. One might ask why, with so little field experience, I would dare discuss the theory of warfare. Well, I am in good company. There is no record that Vegetius ever planned a battle. Carl von Clausewitz never held responsible command. Antoine Jomini, that mentor of Robert E. Lee, never rose above the rank of staff colonel. Certainly Basil Liddell Hart is one of the great modern analysts of war, and he was retired for wounds as a captain. My only actual field command was temporarily leader of a troop of regular horse cavalry, and the first sergeant did the job. Military theorists have not been great captains of the host, and vice versa. The great leaders knew this theory, though, and practiced it.

Since 1949, the literature on war by social scientists has become voluminous. The man-related primates have been revealed as aggressive and violent. Early man has been described as a killer. Aggression and violence, and murder, too, are not warfare. They are not the basis for either submilitary combat, or primitive war, or modern operations. Adam Smith said that the Renaissance invention of gunpowder so revolutionized warfare that it is useless to study what went before. Max Weber corrected this when he said that "the kind of weapon has been the result, not the cause of discipline." A decade after the publication of *Primitive War*, Samuel Huntington's able *The Soldier and the State* stimulated academics into studying war. He said that "modern war" did not really begin until the Industrial Revolution was completed, and that it is profitless to study anything before. Bernard Brodie moved the critical date back to Bonaparte. David Rapoport quotes him as saying that "we have little learned from the purely military strategy of the pre-Napoleonic wars." Morris Janowitz said that modern war really started after World War I. These people, and others, though social scientists, have been obsessed with the weaponry, and are therefore technological determinists.

True war began with the discovery of the principles of tactics which the able commander uses *in toto* in each engagement. It is true that the timorous and unimaginative leaders of World War I regressed in the direction of minor tactics. They were afraid of the new weapons, and failed dismally. The battle of Cannae was no confrontation of two armed mobs. Hannibal won in true war by a tactical foolsmate so old that it is described in the *Book of Judges* and so new that Hindenburg defeated the Russians by it at the Mazurian Lakes. Hannibal had no machine guns. Hindenburg did. Both commanders won by the use of tactical principles, not weapons. General J. F. C. Fuller and Captain Basil Liddell Hart merely rediscovered the art and science of warfare, and as the leaders in World War II had been compelled to read them, the second world war was better fought than the first one. Warfare is a matter of social organization. Warfare *is* social organization. While trying to protect his own, the prudent commander will try to strike and destroy the nerve center of his opposition, the locus of his social organization, his headquarters. This done, all else will fall, whatever the weaponry may be, and whatever the once adequate discipline of his subordinate commands. This happened to Napoleon three times, first in the Near East, then in Russia, then at Waterloo. The great man abandoned his troops in each case, and fatal debacles overtook them all.

Peace is everywhere the preferred norm among all peoples. It needs never to justify itself. War always must. For this reason, there will be no moral judgment on war here. Anthropology must describe the whole of a culture, and warfare is everywhere a vital part of it.

This does not mean that a social scientist must abstain from moral judgments on war. This is a matter of his opinion and the primary groups to which he belongs. Nor does it mean that he may not write about it. It does mean, however, that he ought not sign such a work as a professor of social science. War exists, and has since the Upper Paleolithic, and is with us now. It is an integral part of any people's culture, and should be so described. It must be better understood, especially by those who are against it. How can they, in strict professional neutrality, be against that which they do not comprehend? This book is a modest effort to help this understanding.

Many scholars have contributed inestimable aid, and the following must be mentioned by name. Of the civilians, Cecil Morgan, Dean Emeritus of the Law School of Tulane University, exercised his right as a childhood friend to throw out whole chapters. Dr. Benjamin Riggs, Professor of Psychiatry in the Medical University of South Carolina, gently guided me away from some errors. Dr. Donald Sutherland and Lance Lufkin of the Department of Anthropology, University of South Carolina, have been of inestimable help in correcting the manuscript. Dr. John Greenway, late of the Department of Anthropology, University of Colorado, watched for errors with a keen eye. Of the retired soldiers, Major General Wendell J. Coats has tried to modernize my tactical thinking. Major General Ewart G. Plank, one of the founders of modern logistic practice, has been a patient reader.

And so, in the ringing words of Pontius Pilate, (John XIX 23), quoted in the original Greek because it is more incisive, Ὅ γέγραφα γέγραφα.

HHTH

CONTENTS

Preface 7

PART I. BASIC CONSIDERATIONS

Introduction 15
1. Fundamentals of Behavioral Science 17
2. Submilitary Combat 25
3. The Art and Science of Warfare 46
4. Civil Government as the Warrior 73
5. Military Practice and Social Structure 92

PART II. THE MATERIAL CULTURE OF WARFARE

Introduction 127
6. Human Permeability 129
7. Missile Fire 147
8. Interposition 168
9. Energy Use and Supply 192

PART III. MILITARY PRACTITIONERS

Introduction 223
10. The Soldier 225
11. The Captains of the Host 250
12. The Mercenaries 272
13. The Pretorians 291

EPILOGUE

14. Civilians and Noncombatants 313
    Selected Bibliography 325
    Index 331

PART I
BASIC CONSIDERATIONS

INTRODUCTION TO BASIC CONSIDERATIONS

Each reader has benefited by war. Everyone has likewise been its victim. Now who wants to call quits? Are there more than two categories: those who are surfeited with gain at the expense of others, and those who have been so beaten that they bow their heads and cry, "No more! We have been hurt more than we can bear." Who wishes to debate the issue? Who wants to challenge the Mosaic stricture that the sins of the fathers shall be visited upon the children of the third and fourth generation? The interesting point is that the profits of sin also descend unto generations more than the Decalogue's fourth, and no one is more virtuous than those who are eating the wheat tilled on land fertilized by the blood of the predecessors.

Of Caucasoid American virtue, recall that this was all Indian land once, and while it is doubtful that genocide was often planned, the extermination could have been no more effective had it been plotted. And the Indians cry "Shame" even to this day. They no longer remember nor care that before the Mongoloid population explosion, the Americas were inhabited by other peoples whom they destroyed. The predominantly Anglo-Saxons who did this thing to the Indians had once suffered a similar experience. The Normans landed in 1066, forged the serf's collar around the Saxon neck, and left these Teutons crying in all their subsequent beer mugs. It was convenient for them to forget that but a few centuries before they had descended into Gallo-Roman Britain like the wolf on the fold, destroying one of the sweetest civilizations man ever knew. The universally admired Greeks were not the original inhabitants of Hellas. They invaded the peninsula and islands without invitation, blotting out the surviving Minoans of Crete, the Mycenaean, Helladic, Cycladic and other cultures, exterminating the inhabitants or enslaving them into helots. And they paid! Romans, Crusaders, and eventually the Turks avenged the helots. We have likewise heard a century's lamentation from the French, but if they are French, they are Franks, and

Frankenland is in Germany, not Roman Gaul. Now how far back do you wish to pursue the record, and where?

We mentioned Indians, which suggests the current tears of minority groups, whatever that term means. We will not discuss the Jews. Their own scriptures boast of dashing the heads of children against the wall in Palestine, which means Philistia. As for their current Moslem Arab antagonists, no one asked these people into the Eastern Empire to begin the destruction of one of mankind's few hopes for widespread peace. The splendid Umaiyad mosque in Damascus was built on the ruins of a Christian cathedral, the supposed burial place of St. John the Baptist. Do the Arabs remember that the Nile ran red from the binding of the books of the great library of Alexandria? Colonel Sadat would not have ordered the destruction of the library, but General Amru did.

Yes, we mentioned the so-called Indians. Almost every population when found by Europeans had been invaders and exterminators. You of Algonkian speech did not build the mounds of Ohio, Wisconsin, and other parts of the United States, but you undoubtedly helped destroy those who did. And you warriors of the Plains who vocally hate Custer's name, did you not evict most of the Shoshoneans, and not at a very early date? As for the presently wrathful Navaho, why are the great pueblos from Colorado's Mesa Verde southward unpopulated? Coming like a blight from Canada, your fathers found it easier to kill and steal from the growers of corn than to grow grain. The theft was accomplished by primitive war, but it was rather thorough.

As for other current tears, recall the sub-Saharan Africa was once populated by Stone Age peoples of Soan and Stillbay cultures. There was a small enclave of Negroes who had developed an independent Neolithic somewhere around modern Togoland. By means we need not recount here, the tropical rain belt crops penetrated into Africa from Indonesia, and the Negro farmers swarmed into the now tillable rain forest, in the process all but exterminating the inhabitants. Of course, there are a few wretched pygmies left alive, but not many. Acquiring the arts of iron metallurgy, some moved east, and somehow acquired cattle from India, and again drove south, killing off the bushmen en route. Indeed, the Bantu-speaking folk were finishing this job in the Kalahari Desert when the British colonials made them stop. And now you lift up your wrists so that the world can see the scars of the slave shackles, and your cry of "Shame, shame" rings around the earth. You are looking for roots? Look way back!

But why continue this unlovely story? No people have come through history and prehistory with blood-free hands. Indeed, let us call quits, if we can and dare. First, though, we had better know the nature of the thing we are quitting. Such is the theme of this book.

Chapter 1

FUNDAMENTALS OF BEHAVIORAL SCIENCE

A Review

In pursuing the theme of this book, it might not be amiss to review some of the basic concepts of behavioral science. This is not to imply that the reader is not aware of the principles of the social sciences. It does mean that the probabilities are of unfamiliarity with the author's holistic and systems approach which carry through this book. Many familiar terms will be redefined and used in a manner different from the reader's previous understanding. They will be referred to time and again.[1]

We are going to speak of systems. Everything, everything at all pertinent to this discussion operates as a whole. Therefore, let us begin outward from space inward to ourselves for, farfetched as it might seem, gravity does especially control military systems, from the fatigue of a march to the flight of a bullet.

Consider that turbulence, chaos, and absolute lack of order is characteristic of outer, outer space. The conquest of such disorder is system. System exists in the cosmos. There is the vast spiral galaxy called the Milky Way, and there are other more distant ones. Coming closer to home, there is the solar system, a number of planets organized around a star called the sun. The force which organizes these heavenly bodies is gravitation, the attraction they have for each other. So far as the local situation is concerned, this is called gravity. All human action is the expenditure of energy against the force of gravity, and thinking is no exception. The average weight of human beings and the precise amount of gravity here has made us what we are. So far as is known, these exist only here, so the possibilities of men like us living elsewhere is extremely doubtful.

Each human being, each animal, too, is a system, a collection of subsystems—skeletal, muscular, circulatory, respiratory, digestive, urinary, endocrine, reproductive—all working in cooperation. They are not collections of separate parts. They are one whole, and the approach to wholes was called holism by the philosopher General Jan Christian Smuts. This holistic view is the one of this book, for it is the only tolerable one.

The force which maintains system in a human body was called homeostasis by physiologist William Cannon is his *The Wisdom of the Body*. Whether homeostasis is good or poor is not in point. If it ceases to exist, the organism is dead or dying. A man who is sick in one subsystem is more or less ill all over, no matter where it hurts most. Change is, of course, inevitable, and minor events will occur, but in fortunate cases, homeostasis takes over and automatically makes the adjustment. Taking an example from that physiology from which the concept was developed, if on a bright August afternoon, a man decides to go to the moving pictures. He arrives after the performance has begun, and in the relative darkness, he stumbles over other people's feet, trying to find a seat. Homeostasis then widens the apertures of his eyes so that in a brief time, he can recognize friends several rows away. Leaving the theater at the end, he goes again into the brilliant afternoon. He is almost blinded by the light, but automatically and homeostatically, the correction is made so that he can see again.

Homeostasis is not confined to physiology, but extends to all human relations. It is often called equilibrium in the behavioral sciences: equilibrium of the body, of the personality, of the group. Equilibrium is a static condition, maintained by homeostasis, which is active and dynamic. Lack of acceptable equilibrium is the chief cause of war.

Men do not live alone, nor have they since the extended family appeared in lower primate times. When men from time to time seek solitude, they still wear clothes and use tools which were made in factories, in secondary groups. These social systems are kept in good or bad order by homeostatic systems maintenance techniques—manners, morals, laws and administrative devices—so that minor changes are corrected. Be this stable orderliness—strong or weak, intense or diffuse—it exists or the social system will be destroyed. Systems are always beset by crisis. Now a crisis is a serious situation for which no ready-made answer exists, and for which one must be found or the system will cease to exist in its present form. It is doubtful if a social system will continue as it was after passing through a serious crisis, even if a satisfactory solution has been found.

War is a state of mind and a legal condition. The violent means of waging war is called warfare. It may be "cold" where no direct military action takes place, or it may be "hot" when they do. The essence of war and warfare is to introduce turbulence and crisis into another social system while attempting to prevent a lack of equilibrium within the we-group. This is rather easily done in small systems practicing primitive war, but in long, violent modern wars, the victorious systems cannot remain as they had been before. New methods of overcoming crisis have been found, and they rarely just go away in peacetime.

Men use their nervous systems and related organs to influence each other's behavior. If this does not alter the nervous systems of one or the other, it is called interaction. The simple "good morning" greeting to a passing acquaintance is of this type. If the personalities of one or the other is altered, it is called transaction. Thus, in television advertising, the originators of the program attempt to alter our behavior by transaction, while remaining themselves immune. Groups and social systems are formed, maintained, and broken up by transaction.

Interaction/transaction is called primary if performed with the simple human sense organs, that is, in face-to-face situations. These form and maintain primary groups or systems. If, by contrast, there is the intervention of a third party or a material device, such as the printed page or an electronic invention, it is called secondary interaction/transaction. Our day is characterized by an increase of secondary groups, and perhaps a decline in primary relations. There may be a primary group of bureaucrats at this moment, men whose names we do not know, thinking up a plan which will very much transact our behavior. A squad, then, is a primary group, and a division is a secondary one.

In the classification of traits of culture, Ralph Linton proposed that tools, techniques, and ideas be separated into universals, specialties, and alternatives. A universal is something which every functioning member of a social system understands and can use. The Eskimo, for example, were very fine craftsmen, and made some rather fine tools. Nevertheless, every adult member of the social system understood each one of them. They were all engaged in the same economic pursuits of hunting and fishing. Such universals bind a society together. A century ago there were more universals in our society than there are now. A specialty, though, is the property of certain craftsmen which is not shared throughout. At the siege of Yorktown, soldiers were either riflemen-musketeers and artillerymen, with some uncommitted cavalry in the background. No one today could expect an engineer to operate a tank. An aviator is by no means a mortarman. Specialties are partly disruptive, but ordinarily not seriously so. The disruption comes with alternatives, of different ways to accomplish the same end, and today they very much compete with each other. Alternatives prevent a social system from being as well-knit, as integrated as the Eskimo who had only universals. A man may choose among the competing alternatives or do without them all.

Culture tends to grow and expand. Men seem unwilling to let things be, which brings us to another principle to explain, the Law of Diminishing Returns. This was originally proposed by David Ricardo with respect to agricultural land use, but it now seems to have universal application in the ways of men. Thus, a farmer with a set, given amount of land will apply one unit of labor and one of fertilizer, or capital, to it one year. According to the idea that if one is good, two are better, he will apply two units each of labor and fertilizer next time, and get even more return. Continuing this, he will come to a point where his return is greater, but not in the same proportion as before. He has reached the point of diminishing return, which he may or may not increase until the return will just meet the costs of the additional units. He will stop there, if he is wise. The principle is just as true for urban land use. The capitalist may add stories to a building and prosper. The point is reached where the return does not pay. The Empire State Building in New York City passed far beyond the point of diminishing returns.

The principle needs restating. Now every invention has manifest functions and latent dysfunctions, obviously good qualities and hidden bad ones. When one increases the size and complexity of an instrument, seeking return in manifest functions, he will inevitably increase the latent dysfunctions as well. There were few dysfunctions in the Magdalenian harpoon, just the time and skill needed to fashion it. By contrast, the great ocean liners, the *Queen Mary* and *Queen Elizabeth*, were so increased in size and function that they could not pay their way even with full cargos and passenger lists. Of course, they were designed as troop carriers, each carrying a full division with service troops and equipment to put Americans in Europe to aid the British who built them. The point of diminishing returns was reached in the British battleship *Royal Lion*, but the Americans continued with the greater *Missouri*. She was retired after World War II, but was refurbished and sent as a great gun ship in the Viet Nam incident. She was returned and put in mothballs before that war was over. But return to the main thrust of the argument.

There has been so much research in primatology and the knowledge of almost-man as to amount to an informational explosion. Ordinarily, one would devote an entire chapter to these considerations, but it would become obsolete very soon. Therefore, this will be given the briefest exposition.

And it came to pass that better than a million and a half years ago, a reasonably upright primate made what could reasonably be called a tool. This must be noted, for everything we call human is a function of the upright posture. Humanity must be emphasized, for only arthropods and vertebrates fight as groups, and not many of them do. Most animals fight and kill as individuals, not as groups. The ex-legs and now arms are freed for killing and loving; the ex-paws and now hands can now be devoted to discovering the environment, and eventually to manipulate it. Even before the descent from the trees, the eyes had moved forward, permitting stereoscopic vision and color sense, necessary for a being swinging from tree to tree. Distance must be judged. There must be knowledge whether yonder is a safe branch or one with a brilliantly colored python on it.

Thus, the creature is now on the ground, with the force of gravity keeping him there. Just so much gravity against which his heart must pump blood. Standing upright, he acquired distant vision. The sense of smell was decreased, as the expanding fore-skull crushed the olfactory organs. The human brain was drenched with new information, and it rose to the occasion. There seems to be a culture potential, or a weak power of symbolization, in the whole vertebrate stem, but it was nothing like this. Now a symbol is anything, or anybody, which evokes similar conditioned responses in a group. Certain symbols are selected out to become emblems, things taken to represent a group, but we get ahead of the story by millions of years.

These creatures, then, were relatively weak and defenseless hominids, safe only when operating as groups. Physiologically, they were more closely akin to the baboons, who are gigantic monkeys, rather than to apes. A lone baboon may safely be attacked, but it takes a brave cougar to go for a band of these large, tailed, cooperating monkeys. The genetically related group, then, the extended family, is older than man as man. It must be noted that these creatures were carnivores, or rather, omnivores. Man and the tarsier are the only surviving carnivorous primates, and the latter is so primitive that it takes an expert to classify these prosimia as primates. For thousands and thousands of years, these men and almost-men lived as hunters. Even today, a modern man must have a certain amount of proteins of animal origin in his diet, or he will sicken. Tasty as vegetables are, humans can live without them. The Eskimo proved that, getting the vitamins needed by eating a certain amount of raw flesh. The herbivorous apes will, of course, eat insects and fledgling birds, but this is only snacking. They do not need animal proteins to survive.

Now it took no great change from animal-hunting to man-hunting, the victimization of members of the out-group as game. Both the Pekin type and the Krapina form of Neanderthals split the leg bones of fellow human beings, ostensibly to obtain the marrow, which is generally considered evidence of cannibalism. It was this man-hunting which was the basis of primitive war, or submilitary combat.

Scott believes that the major cause for destructive fighting is social disorganization among such groups.[2] He points out that there is a decade of aggressive violence among adolescent human males between the period when the youths leave the old nuclear family and the time that they form new ones. This violence does not originate warfare directly, but it can be organized by older men, who constitute the leaders. By use of social pressures, this youthful violence can be, indeed must be, transferred from the in-group to the out-group. This can be a highly ritualized and stylized draining of internal hostility from the in-group and directing it to the outsiders. The coup-counting fights of the Plains Indians was of this nature.

Returning to the upright primate, the great visual brain led to the fabrication of tools. According to Iberall's hypothesis, this produced a greater ability for abstract thought.[3] It enabled man to conceptualize time, for he is a time-binding animal. Tools to be used in the hunt must be made ahead of the occasion. They permit an expansion of the developing comprehension beyond the subject-self and object-other towards an artifact, a third concept, which is neither self nor other. A tool is an intermediary. It is a vehicle of social transaction. A weapon is nothing else. (Specialized man-killing tools, or weapons, did not appear until the Neolithic, barring the arrows of the Mesolithic. These latter were hunting tools, but they could kill a man. So can a Boy Scout hatchet, but it was made for another purpose.)

A tool or weapon is an abstraction out of the total reality, and with this power of abstract thought came the idea of the fellow-man as an abstraction. This fellow-human was an abstraction who could be killed without compunction. Although it is different in our day, men in the old in-group were not slain without guilt. This was the theme of the Greek tragedy. Oedipus unknowingly slew his father and cohabited with his unrecognized mother, and had to scratch out his eyes and become a wanderer for his guilt.

Iberall points out that there is no evidence of human group aggression earlier than 40,000 years ago. There was culture of a kind before this, of course, with the first consistently formed artifacts, but he decides that there was little culture in the modern sense before that. He suggests that human speech appeared at the same time. "That is, we suggest that high speed human speech, rich in expressiveness, did not exist in any hominid up to and including Neanderthal man and could not have appeared until a time near the end of the Neanderthalers or the beginning of Cro-Magnon man." (p. 452)

He points out that right- and left-handed tools existed in equal number before Upper Palaeolithic times, in other words, until the Cro-Magnon race appeared on the scene of Europe, and that the predominance of right-handed tools has occurred since Neolithic, or New Stone Age times. Dominant-handedness has been thought to be related to the dyssymmetry of speech centers in the brain. Then, the evidence that Neanderthal man had a supralaryngeal pharynx, like that of chimpanzees and the human newborn, which forbade the pronouncing of the phoneme, the basic sound production required for completely human speech. "There is practically no supralaryngeal portion of the pharynx present in the direct airway out from the larynx when the soft palate shuts off the nasal cavity in the chimpanzee, Neanderthal, and the newborn man."[4]

Neanderthal man completely disappeared from Europe with the close of mid-Palaeolithic, or Mousterian times, and was completely replaced by Cro-Magnon man practicing an Aurignacian-Perigordian culture. A new dimension has been added to this abrupt disappearance. The Neanderthal Mousterian points and scapers, though well made, were tools, not weapons. There is no evidence that they were hafted on poles to form spears. The succeeding Cro-Magnon form had beautifully made javelins and dart throwers, enabling him to stand off and pick off the clumsy Neanderthalers as game. Added to this was modern language, which gave them greater numbers and cohesiveness in the combat group. There could be murder but no war, even primitive war, without the communication provided by language.

Iberall says that modern man has an unstable, or only a marginally-stable brain. This enabled him to have a vast number of ways of behavior open to him, from highly artistic productions to warfare, and the end is not in sight. These include more and more specialties and alternatives, making essentially for greater and greater social disorganization. It is this which produces war.

The genocide of the Neanderthalers, the sneaking Melanesian head-hunting, the outright cannibalism just recently put down, and the type of bison surround, practiced by Crazy Horse on Custer, are treating the enemy as game. It is man-hunting, and it produces only primitive war, or submilitary combat. The appearance of true war requires the use of all the principles of combat in every engagement, sometimes combined in this way, or in that. Tactics are mankind's first social science, and the tactical principles are just that, derived from the stern laboratory of warfare. Tactics were the first social science to enunciate its basic principles which are true without regard for time and place, and they do not change. The manuals of the powers may use a different wording and arrangement. The United States says "surprise," and the Soviet Union says "deception," but they are the same thing. These principles will be discussed in detail later.

The principles are so old that they have been called Alexandrian, after the great Macedonian, but other military peoples have used them. Genghis Khan used them, but that might have been diffusion. The warlike North Pacific Coast fighters used them, and this could not have been. It is thought that both the Iroquois League and the Natchez Empire used them. These principles seem like truisms. This is the wisdom of hindsight, for most of the principles of social science so seem. Now submilitary combat, or primitive war, used a few which were derived from animal hunting. Primitive war remained primitive because it did not use them all.

FOOTNOTES AND REFERENCES

[1] Harry Holbert Turney-High, *Man and System: Foundations for the Study of Human Relations*, New York, Appleton-Century-Crofts, 1968, Part I.

[2] L. Scott, "Biological Basis of Human Warfare: An Interdisciplinary Problem," in *Interdisciplinary Relationships in the Social Sciences*, M. Sherif and C. Sherif, eds., Chicago, Aldine, 1969.

[3] A. S. Iberall, "A Proposed Neurophysiological Basis for War," in *Annals of Biomedical Engineering*, 1, 1973, p. 448. Permission of the author and The Academic Press.

[4] P. Lieberman, E. Crelin, and D. Klatt, "Phonetic Ability and Related Anatomy of the Newborn and Adult Human, Neanderthal Man, and the Chimpanzee," *American Anthropologist* 74, Menasha, 1972, p. 287.

Chapter 2

SUBMILITARY COMBAT

Primitive War and the Sociological Revolution

This chapter deals with fighting among such warriors as the Plains Indians with feathers in their hair, of Jibaro headhunters creeping through the Amazon rain forest, and Australian aborigines forming what could have been called battle lines, but contenting themselves with screaming insults and boasts, and fleeing at the sight of the least blood. It is not meant to entertain with gory ethnological curios. Any military theorist, and hence adviser to leaders in the state and field, must know something about the cultural ancestor of that true war we have enjoyed and suffered for some five millenia of our tradition. Both types of leaders must appreciate the facts and principles herein contained, for the present day confrontationists, saboteurs, terrorists, and guerrillas are primitive warriors in every sense save motivation. Generals Amherst, Braddock, and Montcalm had to discover this in the French and Indian wars that which General Washington already knew. General Grant wondered if he ever could subdue the Shenandoah Valley, confronted as he was by primitive warrior Mosby. The French and Americans took refresher instruction in Southeast Asia, while the British army had to repeat the course in North Ireland.

Submilitary combat, or the fighting of most but not all societies without writing is defective in some of the requirements for truly military operations. Strategy was for the most part beyond such men. Their logistic or supply provisions were practically nonexistent, while their field operations were defective in one or many requirements of truly tactical warfare. Use of the alternative term of primitive war is not resorting to the many weaknesses of the books of the past, volumes on "primitive religion" which was no such thing, on "primitive marriage and the family," practices which were often far more complicated than our own, and so on, and so on, for primitive war is both a cultural reality and a definable concept. It is the collectively approved violence by an in-group (the "we" people), against an out-group (those other creatures), which does not utilize all the tactical principles in each engagement. Its goals are derived from the emotional life of the individuals or small groups, and are rarely economic, as are those of states. It is warfare below the military horizon. Much of the criticism of former works using the primitive adjective was that they assumed that the cultural behavior patterns markedly different from our own solutions to problems of social organization must reflect the ways of human infancy. This simply was not true. By contrast, the simpler forms of primitive war can hardly be anything else. These combat systems will not be spelled out in detail here, as they are readily available.

Let us take up the thread of the previous chapter in order to understand the hypothesis of this one. Man may, and whenever possible does, mix his meat with vegetable food. His health will be impaired, though, if he confines himself to a plant diet, as do most of his primate kin. Great meteorological processes forced his ancestors to become carnivores or die. The human then became the hunter, a pot hunter and no sportsman, and was for millenia nothing else. He survived the fourth glaciation of the Pleistocene in Europe and Asia where little but meat was available to him, and got his greatest evolutionary start in life in such arctic cold that the reindeer wandered as far south as Gibraltar. Food of vegetable origin was in scant supply except in the favored mid-latitudes. The great Pleistocene animals could paw through the snow. They could eat lichens which humans could not, but men could eat flesh. There was plankton in the water which tiny fish could eat, and larger fish ate them to become the food for the great fish which men in the closing epochs of the European Old Stone Age could harpoon.

While the term "primitive war" includes many forms of combat, some approaching the civilized format, one thread runs through them all. This is the treatment of the enemy as a game animal, as something not quite human. The present point is not hard to see. The civilized soldier is capable of treating his enemy like another human being. The primitive warrior, the able ones certainly, is as lacking in sympathy and mercy as the hunter who can bring himself to slit the throat of a wounded doe. The revivers of primitive war— terrorists and guerrillas—have the same merciless attitudes towards those who do not agree with them.

The hypothesis of this chapter is that submilitary combat, or primitive war, is a derivative of animal hunting, and is the progenitor and training ground for true, or political war. This, like any other hypothesis, is debatable, but the negative is invited to familiarize itself with the field material before entering the argument. The *sine qua non* relationship between the rise of civil government and true war is not entirely understood, but some of the possible reasons will be sketched later. The relationship between the twin rise of literacy and civil government might be a little more apparent.

The correlation between literacy and some members of a society and the practice of true, or completely tactical, or political war and the state is a fairly close one, but it is not absolute. The AmaZulu kingdom of South Africa fought true war, to the distress of civilized Boers and British, as well as other black Africans, and these Bantu-speakers were nonliterate. Both the Iroquois League and the divine monarchy of the Natchez fought as soldiers and not warriors, and none of their great men could read. Much of the time the sacred states of Polynesia fought wars properly so-called, and read and write they could not. While the present use of the term primitive war comes very close to being accurate, referring as it does to the simpler phases of the human cultural record, what it really indicates is the combat of societies based on kinship rather than those organized as civil states, which by definition cut across more than one kinship.

The chapter subtitle said that a sociological revolution is to be discussed, and so it is, the first of such in both time and importance. This one is indeed paramount to the thesis of this book, for submilitary combat most likely grew out of it. We will speak here mostly of the kinship, but recall that all social organizations have an overt or covert aggressive-defensive potential for violence, and the "blood relationship" is no exception. Indeed, at the opening of this century, either by law or custom, the adult male members of an American family exercised a right to defend the related group and its property by force of arms instead of calling for the police.

The preceding chapter revealed that cohesive groups were already in existence before man became man. Stable families were known to the upper primates, including the human, and were indeed extended to include more than one generation. Observed groups of related primates are known to be rudimentary offensive and defensive bands, including some adopted members, aggregates produced by sex, and forged into a cohesiveness and mutual dependence by a postnatally conditionable frontal area of the brain. Put even a rudimentary weapon in the hands of the somewhat upright members of the order, and one sees grandparents of this entire discussion.

Grandparents do not carry the active burden of the social task, however, even if it had been better if they had. Achieving full humanity was not without a price, and the final payment is not yet in sight. Yet peace and harmony, equilibrium and cooperation had to be achieved within the related group if a more than infrahuman conquest of the environment was to take place, and it was. The higher primates adapt to their surroundings. Man goes far towards creating the millieu in which he operates. His groups had to become more efficient as hunting and protective organizations, and this was first accomplished by the greatest sociological revolution of them all. Of course, all crossing of social and technological thresholds are revolutions, but the one of which we now speak was the first, and all subsequent ones have depended on it. This is the invention of the twin concepts of kin and community which changed the course of all else on this planet.

While the kinship is based essentially on sex, and the simplest communities might also be, they are not only universals but are the exclusive possession of humanity. The structured family is not a human monopoly, but institutional marriage is. The infrahuman family is bio-psychological, but marriage and the kinship are artificialities. Having no institutions, the apes can have no communities by definition, and Clarence Carpenter reports that they do not. The results of this sociological revolution have been tremendous. Thus, the differences between the sociology of the most talented apes and the organization of the simplest humans is enormous. The infrahuman group equilibria are physiological, while ours is sociological. The action of the primate groups of related individuals is limited by the organism, while culture relieves the weakness of the hominid body, and in doing so, extends the size and power of the group. Subhuman primates fight, but always in the same way. Man, by this basic and subsequent social and technological revolution, has developed so many sophisticated weapons, so many complicated systems of military organization, and battle plans, and maneuvers of such complexity that today no one mind can grasp it all. Having developed beyond the comprehension of the most able general officer, civilized man has invented complex general and special staffs to help him in this, and they have been only partially successful. There would be no defeats otherwise. We get ahead of ourselves, though for we must return to sexual reproduction which is at the root of primitive war just as surely the progenitor of that civilized war which requires more staff officials and supply elements than soldiers in the line.

Sexual reproduction is the immediate source of primate aggressive-defensive groups, but from very, very early in the human experience, sex has been bent and molded to fit the requirements of economics, technology, religion, politics, and all the other expediencies of collective living. Everything humanly sociological takes precedence over sexual reproduction, for the culture-bearing species realizes that it can trust that somehow, somewhere, and in some manner, the adult male and female will get together and according to the local formalities, reproduce the next generation. The requirements of culture, of economics and politics are too fragile to trust to any urge with an instinctive base. Instead of being the essence of society, as it is with the primate relationship, mating became the whipping boy of all else, with some wonderful and fearful results. Bernard Willard Aginsky (*Kinship Systems and Forms of Marriage*) barely listed the forms of marriage known to his research, while he provided only the sketchiest description thereof, this required a fair-sized monograph. Later, George Peter Murdock (*Social Structure*) hardly more than summarized all these kinship systems together with their functions, and this effort produced a fairly large book.

So far as we can see from this distance in time, all this proliferation originated in the invention of the incest tabu. While what is and what is not an incestuous relation varies from culture to culture, nevertheless the sexual avoidance of certain related adults is a culture universal, and while clandestine in its very nature, discovered violation is universally punished. If the human family was to become a training institution, an economic and defensive one wherein some had to give and others to obey orders, the mating of parents with offspring was unthinkable. A mother could not correct a daughter who was co-mate with the husband, nor could the father's authority be effective over a son who is the sexual rival either for the mother or sisters. Father and the brothers had to become hunting and fighting teammates, for the fragility of the family's triumph over or survival in the natural, faunal, and human environment was too great to risk with internecine rivalry. No one understands all the reasons for the incest tabu, but it is certain that all Oedipal tendencies had to be suppressed. This family, and those actually or ceremonially akin to it, had to stand before a world not always friendly. The family may be a biological unit, but marriage is a sociological one, and among other things, it produced a fighting unit, with rules.

The way humanity has twisted the married family into manifold forms has been indicated, but the basic one, the nuclear family, that of the biological parents and offspring, always shines through. There may be rather excessive polygyny, but the more one looks at multiple wives and their children, the more they appear to be constellations of nuclear families with a common husband-father. We inherited the nuclear family from our primate past, of course, but humans have adorned it with many non-sexual functions of which the other nailed forms are incapable. At the opening of this century before urban culture, subculture, or contraculture began eroding it, the nuclear family was the chief source of economic production, education, religious observance, recreation, and status acquisition. It was also the chief source of protection for its members, and if the civil state has taken away the power of the father and older brothers to defend the weaker members, the government really did not seek this role. It fell to it by default.

Extend this nuclear family to the adult children of brothers and sisters, and one has a hunting and fighting unit already organized, accustomed to each other's transactional rates, and able to deliver action. Now every leader of soldiers from corporal to general knows, or should know, that the basic fighting unit is a familial surrogate. The squad and the company are or should be family substitutes of father (the Old Man), older brother (Top Kick), and siblings standing shoulder to shoulder against a hostile world. While this unit is the result of post-enlistment conditioning, it cannot work except as a family of men who know each other intimately, are aware of each other's strengths and weaknesses, and trust each other in offense and defense, with the fraternal necessity of self-sacrifice if need be. The terrible primariness of military transaction, of familistic mutual support, of mutual predictability is older than modern war, is indeed perhaps more ancient than humanity strictly so-called. Why else do we enforce symbiosis on recruits? Why else do they live in the most intimate fashion except to build up this consciousness of kind on which successful combat depends? This writer is heartily in favor of chiefs of state, cabinet secretaries, and generals reading books, but these texts should be of the right kind. The intensity of primary transaction of a fighting unit sets limits to enforced experimentation of mingling persons who rightly or wrongly think of themselves as unlike.

The multiplicity of kinship forms and their designation are not pertinent to the subject of primitive war, but some are. One should, for example, understand the difference between consanguineal and affinal kinsmen. The first term, as the name indicates, refers to a person of genetic relationship, while the second one indicates a sociological relative who is not "blood" kin. Thus, one's father's sister is a consanguineal relative, and is called "aunt." One's father's brother is a consanguineal uncle, but his wife is an affinal aunt. In the bilateral kin count, the offspring of these two pairs are consanguineal first cousins, and could provide one with a squad-sized group of male defenders. This suggests that the bilateral family, one which counts both sides of the relationship, can contain a large number of persons on whom a man might be able to rely in times of violent trouble. No one denies that the "Hatfields and McCoys were brave mountain boys," and adept practitioners of that type of primitive war called the Appalachian blood feud. There are those who would deem such fighting kinsmen as clans, but this is a dubious label in this case. They were bilateral extended families. The clan is a unilateral kin count, either maternal or paternal, and not on both sides bilaterally as we do.

No one should have trouble in seeing that the clan, descended from some mythical, actual, and sometimes supernatural ancestor, would contain more persons bound to help than the bilateral family which does not have a specific name. Thus, without looking it up, how many readers can remember the maiden names of their great-grandmothers, or the names of all these women's children? The annual gathering of the Scots clans at Grandfather Mountain, North Carolina, is good fun, but clanship is not always amusing even in our own day. Everyone actually or supposedly descended from Black Donald is a member of the Clan MacDonald, considering all persons derived from Colin the Great are Campbells, and are therefore actual or potential enemies. If one thinks that the MacDonalds have forgiven the Campbells for the massacre at Glencoe (13 February 1692), he can witness some enjoyable brawls in western Canada if some MacDonald calls out that Campbell in Gaelic means Big Mouth.

Clans are more often than not fighting units in primitive war. Indeed, conscription for the army in ancient Israel mentions so many from the "tribe" of Benjamin, so many from Reuben, and so on. Clans are often stratified in prestige, which has bearing on the rise of the civil state, and some have more military responsibility than others. Thus, all the war chiefs among the Winnebago Indians of Wisconsin were of the Thunder Bird clan. Indeed, the warlike character of some Scots clans is still reflected in the regimental names in the British army. The Argyle (Campbell) and Sutherland, the Cameron, and the Gordon regiments of Highland infantry, with "all their tunes of glory," have fought on all continents wearing their kinship plaids, for even legendary blood is thicker than water, especially when being shed.

Although we are not entirely sure about the origin of moieties in the unilateral kin count, it is a recorded fact that many societies based on descent are divided into two parts. Many American Indian societies are dichotomized into clans belonging to the Above People or to the Below People, under one term or another. The former are usually the war clans, and the latter have supervision of the peaceful, economic pursuits. This does not mean that clans bearing peace names are not required to go to war, nor that the war clans do not have to make their own living, but there is a division of oversight in the social task. In Southeast United States the dichotomy was often between the Red or war clans, and the White or peace sibs. If the predominant population of a village consisted of war clans, the buildings or pallisades were painted red, instead of white, which emblemized the other society. This had an interesting effect on the history of the early Georgia colony, for most of the immigrant settlements were in the jurisdiction of White chiefs who forbade their easy extermination on the sacred, peaceful soil.

Approaching the second man-making invention of our early ancestors, the community, one encounters some difficulty of definition among professionals, most of which need not concern us here. This writer, and many others, prefer the older definition to some of the newer ones, not because of conservatism but because we find it works both as a research and as a method of modern social administration. To many of us, then, a community is a constellation of institutions operating in some kind of equilibrium, successful or otherwise, considered in space and time. The whole discussion hinges on the existence of social institutions, which is the key word of the modern debate. From our viewpoint, Carpenter is quite right when he says that infrahuman primates have no communities. They have no institutions. Among men, by contrast, the community is a cultural universal among all peoples except some very unhappy modern ones. No nonliterate societies are so simple but that they have at least two institutions, the familial on the one hand, and the religious on the other, and they operate in some kind of equilibrium. A brief summary of the requirements of an organization to be called institutional must be reserved for the following chapter, but just as a matter of illustration, note the suburban community very near you. It has one or more food stores which are branches of large corporations, which are institutions. It has one or more drugstores, a clothing store or two, a school, a branch bank, and several churches, all held together by their clientele families, which in turn are members of the institution of marriage. Certainly in the not very distant past, communities were also offensive-defensive structures, and many modern ones are not very hospitable to strangers.

And now for the principle task at hand, primitive war, or more properly submilitary combat. When one terms this type of violence as submilitary, he does not mean that except in the most extremely simple cases it is entirely below military standards. More nonliterate societies than not use some tactical principles, those derived from their hunting past, but none of them fight according to all of them. Nonliterate societies who do use them all are truly military, and are either incidentally or accidentally subpolitical in their social control devices. Submilitary combat, sometimes called primitive war with considerable reason, is a definable concept. It is collectively approved violence by an in-group against an out-group which does not utilize all the tactical principles in each engagement. Its goals are derived from the emotional life of individuals or small groups, and are rarely coldly economic, as are those of the state. It is warfare, then, below the military horizon.

A cultural horizon and an ethnological threshold are for the present purposes the same thing. A threshold is a point in invention where a line has been drawn beyond which there is no turning back. A threshold marks the end of one and the beginning of another cultural epoch, whether recognized at the time or not. It is usually the impact of several inventions, among which the food quest, transportation, and cutting instruments are involved, one or the other, or all. The domestication of plants and animals, textiles, pottery, orderly village life, and certain other minor inventions, pushed mankind out of the hunting and gathering economy of Palaeolithic and Mesolithic into the Neolithic. Man became a food producer instead of a parasite on nature, and the world has not been the same since. Recorded history as well as archeology and ethnology are full of such turning points. Columbus, for example, did discover America in 1492, and the world has not and cannot be what it once was. Powder-armed weapons, the printing press, the deep-keeled ship, double entry bookkeeping, the blast furnace, aviation, automation, and whatever the reader wishes to add to the list, those marked historical turning points. The military horizon was one of these, and consists of the following sociologic traits. These must never be considered as acting separately but as a functioning whole.

1. The existence of the political state invariably accompanies war properly so-called, and is the real cause for it. This book therefore often calls the subject phenomenon political war. Only civil government can command enough men to wage true war. It alone can afford to remove men from productive labor to send them into training camps or the field.

2. Adequate supply, or logistics. Only the state can skim off the product of a large citizenry to feed an army in the field. The inability to do this keeps primitive war in the subject category. Once the food and clothing taken to submilitary combat are exhausted, and the weapons lost or broken, the warriors must come home unless they can steal something from the enemy, and this will provide a short diet. The primitive warrior fights with home-made weapons. The civilized soldier fights with those made by specialists and craftsmen whom only the state or the very rich can pay for not producing peaceful consumption goods. The state must own those weapons it provides, or it will be dominated by those who do, as in the aristocratic military republic of Athens and our own mediaeval period.

3. Definite training, command, and control. The primitive warrior joins a war party on his own recognizance, and departs therefrom in the same manner, usually when the outcome of the venture seems unpromising. His is an undisciplined rabble which really does not stand and die when ordered by some alleged chief. A stand-up battle with quality troops against odds was no more his idea of fun than it is of his cultural descendent, the guerrilla. The primitive warrior, whether he can read or not, loves a sure thing. Turning an apparently hopeless cause into a winning one by valor and skill is not his way.

The command of the officer over his men must approach the absolute, at least during the combat. In primitive war, each combatant can with some reason claim to know as much as his alleged chief, and obedience to orders and commands are foreign to him. The civilized frame of mind did not come overnight. It is the result of training, practice, and exercise. Only the state can afford to devote the time to producing officers and drilling the troops, and only men with the patience of civilization will submit to it. Training is a function of command, which is always weak in submilitary combat. The primitive warrior receives what training provided him from a father, an uncle, or some other kinsman. This is adequate for hunting, man-hunting, but not enough for battle. A chief is merely a distinguished, successful warrior, a person to venerate, to follow when convenient, but not to obey.

4. The ability to conduct a protracted campaign rather than to fight one battle and go home is another prerequisite of political war. That first battle may be a failure, and if so, the common will of the social system must be abandoned, at least temporarily. The art of strategy is that of planning ahead, of study of the terrain not immediately involved but eventually useful, and every factor the future may provide. It requires the movement of troops to the position promising the greatest possibility for eventual success. It is, as Clausewitz defined it, the art of making war on a map. This requires more social organization and individual discipline than mere raiding. Of course, the primitive warrior is capable of planning to drive an enemy from an area, or exterminating him, but the concept of linked up actions is beyond him, even on the defensive. Were this not true, a handful of regular cavalry, equipped with weapons often no better than the Indians had, would not have subdued the valiant Plains peoples.

5. *Completely tactical operations* are the mark of political war, the greatest requirement of them all. Tactics, in contrast with strategy, is the art of handling troops in combat, and it is in this that the primitive warrior exhibits his greatest defect.

The civilian is often bemused or amused with the following statement, smiling about the "rigidity of the military mind," or saying that "generals fight past wars, not present ones," and similarly misinformed generalizations. The doctrine which seems to raise eyebrows is that the principles of tactics, once discovered, do not change. The art of applying them changes, indeed, the application must be different for every engagement. It is obvious that in such a war as the American civil one, with all the room imagineable for operations, tactics were more important than in World War I trench warfare, with both sides statically anchored by Switzerland on one hand, and the Atlantic on the other. These units reverted to minor tactics. The grand Napoleonic tactic was foreign to the small-minded leaders of the day. The military ethnologist and sociologist, of course, knew that many states, rudimentary and developed, have used the classical tactics which could not have been the result of diffusion. The Aztec Empire did, and should have destroyed Cortez had it not panicked and permitted itself to be out-thought by this adventurer of slight reputation. The changelessness of these basic axioms is apparent when one recalls that Lord Allenby, the only cavalry general produced by World War I, and undoubtedly the last of his breed, defeated the Turks at Megido (Armageddon) by using the same tactics as employed in the Biblical battle on the same field. Now the Turk is not only "the only gentleman in the East" but a prime fighting man.

There is nothing mysterious in this. There are but few ways in which successful war can be waged. This is why warfare is man's oldest social science, and the only one which has for centuries been permitted to conduct its laboratory without someone saying, "You must not, you cannot experiment with human beings." You can, too! A lethal laboratory, indeed, and one conducted in deadly earnest.

It cannot be emphasized too strongly that warfare is a matter of men, and not weapons. This includes submilitary combat. Its tools have been far from sophisticated. It did not need fine ones. Warfare is a meaningful action system, and weapons are only its implements. It is motive which transforms action from meaningless expenditure of energy into system, with or without artifacts in hand.

As system, warfare has its goals, motives, and reasons for activity. The weaponry is important, and many subsequent pages will be devoted to it. Nevertheless, the means of implementing any motive or goal are secondary to the primary reasons for action.

No matter how simple the society involved, nor without regard for the high purpose of one as large as an empire, the death and maiming of human beings are involved. This requires reasons to remove them from the charge of murder and mayhem, the existence of which all societies admit. There is guilt involved even in primitive war, and most nonliterate societies have more efficient rituals to resolve it then we do. Of course there are paranoid and schizoid personalities in every society to whom the innocent blood can be viewed with equanimity. We have our overkill men, too, but they are not the majority. For most, there must be ends justifying such means, some of which will now be reviewed. The comparison with civilized war is easy here. This type of combat is political and economic. Whatever the recruiting posters may say, whatever the words of popular songs may chant, the motives of warlike states are rational and practical. Such political structures are unstable and are seeking a new stability. They all involve an attempt to establish economic and political dominance of one social system over another by force, and the resistance of the defenders against such a condition. The motivation of submilitary combat is not that simple. One comes closer to the specific human being here. We are not speaking of the movements of divisions and army corps, but people, and the motivation for even a simple act by an uncomplicated personality is difficult to determine, science being as it is. The following does not pretend to be a complete list, only an important one. Nor does it say that such primitive motives have disappeared in individual civilized soldiers or small groups.

Socially approved violence is an effective tension release. Everyone must face the fact that life is full of frustration at best. Nobody's wishes can be satisfied all the time, but it requires a mature personality to realize this, and to cut his garment according to the cloth at hand. Violence is an outlet for many others, but this must be diverted from the in-group because it weakens the common front against the hostility of the environment, human or natural. Infant mortality, premature death, malnutrition, and several other yet unsolved problems, leave so many nonliterate societies unpopulated for the task at hand. Workers must not be wasted. And so, the more mayhem and murder are condemned within, the more they can be tolerated without, or at least some societies think so. Many nonliterates understand this better than we do that the "uptight" must have an external outlet lest they find an internal one, as the old Scandinavians and modern Malaysians did.

The record of frustrated men is clear for many nonliterate societies. Suicide is always available for the hopelessly frustrated, and in the beserk ethic of old Scandinavia, one finds just that. A man to whom the cold and boredom of Iron Age Scandinavia was intolerable, could seize his weapons, and without warning, start killing members of the in-group. He had run beserk, and kept killing until the manhood of his village cut him down. He was accounted a hero and not a criminal. An almost identical practice existed in Malaysia, where in recent days a man could run *amok* with the same motives and results.

Diverting in-group bred hostility towards violence against an out-group is a homeostatic device in the interest of social equilibrium. This was a common practice among the western Indians. The Flathead of western Montana expected the husband of a notoriously permissive wife to go against the enemy. If he survived, and had counted *coup*, he could return home and humiliate and abuse his wife's lover or lovers with impunity. He had redeemed his place in society. The famous military fraternities of the Great Plains, the Crazy Dogs especially, were enlisted from men who had "vowed their bodies to the enemy" because of their depression regarding life as it must be lived in the village. Does this have a familiar ring? Are the "haves" dedicated enough today to throw themselves into certain death as the "have-nots" have been doing for decades?

Look, too, at the victory gloat rituals common throughout the nonliterate world. They homeostatically permit in-group hostility to be vented on enemy prisoners, scalps, heads, and other memorabilia of combat. They provide tension release for the noncombatant women, especially those who have lost husbands and sons to the foe. They condition the young to the war pattern. This was the real reason why the Plains Indians brought home enemy scalps. According to informants, it was the angriest and wildest women in the village who were the most adept in the post-victory scalp abuse dance. Bringing home a captive warrior provided even better homeostasis for many Northeast United States women. They were experts in prisoner torture, and the children had fun, too. Such captives were relatively fortunate in contrast with Melanesian prisoners, as Abel reported from New Guinea:[1]

"The war party had captured a man and a woman alive. As the canoes neared the home bay the warriors put on their finery. The village was informed of the victory and the presence of spoils by conch shell signals. Joyful pandemonium set in ashore, and the homeguard then began preparing for the feast. Their frenzied joy knew no bounds when they learned that the human spoil was alive. As the canoes neared the beach, twenty or thirty men came dashing into the shallow waters to lift the bound captives ashore on their spear points, taking care not to touch them with their hands, as this privilege belonged to the relatives of recent battle casualties. The captives were flung ashore and dragged to the center of the village where they were tied to two trees. The inhabitants and visitors from friendly villages were by then enjoying the most abandoned dance, which the captives were forced to watch. Women who had lost husbands to the enemy in former battles vied in cursing and torturing them. Tiring of this, the victims were trussed over a fire of coconut leaves and roasted alive. The drumming and dancing went on for days after the victims had been eaten."

Such rituals often cleanse the successful warriors of guilt achieved by killing a human being, as mentioned. Certainly one would not recommend such thorough measures as the above Melanesians used, but there were gentler ones.

Man is a domestic animal, self-domesticated, to be sure, but even if the bars of his cage are of his own making, they still are restrictive. Only domestic animals are capable of being bored. Now, in contrast with ourselves among whom recreation is frankly called an industry, a short primitive war and a merry one is a release from ennui. The nonliterate did not have commercial entertainment to beguile them with make-believe violence. Cinematic and televised violence is an outlet for many of the young, and is deplored by some. Many adults might not find it very satisfying, either. Now let us face this well-attested fact. Submilitary combat is not very fatal or dangerous, whether practiced as of yore or now. It does not intend to "play fair." It rarely attempts to alter the social status quo, at least not until our own rediscovery of the trait. Stand up opposition of unit against unit, or man against man is characteristic of political, not kin-based organizations, and very few soldiers consider it recreation.

Combat as a technique of social climbing was once a powerful motive, and it is far from dead. Every social revolution promised liberty, equality, and fraternity, and none has more than partially fulfilled its pledge. We have already said that the higher primates are not egalitarians. Status acquisition and maintenance are ancient human needs, and we have many techniques of achieving them, but warfare is the present theme. Really, there has never been a more powerful role invented by humans, ancient or modern, than that of general. The wish for recognition runs through us all, in some strong, and in others weak, but it is always there. Humility is considered among the Christian virtues. Perhaps that is why there have been so few saints. Psychology has never plumbed man's wish for prestige. The ancient violence which we pretend to abhor is always available, and is always rewarded by some segments of the population.

Many nonliterate populations are so weak socially and economically that primitive war is the only avenue to positions in which one can look down on some, and be looked up to by others. This is still true among modern primitive warriors, the marginal groups in our own society which fill our journals' headlines. They, too, are substandard, or mirror the structural weakness of official society. As for their predecessors, there is very little one can say about the American Indian as a whole, but the sense of military aristocracy runs through almost all their systems.

The North Pacific Coast Indians had three major methods of status ascription. One could either be nobly or base-born, and very little could be done about that. One could become rich through their potlach, or wealth rivalry system, and much could be done about that. For the poor and non-noble men, success in war was a sure ladder of upward social mobility. As for the Great Plains, the coup system is too well known to require much discussion here. No matter how wise and eloquent a man might be, no matter how successful a hunter he became, even if the spirits showed him how to acquire supernatural power, he was still considered a boy until he had gained a ceremonial war honor. This is really talking beside the point, though, for among the Plains and Plateau Indians this writer knows, the reasoning proceeded in this fashion. If a man had acquired spiritual power, he would be successful in war. If he were a military success, he gained many horses. Having many mounts, he gathered other wealth, and no self-respecting girl would marry or otherwise mate with him without these marks of virtue. The coup was so highly stylized that it cannot be discussed at length, but personal aggrandizement remained its key motive, not winning a war. Capturing ten fine enemy horses in open battle was an economic and military success, but it did not confer a coup feather on the captor. Creeping into an enemy camp and stealing one prized and guarded horse conferred a most honorable coup. Adult male preening of this sort is contrary to the intense teamwork required for civilized war. Actually it constituted a brake in the progress towards civilization.

We need say little of the revenge motive in submilitary combat. Individuals, families can be humiliated, and enemy blood is an efficient erasing solvent for humiliation. It is true that national revenge has been common enough among rudimentary states, and has been known in the twentieth century. This latter may have been a pretext for something more practical to the secret councils of state. In any event, revenge fighting on the part of individuals, families, and clans is an obstacle in the search for civilization. It took a long, hard pull to eliminate it in our own political history, but we finally succeeded, perhaps too well. Vengeance is mine, saith the Law. I will repay. And so, we have surrendered the ancient right of private vengeance to that law, which in turn has renounced public retaliation in favor of rehabilitation which, it could be argued, it understands and practices rather poorly indeed.

Everyone who has had experience with little boys, and this includes at least half of humankind, knows that the chief ambition of the normal ones is to shed that status and assume that of men. Every social system above infrahuman levels makes provision for this by meaningful rites of passage, by ceremonial change from a play to a work role. The silver cord has to be severed in any society wherein men are supposed to be male, and the passage from childhood to warrior status has always been a most important channel to manhood. This is a mark of primitive war, indeed, but it did not disappear with civilization. The fighting class in mediaeval Europe was the most important one. Wealth was very desirable, then as now, but only the mounted soldiers were gentlemen. Their sons endured a harsh training, from pagehood in a house not controlled by their parents, through the rank of esquire, to the eventual accolade of knighthood. The system undoubtedly had both pedagogical and sociological weaknesses, but it did make men, and gentlemen. A society which has either accidentally or purposefully abolished the postprimate ritual manhood acquisition should not be surprised if its youth takes to violent street action, gangsterism and guerrillaism, to achieve a masculinity otherwise denied.

The greatest contrast between primitive war and the civilized kind is in motivation. The economic motive is paramount in civilized, or at least political social systems. Many nonmetallurgical societies simply lacked it entirely. Many, though, had a rudimentary concept of economic war. Most mammals have an idea of private property, which in itself is an inspiration to theft. Armed robbery is still popular among ourselves. Those simple societies with some kind of economic assault on others should have been able to form a bridge into true, or gainful warfare, and why so few did is not entirely explainable. We might otherwise observe, however, that it is the rich, unstable societies on the upgrade of their greatness which are aggressive. Their plateau or decline finds them willing to fight only to retain what they have, and that not always wholeheartedly. They have achieved their stability. Of the nonliterate societies, the most economically warlike are the poor, hopeful, and unstable. The very poor and hopeless are pacific, relying on secret sorcery and other marks of instability to gain their objectives. A people among whom subsistence anxiety is endemic and persistent make poor warriors, which in part may explain the noneconomic content of so much primitive war. The Eskimo, for example, were virtually devoid of offensive combat concept, and were only fairly competent in fighting to keep what they had. Among themselves, they even lacked a clear idea of theft. In the old days, it was practically impossible to steal from an Eskimo. Having entered a man's dwelling and taken a tool valuable because of the time and skill needed for its manufacture, one was only required to praise him for his craftsmanship the next time the taker saw him. Well, for that matter, that was all that was required if one took his wife, temporarily or permanently. These people lived too close to starvation to deny help to a neighbor. Their internal stability had to be near absolute.

The American Indian was more defective than many other folk in the concept of food-raiding. This may be because the poor had poor neighbors. A successful thief must find something to steal. Life is not always worth risking for trifles. If the neighbors were rich, they might also be military. The hungry societies of northern Mexico were not apt to raid the city-building folk unless they were volunteering as human sacrifices to the gods of the Nahua. An exception is found in the incursions of the wild Denè peoples, Navaho, for example, into the pueblo-building territory. Corn was easier to steal than to grow. The pueblo-building folk were poor defenders. They were nonmilitary. Their farming success depended on absolute cooperation and suppression of self for the common good that they could not develop a fighting spirit even on the defensive. Their stability had to be extreme to wrest a living from that environment.

If defective in the practice of food-raiding, the warlike destruction of an enemy's food potential was not unknown on the North American continent. Several Great Plains societies set fire to the grass in the foe's country with the intent to scathe his bison pasture.

Devoted as we are to the politico-economic state and the acquisitive society, it might be easy for us to overestimate the greed of the fighting man and his social system. Napoleon might not have expected to get rich by looting, but he did. (His wife Josephine was superb as an agent of blackmail of conquered towns.) There have been military societies which would have held him in contempt. The gentility of a gentleman in Polynesia and the North Pacific

Coast was enhanced by his generosity, not his greed. Wherever a strong sense of divine monarchy or of a sacred nobility arose, the great man sought loot to give away, not to consume. Social climbing banquets made the great man greater. Lavish gifting bound clients to their chief in many ancient societies. Concerning our own tradition, acquired from the eastern Mediterranean through Rome, the road from nonliterate, submilitary, kinship society to political greatness is the idea of permanent tribute or almost compulsory and advantageous trade relations, not armed theft. Not all of this tribute need be inanimate. Slaves served Rome as well as treasure. In black Africa, too, the royal penchant for massive human sacrifice was economic at bottom, for how else could the agriculturally-minded gods be persuaded to send good seasons?

There is some almost aimless fighting in the world, some of which will be discussed, and very primitive it is. Men do fight, and having seen some reasons for such violence, we must return to the defects of submilitary combat to see how they do it.

As for the Principle of the Offensive, the anti-human violence of culture has long demonstrated that, all other things being equal, or almost so, the offensive should win over the defensive. Submilitary combat is always offensive, and is defensively defective, derived as it is from animal hunting. Only offensive action brings home the game. Nonliterate warriors had about as little sense of the defense as their food animals, which consists of flight. If a folk, such as the Iroquois, erected good fortifications, they are on the threshold of the state. Do not be deceived by the pueblos of Southwest United States. Most of them are poorly sited as defensive positions, even the *casas grandes*, which look like forts.

The revivers of primitive war—terrorists, guerrillas, and such fighters—are magnificent in the offense. Like their prototypes, however, they just fade away should they meet determined, trained, and aggressive opposition. Please do not forget this weakness on That Day. The hunter does not fight his game, but bullies it, and bullies have never been in short supply in any generation.

As for the Principle of Surprise, a successful game hunter specializes sneaking up on animals, giving them as little warning as to how, when, where, and if they are to be attacked. This is good soldiering, too, so much so that it is standard doctrine that a good general may be defeated, but never surprised. The primitive warrior and his modern disciple rely on surprise. It is in this way that a few fairly competent men can disrupt the many, and often their betters.

Counter-surprise, or security, is only good common sense. It is almost amazing how poorly primitive warriors, relying as they do on surprise, protect themselves against it. Any civilized formation on the move, whether in attack or in retreat, protects its flanks, its rear, and probes cautiously forward to prevent its own surprise and destruction. Ambuscade is the hunter's and primitive warrior's specialty, but frankly, they themselves fell into such traps far too often. The modern primitive warrior, too, must have his hideaway, or a population which will protect him and lie for him in case of defeat. He is otherwise very vulnerable, which please again remember should the need arise.

Adequate intelligence, espionage, observation, or by any other means, in either combat or hunting, is essential for success. One should know as much as possible about his enemy, his capabilities and weaknesses, and his means of nullifying the attack. Counterintelligence indicates that one should guard similar knowledge about himself. The primitive warrior is ordinarily superb in gathering and evaluating intelligence. He went to a good school. For example, Custer was under close observation throughout his western progress. He was well served by his Crow scouts, too, but would not believe what they told him. At the proper moment, and at the correct place, then, Crazy Horse served the Seventh Cavalry's first squadron as he would so many buffalo. The modern primitive warrior also survives on superior intelligence, but his counterintelligence is also excellent.

As for utilization of the terrain, almost all primitive warriors try to make the environment work for them against their opposition. It was also a talent with which modern primitive warriors are well endowed. They know their own country better than do the invaders, and they never permit him to forget it.

Mobility is a military virtue which, as man-hunters, the primitive warriors ordinarily understand. There are, however, some instances to the contrary among the subsistence-anxious societies. An observant man knows that the hawk is swift, and that sitting ducks are dead ones. It took a high civilization to think out the Maginot Line syndrome.

As for combining movement with fire, the hurling of missiles, primitive or sophisticated, is only a softening device preparatory to an attack. Victory comes to those who can immobilize the opposition with anything from rocks, through arrows, to chemically propelled hardware. Decisions are obtained by healthy troops closing with those weakened by missile fire. It is difficult to summarize the primitive warrior's observance of this virtue. Fire and movement characterize the successful ones. There are those who, however, merely deliver arrow fire, preferable at safe distances, with the same mentality as the modern civilian who is always striving for, and hoping he has, the means of pushbutton warfare. This seems to be characteristic of the subsistence-anxious on the one side, and the overfed on the other. It is here that whatever praise we can ascribe to submilitary combat must cease, the test being failure to organize. Specialization of task and division of labor characteristic of civilization is beyond the primitive warriors. Intense, integrated division of labor is both a product and cause of civilization, and those below that threshold are defective in this talent in both peaceful and military operations. In civilized warfare, if one has horse, foot, and artillery in his command, he employs all of these to change his enemy's mind. Primitive warriors do not have troop specialization any more than they do in their economic industry. The primitive warrior was too much of an individualistic glory hunter to have more than a glimmer of concerted effort. This requires teamwork, discipline, and command.

Here again, it is not absolute numbers all over the field which counts, but local superiority. The primitive warrior was too inclined to run all over the place, hitting his enemy wherever he could. Concentration of force at the critical point means applying pressure where it hurts the most. As for plans, they often were absent, or too standardized to prevent anticipation. The consistent dawn attack should have been vitiated by defense security. The almost universal surround, characteristic of deer and bison drives, was too rigid. As for correct formations, they simply did not exist. How could they when the ideal of the warriors was, "Come on, boys, let's everyone kill himself an enemy or two."

The tragedy of primitive war is that so very, very often victory was not exploited after so much bloodshed. Crazy Horse and Sitting Bull thought they had done enough to wipe out half of Custer's command. They had counted coup and captured many horses, had they not? Why did they let Reno's squadron escape? With the settlers' protection by "Yellow Hair" gone, why did the Indians only raid the settlements? Why did Crazy Horse, supposedly upheld by the charisma of the Eagle spirit, not lay a trap for the other indifferently led Federal forces?

The question as to why some nonliterate people are warlike and others are peaceful and gentle is not easily answered at this time. The Iroquois were a peaceful gardening folk, and abruptly turned into the most efficient killing machine in North America. This, of course, was due to the impact of Algonkian persecution. But why were the Papago so gentle and the Pima so given to war? Their environment was virtually identical. The latter, as Yaqui, were just recently pacified by the Mexican government's aviation. Again, when the United States abolished the Great Plains war pattern, it destroyed the manhood of these people and took the pith from their culture. By contrast, Gardner, Heider, and others report that when both the Netherlands and the Indonesian governments made the Dani, Papuan groups of the New Guinea upland, abjure warfare, it harmed the culture hardly at all. This did damage to our holistic viewpoint, for war was an important aspect of Dani culture.[2] These people abstain from intercourse with their wives for five years after the birth of a child, and Heider thinks this is due to their low psychic energy expenditure, which may be why they reverted to peaceful ways without trauma. This may explain the pacific nature of more than one people. May be that no one explanation is possible.

But having become civilized, let us put away primitive things. The acid test of primitive war is the fact that its practitioners became colonialized, and remained so as long as colonies paid. The primitive warriors were not put down by force of superior numbers, but by better military organization, usually but not always aided by a superior weaponry. Having become men, we thought we had put away childish things, but we have not as long as confrontationists, terrorists, and guerrillas are around.

FOOTNOTES AND REFERENCES

[1] Charles W. Abel, *Savage Life in New Guinea*, London, 1902, p. 143f. Permission of The Council of World Mission.

[2] Robert G. Gardner and Karl G. Heider, *Gardens of War: Life and Death in the New Guinea Stone Age*, New York, Random House, 1969. Karl Heider, *Grand Valley Dani: Peaceful Warriors*, New York, Holt, Rinehart and Winston, 1979, p. 21. H. Myron Bromley, "The Function of Fighting in Grand Valley Dani Society," *Working Papers in Dani Ethnology*, No. 1, Bureau of Native Affairs, Hollandia-Kota Baru, 1962.

Chapter 3

THE ART AND SCIENCE OF WARFARE

The Tactical Revolution

War itself and its principles, in contrast with warfare, are really the concern of political scientists, and therefore will be given the briefest of treatments. War is in many ways a state of mind, a constellation of hostile attitudes a government and its people may have towards another such political structure. While there may be some modern blurring due to the preference for undeclared war, warfare still has a legal status if organized force is applied. With or without the ritualization of formal declaration, each participant in war intends to harm the other for his own benefit. War is an operation of the social process of conflict in contrast with competition. It is the sociological meaning of conflict, not the tactical one, which is involved.

This conflict need not in itself be the application of organized physical force, although that possibility is always a consideration. The threat of force is present, but its exercise need not be continuous. Thus, when historians write of the Hundred Years War, they do not mean a century of continuous combat. Most realists would recognize that the United States and the Soviet Union have in this sense been at war for many decades, but the struggle has been on the diplomatic, economic, strategic, and espionage fronts rather than by armed combat. Each has attempted to harm and contain the other, and each has from time to time succeeded. As there has been no armed conflict, this type of war has no legal status, but the recognition of strategic maneuvering is publicly recognized by both sides and their allies.

A distinction between war and warfare is therefore suggested. War is a collective mental state more or less openly recognized by all potential contestants. It is a concept of transaction by potential if not actual force, a situation of which both parties are well aware, even if one makes an undeclared Pearl Harbor type of surprise on the other. The United States understood its position on the day before the attack. "Warre...," said Hobbes, "is a tract of time wherein the will to contend by Battell is sufficiently known." Battle and combat, therefore, are only branches of war, not necessarily its fact. Strategy and logistics are the objects of attention long before any expenditure of ammunition is made. Battle is the ultimate clash between the political and military organization of one state and its allies with that of another. It is, as Wendell Coats repeatedly says, the focal point of conflict.

As battle is only a subdivision of war, combat is just part of the battle concept. Fighting may be just a barroom brawl, an expression of the violence originating in the Id. Combat is ritualized violence controlled by the Ego and Superego. Once upon a time, a battle might have consisted of but one combat, but that day is over. Combat is immediate, but battle may last several days, with a diminution of activity over night, or even longer.

The other branches of war and warfare will be given some discussion, but combat, which lies at the very bottom of all this, will be allowed to dominate this chapter. It is the older and fundamental fact, and the others were developed later to implement it. Combat is the armed transaction of structured groups to achieve or to deny the realization of antagonistic goals.

So much for war, which may be only the manipulation of ideas. We must now proceed to the manipulating of men and materials, beginning with the widest of the concepts, which is strategy, insofar as diplomacy belongs to political science. Care will be taken to exemplify the discussion with wars, campaigns, and battles with which the reader is already familiar. The fate of the world, however, has often depended on others less well-known.

Strategy is not as easy to define as tactics, and no one thinks that universal principles for its practice can be enunciated, as with the latter. Too much depends on the situation. Nevertheless, many of the tactical laws can be applied to strategy. The popular press often makes no difference between strategy and tactics, but the professional one clearly distinguishes between the two operations. Lieutenant Colonel Alfred Burne says that "Strategy brings troops to the battlefield: tactics directs their action thereon. Tactics begins where Strategy ends."[1] Carl von Clausewitz said that strategy is the art of making war on a map, which is a bit too simple. For our present purposes, let us consider that strategy is the arranging of the force potential of a state prior to, or short of combat. There can be little doubt that the modernization of war is blurring the ideal distinction between strategy and tactics. Reginald Bretnor, for instance, seems to think that the distinction is obsolete, but the combat generals consulted do not. The term came from the Greek *strategos*, which refers to the field commander, and it may be that at some time the popular confusion of the terms will become real, but not yet.

Strategy is the bridge between civil government and actual warfare. It belongs to war, which is a civil function, and tactics refers to militarily expressed hostility, or warfare. There should be little doubt but that the masters of the polity do, or should, have a greater knowledge of the grand picture than the field generals can have, and so the ultimate decision should be theirs. Generals and their subordinates can complain, though, and often do in writing. Politics must determine the location of the theater of operations, and if there is more than one, which is the more important. Three decisions made by the polity are cited, not always with the advice of the generals.

Many German generals disapproved of the attack on Russia. Hitler had made up his mind, though, and the attack was launched. Once this decision was made, United States Ambassador to Great Britain Kennedy communicated to Hitler that if he would confine his ambitions to Russia and not attack the west as well, the United States would not intervene. Was this done with Washington's connivance? Hitler made two mistakes here. He should either have accepted this proposition or, having invaded Russia without agreeing with it, he should have made an all-out effort on a winner-take-all basis. Russia was partially defeated in the beginning, and could have been more so, or at least reduced to where a holding mission could have contained her. The brilliant German general staff must have known that a second front was inevitable. Hitler might have won had he made a maximum effort immediately against Russia before she could have rectified her lack of preparedness for war, and before the United States could pour in uncounted tons of materials in her aid. His hostility towards Great Britain and France continued, though, and he was bound to lose according to the decision he did make.

Likewise confronted with two theaters of war, the United States government made a decision wiser than Hitler's. Germany and Japan were both strong military powers. The choice was made to defeat the stronger first, if possible, and then assail the second with all maximum effort. This was done successfully, although General Mac-Arthur complained about neglect.

A third World War II political decision is still being argued. Great

Britain wanted the assault on Europe to be from the Mediterranean bases up the valleys of the Danube and Drava, thus rolling up Germany's eastern right flank and containing Russia within its traditional boundaries. President Roosevelt apparently agreed in the beginning, for he spoke of assault at the "soft underbelly of Europe." The chief of staff, General George Marshall, bitterly objected, wanting Germany to be defeated in the northwest of Europe. He won out, and Russia was not only allowed but invited to advance to the line of the Elbe, with results which are only too apparent. By contrast, one captive German general asked why we thought the underbelly of Europe was so soft? "We would have destroyed you in the defiles of the mountains." The present-school solution holds with Marshall by saying that if Germany had been rolled up on its right flank, it would have squeezed her into Scandinavia where it would have been difficult to dislodge her. That conclusion is a bit strange. Hitler had already occupied Denmark and Norway, and had only a most agreeable Swedish government with which to contend.

In humility, then, the generals must admit that the goals of the government come first. It is the overall representative of the people, and it is in their interest that the strategist manipulates the force potential. It must be more obvious now that the political and military goals are woven into a single strand which cannot be separated. Strategy always speaks in terms of defense. Its role is to defend the goals of the state, even if these are indeed very offensive. Raymond L. Garthoff quotes the Soviet general staff doctrine that "The objective of military strategy is the creation by military means of those conditions under which politics is in a position to achieve the ends it sets for itself."[2] In active war, the wholeness of political, strategic, and tactical effort becomes obvious. What, though, if a nation is at "peace?" Be assured that a state may be inactive tactically but feverishly at work strategically.

Battlefield tactics often prefers to conceal its strength at the critical point. Strategy, by contrast, being linked with diplomacy, usually tries to convince its potential enemy of a superior power without, of course, revealing the details, which situation the enemy's intelligence service will try to penetrate. Nevertheless, strategic success without actual or potential tactical strength is almost unthinkable, and the enemy's strategic estimate of just how much bluff is involved contains some very nice decisions.

Strategic planning, attempting to prohibit a possible enemy from interfering with the government's offensive and defensive goals, must be thorough and under almost daily reevaluation. Political goals come first, but they might require alteration by all states as the military potential of either regresses or progresses relatively. All wars are global now, and every nation needs allies. A successful strategy needs foreign bases. Allies, buffer states, and the uncommitted, often exhibiting considerable instability, cling to governments with growing force potential, and become lukewarm or semi-hostile to weakening ones. Spain, for example, an unstable polity, might weary of being a harbor of refuge for the United States in case of an American defeat on the European continent. Neutrals are much like canines watching other dogs fight. They love to jump in on the winning side.

A base, then, either at home or abroad, is of overweening importance, as our later discussion of logistics will show. For the time being let us say that a base is an area from which an army is supplied and replenished. Lack of such kept primitive war in that category.

The arrangement of the lines of communication suggest another strategic-tactical decision the commander must make, or have it made for him by his enemy. Will he fight on interior lines or exterior ones? Burne says that one fights on interior lines when those of communication converge inward towards the base, while on the exterior when such lines spread outward. It might be helpful if one considers that an interior line front is a great wheel, or half of one, with the lines of communication as spokes leading from the base or headquarters as the hub. The commander using exterior lines is not contained by such a wheel. It has been a long time since anyone fighting on interior lines has won a battle.

If a nation or its armies can maintain the initiative, interior lines may have an advantage. The headquarters hub may strike out to any point on its perimeter, and unless the opposition can guess where, it must dissipate its forces all along the perimeter. Sherman, for example, forced Hood to fight on interior lines after the fall of Atlanta, and somewhat to his sorrow. The Confederate general was not called the Gallant Hood for nothing. He was probably the most aggressive commander who wore gray. He simply did not have the strength to sustain the initiative, so his aggression was self-defeating.

In approaching now the more personal forms of war, it is observed again the fundamental proposition of many anthropologists that all cultural invention is a derivative of the organism. The weaknesses and strengths of the human body are permanent realities, and all culture, material and nonmaterial, is an attempt to minimize the former and maximize the latter. Whatever else warfare may be, it is a pattern of culture combining social organization and material artifacts, the goals of which are the infliction of harm on other people while avoiding the same fate for oneself. Since they are not more nor less than a culture complex, military operations—tactics, strategy, and logistics — almost more than any other cultural construct rests upon the correction of the essential weakness and permeability of the human body, and the exploitation of the enemy's essential feebleness.

Please look at this human being who, despite his being one of the weakest and slowest of mammals, has through intelligence and culture almost mastered this planet, and is stretching out for others. Despite this, he is a vulnerable, permeable, fetalized, infantile, unspecialized body, relying only on cerebral expansion for survival. An anthropologist a half century ago said that all human evolution and, in consequence, culture as well, are functions of the upright posture. While this can be and has been argued, yet take a look at this fellow in either an offensive or defensive frame of mind. It is the human body which is mentioned, and no other kind, say like a wolf's. The softest part of the latter, for example, is protected by the whole body, and the fighting teeth and crunching jaws are to the fore where the danger is. If that menace is not overcome, the canine has the advantage of four fleet feet with which to flee. The human being, by contrast, has stood up on his hind legs and exposed the soft parts of his belly and chest to all who wish to strike a blow. His forehead has gone forward to accommodate a mighty brain, but this forced his jaws to retreat backward, so that they and the teeth are of no use in combat above the simplest brawls. His ex-forelegs and now-arms are powerful grasping weapons in love or hate, but they are useless for rapid locomotion in advance or retreat. Being bipedal rather than four-legged, he is more easily pushed over than a horse or a wild boar. The former paws and now hands, though, are wonderful bits of equipment wherewith to wreak evil or good. The diagram in Figure 1 shows two men hostilely facing each other as if viewing them from above. Chest opposes chest. Two long arms stretch sideways in preparation for encircling or delivering a blow. Two men are figured, but the same is just as true if viewing opposing squads, divisions, or groups of armies, each immobolized to some degree by the threat and proximity of the other. The strengths and weaknesses of the body are clearer, of course, when considering just two opponents, for they cannot be masked. Sometimes this is not so obvious in the disposition of large units, but the might-feebleness dictated by the organism is still there, and failure to recognize it has defeated more than one commander.

The strength of each man is to the front, and weakness is in the rear. The arms terminating in fists are designed to strike forward to protect the softness of the belly and the fragility of the rib cage. Each opponent must consider these facts. The first is, I must realize

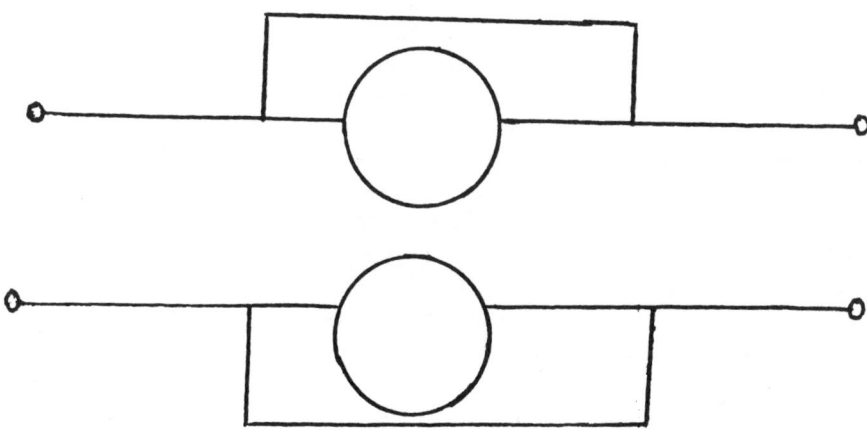

FIGURE 1

that even if I am the stronger, I am easily killed or maimed. My strength lies to the front. I am weak on my right and left sides, or my flanks, and disaster is in my rear. If that other man envelops me on one side or the other, or both, I might be finished. I must at all costs protect my head, or headquarters, from which all my direction comes. The head may sometimes sacrifice a few fingers or even an occasional rib to avoid its own decapitation, and thus the death of the entire organism, or organization.

The second simple truth is the realization that all this is derived from the upper primate anatomy. Simple as it is, it is your first lesson in combat. If you can grasp its meaning, you have gone far to becoming a tactician. If you cannot comprehend it, you never will be.

Warfare is the ultimate technique of war. It is transaction raised to its highest possible degree. It is the systematic, purposive, organized application of deadly force against the personnel, property, resources, and morale of one state against another. One can, by theory, have war without battle, and recent Russo-American experience has shown that theory to be correct. Battle, though, cannot be prosecuted without the existence of a state of war. The last sentence is not qualified by the Japanese attack on Pearl Harbor. A cold war already existed, and if the meaning of "first strike" is comprehended, this act of extreme violence may be only the first of its kind. This, of course, is the theory behind the balance-of-power concept.

The use of the word "violence" requires a memory refresher concerning its meaning. Violence is the partial breakdown of homeostasis of the ordered relations of the body — in society — the extension of physical harm, or the threat thereof, which is random, illegal, emotional, and derived from the primate rage or fear. Force, by contrast, is the rationalization, or canalization and limitation of violence. It is systematic, purposeful and, by international law, legal. The Law of Nations recognizes a state of war or belligerence as legitimate, and as such, it has for centuries enjoyed certain obligations and privileges. One may see acts of violence during combat, baboon-like behavior of overkill and pointless cruelty. Violence is organically animal, and is therefore biological. Force is human organization, and therefore sociological.

When diplomats have had their say, when strategists have attempted to align the space aspect of human relations against their country's enemy, and when logisticians are reasonably content with the bin of men, munitions, and life-sustaining materials, it is fighting which actually decides any question under debate. Combat is the decision-making factor, and all else is auxilliary.

Terming the methods of combat as "principles" has become somewhat controversial of late. And yet such principles probably do exist, and this is the reason for this chapter's title, the art and science of warfare. There may be some wavering concerning both the specific and general application of these principles among analysts, but for the majority of the world's generals and staff colleges, whose concerns include the practical application of force in the field, the following axioms are principles, or even laws. They, like morals, are guides to action. Both are sometimes broken with unhappy results. Probably the reasons for some doubts among theorists such as Reginald Bretnor are due to misunderstandings.

Warfare, not war, mind you, is mankind's oldest social science. It is to date the only one which can summarize its practice by a few general principles which have the effect of laws. The reason for this is quite clear. Fighting is one of mankind's oldest culture complexes. It has had millenial experience with it. It is the oldest behavioral science which has been afforded an almost unlimited laboratory experience, the only one which any group's morality has not forbidden experiment involving the death and maiming of the, shall we say, human laboratory animals. Out of these lethal encounters, certain strong central tendencies have been empirically discovered. This nation or that may state them differently, or some may not verbalize them at all. General J. F. C. Fuller's dictum has become international, yet the fact emerges that regardless of the language spoken or written, the commander who uses them all in a pattern in every engagement almost always wins over the leader who does not. They cannot be called Fuller's principles, for they were first taught to me in my youth by a colonel who had never heard of Fuller. They were called the Alexandrian Principles, inferring that the great Macedonian had conceptualized them. Men have long sought combat principles, and one finds them stated in one way or another by the late Roman theorist, Flavius Vegetius Renatus.

Once these empirically obtained sociological principles are arrived at, they have become invested with certain timelessness. A civilian criticism is that "generals fight old wars, not present ones." This opinion contains some truth without in any way invalidating the principles. The facts are that there are only a few ways to attain success in any complicated procedure. The task of any problem solver is to discover his basics. There is some leeway in making an angel food cake, but not much. You do whip the eggs. You do not use corn or oat meal. You do bake only within a narrow range of oven temperature, and you do not permit loud noises and shock within a certain radius of space. And now for something else. Regardless of the timelessness of cake baking ever since an angel first originated this type of pastry, sometimes the cake is a failure, even if the cook *thought* she had used all of the proper principles. Sometimes she has, but not often. The wise kitchen operative has discovered that at the next baking spree she had better use the time-tested rules again, and not throw away the cookbook.

Will the *apparently* scrupulous observations of these principles guarantee victory? Not absolutely, of course! The other commander may be just as careful. And then there is the "fog of war," a situation which no one could have foreseen. There may be friction in the command, such as the one which cost John Bell Hood the Battle of Ezra Church. Perhaps adequate intelligence has not proceeded from the field to the top, or orders based on it may not be well understood by those who must implement them. An unforeseen change in the weather may favor one side against the other. And then there is such a thing as luck. The superior student carefully preparing for an examination should make an -A-, but this is not always so. Now chess is a game with rigid rules, and with perfect information as to the location and responses of the pieces on the board. Therefore, if two grand masters are playing against each other in this simulated battlefield, White should always win, as he has the first move and hence the initiative. This is not true at all. And the health, and therefore the shrewdness, of great men can vary from day to day. Remember Napoleon's hemorrhoids at Waterloo, and Lee's diarrhea at Gettysburg?

> "There are a few fundamental truths which have been applicable in war from time immemorial and which will continue to be so in future wars. These truths are known as tactical principles, or principles of warfare.
>
> "Though these principles themselves do not change, their application is different for units of different size and varies from time to time in units of the same size."[3]

And says Oliver Spaulding in the same vein:

> "War is war. Its outward forms change, just as the outward forms of peace change. But from the stylus to the typewriter is just as far as from the club to the machine gun — a weapon also known affectionately or otherwise as a 'typewriter.' And the development of tactics is neither more or less remarkable than the development of office methods. Strip any military operation of external, identifying details, and one will find it hard to put a place and to date the story."[4]

The flaw in both statements from somewhat elderly books is that they describe the principles as those of war, which they have never been. They are principles of tactical combat, and need not be defended. History has done that. They are listed here in a somewhat different order than one finds in the manuals of the powers because of an emphasis on the first five, which are usually observed in primitive war, which in turn are derived from animal hunting. The wording is not exactly that of General Fuller. Those eight or nine of universal acceptance are listed in roman, while some others thought to be vital by many authorities are in arabic.

They are, then:

   I. The Principle of the Offensive
   II. The Principle of Surprise
   3. The Principle of Intelligence
   4. The Principle of Utilization of the Terrain
   V. The Principle of Mobility
   VI. The Principle of Objective
   VII. The Principle of Security
   8. The Principle of Fire and Movement
   IX. The Principle of Cooperation, or of Combined Employment of All Forces
   10. The Principle of Concerted Effort
   XI. The Principle of Concentration of Force at the Critical Point
   12. The Principle of Integrity of Tactical Units
   13. The Principle of Simplicity of Plan
   14. The Principle of Correct Formations
   15. The Principle of Economy of Force
   16. The Principle of Sufficient Numbers
   17. The Principle of Exploitation of Victory

The professional staff officer will note that the older manuals have been quoted because they state the principles more completely and in a succinct form. Of course, different branches of the armed forces emphasize some above others, and so do different nations, as Table I shows.

The Principle of the Offensive is derived from primate rage, the power to be dissatisfied, and an ability to hope for happiness through violence. The defensive, by contrast, is derived from the permeability of the human organism. As in animal hunting, the anti-human aspects of culture have long demonstrated that, all other things being equal, the offensive wins over the defensive. As a matter of experience, the defensive can never win. It can only prevent defeat, or postpone it, which is not permanent victory. Now there are certainly times when a force should willingly and temporarily go on the defensive. It is certainly sensible to permit an enemy to knock his head against a stone wall, providing one is convinced of the futility of his attack. Actually, the offense-defense is the same process and not sharply divisable as some think. George Gordon Meade surely fought defensively at Gettysburg, and the consistently offensive Lee lost by fighting at the wrong place, at the wrong time, in the wrong way.

This principle probably has always been misnamed. The most

desirable thing a general can have is the initiative, and he can ordinarily obtain and maintain this by being offensive. Now everyone who has played or watched football and basketball knows that the team which has possession of the ball cannot lose, and that the one without it cannot score. This form of transaction is better called the seizure and maintenance of the initiative which might, at times, become defensive, but only for the time being, and with the deliberate motive of permitting the enemy to hurt himself. It is possession of the initiative which compels the opposition to conform to your plan of action and maneuver. It is therefore a goal in itself. It implies freedom of action for you while denying it to him. It determines how the battle or campaign will be fought, where, and when. Indeed, it seems to be so vital that it is not necessary to state a separate principle of maneuver.

It is obvious that it may not be possible to maintain the initiative over the entire field, especially if one's resources are limited. It is the initiative at the critical point which counts. Indeed, even when compelled to fight a defensive campaign, gaining the initiative at specific points against an offensive enemy may be telling.

The Principle of Surprise is derived from the hunter's sneaking up on animals, giving them as little warning as possible as to how, when, where and if they are to be attacked. Sun Tzu said, "All warfare is based on deception," but he lived long ago. Stonewall Jackson in later days said, "Mystify, mislead, and surprise your enemy," and he was a considerable master of this. So if the Soviets include the word "deception" in their Principle of Surprise, all that can be said is, Of Course! The use of surprise is the control of the space-time aspect while denying it to your enemy, is it not? Surprise is a technique for economizing your own men and resources. Frederick the Great said that "Ruses are of great usefulness. They are detours which often lead more surely to the objective than the wide road which goes straight."[5]

It is possible to effect complete surprise of small units, but in these days of large forces, it has become increasingly difficult to obtain complete surprise over large areas. If not possible all over, it is often possible and decisive to obtain local surprises. Antoine Henri Jomini said, ". . .to surprise an army it is not necessary to take it so entirely unawares that the troops will not even have emerged from their tents; it is difficult to attack it in force at the point intended, before preparations can be made to meet the attack."[6] Yet even in these days of great mass and space, effective surprise can be made. The Japanese caught the American forces in Hawaii in their tents. Again, although British Intelligence had discerned the

Table I

TACTICAL PRINCIPLES, DIFFERENCES IN EMPHASIS

U. S. Army	U. S. Navy	U. S. Air Force	British Army	USSR
Objective	Objective	Objective	Objective	Advance and Consolidation
Offensive	Offensive	Offensive	Offensive	Offensive
Command	Control	Control	Surprise	Combined Arms
Mass	Concentration	Concentration	Concentration	Concentration
Economy of Force	Economy	Economy	Economy of Force	Economy of Force
Maneuver	Mobility	Flexibility	Security	Maneuver and Initiative
Surprise	Surprise	Surprise	Mobility	Surprise and Deception
Security	Security	Security	Cooperation	Adequate Reserves
Simplicity	Simplicity	Cooperation		Morale
	Morale			
	Exploitation			
	Readiness			

details of Von Rundstedt's Ardennes counteroffensive, including the order of battle and objective, the effect on the United States was one of considerable surprise. Neither Eisenhower nor Bradley would believe what they saw.[7] And again, Erwin Rommel failed to surprise Montgomery at Alamein in August 1942, but the latter did completely surprise the Desert Fox as to where he intended to attack. The victory at Alamein was a turning point, and therefore a decisive battle. Surprise still lies at the heart of warfare, and some other human activities as well.

The Principle of Intelligence again derived from hunting, largely explains itself. By espionage, by observation, and by many means, success dictates that one should know as much of his enemy as possible, his capabilities and weaknesses, and his means of nullifying the attack. Counterintelligence indicates that one should guard similar knowledge of himself. This may require censorship of the press. It is said that Lee really did not need the extensive Confederate espionage network. He was an avid reader of the *New York Herald*.

The Principle of Utilization of the Terrain represents the skill of one commander making the physical environment work in his favor and minimizing the efforts of his opponent. "The nature of the ground," said Vegetius, "is often more important than courage." It is not surprising, then, that generals who have been engineers have shown considerable superiority in this ability. Robert Lee's many successes against forces superior to his are cases in point. Obviously, the leader who possesses the initiative should be able to choose the site of battle to the disadvantage of his foe. A fortunate disposition will not, of course, guarantee victory.

This principle is primarily, although not exclusively, one to be considered by the defender. Very often, being on the site earlier, he can choose the rough ground, marshes, minor streams, ruins of villages, and many obstacles which his attacker must overcome under fire. This will disrupt him, fatigue him, and demoralize him as well, and lay him open to that counterattack which any commander worth his pay has planned before hand. The defense must have a clear field of fire. This is ordinarily the military crest of a hill which is that line, not at the exposed top of an elevation, but a curving one somewhat below it which will not provide "dead space" from fire, whereby an enemy may take advantage of gullies and rises to advance with safety. Meade had this at Gettysburg, but he deprived himself of the ability to maneuver, and might have lost that day, for as Carl von Clausewitz observed, a wary attacker will note a nearly impregnable geographic obstacle, and try to effect a turning movement around the defender's flank. That is what Longstreet wanted to do, but Lee thought otherwise. Each side in battle must allow itself a field of maneuver, if for no other reason than room to make an orderly retreat. Fortification is, of course, a cultural device to increase the importance of the terrain, but that can be turned into a trap as well as a defense.

The value of the terrain may vary as to the principal arm of the battle. Thus, an environment chopped up by mountains and broad streams favors infantry, as was shown in the 1943 struggle for Tunisia and Sicily. Flat, open country favors cavalry and armor. The Libyan desert favored the side with the most and best tanks. In any event, the terrain may be used to protect the flanks, and therefore permit the side with the fewer troops to stand against a superior force, as at Thermopylae. Andrew Jackson at New Orleans had his right flank protected by the Mississippi, while his left flank was on the swamps of Lake Borgne which nobody on foot could negotiate. In the same manner, Marshal von Rundstedt, deceived by his espionage, indulged in a fatal bit of wishful thinking when he expected the Allied attack to be over the gentle beaches of the Low Countries, favorable to landing craft. He wanted to contain the numerically smaller enemy on these beaches where he could work his will upon them. He should have known that the temporarily smaller force would have to land on a peninsula, Normandy or Brittany, run across to the other shore line, and with few troops hold the protected flanks until logistics supplied men and materials.

Experts seem to think that the importance of the terrain is increasing in modern warfare. The increased size of units make the loss of the important features of the terrain very disruptive under the greatly increased firepower of today.

The commander should not be lulled into a false sense of security by his control of the key terrain features. If he is tempted thereby into into a static defense, he may have a surprise some day. Mars hates the complacent more than the cowardly.

The Principle of Mobility. "Find him, fix him, fight him, finish him," indeed! The emphasis is on fixing, immobilizing, pinning him. An observant man knows that the hawk is swift, and that sitting ducks are dead ones. Keep mobile as long as you can, even on the defensive. This was the way of the best mediaeval knighthood. The defensive castle was only a pivot of maneuver and a place of refuge. "All day in the field, all night in the castle" was good doctrine. World War I trench warfare degenerated into something never seen before, siege and counter-siege all the time and every day. Complete loss of mobility led to a war of attrition and counter-attrition.

Pershing spoiled that regime. Mobility was regained in World War II, which was a more successful war in every way. The Germans had learned.

Mobility provides the means of either striking a defensive enemy, or avoiding his blows if you are defending. It hardly needs saying that such rapid movement must be controlled by organization. Headlong rushing forward and panic to the rear makes it hard to reassemble and reorganize troops in the interests of survival of the command. This has always been a weakness of cavalry charging other cavalry. The whole action is apt to degenerate into a man-to-man melee wherein control of the troops lost. There were repetitions of these melees in armor before St. Lo.

The most successful battles have been those of maneuver, of pinning and encircling. The old cavalry trooper's description of a battle, "grab him by the nose [by dismounted fire], and kick him in the pants [envelopment by the mounted element]," has always been sound, and was used by the armored cavalry in Viet Nam. The Principles of Fire and Movement and the Combined Employment of All Forces are largely echoes of this one. Immobilize your enemy, harm him as much as you can by artillery, automatic, and rifle fire, while sending your mobile units around either or both flanks. Mobility is absolutely necessary for assault on the critical point, and often determines its position. Loss of maneuver probably means the loss of the battle. A shock action is impossible without mobility, and in the end many battles are decided at the critical point by shock. The Principle of Exploitation of Victory cannot be pursued without mobility.

Our generation has seen the culmination of a long search for mobility in every walk of life, and perhaps an over-reliance on it. Here is a fundamental contradiction in the development of weaponry. If the permeability of a weapon and its operators is reduced by protective devices mobility can be lost. The reverse is also true. High mobility and fragility go together. The late medieval cavalry produced such over-armored men and extremely heavy beasts to carry them that it became slow, ponderous, and subject to fire. Ever since the successful application of internal combustion engines to warfare, the speed has increased to the extent that a fighting airplane today move faster than the speed of sound, and is about as vulnerable when hit as its predecessor, the kite. The best way to fight units specializing, or overspecializing in mobility is to saturate the area they must traverse by fire, which also seems to be true for intercontinental missiles. It is necessary to discover where that area is to be, of course, and have fire superiority over it. Thus, in the

Franco-Prussian War, the Germans with their breech-loading rifles utterly destroyed the French cavalry at Sedan. The German planes fluttered down as they tried to pierce the antiaircraft defenses of London. No cheers were uttered when the slow, armored, heavy bombers (Flying Fortresses) at St. Lo fell like maple leaves in the autumn.

This century has seen the mobility and strike power of military aviation destroy coastal fortifications. The massive firepower of the battleship has been invalidated, but its lumbering, in-between missions transportation, the carrier, is plainly threatened. In fact, and in praise of the air force, it might be in process of confirming its own obsolescence. As for warfare in general, the old mounted maxim is still true, "Cavalry can take but cannot hold." This is even more true of modern weapons which are so specialized in mobility that they become only highly effective and mobile artillery. Winning a war is more than destruction. There are people down below who, battered though they may be, must be considered. They may have listened to Bretnor's advice, "Disperse, take cover, or die," and may be angrily waiting at the shore to greet those who have hurt them so.

The Principle of Objective is the one which usually heads most lists, and it should. It is the place here to mark the cut-off with the man-hunting mentality of primitive war. If the bedecked warriors ever profited by it, it was by luck, and not from intent. Indeed, it is so obviously virtuous that it should not require mentioning at all, except that many a captain of the host and a plethora of statesmen have come to grief by its nonobservance. The role of bird dogs is to retrieve shot fowl. That of the foxhound is the demise of foxes only. Both types of poorly disciplined canines will run off for an easy victory over rabbits, and so have some generals.

What is the only legitimate objective of the armed forces in the field? It is the implementation of the ambitions of the state they serve. And what is the way to do this? There is only one. It is the nullification of the enemy's armed might which stands in the way of the victor's wishes. The objective of the land forces is the enemy's army, not his real estate. Napoleon's only objective was the destruction of Kutuzov's army, not golden-domed Moscow. Grant knew that his objective was Lee, not Richmond, as McClellan foolishly thought. Seek ye first the enemy's disaster, and all these desirables shall be added unto you. General Bernard Law Montgomery at Alamein found that his Eighth British Army had surrounded a mass of Germans. Old foxhunter that he was, he recognized this force as a rabbit. He refused to be committed. His real fox was the Desert Fox's Panzers, which if allowed to escape would have prolonged the war in North Africa. He went for the German tanks, and after their decisive defeat the Germans had only one choice, an orderly withdrawal.

The Principle of Security warns that even successful troops and nations must protect themselves. Napoleon protected himself poorly in his invasion of Russia, forgetting that his fellow dictator, Julius Caesar, warned that contempt for the enemy is dangerous. It has already been said that it is a mistake to consider the offensive and defensive as poles apart. They are two faces of the same social process. A vigorous counterattack may be the only defense left.

The defensive is an integral part of warfare, and must be provided for in the planning. No great fenced city, for example, was ever taken by storm from the very beginning until the fall of Constantinople to the Turks. William the Conqueror did not attempt to storm the London of his day. No competent leader, from sergeant to field marshal, fails to organize his defense, and in as much depth as he can.

Security includes counter-surprise. Any civilized formation on the move, whether in attack or retreat, protects its flanks, its rear, and probes cautiously to prevent its own surprise. This much is clear. Most animals will fight more ferociously when on the defensive than in aggression, and this is true for civilized states. Indeed, more than one military theorist, from Carl von Clausewitz to Wendell Coats, sees the origin of true war in the defensive, in the maintenance of the security of that *status quo*, more than in aggression. No modern nation entitles its war ministry as the Department of Aggression, even if it is. It is still true, however, that in open war, and diplomacy as well, the defensive only postpones defeat in the face of a determined enemy with a long time view. The offensive dictates the time-place factor, to which the defensive must at least temporarily conform.

The vulnerability and permeability of human beings dictate the following subprinciples of security. They are few, but experience throughout history has added no more.

1. Obstruction, which was mentioned under terrain protection.

2. Mobility may be used as a security measure. It is often wise to get away from a certain site with alacrity, in good order, of course.

3. Concealment. Using forests, high weeds, fields of grain, etc., may confuse an enemy as to where to deliver his fire, cause him to waste it.

4. Dispersion. General Gage learned a sad lesson at Bunker

(Breed's) Hill, but the British had to take the course over again on many a subsequent bloody field. A point that horsed cavalry's enemies, who can never see anything but a boot-to-boot charge, never cite that its soldiers can be dispersed more rapidly, controlled when dispersed, and reassembled faster than infantry. Franco's Moorish cavalry in the Spanish civil war on several occasions dispersed widely to attack the Republicans. The latter sited their machine guns at levels deadly to infantry, and were the last field soldiers to die under the sword.

The Principle of Fire and Movement may not be a principle in itself. It may be a sub-axiom of the concentration of force at the critical point. Its wisdom has been apparent since the days of the longbow. Confuse and harm your enemy as much as you can by missiles, but never stand still. Advance towards him as constantly as you can, or retreat from him if necessary, but MOVE. Fire superiority over the entire terrain may not be possible or necessary, so try to obtain it where it will do the most good, but remember that battles are won by closing with the opposition, or keeping him from closing with you.

The Principle of Combined Employment of All Forces simply means that ever since the specialization of forces, there have been horse, foot, artillery, and engineers, and all should be used in every engagement, combined according the mission to achieve victory at the critical point. This is closely related to the Principle of Correct Formations, and to the terrain. Probably the most magnificent exemplification of this principle is found in the Allied invasion of Normandy.

The Principle of Concerted Effort spells the same lesson. An old and dedicated master sergeant who, due to the fortunes of World War II, was promoted to lieutenant colonel, was heard to say during his officers' call, "Infantry fights infantry. Cavalry fights cavalry. Artillery fights artillery. Aviation fight aviation. Then what is left over jumps on the enemy." One wishes that the theory of battle were this simple, but it is not. The commander must determine the position of the critical point, and use all his resources in a pattern for its destruction, or for the protection of the troops who will accomplish this mission. It is not surprising, then, to find that one of the originators of the modern holistic philosophy was a general, Jan Smuts, for he had discovered that one must think in terms of whole systems and not of parts, of patterns and not fragments, for in battle the totality of force is stronger than the sum of its separate parts.

This is a thing easier to write about than to accomplish. There is such a thing as friction in a large command. Confederate General Hood had a subordinate in General Cox who disliked him personally, and by dragging his feet in following his commander's orders, at Ezra Church, particularly, he spoiled Hood's chance of wresting the initiative from Sherman, and Georgia was lost, and probably the Confederate cause as well. Sherman suffered from the same disease, but not as fatally. Longstreet knew that Lee's plan for Gettysburg was wrong, and was not exactly speedy in prosecuting it. The Union commander, Meade, by contrast, had a subordinate in General Winfield Scott Hancock who loved his job that day, and did it crushingly well. James Longstreet had never heard of Napoleon's advice in such matters. If a general cannot change his superior's mind about marching into folly, he should resign his commission on the spot, and let someone else take the blame for the disaster.

The Principles of Concentration of Force at the Critical Point is what it is all about, and is distilled by Nathan Bedford Forrest's supposed maxim, "Get thar fustest with the mostest." Get where? At the point where it will hurt your enemy the most, where his situation is the weakest, and do not fritter away your attack or defense all over the field. Clausewitz said: "The theory of war tries to discover how we may gain a preponderance of physical force and material at the decisive point. As this is not always possible, theory also teaches us to calculate moral factors; the likely mistakes of the enemy, the impression created by a daring action... yes, even our own desperation...."[8] Again, according to Napoleon, "The art of war may be reduced to a single principle—to unite on a single point a greater mass than the enemy." This implies, does it not, that the point can be created. The British analyst Alfred Burne criticizes Sherman for not doing this time after time in the Atlanta campaign. Colonel Burne strongly implies that Sherman would have been defeated if Hood had commanded from the beginning instead of Joseph (Fight-and-Fall-Back) Johnson, who also had a talent for frittering. The principle is also true for the defensive, too, for as Petain said, "He who defends all loses all."

A battle is not a struggle for absolute strengths but for relative ones. It is at the point of decision where strength counts, and one cannot be too strong there, wherever else one is weak. Remember that one can win a battle, even numerically more battles than the enemy, as the Confederacy did, and still lose the war. The test of battle, then, and of campaigns as well, is the concentration of force where it will hurt the most.

Force must be effective, on target, destructive, penetrative where it counts, and conserved where it is not needed. It is applied where the enemy is off balance, where he can be thrown into that condition, where his equilibrium of system is the weakest. Every successful courtroom lawyer knows this, and disrupts with surprise testimony where he can. It is true in any political campaign, any diplomatic, economic, cultural, and psychological effort wherein one side is apt to lose something valuable. The more complex the system, the harder it is to maintain organization.

The critical point must be determined for each engagement, and there is no infallible formula for doing so. One must ask, where is it? Can I get there in time? What will be my costs in fatigue and casualties in getting there? As much work as possible should be performed ahead of time: map study, reconnoiter, and intelligence. It is well to intercept or guess the enemy's order of battle, for the personalities of opposing subordinate generals are well worth study. Results of this beforehand study may collapse if the enemy has unlimited power of maneuver. He may refuse battle until he, not you, wants it, making the find-him-fix-him-fight-him formula a bit simplistic. Indeed, such a point may never develop, as in the protracted trench warfare in World War I.

The critical point will usually reveal itself if the initiative can be kept. If continuous pressure can be exerted, the opposition's organization will tend to disintegrate somewhere, and that is probably the critical point if the area involved is important. This weakness may be a feint, however, and one must beware of being drawn into that ancient booby trap of the pretended weak center. This is so old a trick that it is described in *Judges* 20 for the campaign against Gibeah. If the enemy is overextended, it may be the center. A commander, though, ordinarily makes his center strong, for he fears being penetrated and cut in two.

More often than not, the attack will attempt a turning movement, suspecting that one or both flanks constitute a decisive point. Flanking may cut the enemy from his base and support troops, and permit one to enfilade him and roll him up. He knows this, too, and may protect his flanks with cavalry or armor.

The possibility of nuclear war has not diminished the importance of the critical point. Nuclear weapons are too expensive and destructive to waste in widespread, indiscriminate showering. Besides, if the aggressor intends to occupy and exploit the defender's economic land, that is, his natural resources, it would be unwise to make them uninhabitable. Battlefield use of atomic artillery is surely under consideration. Shelling by it could isolate the opposition units, inhibiting their cooperation, and immobilizing their reserves.

The Principle of Integrity of Tactical Units may not be a battle principle at all, but a strategic one. It is certainly one of social psychology. It means no more than that able commanders long ago recognized that a unit is a system of primary transaction of the family type. The men are already conditioned to each other, in small units at least, and are accustomed to each other. Battle casualties are best filled by individual replacements so that the old unit pride and tradition may be maintained. Morale is a battle weapon, and cannibalizing a unit and distributing its members around the command, except as a means of disciplining an unsatisfactory unit, is folly. Old Civil War units, based on kinship, neighborhood, and social position, kept their morale.

The Principle of Simplicity of Plans is a primary consideration. A battle, like all complex transactions, requires intense study of all possible contingencies. It may be that a bad plan is better than none, but not much, especially if fighting an able opponent. There is such a thing as luck, too, and the staff planner must keep in mind that such fickleness of fate might favor the other side. There are almost always unforeseen and unforeseeable circumstances called "the fog of war."

Ever since units have increased beyond the personal control of the commander, a bureaucratic structure of a staff has been necessary. Even the mind of a military genius cannot discover, evaluate, and remember all the necessary details, and in no place does intelligence, industry, experience, and dedication pay more than in the aforesaid master's general and special staff. It is no place for culls. Staff plans must be made in peace against every potential enemy, and must be constantly revised. Thus, you may be sure that if you live in an important place, there are brilliant men who have a plan for the reduction, destruction, containment, or occupation of your home city, plans made by bright men who do not know your name and could not care less. Count von Schlieffen's plan for the defeat of France was made long before August 1914, and was almost foolproof. A fool did get involved, however, when the field command was given to the younger von Moltke, a neurotic who could not follow through.

Even a good plan must be flexible. Granted the possession of command and staff genius, the unforeseen can happen, and there must be an alternative. Furthermore, if the enemy perceives that you are capable of erecting only one plan, or very few, he really has focused the microscope of military intelligence on you. Napoleon used to boast that he had worked out every detail of a campaign before entering it. Actually, he was much more flexible than this, but nevertheless Wellington had seen through him and predicted his behavior before Waterloo was joined. Soviet Russia, who had never fought a major power, held to such rigidity of method and plan that the Germans defeated them handily. When the Russians saw the wisdom of this and began fighting like Germans, they saved their state.

Plans must be as simple as the conditions permit. Language is at best an inadequate means of communication, as you well know. Every active person is partially misunderstood every day. The more intricate the plan, the greater the possibility of misunderstanding, in delay of following through by some subordinate, of failure to integrate all the pieces into an operating whole. The more complex the plan, the nearer these faults become inevitabilities.

Any pair of human beings, or any group thereof, who intend seriously to influence one another must, in popular parlance, "size up each other," especially if one seeks an advantage, even a minor and gentle one, to the disadvantage of the other. Most of us have, for example, resisted the blandishments of a salesman who failed in his evaluation of us. Success follows a rational judgment as to one's own capabilities and those of the enemy, and is called in American staff language the estimate of the situation.

The steps of arriving at an estimate of the situation are described for the United States in Field Manual 105-5, and follow a fairly rigid ritual procedure. This rigidity does not flow from a love of formal inflexibility, but is the construction of a program to avoid forgetting some essential step. Actually, serious problem-solving in civilian life had better have such a routine, and for the same reason. The following questions are not quotations from this routine, but are matters of advice.

The first step must be the intelligence estimate. The commander must have the best possible information about the enemy, which must be carefully evaluated. It might not all be true, nor even as near the truth as possible. In the meantime, until his intelligence sources provide him with better information, he must assume that his enemy's troops are as able, as well led, as well armed, and of as good morale as his own. The commander must then solve the time-space-environment situation. In other words, Where am I? What is my own and my foe's terrain for operations? He must then ask himself, What do I intend to do? What are my means of accomplishing this goal? What are my enemy's means of frustrating my wishes? The commander can make no successful plan until he has at least a fair knowledge of these factors. He cannot estimate the position of the critical point, where he or his opponent may seriously be out of balance.

Obviously there must be alternate estimates and subsequent plans.

One says obviously, but this is a hard lesson to learn for any person apt to fall in love with his own wisdom, and this includes many directors in all fields of endeavor. Battle is only more serious for, if one plan fails and is persisted in, destruction may be the alternative. A business-head may fail financially, and a university department-head fall short of professional success, but death of other people may follow a general's or surgeon's *amour propre.* "The eye sees what is in the mind," said the criminologist Bertillon, but the opposition's mind-set may see a different picture.

The Principle of Correct Formations is hard to generalize about in this day when the tables of organization are changing rapidly to fit modern conditions. The correct formation must be determined for each engagement. Too much standardizing on a nation's part may be fatal.

The Principle of Economy of Force can be simply stated by the advice not to send out a man to do a boy's work. You may need the man somewhere else. This is a truism, of course. There is more to it, though, than the simple arithmetic of the personnel required to attack or defend. It is hard to think that there can be too many troops at a preselected critical point, but unless an adequate number is withheld until the point of decision is determined in the course of the battle, one had better keep as strong a reserve for the moment of truth as he can. General von Arnim committed his entire reserve in the Battle of Ypres in 1914, while Sir Douglas Haig with his slim forces kept a little reserve which he skillfully committed at this point, and started scraping up the rear area for any soldier he could find to form a greater reserve. Seemingly complacent about the need of any reserves in depth, Eisenhower was attacked by Rundstedt in the Ardennes, and the bottom scraping of cooks, bakers, clerks and typists was wonderful and fearful, but it helped turn the tide. His strategic reserve was out on pass in the Rheims region.

The Principle of Sufficient Numbers, or of *Mass* is only a corollary of the foregoing one. One should not send out a boy to do a man's work. It does not mean overall and overwhelming numbers everywhere. Local superiority where it counts is what must be sought. Good small armies have time and again humiliated large masses. Clausewitz said: "We must select of the enemy's position for our attack...and attack it with great superiority, leaving the rest of his army in uncertainty, but keeping it occupied. This is the only way that we can use an equal or smaller force to fight with advantage and thus with a chance of success."[9]

The Principle of Exploitation of Victory is a sad one insofar as it has so often been neglected. Why all this bloodshed to win a battlefield victory unless one intends to convert it into a shortening or finishing of a war? Indeed, the axiom is so much one of common sense that perhaps it should not be cited as a principle, but it seems that common sense is a bit uncommon. Under the title of Pursuit, Clausewitz thought that it is a principle. Once you have defeated him, never let him go. Maintain vigorous contact, for unless he is utterly destroyed and demoralized, he will regroup, lick his wounds and make another attempt against you. Before you rank Wellington among the greatest captains, tell why he and his Spanish allies, having thoroughly trounced and discredited the French in the Peninsular Campaign, permit them to leave Spain to become Napoleonic nuisances later? He could have prevented this escape, but he did not make this mistake at Waterloo. Rowan Robinson is quoted by Alfred Burne in saying, "for 150 years prior to the Great War, Jena, Waterloo, and Tel el Kebir [*in the Egyptian campaign of 1882*] furnish the only examples of complete victory by pursuit." Why did Howe, after thoroughly defeating Washington at the Battle of Long Island, let him escape destruction? Instead, Howe permitted him to gain the mainland, while he himself retired to enjoy the pleasures of loyalist New York. Why did Meade allow Lee to escape after Gettyburg? His infantry was tired, of course, but where was his underemployed cavalry? He must have known that J. E. B. Stuart was too far away to help Lee. Meade permitted Confederate Imboden to gather up some scraps of horse, and drive the halfhearted Union cavalry pursuit back to its horse lines. Did George Meade know he had beaten the renowned Robert Lee? Lee recovered and continued the war for a long time. Why did not Braxton Bragg, whose army had thoroughly beaten the Union, permit them to withdraw? Both Bragg and Buell were so inept at Perryville that neither knew that their armies had been engaged, and that a decisive victory-defeat engagement had been fought in Kentucky. Why did not Jefferson Davis sack Bragg? We know the answer. He loved him personally.

Violation of this vital principle is a politician's illness rather than a general's, leading to an indecisive war. Why did Woodrow Wilson stop his armies at the Rhine, and thus become the architect of World War II? Why did Franklin Roosevelt, or was it Eisenhower's almost complete lack of strategic sense, halt the armies at the Elbe, and wait for days for the arrival of the Russians? The Russian lines of communications were overextended, and after the Ardennes, the American ones were taut as a well-wound mainspring. Why was General George Patton recalled from Czechoslovakia and sent on a wild-goose chase against a nonexistent Alpine fortress? Why did

THE ART AND SCIENCE OF WARFARE 71

Harry Truman (Colonel, USAR) stop Douglas MacArthur at some Korean parallel or other, to become a co-planner for Viet Nam? Had he been warned by Intelligence that the Russians would join the war in force? Probably not! Why did Lyndon Johnson (Lieutenant Commander, USNR) stop William Westmoreland when he could have won the war in southeast Asia?

And so, civilians know this much from life. Be offensive even on the defense. Do not "telegraph your punches." Know as much about your opponent as you can, and keep your secrets from him. Use the natural environment to help yourself, and to hinder your ill-wisher. Keep pressing in this direction, but do not confide your desperation to your foe. Protect yourself whenever you can, for everybody is vulnerable, even the strong. Distract and confuse your opponent with missiles, but try to get close enough to him to change his opinion. Use all the resources at your command, and all at the same time. Strike where it hurts the most, and not just anywhere. Respect the integrity of your helpers, and do not consider them just so many faceless bodies. Get the best information you can, then plan your actions calmly, and do not devise a recipe for action that your subordinates cannot understand or carry through. Use only the combination of things most likely to succeed. Do not waste a man's strength on a boy's job, and keep a few men around to help the youth if he gets in trouble. And if you have won a poker game, do not pack up and go home. If you do, they will surely ask you to play again, and on their terms, and with a stacked deck.

Is all of this so very profound? Apparently it is, for in war and peace so few are able to keep these simple precepts in mind. There is something of which we may be very sure. If your chiefs cannot conceptualize these simple principles, they will ask somebody besides themselves to pay the bill, and this could be you.

FOOTNOTES AND REFERENCES

[1] Lieutenant Colonel Alfred H. Burne, *The Art of War: Illustrated by Campaigns and Battles of All Ages*, Harrisburg, 4th printing (revised), p. 23. With permission of Stackpole Books.

[2] Raymond L. Garthof, *Soviet Military Doctrine*, Glencoe, 1960, p. 1f. With permission of The Rand Corporation.

[3] *Tactics and Techniques of Cavalry*, 6th edition, Washington and Harrisburg, Military Service Publishing Company, 1935. With permission of Stackpole Books.

[4] Oliver Lyman Spaulding, Jr., Hoffman Nickerson, and John Womack Wright, *Warfare: A Study of Military Methods from the Earliest Times*, New York, 1925, p. 3. Harcourt, Brace and Company.

[5] *Frederick the Great, Instructions for His Generals*, translated by Brigadier General Thomas R. Phillips, Harrisburg, 1944, p. 58. With permission of Stackpole Books.

[6] Brigadier General J. D. Hittle, ed., *Jomini and His Summary of the Art of War*, Harrisburg, p. 117. With permission of Stackpole Books.

[7] The reference for this, and other remarks regarding World War II, is B. H. Liddell Hart, *History of the Second World War*, New York, G. P. Putnam's Sons, 1970.

[8] Carl von Clausewitz, *Principles of War*, translated and edited by Hans W. Gatzke, 1942. With permission of Stackpole Books.

[9] *Op. cit.*, p. 21

Chapter 4

CIVIL GOVERNMENT AS THE WARRIOR

The Political Revolution

The sociological revolution resting on the kinship and the community made men out of talented monkeys, but that was not enough. Not enough to create civilization, for that term includes or really rests on the political revolution which brought the civil state into being. When some societies organize themselves into civil governments, they cross an irreversible threshold. Nonliterate men could live in kinship dominated societies, but we cannot. We are committed. Perhaps a few can drop out like Thoreau and live at Walden Pond, protected by the rest of us who must take the bitter with the sweet.

The revolution now to be considered is the political one. Society became riven into classes, each with its own manners/morals code, and informal controls would no longer suffice. The overall civil state was invented in more than one place, and diffused from others. Thus, at the opening of the twentieth century, the majority of mankind lived happily without civil government. This is no longer true. Everyone is now organized into civil states, even the most unlikely. This is mightily the present concern, for the civil state and true, or tactical, strategic, and logistic warfare has twin births. Wherever there is the one, there is the other, and there are no exceptions.

Human society, among other things, is a technique for survival. Many nonhuman groups are also survival oriented, and observations of prides of lions show that such social structures are not confined to primates. The infrahuman primate group was adequate for the demands put upon it until for good, evil, or both, one species of the genus stood more or less upright and held a sharp instrument in its hand. By that event the transacting human group found an ever increasing task of maintaining existence on this kind of a planet. The animal group is based on physiology and sex. It is structured, indeed, with each member knowing his "place," but this is an organization derived from experience and the conditionable response. These two were not abandoned with the acquisition of real humanity. Actually, they were sharpened, but still they were not enough for a creature whose hand could grasp some other animal's fibula as a club, or a sharpened bit of flint as a piercer. The human group had to elaborate the rudimentary animal normative system, for it had now not only to survive in the natural environment but a human one as well. And so, the individual person had to learn to live in a homeostatic normative system, from simple to complex, from manners and morals to the law, eventually to bureaucratic procedures, guide lines, and administrative regulations.

The human group had to systematize its norms over the rudiments thereof found in animal aggregates, who has the right to peck whom, who eats first, who protects whom, and so on. Norms in this sense are, of course, standardized ritual procedures such as manners, morals, law, and administrative regulations. The older types of norms are rather successful attempts to predict the behavior of one's associates, for utter unpredictability forbids the existence of even the simpler human social systems. Manners or etiquette patterns are only niceties, little rituals which are designed to keep us from irritating our fellows so that adequate transaction for group maintenance is difficult. Manners are not matters of group survival, and their violation is punished only by limited withdrawal from the transactional pattern of the offender. They are taught to children with such insistence that they are made part of the personality of members of a social system, and are obeyed almost automatically.

Morals are more serious concepts than manners. They are conceived of as survival rituals. Most of them, according to William Graham Sumner, are derived from older folkways, or etiquette procedures, but a public welfare aspect has been added. Probably due to the increasing complexity of a social system, a group comes to feel that certain norms *must* be observed if the system is to survive. Immorality is punished by complete withdrawal from the offender, and not infrequently inflicting an unspecified amount of violence on his person and property. Manners and morals do very well until a society is deeply riven by social classes and many institutions. A more formal and authoritative normative system is then required.

The law offers a predictable and exact amount of punishment against the offender's person and property. As a result of the search for stability, it is in many ways the most glorious sociologic invention of mankind. Manners and morals are characteristic of specific kinships, communities, and social classes, and are really only valid within them. The law cuts across such structures. The law is the standard of minimum good conduct expected of a reasonable man, a rule which cuts across all kinships, classes, and communities of a social system. Ideally, it is a rule of *minimum* good conduct, for as the Romans said, *de minimis non curat lex*, the law is not interested in trifles.

The law is the handmaiden of the state, and where you find one, you usually find the other. There are some minor exceptions, of societies which have rudimentary law but not civil government. The Ifugao of the Philippines are one exception,[1] and certain Nigerian peoples are another.[2] As a working rule, however, we can say that the law is the decree of the state. A political scientist would say that.

In any event, the civil state is one such technique for survival, and as there is apparently something inherently distasteful about systematically killing other human beings, the survival motive is almost always invoked for war, even if the state's real motive is expansionist or even predatory. It is true that the origin of the state sprang from an in-group wish for economic welfare, the human being has added something non-animal to his psyche, a compulsive expansion of his wants and the tools wherewith to satisfy them. Remember that while fighting may be instinctive, war and the tools of war are cultural constructs. Expansion of the level of consumption, or the maintenance of one far beyond the needs of survival or comfort, is often confused with the needs of life and death. A survey of states ancient and modern yields the impression that they would rather accomplish their survival/expansionist goals by peaceful means, and often do, nevertheless the state is a sociological means to obtain what its clientele *considers* requisite and necessary for the body as well as the spirit. It is, among other things, a device for applying lethal force against nonmembers, and members if need be, in the satisfaction of these goals. It may be as Herbert Spencer and others have said that the number of wars has decreased over the centuries, but their range and lethality have increased. War and politics are apparently inseparable concepts, and if one hates the one, he must loathe the other, which is not too difficult to do at times. Yet the nihilist alternative of a slow death by starvation rather than a quick one of the sword is so unappealing that most of us elect to bear the burden of the state. All social organization is repressive of the organism. This dictum of the great French sociologist Emile Durkheim is hard to swallow, but there it is.

The existence of an armed police force in stateless social systems is rare, but it has been known. Of course, a power to protect the internal welfare is inherent in all social systems, but an organized, ritualized armed police force in the popular sense can be cited. The bison-hunting Indians of the American Great Plains had such military police forces, and needed them. They were in almost constant combat footing, or were on the communal buffalo hunt. The impetuous young men had to be restrained from rushing and prematurely stampeding the game animals, and thereby threatening the band food supply. They had also to be kept from rushing the enemy in battle before the right moment. All such behavior was contrary to the public welfare. These Indians were so stateless that they lacked authoritative chiefs in combat, but they had the famous police associations—Crazy Dogs, Kit Foxes, and others—who could exercise lethal force against the offenders if need be without fear of retaliation. These are exceptions, but need can inspire exceptions to general principles.

Nonliterate rarities are not under discussion, but the state is. Now it is the state which gives the most, and it also exacts the most, and back of its exactions lies the possibility of force. As neither the army nor the police force can exist without the state, this survival is mutual. The Law giveth, and the Law taketh away, and this extraction may not necessarily be gentle. The state would much prefer that everyone acknowledges and conforms to the public welfare function of its police power, but be not deceived. Back of the benevolent decrees of the state stand the troops with loaded weapons and fixed bayonets. The Federal government militarily enrolled a student at the University of Mississippi at a dollar cost comparable to its capture of the forts of Vicksburg in the same state.

This effort was not a novelty in American history. Having frustrated the British government which wished by force of arms to make its civil writ obeyed throughout its thirteen colonies, the new United States government, born in turbulent instability, was faced with the same internally. This is after the manner of revolutions. With a population suffering from war fatigue, it had reduced the regular army to less than three thousand men, but it put down Revolutionary War Captain Shay's Rebellion, and the Whiskey Rebellion, with force of arms.

Durkheim's dictum tells only half of the story. Sociopolitical organization is repressive, but it is also permissive of the organism. It gratifies our most fundamental needs, survival being the greatest.

The synonyms state, civil government, and polity have been used so much in the preceding pages that a definition is now in order. It is *a system of ritualized social control exercised by full-time specialists. It does not terminate to a higher system except under compulsion, and its power of originating is strong enough to make its clients aware of this subordination to it either by inducing or compelling them to support it out of the surpluses of the productive classes. Its external relations subsystem contains both the right of embassy, and true, or tactical warfare.*[3]

The orgins of this master repressive-permissive institution have long intrigued social theorists. Most of the elder practitioners have had to unlearn much, and it is not pertinent to map the blind alleys once trod. There were many schools of thought, largely based on the wishful thinking of the political bias in fashion, but the works of Karl Wittfogel and others have eroded so many of these charming prejudices.

It is stated here, with perhaps too much simplicity, that the origins of the state are not to be found in war but in the public works of peace. Furthermore, the early states were divinely charismatic. It is secularism which is a political afterthought. The archaeological record for both the Old and New Worlds is fairly clear. Certainly it is not the old war chiefs who made themselves politically paramount. The study of primitive war has shown their incompetence for complex organization. They may have had their part in all this, but the state could not be and was not based on some vague war leadership. The first pictures of drilled troops were contemporary with those very early kings who look more sacerdotal than military. The oldest known drawing of a military unit working under an officer was made by the Sumerians, so long dead that these "after the Flood" Asians who migrated to and helped civilize the Tigris and Euphrates Valleys are still largely a mystery people.

The state was probably fabricated out of many materials. There are some irreducible requirements for it, but each truly political people had to meet their own needs according to their own genius and traditions. Only the most ardent diffusionist would claim that civic orderliness was invented in just one place and time, and then spread throughout the civilized world. In spite of several variables, not perfectly understood, please consider these basic ideas. The political organization did not first occur on the best land, the most fertile and naturally productive, but on relatively unpromising terrain. A highly productive cultivation on superior farmland is a later development. Again, it was the commercial man, not the war chief, who lay at the core. It was he and his prospectors, smelters, and smiths who brought in the high Bronze Age, which was one of implacable war. Military-industrial complex? It is an ancient friendship. Except for Middle America, it was the bronze blade which severed the umbilical cord connecting humanity with the kinship. This was done in the name of whatever god or gods there were, and in several times and places.

Look at these semi-arid lands populated by able folk: the Valleys of the Indus, Tigris, Euphrates, Nile, the coastal lands of Peru, and the highlands of southern Mexico, and very unproductive places they all were for people who had just learned to farm. Nevertheless, with late Neolithic stone and early Bronze Age hatchets, it was easier for them to fight aridity than the forests of the rainier regions. Wittfogel calls these early states hydraulic civilizations and, based on irrigation as they were, his term is descriptive.[4] And there were gods served by priesthoods, a late phenomenon in mankind's prehistory. This is not the place to trace the development of vague, local spirits into divinities with identifiable personalities and names, and their servants from shamans or medicine men into liturgically-minded priesthoods. It is a fascinating story, much of it hypothetical, but it is sufficient here to know that it happened in each of the regions just mentioned. The oldest states were divine: they were bureaucratically absolute; they were economic enterprises; their authority was backed by force of arms.

Mesopotamia is a desert except where watered by irrigation from the two rivers. Egypt is one of the worst deserts in the world, the Sahara, really, except where the Nile's irrigation ditches relieves it. The coastal plain of Peru was and is a wretched country from a farmer's point of view. The highlands of southern Mexico, the valleys, the high and arid plateau between the two principle mountain ranges were good for the simplest farming, but not adequate to maintain a large population, and the rain forests of the Yucatan peninsula were too difficult for the culture of the time. The Maya eventually conquered the lowland rain forest, and the ancestral Peruvians moved to the high valleys where by irrigation they could utilize the snow meltage of the Andes.

Each of these areas discovered the benefits of irrigation, but this demanded a social organization and authority beyond that of the clan. Thus was civil government born, cutting across kinship lines and taking precedence over it. Thus the little shamanistic spirits became godlets, and they developed into pantheons of mighty gods with splendid temples. This demanded priesthood, not shamanism, and with this trait came recurrent feasts and fasts, always beloved by the liturgical clergy. This required record-keeping, and as the religious cycle of worship was based on the heavenly bodies, astronomy and mathematics were also born. Only a rudimentary state can exist without record-keeping, but we are speaking of divine, productive, bureaucratic monarchies here, and authoritarian states and their bureaucrats must and do keep meticulous records. Craftsmen gathered around the temples, for the gods need fine things. The sacred workshops demanded storage space, and the temples became warehouses for the contributions of food needed to maintain them and their works.

The charisma is the present subject. The most important priest of the ranking god became not only the chief hierarch but king. Was Melchisedek not only priest but king in Salem? Did not even the much later King Solomon offer the first sacrifice in the new temple, and not the sons of Aaron? Does the role of priest-king offend you? If so, you are betraying the lateness of your birth. It was a terrible burden for the people to build and maintain the irrigation systems, but the totalitarian monarchies were divine. Obedience to them was demanded by the gods, and disobedience was sinful as well as criminal. The charisma is cheaper than force, but that was there, too. The first troops were obviously pretorian ones to keep the workers dedicated to their task. Food and consumption goods must be produced.

Civilization was born thus, which does not mean a society of the sweet, loveable, and cultivated, but a configuration of culture which contains cities, metallurgy, institutionalized politics, a system of keeping records, priestly religion, institutionalized commerce, and tactical warfare performed by professionals. The priesthood may be weak or abolished today, but the rest of this sociological nosegay is still with us, to feed us, to organize us, and the army, now one dominant, now another, but all working in a functionally dependent pattern.

Self-protection may have contributed to the rise of some military states, for this happened right before our colonial eyes. The Cherokees were a loosely related group of kinship villages when the Europeans landed on the coast of what is now the southeastern United States. The colonists pressed westward and encroached on Cherokee lands. Treaties were made with the Indians and broken. Their rights were protected by the British Crown, which enraged the white settlers against this overseas monarchy. Very swiftly and in order to maintain themselves, the Cherokee invented the sacred priest-kingship protected by a military nobility right before the history-writing American eyes, and in vain.

This chapter takes the position that some sacred monarchies were invented independently, but it does not deny the possibilities of diffusion in some instances. The Cherokee incident suggests as much. It is not unthinkable that the extremes of the sacred, military naive states of Polynesia were in part diffusions from the mainland of Asia. One of the most powerful divine military empires of North America, that of the Natchez, has too many Mexican features to have been the whole-cloth invention of the lower Mississippi Valley. The sacred kingdoms and empires of black Africa have too many resemblances to Pharaonic Egypt to be completely independent. The hypermilitarism of some of them was probably due to the inspiration of the early European colonists, and it is certain that the royal war machine of the Zulu was. Its founder, King Dingiswayo, knew about, admired, and attempted to emulate Napoleon.

As for our own tradition, the Indo-European speaking folk swept over the world as they knew it. They had also heard of priest-kings, and the Greeks began filling each valley, conquering and enslaving the natives by their secret weapons, the horse and the iron sword. The head of the most sacred clan became a little king, and the patriarchs of the most prestigeful ones became the noble, military companions and protectors of the court. The country folk came to the little *polis* with their gifts, and in the palace they could be fed and entertained. Here they could find justice of a kind, but why continue? It is all in Homer. Their kinsmen in India made the noble companions into the *kshatriya* caste of professional soldiers. It happened in Ireland, and wherever the old language family was spoken. The limited, defensive wars did not satisfy them forever. The Greeks looked across the commerce-controlling Bosphorus and saw the fortress of Troy which had to be destroyed if Hellenic prosperity was to increase, and King Agamemnon was a forward-looking man.

The civil governments along this royal line were city states. Our word civilization comes from the Latin word for city, *civis*, while politics is derived from the Greek word *polis* meaning the same thing. Here were the priests who encouraged craftsmen and invented and improved writing.

City air makes free, as our mediaeval ancestors said of their mercantile revolution. Free from superstition, which is only the country people's beliefs. Free from trammels of kinship, for who in any city cares who your clan or family might be? The unsibbed, uprooted, defamilized countrymen are all jumbled together into the only important relationship, the efficiency of production and distribution which the old tribal militia was incapable of defending. It was in the cities that the state religions were conceived and enforced, but within the walls people began doubting the not very credible gods of Athens, Rome, and elsewhere. Here began the worship of the state for its own sake, and the senatorial military republic was born. The office of priest-king, of the high priest of Jove or *flamen dialis*, or in Athens the *archon basileus*, became a nice sinecure for somebody's nephew, and the republic was due to have its day.

The very term "republic" is hard to define, and becoming more so. Ordinarily one thinks of a state whose chief is elected either by the people or the legislature, its holding office by the popular will. Republican Carthage was none of these, nor was Rome, nor Athens, either, during its heyday. The modern "people's republics" meet none of these terms. Introducing the concept of democracy only muddles the picture. The Most Serene Republic of Venice never claimed to be a democracy, and the Republics of South Carolina and Texas could hardly be called that when they joined the Union. Be content by saying, broadly, that a republic is a state wherein the chief is appointed by election rather than by hereditary right. Recall, though, that the all-powerful electorate might be a very small segment of the actual population, and not "the people" at all. Even here there is a difficulty. Before it was dismembered by its neighbors, Poland called itself a kingdom whose monarch was elected by a numerous nobility. The old papal state never claimed to be a republic because its head was elected by the cardinals.

Developed senatorial republics have had a way of becoming noble military ones, fighting defensively until their position and territory are secure, then turning towards expansionism. Athens and other Greek city states on one side of the Adriatic, and Rome on the other, began as pastoral priest-kingships, but the aristocratic clan chiefs overthrew the monarchies early in their recorded histories. Athens has often been called a democratic republic by western historians, but this was far from true. One has to deduct the disenfranchised, haremized decent women from any population estimate. The bulk of the Athenian population were slaves, or peonized descendents of the aborigines, and the strangers. The latter term included many people whose families had lived in Athenian territory for generations, but since they were not descended from the original invaders of Attica, they were political nonpersons. Actually, Athens was a noble senatorial republic, the legislature being a town meeting of all the free, properly born citizens, a small minority of the population of the city. The common people were not considered fit to join the army except as unimportant auxilliaries and camp servants. A very wholesome theme is perceived in Athenian warfare. The senators alone declared war, and they fought it as hoplites, or the heavy infantry line. Having in a not very clean way forced itself to the head of its allies, Athens turned towards empire with disastrous results.

Rome was likewise ruled originally by a royal priest. King Numa Pompilius not only regularized the official theology but wrote the basic tables of organization for the old army. As is known, the priest-kingship was overthrown by the noble chiefs, and the senatorial, or perhaps the patrician military republic was on its way. Very incorruptible and high-minded the old senators and consuls were in the early days, although Brutus, Scaevola, and others were just too, too noble as described by Livy to be quite credible. The aristocratic senators, however, allowed the plebs and farmers to fight in the army, although retaining commissioned rank for themselves. A very successful military machine it was, as we all know. Its degeneration into senatorial venality, selfish power structures, tyrannies, and dictatorships was so complete that Julius Caesar and his grandnephew Octavius (Augustus) overthrew it without too much difficulty.

It is not expected that the next republican type in western history will be accepted as such by everybody. Yet what states as were left between the collapse of Roman imperial authority and the rise of centralist, absolutist monarchies in the renaissance were likewise patrician military republics, this time, though, on a cavalry instead of heavy infantry model. The survivors of the Roman military system rallied some troops and free farmers for the defense of Gaul against the barbarians. They were former barbarian mercenaries themselves, and knew what to expect from the invaders. Their tenants stood and died side by side with them, but they won, and passed a kind of Roman civilization down to us. The free farmers lost much of their liberty in that search for military and economic stability, but it is well to remember in these post-Rousseau days that feudalism was once a blessing, and one without which we could not have survived.

Oh yes, there was a king around somewhere, but who paid any attention to him? The Capetian kings of France received no financial support from the baronage. They lived on the products of their own estates, like other feudal lords. One such king told his son and potential successor that if he could look from the walls of the castle of the Louvre and see no fires between him and the not distant tower of Montlhery, he could count that a lucky day. The Dukes of Burgundy, Brittany, the Kings of Navarre, the Counts of Foix considered themselves sovereign, and the Count of the civilized Visigothic state of Provence had to be the subject of a holy crusade to bring him to obedience to the French crown. The Duke of Normandy and Count of Anjou, inheritor of the lands of Eleanor of Acquitaine, who was incidentally King of England, sometimes did homage for his lands, but was the implacable enemy of the Capet, and usually fought to take away his crown. It is certain that whenever the great magnates got together in the name of something called France, they were a mounted, armed senate, and did about as they pleased.

England, although William the Conqueror tried to have a more centralized government than France, was as much a military noble republic as the latter. The armed barons actually elected the king, and deposed him when they found him unsatisfactory. Unfortunately for his survival, he was the anointed of the Lord and really could not be deposed. He had to be killed. The following list shows that many were.

This is the list of the impeached. (1) William the Second Rufus, a far less exacting man than his father the Conqueror, shot by a knight who was never punished for the act. (2) Edward II was defeated, imprisoned, and murdered by the baronage. (3) John I who wished to erect a modern government and halt the papal financial and political exactions, defeated by the baronage and forced to sign the Magna Carta. Persons who think this instrument was the foundations of democracy had better read it in the context of its times. (4) Henry III, a reactionary king, was defeated by the more modern and tactically efficient baronage under Simon de Montfort the Younger, the Good Earl Simon, at Lewes. (5) Henry VI was deposed by the baronage. Richard II might have been an ineffective king, but he erred in sympathizing with the peasants' rebellion. He was deposed by the nobility and murdered somewhere, probably in Pontrefact Castle. (6) Richard III also made the mistake of holding a liberal parliament, and was betrayed and murdered on Bosworth Field. There is no evidence that he imprisoned and murdered his nephews in the Tower. The succeeding parliament held by his enemies, composed an impressive list of charges against him, but did not accuse the dead Richard of this crime, which they would have been delighted to do had it been true. The baronial parliament then elected the Earl of Richmond under the title of Henry VII, a man with less royal Plantagenet blood than many readers of these pages. (7) Then there was Charles I, defeated and executed by the House of Commons for refusing to accept a nominal monarchy and abolishing the Church of England. The sentence of death passed the court by a vote of one. (8) James II was perhaps the most morally impeccable man ever to bear the title, but he was unyielding in his devotion to the Roman Church. The London merchantdom had him deposed. Parliament elected Mary Stuart and her husband William of Orange, who defeated James II at the Battle of the Boyne, Ireland.[5] (9) At the death of William and Mary, the legitimist Prince Charles Edward Stuart was defeated at Culloden, and Parliament elected the Elector of Hanover as king. (10) As a matter of legal fact, Ernest Elector of

Hanover had a better claim to the crown at the death of William IV than did Victoria, but the establishment objected to his morals, and with some reason, and a young girl was elected. (11) Times will change, and belief in the charisma can fade, so Edward VIII was not killed but deposed by the establishment and exiled. In any event, this is a rather impressive record.

Of time-space-energy, the first two are now under consideration. The American and Russian peoples have lived to see these ancient man-making concepts collapse around them under the threat of inter-continental nuclear bombardment. The formalities of the declaration of war and peace, are probably obsolete. Decisions may have to be made in minutes if the nation and its people are to survive. The power to make war and peace are essential to the concept of sovereignty, and if a government is thus vested in the people, we may have to rewrite the dictionary.

There is only space to remark certain characteristics of superstates. Every step in the march towards them cannot be traced, and it is doubtful if they have always been the same. It is nevertheless necessary to remind Americans and British readers, with their two brief centuries of *laissez faire* tradition, that the prime reason for the invention of the state in the first place was the acquisition and utilization of energy resources and their products in the interests of the clientele. The ancient polities of the Indus, Tigris-Euphrates, and the Nile Valleys began as bureaucratic despotisms, and for this very reason. If the increasing complexities of energy sources have become more complicated, be not surprised if recent trends are in the ancient tradition. This seems to be the only way that the greatest good, not for the greatest number but the total number can be achieved.

It is true that the patriarchal, pastoral priest-kingships of Indo-European speech did not begin as Oriental, despotic war states, but those which survived became such. Athens failed because her imperial ambitions took the wrong geographical turn frittering away her strength on Mediterranean islands instead of incorporating the then little Roman city state. Rome in her turn did not fail. The Greco-Roman civilization carried the vegetable-energy system and infantry jugernaut as far as they could go. Great Britain, from an insignificant kingdom on the edge of the known world, carried the solid fossil energy system as far as the inherencies permitted, and became the greatest oligarchically controlled commercial and militarily enforced empire thus far. Today, though, if coal is king, it is a sick one. The Marquess Curzon of Keddleston saw the obsolescence of the coal-driven war fleet, and pushed Great Britain in the direction of the Netherlands East Indian petroleum reserves. Lord Curzon's Britain was out-competed by her American elder daughter, with apparently limitless energy resources, set out on the great fossil fuel adventure. Starting as a have-all nation of almost continental size, the United States is now facing the possibilities of a have-not economy, and her domination of the ocean's oil-path by her fleet is threatened. She must find new energy resources or, like her Britannic mother, become a haven for tourists viewing former grandeur. But then before, British troops set foot on every profitable and defenseless shore seeking raw materials and markets. Britannia was truly ruling the waves with numerous no-nonsense cruisers.

Never forget that the state has become a residual institution. It cannot delegate its functions to any other without diminishing the political nature of its very being. By contrast, if any other institution drops a function the clientele believes essential to its wellbeing, the state must assume responsibility. All institutions are subject to the aging process, for their very conservative nature makes it difficult for them to replace their moribund parts with vital ones. The cultural lag, as William Fielding Ogburn termed it, is a reality. Invention is also a reality, and the faster the tempo in any generation, the more rapid is the morbidity of the traditional institutions. A fast rate of invention will create new functions which must be institutionalized in the public interest, and the government is usually the agency to do this, for ever since the invention of the printing press, it has had a seemingly indestructible supply of funds and an unlimited source of candidates for the bureaucracy.

This is deliberately putting a good face on the progress from the democratic, representative polity towards the superstate. It is not always possible to be this cosmetic about the political countenance. Most states are power-hungry, and not only rush in to solve emergencies but have been known to create a few. Simplistic stability is characteristic of lack of natural resources, technological skill, and inventive talent. Ever since the dawn of civilization, at least, primate dissatisfaction and boredom will push towards a higher standard of consumption, at least for those in power. Where is the proper point of control in all this? Total government control of the inventive-productive process stultifies, and a complete *laissez faire* is callous towards basic human needs. No one has solved this one, old as it is. Since the original polity was the superstate, it has been here long enough to be better understood than it is. It concerns the subject of this book vitally, for all such political structures have been accompanied by an application of external and internal force.

For the purposes of the present analysis, the superstate comes in two forms which will be called the Leviathan on the one hand, and the imperium on the other. These unfamiliar terms have been chosen because they are relatively value-free, and offer less emotional trauma to those who may not want to recognize that they live under one or the other. Karl Wittfogel calls the first the Oriental despotism, and this offends, although both he and Herbert Spencer state that the despot is not necessarily an evil ruler. He is only a complete one, and he may rule with justice as his subjects understand it. The Emperor Hadrian was a despot, and was a just, compassionate man. The term the Leviathan, as coined by Thomas Hobbes, is therefore preferred. The imperium, is, of course, only the Latin word for empire, but note that the original meaning of its ruler, *imperator*, does not mean emperor in our sense, but supreme military commander. The Latin word is used here because few modern men enjoy being called citizens of an imperial military Caesardom even when they are. Theoretically, these two types of superstates are not identical, but one has to search for examples where they do not merge, if given time.

The state itself, even a rudimentary or weak one, is tangent to all institutions within its territory, as said. When it becomes stronger than and able to resist all the forces in the society it controls, there is Leviathan. Ideally, a Leviathan rises when the state penetrates, absorbs, consolidates, and centralizes at the expense of structures within the internal relations set. An imperium, by contrast, behaves in the same way at the expense of peoples and institutions not formerly part of its state system. It is seen, though, that once a Leviathan has set its own house in order, foreign adventures are too tempting to resist. While it may have effected economies within its borders, it is necessarily an expensive type of organization. It may have to expand at the expense of others to pay for itself and keep the clientele satisfied. The latter, too, may have become accustomed to a rising standard of consumption and may push the masters of the Leviathan into foreign expansion. They, too, may become enthralled with the concepts of Victory and Glory that a static condition is unacceptable to them. A Leviathan and its people tend to exhaust the natural resources with its legitimate borders, and tend to look outward for the means of maintenance. Anthropologists and historians usually term successfully expanding superstates conquest empires, and so they are.

One of the first steps towards Leviathan is the depressing, and then destruction of local political autonomy, and not always by force. The United States government with great and costly effort subdued certain of her rebellious states who wished to stand by the old ways, and then set about destroying the Indian societies which stood athwart her march to the Pacific. She conquered and detached the territories of Texas, Arizona, New Mexico, and California from Mexico, but at the time gave them statehood on equal terms with the old members. Since then the erosion has been gradual, persistent, but gentle. Since Abraham Lincoln invented the "shin plaster," the national government can finance its peaceful and military ventures with paper money, but the state banks and their power to issue currency have been abolished, and today the Federal Reserve system controls all.

The Federal government had to absorb the part-time pretorian troops of the individual governors in the name of national security, but in any event, the state militias were transformed into the National Guard, the second line of defense, not of the states but of the national government. The costly weapons are donations by the Federal government. The final test came under President Eisenhower when the National Guards of some states were "federalized" in peacetime lest they be loyal to their governors. Let lawyers argue about the constitutionality of this act.

Military corps areas were set up just after World War I to preserve not only the Federal garrisons they contained, and the Federal army reserve units resident therein, but they assumed the training and advisory oversight of the National Guard. The policing of the various states has not very gradually been assumed by the Federal Bureau of Investigation and with the permission or enthusiasm of the local authorities.

None of this is new, and the Americans have not yet reached Incan levels. While the pre-Colombian Peruvians could not read nor write, they kept meticulous records by knotted cords. A civil servant visited every community of the empire at least once a year, and skimmed off two thirds of the product, one third going to the maintenance of the central government, one third to the state religion, and one third left for local consumption. The Incan was a benevolent government, it is said, for there was no poverty or want among its clients. Crop failure in one region was compensated out of the vast store of food and clothing in the government stores. Overpopulation was kept under control. The visiting civil servant estimated the product of each community and confiscated any excess children over the possibility of maintaining the official standard of living. These children were reared by and for the state. The beautiful girl children were put in the Inca's harem, and when grown, were given to successful military commanders in lieu of little bits of ribbon fashionable today. The plain ones were sterilized by being immured in convents to the Sun. The brilliant boys were reared as civil servants and engineers for the extensive irrigation system, the second order of intelligence were put in the regular army. The lower orders of intelligence were put to work in the extensive public works. According to Garcilaso de la Vega, the half-caste son of an Incan princess, this benevolent, bureaucratic, divine Leviathan worked smoothly and perfectly. It was immune from attack from within or without as long as South Americans were concerned, but please remember the name of Francisco Pizarro when the subject of military vulnerability of a centralized government comes up.

France began its centering march towards Leviathan subtly under Richelieu, then violently under the Revolution. Even the old names — Auvergne, Artois, Brittany, Picardy, etc., etc. — were abolished in favor of administrative departments named after river valleys. The nation was rapidly developing into a Leviathan under Bonapartist enthusiasm, but with Napoleon's downfall, the individualistic temperament of the French peasant ground this to a halt. In Great Britain the independence of Scotland and Wales has disappeared save for a few local legal practices in the former. The partial independence of such magnates as the Duke of York is a thing of the past. The Bishop of Durham, as Count Palatine of the North, surrendered his princely coat of arms, which had long been an empty symbol, to Queen Victoria. The same sovereign lady brought even the title of King of the Isle of Man from the princely Kelley. Unlike in France, the counties keep their ancient names, but the High Sheriffs thereof have become merely ceremonial officers and administrators of the decrees of civil courts instead of the sources of armed force. The day of the mandarins on the one hand, and of the warlords on the other, is a part of Chinese history. The Peoples Republic of China does not pretend to be anything but a charismatic, bureaucratic, military dictatorship, and it is difficult to believe that the constituent republics of the Soviet Union have any independence when officially independent allies are disciplined by armed force.

A vital element of the progress towards Leviathan is observed in the growth of personal rule, abhored by some, but tolerated by the effective majority. From the assassination of Julius Caesar to the reforms of Diocletian, the growth of Caesardom was fertilized by the public welfare motive. Even in the later republic, the plebs persuaded the senate that they needed a protector against their own government, and the office of Tribune of the People was instituted. The title of this Latin *ombudsman* was preempted by Caesar and added to that of *imperator*, or general-in-chief of the armed forces.

Only the mention of Soviet Russia is needed in passing. The original Soviet constitution was perhaps the most democratic ever written, but Stalin had not risen to power. Who now has the power of making war and peace? The Supreme Soviet?

The Americans set themselves on a path from their constitutional beginnings when they conferred the role and function of commander-in-chief of the armed forces on their elected president, a power which no non-royal chief of state has held in the West since the collapse of Roman administration. That certain presidents have used this as a war and peacemaking power without consulting the Congress is too well-known to require the listing of foreign armed adventures of President Wilson, President Truman, and Presidents Eisenhower, Kennedy, Johnson, and Nixon. Not only were the logistics supervised in the Viet Nam affair but the tactical and strategic details thereof were absolutely in the hands of the executive branch. Of course the Congress supported this venture financially, but the Senate and the Roman People did the same for imperial Caesar.

Abraham Lincoln set a precedent when, as a wartime measure, of course, he suppressed the right of *habeas corpus* and issued the Emancipation Proclamation on his own recognizance. This has ended in a massive bureaucracy responsible only to the chief of state. That this grows out of control even by this chief is an historic fact. The Tsar Alexander II, who was in title and in fact The Autocrat of All the Russias, complained bitterly that he could neither understand the Romanov bureaucracy nor control it.

An imperium is by definition expansionist. Its population can be persuaded to bear the burden of conscription and financing expensive mercenaries if it is winning, and with the promise that eventual economic gains will benefit the citizenry. The stabilizing of an imperium's efforts, which has so far been a prelude to defeat and retreat along the frontiers, can be fatal. The fall of the Spanish empire could have been foretold when it ceased to expand, and when the flow of gold from the colonies produced more inflation of the currency than prosperity for the population. Imperial wars have always been more frankly economic than those of other political types. The Russian imperium, Romanov or Soviet, has never pretended anything else. In this the United States has a valid claim of not being an imperium. The Soviet army has rarely hesitated to discipline an unruly satellite, while the mighty American force was ousted from France by the puny and defeated forces of Charles de Gaulle. Actually, once having conquered the west, American economic expansion by military force has been moderate. Cuba, and later the Philippines, were given their political freedom. So far, American technological, marketing, and an almost monopoly of managerial skills has permitted economic penetration not backed by force. This has been the Coca-colonization of the world so deplored by President de Gaulle, who was unable to stop it. The United States is presently worried about these laurels. Her economy is being more penetrated by her ex-enemies, Japan and West Germany, than she is economically invading anyone.

The foregoing sentence hardly needs emphasis. Imperia are conquest empires for economic reasons with but few exceptions. It is hard from this distance to see the advantage of expansion for the Natchez. It is possible, too, that the Empire of Ethiopia grew out of an alliance for mutual defense. The myth of the founding of the Kitwara Empire of the Baganda, Banyankole, and Banyoro in black Africa is known, but what advantage was it to anyone? Perhaps that is why it did not last. The Plantagenet empire was another short-lived one. It ruled from Scotland to the Pyrenees, and was frankly economically exploitive. Strangely enough, grasping as some of its princes were, the Plantagenets had a way of being politically ahead of their times, which might account for their downfall. The British, Incan, Roman, and Romanov imperia were unashamedly economic in motive. One might note as a parenthesis that it is easier to spread an imperium if it has an ideological base, or pretext, as the case may be. Charlemagne had a Christian missionary motive for his conquests, while Soviet expansion invokes the Marxist liberation of mankind. The attempted expansion of the Hohenzollerns lacked an appealing ideology, but Hitler rectified that.

Before leaving the subject of the superstate, one must consider some of their inherent weaknesses. The first is that by its very nature it is made of too many divergent materials. Whether or not its ideology admits it, it is composed of many social classes, and it is impossible to please all of them all the time. Leviathan fears civil war more than any other kind. The evidence is good enough to hypothecate that the old Oriental despotisms invented the regular army as a device to keep their populations peacefully at work rather than to fight foreign wars. Do not ask if the Soviet Union would dare reduce its military strength to an adequate border guard. The Romanov Leviathan could be maintained as a police state for a while, but not long. The Russian people are highly productive of intellectuals, who will write and talk, and who will eventually affect the army as surely as the conquest of the Western military force by the Christian ideology was no help to Caesar.

With all their military might and economic success, imperial Leviathans contain a menace heretofore unresolved. No emperor, king, or senate, or even court can repeal the law of diminishing returns. Information must go up to the bureaucracy to be sifted and summarized for the chief. True, the old superstates had to depend on messages transmitted with the speed of voice or sound, or by foot or horsed courier, while modern ones can transmit their business with the speed of light. Nevertheless, the more hands materials must pass through, the greater the distortion and loss of accuracy and emphasis. Again, the state must be reminded constantly that it exists for the benefit of its citizens, and not for its own sake, Achille Loria and other fascist philosophers to the contrary. It is suggested that external expansion, military or otherwise, can go only so far without producing such an internal complexity that social problems and dissidence within will increase. No matter how sophisticated even the modern computers, a government is a rule of men in primary transaction, and no mathematical device can program the solutions for real or supposed frustrations in human minds. Even good will in an overstretched polity is not enough. The good Emperor Hadrian was confronted with the fact that even under his enlightened rule, the Roman social system was decaying at the core. He withdrew the legions not because he wanted to, but because it was the wise thing to do, and he set Rome on its long, downward trend.

FOOTNOTES AND REFERENCES

[1] Robert Thomas Barton, *Ifugao Law*, University of California Publications in American Archaelogy and Ethnology, Vol. 15, No. 1, 1919.

[2] John C. Messenger, "The Role of Proverbs in a Nigerian Judicial System," *Southwest Journal of Anthropology*, Vol. 15, 1959, pp. 64-73.

[3] Harry Holbert Turney-High, *Man and System: Foundations for the Study of Human Relations*, New York, Appleton-Century-Crofts, 1968, p. 364.

[4] Karl Wittfogel, "Developmental Aspects of Hydraulic Societies," *Irrigation Civilizations: A Comparative Study*, Social Science Monographs, Washington, Pan American Union, 1955, pp. 43-52.

[5] Many if not most of Ireland's noble fighting men renounced their country forever after the Boyne, and took service elsewhere with great distinction. Count Alejandro O'Reiley was governor of both Spanish Louisiana and Puerto Rico. The adjutant general of the Hessian forces in America reported to his superiors that on 14 August 1778 Lieutenant von O'Brien was doing well. General Bernardo O'Higgins was the liberator of Chile.

Chapter 5

MILITARY PRACTICE AND SOCIAL STRUCTURE

The Development of the Western Tradition

The first task here is to classify wars, and then proceed to the development of social structures which used them. It has become a convention today to speak of (1) Limited War, (2) Unlimited War, and (3) Total War. And then there is (4) Irregular War. These terms will be used. There are several types of these, as will be seen.

A limited war is fought against the armed military strength of an enemy. Such an attack is not directed against his civilian population, nor does it intend to penetrate or destroy either his economy or social system. Its target is as limited as its method, and is usually directed at the top level of his government. It specifically abstains from applying the maximum force. If both sides are playing the same game, there is often a conscious or unconscious, formal or informal agreement to abstain from the optimum application of the available weaponry.

The cause of modern limited war, save for a peaceful country striving to protect its borders, is fear of the opponent and his allies, that is, lack of adequate intelligence information. One suspects that such wars will continue as long as each side is unsure of its opponent's saturation potential. It is unlikely that a limited war will ever be fought by one imperium against another directly, for the risk of escalation is too great. An imperial limited effort against a relatively weak nation is something else, especially if it is a real or suspected satellite of another imperium. At the present moment of writing, there are reasons to think that limited warfare will increase among small powers, and between strong second class powers which lack the weapons for total saturation, and will continue as long as strong powers supply a controlled amount of weapons to the military midgets.

All of this is very well indeed if both sides agree upon the game being played. The British Crown fought a limited war against its rebellious colonies, while the revolutionaries fought total war, with unhappy results to the former and its American civilian adherents. Again, in American history we see a failure of both the Union and the Confederacy to agree on the type of war in progress. The latter planned only a limited war of defense of its own borders, and waited for the Union to strike, which it did. Unionist General Don Carlos Buell was defeated by the Confederate Army of the Tennessee at Perryville, Kentucky, which could have swung eastward. Its commander, Braxton Bragg, was not an offensive man, militarily at least. Surprised at having won, he retreated as fast as he could on Chattanooga. William Tecumseh Sherman lived off his enemy's country. Why did not Bragg try? Again, the Confederacy could have made at least a token invasion of the North after First Manassas (Bull Run). Its enemy was not only defeated but demoralized, and its nearby government was without protection. What troops did reach the pontoon bridge into Washington were recalled. Even if Beauregard's infantry was exhausted, his excellent cavalry had not been committed to action. Jefferson Davis is probably to blame. By the time the Confederacy decided to take the war to its enemy, a few crushing victories such as Chancellorsville had convinced Robert Lee of the invincibility of his infantry and the ineptitude of his opponent. He met a worthy foe at Gettysburg, and his admirers have tried to blame Longstreet ever since. It was not Longstreet who ordered the willing George Pickett to rest his troops overnight instead of ordering them into the line for an early morning attack. Lee took all the blame, as he would, and should.

Leave it to history to excuse the Japanese for turning east and south after Pearl Harbor, content with destroying their enemy's naval power to harass their rear. If they had only limited war against the United States in mind, they paid for this error.

The Americans later paid a similarly bitter price. After the brilliant stroke at Inchon, their field commander, Douglas MacArthur, thought in terms of unlimited war and was sacked for his pains by President Truman. In time so short that officers were engaged in both wars, the United States fought another limited war in Viet Nam. The North Vietnamese thought in terms of total war, as revolutionaries always must.

There may be some who will disagree with the following statement, but not many soldiers will. War in any event involves the attrition of men, materials, and treasure. It would seem that a state owes its dead, wounded, prisoners, and civilians the wish to come to a decision, and every effort should be made to implement this wish. Long ago both the Roman and British imperia fought limited wars on their distant frontiers without disrupting their social systems, but Americans seem to lack the talent.

To proceed in the direction of severity, unlimited war attempts to penetrate and destroy the enemy's social system by assailing all his manpower, and all his natural resources. The victor has no intention of permitting the status quo to survive. All available resources and weapons are inflicted on the enemy's tactical and strategic forces, and his logistic ability must be brought to naught. In such a situation there is a tendency to disregard treaties when one side or the other finds them inconvenient.

Total war has all the elements of unlimited war, but it is directed not only against all males who are or could be fighting effectives but against the entire social and economic systems of the opposition. Every member of the enemy population without regard for sex or age assumes a target status. The American revolutionists had total war in mind, as said, but surely the War in Lace, the polite limited war of the seventeenth and eighteeenth century monarchies came to an end at Valmy. By contrast, Grant invaded the Shenandoah Valley with some remarks about starving out the crows. Sherman considered no property too insignificant to destroy, no population too unimportant to terrorize. Poised on the banks of the Savannah River after his visitation of Georgia, he wrote to his chief of staff, "The truth is, the whole army is burning with an insatiable desire to wreak vengeance upon South Carolina. I almost tremble at her fate. . . . If Georgia has been scourged with whips, now South Carolina will be scourged with scorpions." Hitlerist Germany fought total war against every soldier, ships, factory, and school building in Great Britain. Booby-trapped toys were left in the streets, so that the constabulary had to warn children that valuable toys are not left on the sidewalks. Germany was destroyed by her own methods. In the foreword of his *The Destruction of Dresden*, Air Marshal Sir Robert Saundby says that 135,000 persons were killed in the February 13-14 raid on that city, 83,793 so-died in the American raid on Tokyo, while 71,379 perished in the nuclear attack on Hiroshima. It is doubtful if many of these Japanese dead were soldiers. The civilized world strove hard to realize the concept of the civilian, but the unselective power of long range artillery and aviation has made this idea obsolete.

Applying all available resources, human and technological, to an entire population is an expansion of fighting against the total strategic ability of an enemy, of which the civilian is a part. As in psychological warfare, the will to resist rests as much on the civilian population as on the soldier.

The very name of total war seems to be repulsive to Americans, though it should not be. It is their very own, and always has been. The European settlers soon to be called Americans left lacy war behind, and adopted the concepts of their abler Indian opponents, and the tradition has never died. Total war means not only the destruction of the enemy's fighting effectives but of all that supports them: economy, resources, the morale if not the bodies of noncombatant men, women, and children. In contrast with the limited war in lace, total war is the penetration and annihilation of the enemy's economic, political, and social systems by any means possible, including the holocausts of one's own troops and resources.

Space is not available for a summary of this position presented in Professor Weigley's book, soon to be quoted in another connection. If this point seems controversial, ask the American Indians, the American Tories, the Confederates, the Germans, and the Japanese.[1]

Long total wars between powers of comparable strength have taught at least one lesson. The destruction of the loser's system is accompanied by vast changes in that of the victor. The Union entered the war under the gentle rule of mercantilism and incipient industrialism, and ended under the regime of the financial-industrial "robber barons." Both sides went with the wind. Both World Wars altered the American system mightily, and destroyed what was once Merrie England. The final impact of the United States adventure in Southeast Asia is not yet in sight.

A special type of total war is called *blitzkrieg* after its German inventors. It is pursued by an aggressor who knows that he lacks the trained manpower and logistic strength to conduct a lengthy general war. It is a design for a quick overwhelm, which if successful, could instill fear into his victim's potential allies. Although the massing of men and materials can hardly be kept secret, the blitzkrieg concept attempts to use the Principle of Surprise against an unwary enemy, or one lulled into a feeling of false security, or suffering from war fatigue from previous encounters. All potential victims should see this stroke for what it is, a confession of weakness instead of strength, and take proper steps.

Hitlerist Germany massed its every military potential and invaded Poland. This effort left an inadequate force to protect its rear. Great Britain and France had guaranteed the independence of Poland, and promptly declared a war which they had no idea of prosecuting. This was *La Guerre de Blague*, the Phoney War, and both the British and the French paid dearly for their joke. The Polish adventure should have caused the Germans hardly more casualties than a full-scale spring maneuver, but it was so poorly organized that it exhausted the Reich's potential, at least temporarily. Almost all of its tanks and aviation had to go to the shop for repairs. Spare parts were in inadequate supply. Its trucks were similarly worn out. The gasoline supply was at low ebb. The German generals knew this even if Hitler did not, and it is impossible to believe that the superb British and French intelligence was not as well informed. Russia was trembling in its boots, and was happy to believe that Hitler would not continue his eastward thrust. Its huge army could have crushed Germany at this phase, but Stalin was content with a slice of Poland as a bribe. Germany was defenseless on her western frontier, but any tendency towards political and military action had departed from France. Great Britain had permitted its army to be reduced to insignificance. Nevertheless, the combined forces of the French and British could have invaded Germany with only token opposition. Instead, they both waited timorously to be attacked, and were. Russia could have been the anvil, and the Anglo-French forces could have been the hammer. This is the well-considered opinion of one of the greatest military theorists of our day, the late Sir Basil Liddell Hart.[2] Oh well, even the wary forces of Cornwallis could have been the anvil, and those of the somnolent Clinton and Howe could have been twin hammers. Empires are lost in this way, and no one should either forgive or forget such timidity.

It is well to understand the blitzkrieg in spite of its German failure. It might become the war of the future. That is what the potential of a nuclear shower means.

While the world has known the phenomenon for centuries, we thank Reginald Bretnor for coining the term "indecisive war" as a category.[3] Such a war is one in which the aims of the victors are not achieved when they might have been. One might also include a struggle wherein all the tactical and strategic objectives have been accomplished, but at a cost disproportionate to any or all benefits acquired. Indeed, such a Pyrrhic victory which might be so costly as to injure the victor's internal social system that it might never recover its former stability, even over and beyond the expectable war fatigue.

The indecisiveness of a war, or a battle, may be the fault of the field commander, his subordinates, and his troops. It is the politician, however, who is the master of this sort of war. World War I was fought as an unlimited war in the field. It could have been a complete victory had not Woodrow Wilson and his colleagues decided to accept virtually nothing in exchange for all the tremendous costs expended. The Hohenzollern personal rule was exchanged for one less palatable. It was the British economy which never recovered, not the German, and the stage was set for World War II. The latter was a total war, of course, and of global magnitude, but who ordered the fit United States Army to stop at the Elbe and wait, Roosevelt or Eisenhower? They should not have stopped at half measures.

Any distinction between civil and revolutionary wars present some complications. One aspect they have in common, though, is that both are considered criminal actions by their target governments and ruling classes. Legitimation comes with success, and often with the recognition and intervention of foreign governments. One might say that civil war aims only to replace the personnel of government, or to alter its form, or to terminate allegiance to the same, but not basically to change the social status hierarchy or class system. In this sense the American War for Independence was a civil rather than a revolutionary war with the allegiance of the colonial population split between the contending sides. This was indeed a tactical, strategic, and logistic war, and a total and decisive one with clearcut victory and defeat, but hardly an ideological one of great importance. The old social structure was maintained even though the form of government was considerably altered. A revolution, by contrast, has an ideological base which has the altering of the class system as the prime motive for bloodshed. There are those who deny the status of war to such operations, claiming that these are internal rebellions and collapses from within. Since apparently successful ones usually produce strong counterrevolutionary action, one thinks that they are actually wars of a civil nature. The French Revolution is aptly named, but when the revolutionary army had to direct strong military measures against the equally French populations of Brittany, Normandy, Toulon, and the Vendee which did not sympathize with the anti-royalist rebellion, there can be little doubt about the military nature of the revolution. The same may be said of the Russian Revolution, which took some time to put down the counterrevolutionary forces of General Denekin and Admiral Kolchak. The American Civil War was in this sense a counterrevolution on the part of the seceding states. The victorious Union surely revolutionized southern society, completely and almost permanently.

There are a few features of both these types of war which merit considerable reflection. The first is that every major war is in part a civil war. There were several prominent northerners who accepted Confederate commissions, John Clifford Pemberton being the best known. By contrast, Union General Oliver Howard was a Virginian of the same social class as Robert Lee. Some prominent South

Carolinians were always pro-Unionist, while whole counties of western Virginia, North Carolina, and Tennessee were anti-secessionist. None of the Acadians of south Louisiana thought much of the war, and contributed nothing to it. The New York City draft riots indicate that Lincoln's cause was not entirely popular in that metropolis. The term "Copperhead" for pro-Confederate northerners was a bad word in its time, while the opprobrious name of "Tory" can still be heard in the older portions of the United States. It is no secret that many American, British, and French citizens were Nazi sympathizers in World War II, while violent demonstrations carrying the North Vietnamese flag in the capital city of Washington are of recent memory. There were prominent German officers, the "White Germans," who were secret Allied sympathizers and, in whatever way they dared, assistants, is not so well-known. There is a solution for this problem. When asked if he feared a "Fifth Column" of pro-western sympathizers at the outbreak of World War II, Stalin replied that he had taken care of that, and so he had.

Every complex society has marked social classes with their own attitudes and values. This is equally true of the Soviet Union which sought to destroy all class systems by the Marxist technique of attributing all power to the proletariat. Now what must be faced is that sometimes class loyalties and emotions may be stronger than national ones. There will be some who identify with their own class over national and military lines. This must be carefully considered by a nation about to engage in a major war. Indeed, consciously or otherwise, it might be one of the reasons for the increase of limited wars. Large wars do erode the social systems of all contending parties, and each side might attempt to penetrate its opponent by way of the back door.

The next consideration is that, if such warfare is prolonged, both civil and revolutionary wars may cease to be local ones. Foreign nations may find it convenient to pay off old scores. One cannot guess what the results of the American Revolution might have been without French and Spanish intervention. Vicomte de Rochambeau at Yorktown had within a few hundred effectives the same troops strength as General Washington, but the former had seasoned professionals, and the latter was encumbered with a considerable militia. No one denies that the deciding factor was the French West Indies fleet under Comte de Grasse. The British Prime Minister and many members of Parliament were for active intervention in the American Civil War, but public opinion was against them. At that, the famous CSS *Alabama* was built, armed, and largely manned in England.

The next consideration is that there can be no civil or revolutionary war if the intellectuals—writers, editors, clergy, artists—remain loyal. If this class had defected or become halfhearted, a nation had better take stock of itself. It is proposed that if they and the army remain loyal, no ruling class can be overthrown. There is a temptation to put the role of the intellectual over that of the soldier, for the latter does read what their contemporaries write and are not to be convinced by them. Noblemen Bonaparte, Lafayette, and Rochambeau became revolutionists, and Comte de St. Simon, who served well in the American Revolution, became the founder of French socialism. And please remember that in its early phases, the Bolshevist Revolution was inspired and led by Russian noble officers who had read too many books for the Tsar's good. They were taken care of later, of course. Radicals do not trust liberals, but who does in a combat situation? It may be that the truth is gray, but in revolution, both sides harden into jet black and lily white. Rochambeau died at the guillotine. Lafayette was condemned, but the executioner forgot to call for him. Napoleone Buonaparte was on thin ice for a while, while his future wife, Josephine Tascher de la Pagerie, Vicomtesse de Beauharnis, had been condemned. All of these reasons point to the importance of psychological warfare, which might be the most important kind.

Psychological warfare may be an inaccurate term, as all war is a struggle to win the minds of men. It is a technique for reducing the enemy's will to resist. This is a psychological process, accompanied by whatever means available. Indeed, diplomacy cannot purge itself of this motive, for conferences with potential enemies always contain a force threat, no matter how suavely administered.

The first psychological target is the state's own citizenry. War is a dangerous and expensive business at best, and a nation whose productive, civilian population is halfhearted in making the sacrifices of treasure, of increased economic effort, and of contribution of sons, husbands, and other valued males had better try to resolve its differences abroad, and wait for a better day. That the feminine element must be given special attention hardly needs saying, or else the nation may approach the situation caricatured in the *Lysistrata*. Certainly the women are targets in total war, for only strong ones can resist the threat of terror and the necessities of life for their children.

Too many books have been written on propaganda to need reviewing here. Every beginning textbook in sociology discusses the problem. So, let us say that the effective majority of a nation's population must accept the official doctrine of the utter villainy of an actual or potential enemy, and the total purity of one's own cause. It is better that this propaganda contain some truth, which is not too hard to discover. Almost any potential enemy has some chinks in his moral armor which can be exploited. The Big Lie, total and flagrant, still has its uses. Hitler taught and demonstrated that if it is repeated often enough, and loud enough, it will in time make converts. This and all other types of propaganda must be continuous and repetitious. There must be no pause in telling the story, whether entirely true, partly so, or entirely false. Such seed sown on the ground of an already existing prejudice system has good chances of success. Thus, a Vichy-inspired propaganda poster seen in the Normandy invasion showed a sorrowful young widow, whose little son looked up to her and asked, "Mama, why is Papa dead?" The maternal reply was, "It is the fault of the English."

A nation which has complete control of the educational system has a distinct advantage. The ambitions of the chiefs of state may not be practical until an entire generation has been exposed to the official line of reasoning. Indeed, it may take a little longer, as the parents of the children may act as a negative influence unless they are threatened with real punishment with their children acting as informers, which happened in Hitlerist Germany. A totalitarian state, then, enjoys many advantages of this kind, and especially if its armed forces constitute an important part of its educational system. If the state has but one legitimate party, and an ideology markedly different from that of its potential enemies, it can rely on both its civilian and military systems, but it suffers from a relative inability to export its ideas.

The most important target is the young manhood of one's own state. Whether recruited or conscripted, a soldier lacking faith in his nation's cause is a weak reed on which to lean. If warfare can be made to appear as a jolly trade, so much the better.

The enemy troops are, of course, a prime propaganda target. They must be made to feel that their cause is hopeless. This must be cleverer than than the efforts of "Tokyo Rose" and "Lord Haw Haw" in World War II, who entertained the Allied troops rather than influencing them. The enemy prisoners of war constitute such a captive audience that it is now necessary to insulate them against "brainwashing" as part of the recruit training program. The stick-and-carrot treatment can be effective. Abuse and neglect of the intransigent and favoritism towards the uncommitted is as old as the Latin phrase *divide et impera*, divide and rule. This was aptly used on the German prisoners of the Convention Army captured at Saratoga. These men would not break their oaths to the British Crown, but did volunteer to Governor Patrick Henry to protect the

Continental left wing against the British Indian allies, if rearmed. While this did not entail direct combat with Cornwallis, it released Virginia troops for this purpose. As a reward, these collaborating Brunswickers and Anspachers were given vast land grants in western Virginia, where their descendents still live. The Union tried this method with great severity on Confederate prisoners at Rock Island, Camp Chase, Fort Delaware, and other grim camps. The "rebels" would not take arms against their own kin, but they did enlist in numbers to fight the Indians who were harassing the western frontier. This permitted that withdrawal of good regulars to give sinew to Grant's efforts. This device never occurred to the Confederate government, or it might have held Arizona and New Mexico. The privations at Andersonville, Georgia, made the southern name a loathing among the survivors, and did nothing to ameliorate the severity of reconstruction.

Psychological warfare directed against enemy civilians is not all blandishment. Fear is a weapon, and a good target for the terrorist is the helpless and defenseless. Many North Carolina small-farmers wanted to join Cornwallis, but dared not leave to the mercy of the terrorists their homes, wives, and children. Even though he probably did not know this, William Tecumseh Sherman needed to read no history book in his march through Georgia. He was shrewder than President Lyndon Johnson, a man who wanted to be loved, who ordered the first psychological warfare in Viet Nam to be a shower of aviation distributed pictures of himself with a tender message. His enemy gathered these leaflets, altered the kindly remarks appended thereon, and re-disseminated them.

A fertile field for psychological warfare is war fatigue. A population may weary of war, of sacrifices, of the oversell of propaganda, and the breast-beating politicians. A short war and a merry one might be fun, with the casualties accounted as heroes, but that is a thing of the long distant past. The vanquished know this well, but the victors are just as susceptible. Violent contact with the enemy reveals to the common soldier that they are people, too. Allies cease to be heroes, and peace makes the citizen and soldier wonder if it was not all in vain. Propaganda raises a population to a moral level which they cannot maintain, and peace not only lets them sink to their former level, but even lower. The *Kriegsherr*, the Emperor William, marching abreast with his handsome sons with their feathers fluttering was a brilliant promise which was answered by the Versailles Treaty, followed by the defeat of a Reich which was to endure for a thousand years, then occupation. *Nie wieder Krieg*! Denazification indeed, which produced a German army on which the

Americans would like to rely. At the moment of writing, the German regular army outnumbers the American NATO forces in their country by 6,000 men who do not want to hear any more about death camps. Denazification indeed, or should one speak of demilitarization of the Germans who crushed the Roman Varus at Teutoberg Forest. The command function has been so diminished that even military offenses are tried before civilian courts. No experts, including their own, consider this army an effective fighting force even on the defensive. The Americans have similar emotions about the de-Shintofication of Japan, happy under the military umbrella of the United States while penetrating the economy of their erstwhile enemy.

The question of the time to exert extreme pressure on a nation involves what Reginald Bretnor calls the point of critical imbalance of power.[4] An undoubted factor in this is a situation when the target nation is suffering from war fatigue providing the aggressor is free from the ailment. It is assumed that the professional or mercenary soldier is not so afflicted, but the citizen soldier is something else, especially in his mass-man aspect. He is really a civilian at heart, and all civilians are prime targets today, if not of battle, then of war. There is much talk today of civilians being hostages in the "balance of terror." Since when has this not been true? There is no non-ecclesiastical building in the princely city of Liege dating from the Middle Age, for the troops of the Duke of Burgundy levelled them all, and put the population to murder and torture. Rome has never recovered from its sack by the Lutheran troops of the Catholic Emperor Charles V. Even today it is sickening to read of the rape, murder, and torture of the Roman innocent. Only the means of accomplishing the terror have improved, not the idea. It has now become theoretically possible to destroy the civilian bulwark of a state before harming the armed forces in the field. Perhaps we should rephrase Clausewitz's definition of strategy and call it the art of waging war without really fighting.

War, like chess, bridge, and sales, and political campaigns rest on the fact of the universal scarcity of desirable items. There never has been, and is not now, enough of these desirables to satisfy the wants of everyone who values them. Victory is a technique for acquiring these values, even at the expense of denying them to others. This frustration is just as much an affliction of large social systems as it is of individual persons.

A person, a small institution, or a nation, lacking what they think they should have, and can have, may start striving toward acquiring these goals by industry, by skill, by cooperating with others, by diplomacy and chicane, by marshalling and expanding their resources. This is economic-diplomatic strategy. Their goals and their vulnerability are surely obvious at this point to those having control of these desirables. The have-nots are in imbalance, as Bretnor would say, but their fat rivals are often lulled into a false sense of security or a fatal contempt for the puny. The weak state may even proclaim what it wants, and how it intends to proceed as, in all honesty, did Japan, Hitlerist Germany, Soviet Russia, and later, Cuba, and no one took up cudgels against them in the days of their imbalance.

We need not go abroad for examples. The young United States made no secret of what it wanted. France was too feeble from the Revolution to do anything about it until Napoleon III tried to take advantage of the American Civil War by trying to take Mexico. The Spanish Empire was disintegrating, and the United States forgot that it was a useful ally in its War for Independence. Florida was a thorn in the British foot, and Governor Galvez pinned down a British division at Baton Rouge which Cornwallis sorely needed. The Mother Country, still smarting from the humiliation of Yorktown, was no lover of the daughter republic. She tried to keep the new machines from the New Englanders, and failed in this effort at economic colonialism. She succeeded in maintaining this economic overlordship in the cotton states. The Monroe Doctrine was proclaimed for Latin America, which was enforced by the British, not the American navy. This was an inexpensive device, and America was feeble.

Britain woke up too late. The liquidation of economic colonialism was accomplished by insisting on the payment of war debts from World War I. That war left the United States, a nation which was "too proud to fight," as the strongest military power in the world, or almost so. It is no great secret that many powerful figures in the British government, the rising Winston Churchill being one, seriously considered a war against the increasing commercial and military strength of the United States in the late nineteen-twenties. Control of the Caribbean could have been the *casus belli*. The sugar beet had impoverished Britain's Antillean islands, and she more or less let them go by default. Discovery of oil in Venezuela and the success of the Panama Canal were something else. The British ruling classes, though, wisely refrained from fanning this disagreement into a war. The two nations were too closely in balance by that time to take the risk.

The Americans were not deceived by this. They sent their Atlantic fleet into the Caribbean, and rushed the completion of three battleships. The British capital ships were aging. They refrained from overt war, nevertheless, but won a brilliant diplomatic coup. They persuaded the United States to enter a disarmament conference wherein it was decided that a battleship is a weapon of aggression, but a cruiser is a protective device. Having liquidated the imperial German battle fleet, and not being impressed with that of France, she had all she needed to protect her modest shoreline. She wanted no rival to arise. The Americans, by contrast, had a vast coastline to protect with these massive floating batteries, for the power of aerial bombardment was in its infancy. Britain needed cruisers to secure her commercial lifeline and far-flung empire. The United States was most accommodating. The nearly completed capital ships were towed to sea and sunk by naval gunfire, a rather expensive target practice.

One notes that when balance of power between two rivals is achieved, the times are marked by slow attrition and indecisive activity. Each side may now try to throw this equilibrium into imbalance. In this strategic and diplomatic phase of hostility, Bretnor says that it becomes critical when one side's vulnerability is increasing and his force potential is deteriorating until at last a threshold is reached beyond which there is little hope.

And so, the review of the types of states and the war they fight, beginning with the nation-at-arms if for no other reason than simplicity's sake, is undertaken. It is one wherein the demands of war and politics are so nearly identical that the means of teaching a man to be a good soldier and good citizen are virtually the same, and where every man is required to be a full participant in both the political and military processes. David Rapoport and others who have popularized this term know that it is not a new phenomenon. The Swiss Confederation and Paraguay are such nations which have survived in spite of powerful neighbors. For brevity's sake, the Jewish state is too much in memory and present knowledge. The Israeli have proven that they can defeat any and probably all of their hostile neighbors if foreign "volunteers" and "specialists" are kept out of the dispute.

If the adjective is carefully used, the nation-at-arms can be considered a democratic device, although something very far from the mass-man army popularized by the French Revolution and its neo-democratic successors. The nation-at-arms is sociologically describable as a social system without great cleavages in the status hierarchy. The nation is relatively poor. The economic differences between the classes are not great, and neither is the standard of education. The institutional structure is integrated, comprehensible, and supported by most of the non-criminal. The value system of the society is simple and understandable to such a proportion of the population that almost everybody feels that he has a share in the state's survival. It hardly needs saying that the requirements for the nation-at-arms can be met only in geographically small, sociologically compact, and culturally homogeneous social systems.

At the dawn of our own tradition, the early Greek polities were organized as nations-at-arms. Later the rights and duties were confined to the upper, and later, upper middle classes. Originally, though, the Hellenes came as invaders and expelled, absorbed, or enserfed the indigenous population. Each kinship populated a valley, or small series of them, or settled on fiorded bays. They were clan-oriented on the patriarchal, patrilinear, and patrilocal base. The patriarch of the most noble clan was chief of the system, and later became a little Homeric king. The land was divided up among the clans, and in early times, no man thought himself too good to do his own farming with the help of a household slave, if he were fortunate enough to have one. Even the king's daughter considered herself the head laundress of the palace, as the pretty story of Nausicaa shows. This idyl did not last. Money, legendarily invented by Midas King of Lydia, destroyed what remnants of equality as was left.

The fundamental fighting unit of the Greek senatorial states was the phalanx of heavy infantry, the elite of the elite. These were the hoplites, and only men of wealth and standing could serve in this line. The societies of city-states were divided for military and voting purposes into three strata of property owners. The richest formed the center of the line, and the other two the flanks. The phalanx was usually formed four ranks deep, the best being in the front one. This was the battle line with its long, heavy spears thrust forward, and the large hemispherical shields overlapping. The second rank stood ready to take the place of individuals who might fall, but their lances, too, jutted forward under the shields of the first. The third rank tried to push theirs over the shoulders of the more forward ranks. Capped with almost impenetrable helmets, clad with metal cuirasses protecting the front and rear, fitted greaves protecting the legs and ankles, this walking pincushion was the world's best example of the government under arms.

The hoplites *were* the lawmakers. They not only declared wars but fought them, and a worthy ideal, that. They were the rich and respectable, the top of the educational heap of their day. The great Greek classics, dramatic, poetic, philosophical, were written not only for them but by them as well. The father of Greek tragedy, Aeschylus, fought at Marathon and Salamis. This system shifted from the nation-at-arms to the patrician military republic, but it was the rich who defended their wealth with their *own* blood, not that of the humble. Men who could not qualify by wealth and birth for a place in the hoplite line were peltasts, lightly armed slingers and javelin men who were really never used, and rarely made the sacrifice. The Greeks never appreciated firepower and light infantry. The hoplites were the legislature-at-arms, and as for being politicians, they invented shady politics.

The fighting Greek legislators were gymnasts. When they were not in the council halls, or having drinking bouts, or listening to the noble dramas of Aeschylus, Aristophanes and Euripides, or sporting with the high-grade prostitutes called *hetairai*, they were at exercise in the gymnasium, and no one was exempt from military service until age fifty-nine. Pot bellies were for the base-born and the elderly. Even today we know one of their greatest philosophers by his athletic nickname of Plato, or "Broad." We are not sure what his real name was. Of course the decisions of the patrician military republicans were not always honorable. These men were not gods, but by the gods, they were men.

It is well that their manners were superb when fighting among themselves. These embattled legislators could think of no better marching column than single file, which stretched a phalanx in motion over several miles. The phalanx was excessively vulnerable on the march, but it was considered bad form to attack a marching column. (The Romans, who had such bad manners, knew better than this.) Battles were fought almost on the "by appointment only" basis, neither side attacking until the lines were formed. This almost impenetrable armed legislature was to be challenged by two social systems of lesser education. One they overcame, and the other overcame them. It is well, to take another look at the battle line, for it was almost duplicated by ourselves in the renaissance.

The battle line of Greek hoplites was by battle test a sucessful heavy infantry formation. Being defective in firepower, it was primarily a defensive line, being defective in mobility. The clash between two such defensive lines seems to have been postponed as long as possible, each hoping the other would commit the folly of attack. The clash of lines, when it did come, was terrible, and given equal equipment, training, and devotion, the decision was rarely made in the center. Other things being equal, the longest line would win by envelopment. Lines being of equal length, the right of each opponent, being the stronger, would crush the left of the other, so that the battle line ended in something like the letter S. The victory then went to the most able and strongest in manhood. But look below for the test with foreigners.

Unlike the Greeks, the Persians specialized in arrow fire, and were mobile and flexible. Greek formations were primarily holding devices, while the Persians better observed the Principle of Offense. The Greeks had something to defend, wealth and liberty, and were a devoted band of the Rich, Resepectable, Disciplined and Masculine.

Persian fire was wasted on the Greek heavy shields, and the cavalry charge could not be driven home against the Greek forest of pikes. The test was decided by sociological, not tactical considerations. The freeman won over the armed slave, and even if the free were but few, they were adequate. The Greco-Persian wars were the first test of mass-man against an elite corps, and perhaps should have been the last.

The Greeks usually fought limited wars of trivial economic importance. Excluding the defensive war against the Persian imperium, the political goal was the strong against the weak. It made little difference to the common man and noncombatant element which well-greaved snobs ruled them. The legislators-at-arms could not play fair with their allies, and Athenian behavior was the shoddiest of all. The rightist and leftist parties gagged at nothing cheap or selfish. All this ended by Philip the Macedonian Madman dancing over the corpses of the Athenian defeated, and his son, Alexander the Brilliant Alcoholic ruling between the Indus and the Nile. The ancient Greeks were capable of becoming foreign mercenaries if the price were high enough. Xenophon, the biographer of Socrates, was one. They could produce collaborators of such brilliance that the name of Aristotle will be known as long as men can read and write. Something stronger, if less intelligent, was rising in the west to maintain the tradition of the armed levy of citizens.

The early Italic people were kinsmen of the Greeks, both speaking member languages of Indo-European stock, both originally hill people from somewhere in south Russia, both descended from the horsed Battle Axe Folk who began filtering into Europe by the end of the Neolithic. Like the Battle Axe Folk throughout the world, both had been nomadic cowboys who imposed cattle culture on the farming one they took over from the folk they conquered. Thus, from Ireland to India, one finds the tremendous respect given to the horse, and from worship to irrational regard bestowed upon cattle. Both started their military careers by trusting the cavalry of the well-to-do and noble, a trait they both gave up for the solid infantry line. The military aspect of both social systems was characterized by the citizen militia, which made both famous and, in the end, both gave up this fame-creating orientation for the mercenary and the professional, and for the same reasons. Both began as mixed people who boasted of their racial purity. Italics had less of this than the Greeks, and soon renounced ethnocentrism. The mystery Etruscan people, the Indo-European Italics, the Celt-Iberians, the Ligurians, and Semitic Phoenicians, and many others, contributed to what we call a Roman. By their own legend, the City was founded by displaced persons from Asian Anatolia, flying from the sack of Troy, and intermarrying with the natives of Alba Longa and the Sabine state.

It was the dissimilarities, not the likenesses, which gave the world to the Romans rather than the Greeks. As the Greek city-states were ethnocentric, and refused to assimilate the foreign elements they so badly needed, the Romans welcomed all. First they absorbed the Italic villagers, then all Italians, then Greeks, and eventually Jewish intellectuals like St. Paul. In contrast with the Greek states, the Romans treated their allies as equals and absorbed them. No ally ever broke away from Rome. None clove to Athens, Thebes, or Sparta except under the compulsion of armed might. Roman law and justice appealed to the world, and Greek political trickery did not. Rome also began as an insignificant city-state, but was never content to remain so. Like the Greeks, Italics would fight, but unlike them, they would also work. No Roman unit rested for the night without creating a heavily fortified camp with ditches and palisades. The Principle of Security was as foreign to the Greeks as hand labor was to the perfumed, gentlemanly hoplite. Both were militias of citizens, but citizenship was restricted to the Greek upper and upper middle classes, while the Roman citizen was a work-hardened farmer who needed no muscling-up in the gymnasium, and was commanded by an upper class whose hands were not strangers to the plow. Both rose to glory by considering the state and the army the same social structure, and both ended up as something else. Both started out with priest-kings as civil executives and field commanders. Both tended to replace the limited monarchy by patrician military oligarchy. Both distrusted an executive vested in one man. Rome gave this role to two elected consuls ruling jointly. This carried over to the military, for in the early republic one consul commanded the right wing, and the other the left.

The most important distinction of all is that the Greeks, the Macedonian barbarians excepted, always fought limited wars. The Romans fought unlimited and total war if they possibly could.

The levy of farmers called up for war was originally the assembling of the *gentes*, or clans, as indicated by the word for a tribe, or *legio*, or legion. Reading Livy, one is inclined to believe that the old regal state was composed of three tribes, each of somewhat different racial stock. These were divided into thirty *curiae*, or phratries, which were bases of both civil social structure and military organization. Each curia furnished ten horsemen and a century of footmen led by a centurion. Thus, originally, a legion consisted of three centuries of organic cavalry and thirty centuries of infantry, the cavalry being the basic arm. This false idea was given up long before the end of the republic, and only allies formed the mounted element. Indeed, "equestrian rank" came to designate the rich middle class whom the military upper-upper class scorned. King Servius Tullius did away with the kinship idea of military organization, and Rome was on its way.

The legion was originally based on the phalanx, but a much more flexible one than the Greeks could organize and fight. Progressive and able to learn from experience, the Romans were constantly experimenting with the legion organization and disposition, from the phalanx legion, to one grouping centuries into maniples, to the cohort legion. This is a technical discussion too long for present purposes, and is cited to show the Roman ability to learn and adapt. The legion was a heavy infantry unit, but experience demonstrated that armor should be lightened in the interest of mobility, and so it was. The Romans always fought by fire and movement. The heavy Greek lance was reduced to a throwing javelin, the *pilum*, equipped with a soft head. This would detach from the shaft and fix in the defense's shields, thus reducing their usefulness. Romans advanced behind a line of light infantry, slingers and archers, and closed with a shower of pila. They did not rely on the push of the pikes, but were primarily swordsmen. Knowing what every child should know, that the point of a weapon is more dangerous than the slashing edge, the legion advanced behind its shields, and jabbed with their short swords, as good boxers should.

Such was the old Roman citizen army, a far cry from the hardcore professional one of later times. Defective in high command, perhaps, and run at the top by a board of directors, as was the civil state, the old Roman army of hardened farmers was led by the country gentry whom they knew, and who knew their men. It was a citizen's levy willing to submit to iron discipline and drill, drill, drill, and loving spit and polish of equipment for, being poor men, they knew as the able poor always do, that clean equipment lasts. This was the nation-in-arms, but the patrician military republic, and later something even less democratic, was on its way.

Professionalism set in towards the end of the republic, as it was bound to when Rome became a successful imperium. First, the centurions began objecting to being mustered out, then recalled from their farms to begin once more as privates in the ranks. They became Rome's first professional military class, and their downward social mobility from the status of officers towards that of master sergeants began. The long campaigns from Spain to Greece took so long that the ordinary legionary infantryman lost interest in farming, his land had gone to pot in this period anyway, and soldiering became his life. Commanders were not slow to see the value of these old veterans in contrast with part-time levies, and a new Rome was in sight.

Successful warfare, even with purely political goals, collects wealth almost in spite of itself. Rome's wars began as mere political transactions, but soon developed into loot and tax operations. Rome became rich. The new wealth was distributed with neither much wisdom nor old Roman justice. It landed periously into the hands of the politically powerful. The free farmer disappeared into the welfare state of the capital. The country gentleman was ruined. Farming was first entrusted to slave-run plantations which overcultivated the land and spoiled it to this day, as latifundia slavery always has. Rome became the military robber's roost of the world, extracting grain from others rather than growing it. Horace might sing of the innocent joys of his Sabine farm, and Vergil compose hyper-refined buccolics, but neither political poet ever touched a plow, as did General Cincinnatus of old.

The state, and then the army, became bureaucratic. Administration had to become important as complexity increased, and the influence of civil servant quaestors, starting as administrative officers and ending as warrant officers, grew into something familiar to our own day. The armies on the frontier, no longer self-sufficient militias, had to be equipped, fed, and paid. The veterans had been away so long that the Roman matron, a figure of formidable virtue, had become emancipated, was without work, was politically powerful, and sexually permissive. Rome finally having conquered and taxed most of the known world, kept some virgins in the Temple of Vesta just to let people see what it used to be like.

If there is a rhythmical aspect in the development of warfare, this marked the end of such a cycle. The legion had shot its bolt, or pilum, if you will, and cultural perfection means decay and shift. Augustus, that master organizer, while trying to keep or even revive the old forms of society, actually reorganized the state so that it lasted for centuries and survived some very incompetent emperors. The army was professionalized, the citizens disarmed to enjoy their leisure and lack of responsibility. This was the *Pax Augusta*, an epoch of war fatigue of great depth. It was an imperial Leviathan sick of foreign and civil war, and weary of the strain of patriotic emotion. The line of the empire should have been set at the Elbe, but contented itself with that of the Rhine and the Danube, and lost forever the chance to control and acculturize the Germans. The defeat of the incompetent Varus by Arminius proved permanently decisive.

MILITARY PRACTICE AND SOCIAL STRUCTURE   111

War fatigue is a luxury which exacts a bitter price. Loss of initiative indicates a permanent war on the defensive. Successful application of the Principle of Objective in the field, and its disregard on the political front charges a price which should wring no tears from the eyes of wise men.

The Roman professional core, first consisting of Italians, then of allies, then almost anyone hungry enough to serve on the outskirts of the civilized world, could not hold when even the incompetent barbarians began pushing. It was not Teutonic strength which induced Hadrian to withdraw the legions, but internal maladjustment, the destruction of the currency necessitated by the waste and extravagance of a centralized superstate which had passed the point of diminishing returns long before. Many military analysts have remarked what seems to be a general principle, that even a competent professional force is very vulnerable unless backed by a warlike population. This means that the attitudes, values, and goals keeping the professional force under arms must be those of the effective majority of the civilian population. The state, as has been said, is tangent to all other institutions, and the military is only its force arm. Lack of integration of the important institutions leaves even a competent professional army menaced from both front and rear.

Lack of consensus of goals, and the presence of a tight-knit and selfish oligarchy brings in a phenomenon praised by a few. We refer to the "pretorian state," and few pretorian guards have militarily been worth their rations. Pretorianism is military statism *par excellence*, and so important that a whole chapter will be devoted to it. And so Rome in the West "fell," as they say, although many fine generals, emperors, and troops survived long in the East. The last Western emperor was Romulus Augustulus, slain by the barbarian Odoacer in A.D. 476.

The face of Mars did not change in the process. Once settled, it can be argued that it never does. Mars changes his garb, however, and we may now speak of Gentlemen in Steel. And look at them carefully, please, and see if you do not see a reversion to petty, local monarchies in fact if not in name, defended by heavily armored gentry leading a popular levy of citizens. A great tactical revolution which was also a social one now lies ahead. The rise of this class illustrates the error of not considering material invention organic to culture better than almost any possible novelty. It was such a small invention, but it changed the face of the western world, and gave us such fine words as gentleman, squire, chivalry, courtesy, and a new meaning to the old Latin word honor.

The legionary steamroller conquered and held from Gibraltar to the Near East, from the Rhine to deep into Africa, and infantry seemed established as the Queen of Battles. After the first civilized try, cavalry was considered of little use to the western world. The reason for its decline is clear. All the friezes and statues from the Parthenon to Rome teach that the Greco-Romans rode bareback without stirrups. No intelligent cavalry command would charge a solid line of hoplites or legionnaires behind their shields and their spears or swords jutting forward. Bareback riders cannot carry long spears or long swords, nor wear heavy body armor. Any good infantryman could kill any good cavalryman by dealing the horse's head a smart blow with his spear, causing the animal to swerve or rear, upsetting the horseman who received the other end of the spear. And then toward the end of the Roman administration, the simple little device of the stirrup began changing the world.

The invention of the stirrup is shrouded in too much mystery to be discussed here, but the Eastern Empire probably got the idea from Scythian sources. We know that the able Emperor Maurice made it standard equipment for his army, and from the Eastern Empire the little device diffused throughout the civilized world. And look what happened!

The horseman could no longer be jerked from his seat by a legionary grabbing his ankle. The infantryman could not even get close to the horse. The cavalryman could lenthen his sword and lance. He could completely take his hands away from the reins of a trained charger. The horseman could not only keep his seat when the horse reared and plunged but actually trained it to do so in order to mash down the infantry in front of him. He could wear body armor, and increase its strength until he became almost impermeable. So behold the walk-trot-canter-CHARGE of the armored cavalry line. A new steamroller appeared before which neither the European line of foot swordsmen nor pikemen could stand for centuries, and which could brush away the Saracen light horsemen. True, a circle of heavy infantry pikemen could provide a haven of refuge for a tired horseman, but like it or not, infantry was often not brought into the field at all.

Mediaevalism, or feudalism as a status hierarchy, including villeinage, sefdom, subinfeudation in lieu of money payment, and all the rest, were functional dependents on the invention of the stirruped *kataphract*, the knight and his men-at-arms, who ruled Europe for centuries.[5] It was not Germanic infantry superiority which defeated King Arthur. He could arm his young men as kataphractes, but he could not discipline them into soldiers nor keep peace in his own family. English therefore displaced Gallo-Latin as the mother tongue of most of Britain. But the Anglish had their turn. The Saxon hardly learned how to handle the new device before the Battle of Hastings (Senlac), which William himself knew was a poor place for a kataphract battle. Harold's good cavalry was fighting elsewhere at the time of Hastings, so he had deprived himself of the advantage of the Principle of Combined Use of All Forces. He placed his good infantry well according to the Principle of Utilization of the Terrain, but he could not restrain his troops from breaking barbarian-fashion and running forward to loot the wounded and Norman dead into a country where they could be ridden down. Hence we use serf language, that is, Saxon, regarding "sheep" and "cow" and "swine" for animals in pasture, but the French "mutton" and "beef" and "pork" when served at the master's table.

Neither firearms nor the longbow really brought the kataphract to ground. It was primarily social organization which did. The rise of towns and the new commerce taught discipline, self-discipline, to the common man, to the lower middle, as we say today, and so did the mercenary captain. Shoulder to shoulder, hold fire until useful, fire by units systematically into the French gentlemen's horses, and our fine old words, *noblesse oblige*, chivalry, honor, and perhaps gentleman too, were relegated to lexicographical curios. But we get ahead of the story.

The Dark Age is discussed now, as the ultimate rescue of our civilization, before the High Middle Age, also called "dark" by those who profited by its overthrow. Gratitude is hardly expectable in sociocultural affairs, but those to whom "feudalism" is a term of opprobrium are the beneficiaries of that remnant of Roman discipline and order. The Eastern Empire did indeed find security of a fashion, but the West is under discussion here, which is our own civilization and our cause. The roots of feudalism go back to the time when the Western Empire was fairly safe, and when with the blessing of The City, the general over a wide area (*dux*-duke) was also the civil governor. This privilege, indeed, obligation was delegated downward to subordinate commanders (*comites*, counts, *vice-comites*, assistant counts, or viscounts, *barones*, or roughly company grade officers, *scutarii*, shield bearers or esquires), but no one expected these ranks to become hereditary. Under the professional system of the later empire, these leaders were generally barbarian themselves.

The Dark Age, properly so-called, was the lowest ebb our side has so far seen. Our ancestors, however, found a source of new vigor. The Dark Age meant that whatever remnant of Roman order as was left was beset on all sides by the turbulence of robbers, guerrillas, Saracens, Magyars, and worst of all, the Scandinavians or Vikings. Contact with Rome was cut off. Indeed, The City had fallen to the robbers. The barbarian field commanders in Roman pay often took over what social control was left. There was no money, or too little, so the overlord, or commander, paid his kataphracti by giving them control over land. These knights paid their subordinate ones with land, and the latter paid their tenants by protection, agricultural administration, and the maintenance of courts of justice. How well did this work? The only answer is that they were far from perfect, but we were not overwhelmed. We are here to tell the story. The valor of these men gives us heart for what we may face.

The story of the feudal wars is too long for discussion here, but a summary will be made. They were limited wars, as logistic difficulties made it impossible to carry fire into the territory of the Saracens, Magyars, and Vikings. The Principle of the Offensive was discounted. Vast sums were spent on defensive armor and castles. The beginning of feudalism was a *de facto* revival of petty, local monarchies backed originally by the infantry militia of the armed citizens. It became something else, of course, but in the early days the lord was the only mounted professional, and whether or not he defended his own territory, or was brought with his tenants into the temporary service of the overlord, the armed tenant and his lord won their war. The back of the guerrilla raider was broken, as it always is if the forces of order dare to go all the necessary way. We go to schools and churches, and we deal in markets. We go to courts with law and justice as ideals if not always facts. Indeed, we have the rights of citizens of the Empire or, what we have called since Constantine, Christendom. The feudal system would not please us, but we its inheritors might doubt just how cruel it was. Before we ethnocentrically condemn, the following questioned must be answered. Tenants and vassals, time and several thousand times over, stood with their lords to beat off the invader, and the lord's rivals. Men cannot be flogged into doing that, but the final question is this. Who dares say that the modern factory or office worker would stand up and die for the defense of his chairman of the board of directors, or bureaucrat, or elected legislator?

Mediaeval war did not become vicious until the end, when total war became the rule, and the patrician military republic was yielding to nationalism. Mediaeval armaments and tactics were still used, but the early renaissance goals were civil war and the attempts of kings to destroy feudalism in the interests of the new nation and commerce. Duke Charles the Temeraire butchered the harmless citizens of Liège because their prince-bishop's sovereignty stood in the way of his dream of a large Burgundian state. Chivalry sank so low that Dunois, Joan of Arc's field marshal, was condemned for the most brutal and bestial witchcraft on the corpses of children, and political as it was, it is not certain that the Maid's condemnation did not have some justice in it, if one believes in witchcraft. Saints do not associate with Dunois, nor do they have hysterics at occult wells known to have been such for centuries.

Barring the crusades, the warlike character of the mediaeval period can be exaggerated. Once the barbarians were stopped, the feudal age was one of prolonged peace until the King of England decided to take over much of France. The rule was pettifogging local wars of short duration, and more attention given to the pomp of tournaments than to victory on the battlefield. The militia of citizens had not been in force for centuries. The feudal regime reached for perfection, found it, and withered.

Now was a return to royal absolutist Leviathan. Philip Augustus of France began eroding feudal semi-monarchies, and his successors ably followed his path. Even when the lords were loosely organized into the patrician military republic, they were in the way of business, which was to rule the future. Strangely enough, it was the commercial men and the kings which formed partnerships to destroy feudalism and usher in the age of royal absolutism, but both the Kings of England and France were to be decapitated when they, too, got in the way. Thus, then, another cycle of politics and war. Its beginnings can be called the era of the Common Man in Tights and Fancy Hats, for the costume of the mercenaries was as flamboyant as anything else in the renaissance. The great rebirth was, in a military sense, the revival of all conceivable viciousness and cruelty. The visible head of western man, the Emperor, held an empty title. The late mediaeval Church could not maintain the moral headship of Christendom. The feudal nobility was weak, venal, and without moral authority. No one could keep the common man suppressed now, and some of them indeed burst forth. This is the first record of that democratic phenomenon, popular ideological passion. Kings of relatively humble lineage, like Francis I of France and Henry VIII of England, turned the courts into royal bordels, which was bad enough, but the last Valois King of France, Henry III, and James I of Great Britain converted the palaces into regal homosexual rings. The King of Sweden was a gangster chief ready to kill for anybody's gold. A new merchant class became rich, men without responsibility to anyone. Wars were fought by mercenaries in colorful tights whose officers were worse than their men. They were not too fatal for these dandies in codpieces, but they were total wars from the civilian point of view. Having come from the masses themselves, officers and men considered an occupied town theirs, not only for loot and rape, which became almost respectable, but for torture and cruelty of madness.

The new firearms put great power into the hands of these mercenaries, for artillery was first fired by civilian engineers. Although not much of a soldier, the common man arose in the name of whatever religion, and his savagery under no control at all, exceeded the bestiality of even the mercenaries. France fought eight civil wars in about thirty years. The murder of Protestants by Catholics on St. Bartholomew's Eve has made the Roman apologists blush ever since, but few have apologized for the prior massacre of Catholics under the Huguenot Queen of Navarre, Jeanne d'Albret. Beginning with Burgundy's sack of Liège, and continuing through the Thirty Year's War, the population of Europe was sadly reduced, just by what percent is beyond the ability of statisticians to estimate. It is a period best passed over, for such turbulence could not last. Man must have some stability in his human relations. The publication of the international law by Grotius, and another great period of war fatigue, could have been anticipated.

The renaissance and reformation period showed the world what the unleashed common man could do in his wars of religion. True, the actual political wars were fought by mercenaries, and not very numerous ones at that. The officers of the period had been indoctrinated into no more code of responsibility than his men. True, the semi-religious code of knighthood was often breached, but it did exist as an ideal.

Much of the so-called military activity of this period was by men unleashed from an loyalty, fighting other groups as train-bands, actually mobs under no adequate control, frustrated by centuries of repression, and dangerously imbued with religious ideology. No more dangerous killer has ever lived since the extinction of *Tyrannosaurus rex*. Turbulence produces misery, misery needs the tension release of art, and the renaissance produced the best art that was needed, the most violent and unintegrated social systems contributing the best.

The common man was put back in his place by those who had the means to do so, the former peasants who had risen by the renaissance techniques of social climbing to the new position of mercantile and political power. War fatigue again set in so strongly that it did not fade until the French Revolution. All nations reduced their field forces. For example, England disbanded Cromwell's strong army to four small regiments of infantry and two troops of cavalry under Charles II.

And so began the absolutist monarchy and its limited *Guerre en Dentelles*, the War in Lace, of which some historians have made such fun. True, at the beginning of the baroque period, officers did wear some lace collars over their light armor, but they gave up this costume, so it should be called the war in hair ribbons, or flashes. In spite of the fun-poking at the baroque and rococo, some of the greatest captains of Europe made names for themselves during this era. War just ceased to be bloody, and became one of both field and council chamber maneuver. Everything in the age of the minuet, though, was in good taste, including the art of killing people.

It is necessary to examine the reasons for this lack of lethality, for this was certainly not a period of political stability. War weariness was real in those days, and this was a ruling factor. Another was the regular armies, which had come into full flower, were expensive, and royal treasuries were definitely limited. Louis XIV had drained his resources, and while he did not quite wreck his country, he was the most extravagant prince of the era when gentlemen wore perfume. The third and perhaps the most important factor was that war was given over entirely to professionals. It took a very long time to perfect an eighteenth century infantryman in the complicated musketry and related close order drill of the time. Such men were treasured by a general who wished to risk the lives of as few as possible.

This was the Age of Reason, which the eighteenth century had thought it had invented. This was the era dominated by the mathematical niceties of Descartes and Newton. Thus, reasonable men fight reasonably. Their maneuvers should be mathematical and precise. Indeed, Vauban, the greatest military engineer of all time, built his new forts with mathematical perfection, beautiful and geometric to see even in this day, and designed to save the lives of the people within their walls. Generals distrusted, and reasonably, the raw recruits of their time, so veterans must be spared.

The generals had something to fear. The improved musket with the caliber of a modern elephant gun, was deadly at the close ranges used. An engagement, if one had to be fought, could be costly. The Allies lost thirty-three percent of their forces at Malplaquet alone. This was the perfection of mass fire invented by the English archers. Infantry had to stand shoulder to shoulder and fire by platoons to be effective, and such fire was effective. Indeed, he who fired first was at a disadvantage. Troops were helpless while they were reloading their pieces in face of enemy fire. Hence, the famous remark at the Battle of Malplaquet, "*Messieurs les Anglais,* fire first." This was not French courtesy, nor even a taunt. It was an invitation to folly.

As the close order needed for mass fire could tolerate no breaking of the ranks, the constant drill, drill, drill was not for parade purposes. A man somewhat ahead of the ranks stood a good chance of being deafened by the noisy musket of the men on his right and left. If he were behind his line, he would deafen his comrades. This devotion to close order drill yielded pretty results. The precision of infantry maneuvering at half-step to the tune of their field music, with their officers' hair flashes flapping in the breeze, their wheeling and countermarching was not a minuet, nor entirely for the formation of symmetrical lines. It was maneuvering for the best position so one could greet the foe with, "*Messieurs, les Anglais,* fire first and die."

A reasonable period for reasonable men. Bishops in their powdered hair and lacy rochets knew full well that the central authority of God was not recognized by the snuff-taking gentlemen, although some became so weary of being courtiers that, like Abbot de Rancé, they refounded the hard Cistercians and called themselves Trappists. If Aquinas's God was gone, or shadowy, his reason was the central core of polite society. So, do not abuse your enemy in state papers, even if you think you are right. It is unreasonable to destroy his state, for this is expensive, so keep him in a pleasant frame of mind. He may have to attack you some day, and you do not want him filled with revenge. Promote the general who by bluff and maneuver can bring your enemy to terms. Look coldly on the one who risks battle. Demote the rash one who fights unnecessarily, and unless he is in the best possible position. If he is in that fortunate situation, the reasonable enemy will see it, too, and withdraw without harming himself or you, as he has lost anyhow.

The officer class had been revived, and only the supernumerary sons of the nobility were commissioned. The professional common soldier, though, came from the poorest ranks of society, but treat them well, and pay them liberally. Keep them under strict discipline lest they desert, but make them happy so that they will not want to run away. Make them love you, so if a fire fight cannot be avoided, they will suffer great losses without breaking ranks. Discipline soldiers harshly who mistreat civilians. The troops are well paid, so do not permit them to be anything but helpful to the civilians of the enemy country you are passing through. This is the code of the gentleman of honor. And furthermore, do you want to encourage them to give intelligence to your enemy, to rush to his standard,

MILITARY PRACTICE AND SOCIAL STRUCTURE

to scorch the earth before and behind you, to kill your wounded? Let us be reasonable about all of this. A later chapter will cite the doctrine of the great Vauban, which is to contain your enemy in a fortress, protect your own troops by trenches. Dig another one, a "parallel," by night. If it takes you a season to get close to his works well let it be. You have him invested, have you not? He cannot get away, and you can rest your men. Do not rush that breach in his work. This might cost you a battalion. Keep your engineers digging, and wait a month. Your reasonable opposition knows you have him, that his situation is hopeless. Then he will surrender, then both sides can have a fine dinner together, as the French and British did at Yorktown.

It is not necessary to subscribe to the age's detractors, but some of the defects of the period must be pointed out. First, which specializing in warfare by maneuver, marching and countermarching to gain advantage, the beginning of the era was marked by violation of the Principle of Fire and Movement. Good troops *like* to close with the enemy, but this was rarely done until a smith at Bayonne invented the bayonet. From then on it was fire, then rush. Like the Roman legionary, these veterans in pigtails stood and took fire punishment until the right moment, then closed with the bayonet.

The devotion to precision of lines drilled into the troops by sergeants violated the Principle of Correct Formations. There was only one, too rigid to meet men not so well drilled, as when the Duke of Brunswick met the French revolutionaries at Valmy. The unimaginative generals overlooked the Principle of Sufficient Numbers, or mass. They felt that if they could parade their troops so that they could assume the most advantageous fire at the critical point, a few could defilade the mass. And so they could, if that mass were dancing a counter-minuet. As they could operate only on a beautiful meadow, the Principle of Utilization of the Terrain became a thing of the past. Surprise was out of the question, of course, and intelligence, carefully followed, was by spies in the council chambers of the opposition, not in the field. Victory was rarely exploited to the full, for that would irritate a gentlemanly enemy into resentment which he might avenge a decade later. Besides, you might want him for an ally at the next session.

Has all this anything to do with us? Unfortunately, it does. It laid the foundation for the tragic myth under which we have, do, and yet may suffer.

Braddock was out-danced by the French and Indians. Pakenham allowed himself to be joked into attacking too soon at New Orleans with his parade troops, who still lie at Chalmette in death. These were good units which had just whipped Napoleon at Waterloo. The myth seemed justified. Kentucky backwoodsmen, along with Lafitte's pirates, aided by some United States regulars who are rarely mentioned in the high school history books, destroyed Sir Edward Pakenham who had gained distinction against Napoleon. In fact, the British began losing an empire before that when Thomas Gage forgot about the Principle of the Terrain and tried to take Breed's Hill in a parade. Take it he did, but at what a cost! He helped establish the doctrine that patriots in linsey-woolsey usually defeat regulars. The Allied commander in the French Revolution deployed only 14,000 men over more than twenty miles before Hondschoote in Holland. Perhaps the French revolutionists were only schoolboy levies, but their officers had served in America. Attacking, the Hessians and Hanoverians at Hondschoote fired, and most French amateurs started for the Mediterranean. But not all! As Colonel Nickerson has said, the French were, and are, a nation of poachers. Some French took cover behind hedgerows and ditches, and let the royal Germans have it. The infantry lines of skirmishers was something learned late. Indeed, George Pickett stopped to dress his lines at Gettysburg instead of getting the "flower of Virginia" (and North Carolina) to advance on their knees while their fellows protected them by fire. Gallant Brunswick, Gallant Braddock, Gallant Pickett!

It has been the resulting myth which has been fatal, and it goes like this. Amateurs always defeat regulars if they have enough enthusiasm for the "right." Warfare is not a profession, but an avocation which can be learned in a few weeks. Generals need no experience, so promote lieutenant colonels to lieutenant generals in a year. Your green Americans, even if poorly deployed, can win against the flower of Hitler's Afrika Corps at Kasserine Pass, especially if a seasoned British army is available for rescue. The myth persists to this day, in spite of the thousands of American white crosses which dot the world.

The stately limited wars came to an end when the last regiment cut off its pigtails, and the rush towards unlimited war, towards total war, towards the physical insecurity of every child in the world, has been breathtaking. Social scientists know that no villain need be distrustful as they are of the great man theory. Even if this particular scoundrel did not exist, another opportunist would have oozed into the position of irresponsible power should the social structure reveal a big enough chink.

It is doubtful if a single reader of these pages fails to subscribe to democracy. If so, he must realize its latent dysfunction of mass armies and mass slaughter. A price has been paid, and liquidation of the mortgage is not yet in sight. The humanism of the eighteenth century could not change, and non-humanists have taken over. War has not been "reasonable" but ideological since a hundred and a half years ago, and hence it has been amateurish and murderous. *Liberté, Egalité, et Fraternité* were bought at too high a price to sink into *Liberté, Stupidité, et Venalité*.

The new war has been mass-man war. It is not a revival of the nation-at-arms. It is a Leviathan-dominated war of half-trained conscripts, not that of a trained and disciplined citizens. It is a war of the logistic overwhelm and counter-overwhelm.

The tactical discussion of modern times, which came to an end at the American rest at the Elbe, is too well known to warrant discussion. The Napoleonic wars are too well written, and the plethora of books about the Americans' war among themselves is perhaps the largest literature of its kind in the world. Ours has been the age of conscript infantry with improved weapons, backed by artillery of tremendous power, with the death of horse cavalry at the charge of the French against the Germans at Sedan in the Franco-Prussian War. Modern war, democratic war, has been mass murder, and the record needs inspection.

Barring the little wars, modern war is either unlimited or total, as practiced by Ulysses Simpson Grant and William Tecumseh Sherman. Instead of political interpenetration and conviction, such as the period in lace, it is aimed at the complete destruction of the political system of the opposition. It has already been noted that overt total wars have covert civil war as their latent dysfunction. This helped bring Napoleon down, was present on both sides in the American Civil War, belatedly did as much in the Russo-Japanese War, and changed the social systems of both sides in World Wars I and II.

Seeing that political democracy yielded to the dictatorship of the First Consul in France, Napoleon kept its name and invaded his world. His people were in a ferment of upward social mobility. Nothing was impossible for them. When the general, or emperor, had exhausted his good troops inherited from the royal army, he knew that he had an uncounted mass of Frenchmen he could sacrifice, and did. Invading Russia, he managed to bring his enemy to battle just once, at Borodino, and lost 33,000 in one day, and still his foe withdrew in good order. The Russians lost about 11,000 more, and fat, aging, half-blind Marshal Kutuzov knew he could not afford another such bloodbath. The "old dowager," as Napoleon called him, decided to permit arson, winter, harassment, hunger, and Napoleonic bad judgment to destroy the Grand Army, and he succeeded.

Imbued with great democratic ideals, northerners and southerners slaughtered each other in massive terms. Grant did not invent the saying that one cannot make an omelet without breaking an egg, but he was a master at egg breaking. He lost more men in one month in 1864 than Lee had in the opposing army. He had suffered similarly at Shiloh in 1862. The overwhelm from an inexhaustible reservoir was a substitute for skill. Billy Boy and Johnny Reb were brave, as people imbued with ideological fervor are, but it should not have happened to them.

Grant was superior to Lee in only two things, and he knew it. These were men and materials, and he liberally expended both. What happened to the Union in the crater at Petersburg should have happened to no one, and would not have under the proper leadership. Grant was not alone. What Burnside allowed Longstreet to do to his troops at Fredericksburg should not have happened to gladiators. The Confederate army would have ceased to exist as a fighting force if it had endured the massacre suffered by the victorious Union at Chickamauga.

Again, aroused to anger after the destruction of the *Luisitania*, the Americans landed in France for World War I. The Germans wisely retired as soon as they saw that the United States could land material and personnel in such quantities. They lost their regular army, and had only conscripts with which to fight, but both the French and the British were in the same condition. The German general staff knew that the Americans had more green troops with which to overwhelm their equally green ones, and they quit. The French upper and upper middle classes sought a negotiated peace, and have never forgiven the Americans for coming in.

Someone has called America's war in southeast Asia the Living Room War, insofar as it was partly televised, corpses and all. Television should have been at Salerno, Anzio, Omaha Beach, and the Normandy hedgerows. Even what they have been told has so depressed the Americans that they longed for a war of material only, a pushbutton war. This was a vain hope. They got Viet Nam. American atomic artillery may prove its own worst enemy. One more attempt at cannon fodder may be made, but it surely should be the last one, for its successes have been limited. And surely the mass-man myth should be scrapped once and for all. Like most other cultural inventions, the conscript army developed a drive towards perfection, and exhausted its potential and ability to meet new conditions. Its unbelievable complexity has provided a phenomenon which no general or staff can completely understand or control.

The mass war of the nineteenth and twentieth centuries was the steam factory's war. Analysts have been so preoccupied with the founding of industrial capitalism that they have overlooked the army which appeared as part of the politico-economic pattern. The myth of the early period was free enterprise and Ricardo's Iron Law of Wages. Mass-man was therefor drawn into the proletarian army, and treated like the swarm of country people needed to feed the maw of the new factory and mine. The soldier was a replaceable labor unit, completely expendable due to the exuberant birthrates of the powers. This was the war of the bureaucratic Leviathan, and it is doubtful if it can survive in the approaching welfare imperium. Ricardo really is dead, and none too soon, in either the army or the automated factory.

Leave the bulk of "youth" alone to enjoy their suburban permissiveness. They only get in the way of soldiers. And inspect, then, the higher command. Due to the ideals of corporation status seeking, the modern army has very few basic privates, but enough general officers to command the armies of the world. Hidden in this bestarred mass, however, is a small group of eminently intelligent, highly educated, cold-eyed generals who know who they are, what they are doing, and what the right alliances are. They probably hold the key to the future.

One hardly expects a change in the basic principles of warfare. The ways of applying them will change as the interlocking technological and political systems change. One may hope for an abolition of war. The current anarchist revival may hope for the disappearance of the civil state, but it shows few signs of withering away in any foreseeable future. If civilization lasts, that concept includes civil government. We can expect to retain institutionalized politics, and with its structure, its ultimate appeal to institutionalized force. The state's clientele had best adjust to this political reality.

FOOTNOTES AND REFERENCES

[1] Reginald Bretnor, *Decisive Warfare: A Study in Military Theory*, Harrisburg, Stackpole Books, 1969, p. 15f.

[2] B. H. Liddell Hart, *History of the Second World War*, New York, G. P. Putnam's Sons, 1970, Ch. 4.

[3] Bretnor, *op. cit.*, p. 15f.

[4] *Ibid.*, Ch. 4.

[5] These are the men who wore the *kataphrax*, the mailed shirt, or hauberk.

PART II
THE MATERIAL CULTURE OF WARFARE

INTRODUCTION TO THE MATERIAL CULTURE OF WARFARE

The techniques of warfare are those of social interaction, or better, transaction. This is a core concept which must not be forgotten, and often is. Transaction is the impact of one or a group of human personalities upon those of others. Warfare differs from most types of the phenomenon by adding the possibilities of permanent or temporary elimination of the targets. What is in the mind dictates behavior to the hand, and if need be, to whatever artifact is therein contained. Perhaps enough corrective suggestion has already been made to those who confuse the arts of warfare with its tools, perhaps not. This is the opinion of most combat-experienced officers, and the position of one will soon be quoted.

Warfare is a social science. The development of weapons is technology, engineering, and other practical applications of physics and chemistry. There is but one Nature, one cosmos, and the separation of reality into physical, natural, and behavioral sciences is only a matter of human convenience. The same is true of the separation of the latter into studies of material and nonmaterial culture. A culture is a whole thing, and operates as such. Nevertheless, it is very easy for one fraternity to lose contact with the needs of the other, and the world is not well served by that.

Because of the difficulties of verifying the validity of innovations in the nonmaterial culture, in contrast with the ease of doing so in the material realm, there are times when materials surge ahead of the nonmaterial, creating the confusion William Fielding Ogburn called the cultural lag. We live in such times. By contrast, there are those times when social organization develops ahead of the material. The revolutionary Christianization of the Roman Empire was one of these. Another was the Franco-Burgundian Revolution which changed western life from the rather dark early mediaeval period to the civilization of the High Middle Age. Neither did the renaissance rest upon any significant improvement in the material inventive process.

It would be folly to say that the material culture of warfare is not worth consideration. Even an extreme transactionist would be more apt to conform to the suggestion of an originator with a pistol than to an unarmed man. It is for this reason that the following discussion of the material culture of warfare is included. But keep it in its place, and the opinion of a great captain is quoted on the point. General George Patton said,[1]

> "History is replete with countless other instance of military implements each in its day heralded as the last word—the key to victory—yet each in its turn subsiding to its useful but inconspicuous niche. . . . New weapons are useful in that they add to the repertoire of killing, but, be they tank or tomahawk, weapons are only weapons after all. Wars may be fought with weapons, but they are won by men. It is the spirit of the men who follow and of the man who leads that gains the victory. In biblical times this spirit was ascribed, and probably with some justice, to the Lord. It was the spirit of the Lord, *courage*, that came mightily upon Samson at Lehi which gained the victory—not the jawbone of an ass."

The jawbone of an ass is now under discussion.

FOOTNOTES AND REFERENCES

[1] Quoted in Ladislas Farago, *Patton: Ordeal and Triumph*, New York, Dell Publishing Company, Fourteenth Printing, 1975, p. 107.

Chapter 6

HUMAN PERMEABILITY

The Penetrative Revolution

Fighting is no human monopoly, but war is. That the human being is at the core of this violent phenomenon is a position so obvious that it should not need stating. War is a technique of manipulating men, their minds, and their social systems on the part of originators of action, and of preventing the same from the responder's point of view. All of the great captains have recognized the primacy of the human being. They have never confused war with its implements. It is strange that civilian writers have time and again set weapons at the center of the discussion, and have put men and the minds of men around the periphery. Napoleon said, "The moral is to the physical as three to one," an exaggeration, perhaps, but Bonaparte was a soldier of such enduring reputation that his word should be taken for something. He knew that warfare is the method of reducing the enemy's will to resist by whatever available means, and so must we all.

It might be theoretically possible to have a battle without weapons between small forces, each in a high state of leadership, morale, discipline and skill, and the victory would go to the side best endowed with the aforesaid virtues. It is not necessary to consider such an extreme, however, for no one can recall such a situation. Skilled and well led soldiers can defeat rabbles better armed than they, for not only history but relatively recent news media have provided examples. A culture is a unity with two aspects, the material and the nonmaterial. These are two faces of the same coin, always interacting and influencing each other. The body of man and the personality it encases is paramount, and tools are but extensions of the human body, and used to achieve its goals, wishes, and desires.

Of course it is folly to neglect the instruments of warfare. Parity or superiority in the weaponry is essential to any political system that wishes to survive and maintain its way of life. It is true that in our thermonuclear decades the material culture of political disagreement has seemingly been gaining in importance over the nonmaterial, and humanists and social scientists are bitterly deploring the trend for a very real reason. They are now sharing the target characteristics of the field soldier. No one should be surprised at the growing importance of military technology. The comparative expansion of material culture contrasted with the nonmaterial has for years been characteristic of every walk of life in western civilization. This has unexpectedly resulted in a proliferation of secondary social transaction over the primariness of happy interhuman relations, with some less than lovely results. The field of warfare presents no exceptions to this drift, but in it men are still at the center. There are superior types of human beings, perhaps — designers, inventors, engineers — but soldiers are still there with their commanders, and according to the needs of the times, their quality must likewise improve. Cannon fodder was all right for the days of the cannon, but that smooth bore weapon lies in the past as much as the arbalest.

Returning to man as nature left him on this planet, look and see if this is not a weakling. Individuals, varying as they do in sex, age, health, and physical fitness, present a respectable range of strength, but the basic and often bitter fact remains. Men are weak, feeble, and left defenseless by nature in an environment often indifferent or hostile to their happiness. Nature's chief lesson to *Homo sapiens* is adapt or die, and much of the homily which evolutionary biology has spoken is that superior protoplasm adapts. Much of this adaptation consists of mankind's interposition of a tremendous warp and woof of culture between the environment and his weakness, only to discover that every manifest function has a latent dysfunction, or to speak simply, every rose has a thorn. All culture, even civilization, is a corrective of human weakness, as its inventors appreciate and conceive of it, but there is no thornless rose here. As the house dog often intentionally or otherwise harms his master, or the tabby scratches and infects its little mistress, his own cultural devices often bite mankind to the bone.

There is no reason to think that anatomically, physiologically, or mentally this weakness is decreasing. The human is as vulnerable as he ever was. His evolution is finished in that direction, if indeed a reversal is not in prospect. Culture and kindness have interfered with natural selection, have conspired for the survival of the unfittest. Mankind's greatest protective equipment, his superb brain, must soon tackle the problem, which is as yet only dimly understood.

The whole range of human feebleness cannot be discussed here. The present specialty is the permeability of the human organism, and the personality and groups with which it has surrounded itself. Everyone has in part grasped the reality of this permeability. Everyone has barefootedly stepped on something sharp. Everyone has cut himself with his own knife. He did not need Laura Thompson to teach him of the painful and disabling nature of such experience. She was, nevertheless, and so far as the present writer knows, the first behavioral scientist to emphasize the fact that the human body and its personality are so subject to invasion and penetration that permeability is a dominant force in existence.[1] This does not mean that all of this is unpleasant or threatening. That the environment can penetrate the individual through the openings of his body — his eyes, ears, mouth, and nose — in the basis of learning and even more delightful experience. Delicious food may be ingested. It is because the male can invade the female that we as a species survive, and that we have such a needed source of tension release. We speak here, though, of the threatening, the dangerous, and the deadly. On the recognition of menace and its correction rests the tactical Principle of Adequate Defense. No matter how valiant he or it may be, a sufficiently penetrated man or unit is finished, at least for now.

Look at man as nature left him once more. His skin has shed its visible hair, so that it no longer protects him against sharp objects and missiles enjoyed by shaggy dogs, or heavily feathered birds, or toughly plated reptiles. This skin system is far more useful in protecting his interior from the assaults of temperature changes than from splinters, nails, and aimed weapons. It is almost but not quite useless as protection against an unfriendly natural or social environment. Perhaps it is better so. The huge sea turtle is heavily armored and of low intelligence. Its human enemy can turn it over and render it helpless. Many a heavily armored tank has suffered a similar fate. Chop off the paw of the armored turtle and its mobility is greatly reduced. By fire or projectile, knock off the tread of a tank, and it is as vulnerable as the leg-chopped turtle.

The greater the defense, the less the mobility. There is a point of diminishing returns in protection. And there stands mankind, soft, penetrable, rising upright and presenting its tender belly to its enemy. If that enemy is human, that one has but little penetrative capacity given him by tooth and fingernail. Something had to be done about this, and something was. That is why this chapter deals with the penetrative revolution, a cultural and not an anatomical fact. This cultural revolution has never been completely successful from either the offensive or defensive aspect, and there is no reason to think it ever will be. The heavily armored knight became practically impermeable to his mounted enemy, but his horse was not. Neither was he invulnerable when unhorsed. An upturned knight on the ground was the goal of a foot mercenary with either ransom or murder in mind. The heavily armored battleship hull was for a time impenetrable, but General William Mitchell tried to tell his superiors that the deck was not impermeable to an airplane, itself the most penetrable product of inventive genius since the invention of tissue paper. Mitchell was court-martialled for his impertinence, of course. There has been success in the search for impermeability, but do not expect perfection in the ways of men.

If warfare, then, were reduced to its bare essentials, one of these would be the permeability of man and his works. Thus, an enemy state and its masters attempts to penetrate the social system of its opponents. This may be done without force of arms, for economic competition, diplomacy, propaganda, and espionage are mighty weapons when skillfully used. In the last analysis, the enemy's civilian and noncombatant population is the ultimate target of overt or covert hostility, and the minds of men are essentially penetrable. This is a direct result of the evolutionary depression of human instinct, and since the invention of writing or modern electronics, the tools to impact and penetrate the learned responses of people have increased faster and more efficiently than the defenses against them. The essence of warfare and salesmanship is the reduction of the opposition's will to resist, and the technique thereof is called invasion and penetration. This penetration of both the enemy's mentality and his battle lines is the basis of the tactical Principle of the Objective, of the Offensive, of the Initiative, and of Fire and Movement. This thread will run throughout this book, but the present problem is the technique of penetrating the skin, muscles, viscera, and skeletal structure of the opposition's armed personnel, and the tools for implementing this technique are called weapons.

The situation from the present viewpoint may be summarized in this manner. Human natural vulnerability, or to use a more basic word, permeability, cannot be reduced. This is a prime factor in warfare, as it is in many peaceful pursuits. The strong man is just as permeable to the sword stroke, arrow flight, or bullet impact as a weakling. Reginald Bretnor was one of the first theorists in plain language to insist on permeability (he calls it vulnerability), although all but the most mechanistic social scientists have realized it. So have all competent tacticians, for the Principle of Security rests on its realization. Think, then, along the following lines.[2]

All mankind, every individual, is vulnerable because of two features to be found in all living things.

1. Aging alone will destroy every equilibrium, homeostasis, or balance unless the senescent or obsolescent parts of the constituent whole are almost constantly replaced. If the quality of the replacements is better than the replaced, this can be called growth. If the replacements are inferior, or not available at all, this is dying. This is true of every organism, most tools, every social structure, and every weapons system.

2. All mankind, every individual, is permeable by violence. If this is unorganized, one may call it accident. If the violence is organized and ritualized, it should be called force. One prefers to call it force if directed against himself, and strength if it is his own, but euphemism will not decrease the fact or pain. Therefore, whether one is indulging in the penetration by peaceful competition which is often conflict indeed, a game of cards or athletic contest, one must measure his own strength and permeability with his opposition's defense, his power to realize this strength, and to reply by force. This is the essence of the estimate of the situation: unless the player is willing to prepare meticulously, he would better not enter the game at all, unless compelled against his will. This and similar books constantly call attention to the ambivalence of man, his behavior, and his works. Every situation has an ambivalence with at least two faces, one good and the other undesirable. In this case, one is speaking of the positive or force, and the negative or vulnerability.

This is the fundamental ambivalence in war, which also exists in almost every other human activity. There is a vulnerable or negative aspect in much of our living which would destroy us if it were not for the forceful or positive. Every tool, structure, or social relationship has both functional or desirable aspects, and dysfunctional or undesirable ones. What so few are capable of understanding is that when one augments the complexity of the desirable, he will increase the deplorable as well. Few of us, for example, would like to do without the self-starter on our automobiles, but there is inherent in this muscle-saver more chance of malfunction than ever existed in the old hand crank. All inventors and first users are essentially optimistic. This is the curse of the convenient. The flaws show up later, and much if not most of the subsequent improvements and secondary inventions are directed to the dysfunctions which the originators would not or could not anticipate. There is nothing perfect or absolutely perfectible in mankind, his works, ways, or relationships, but it requires a mature personality to realize this. The others cry, "What happened?" when they should have known all along.

And so it has been that men have set up weapons systems, simple or complex, and trained others to use them as protection against their weaknesses. All of these are not only accompanied by dysfunctions in general but have nuisances and disasters specific to the particular weapon, tool, or organization. In the old cavalry days, for example, the swordsmen were defenseless on their left and rear, while lancers were vulnerable on their right, left, and rear. The eighteenth century infantry, close-packed to obtain massive firepower by musketry, was defenseless on both flanks and rear. Artillery has always been so defenseless on its right, left, and rear that it has been necessary to provide it with cavalry or infantry to protect it. A single machine gun is vulnerable on every point except the one defined by its muzzle. Indeed, this instrument is so delicate that few machine gunners like to fight with it unless paired with another one. Breakdown in one of the two is from expectable to inevitable. Four footmen have destroyed many an isolated machine gun, its emplacement, and crew. The amount of ammunition the weapon consumes produces logistic, or supply vulnerability. Each weapon, then, has a built-in weakness peculiar to itself. Thus, a half pound of sugar fed to a cavalry horse produces a blissful quadruped, but when introduced into the fuel tank of its automotive successor by a saboteur, only disaster can result. There is something new under the sun, though, for those mistresses of modern war, the airplane and submarine, have four-dimensional vulnerability. They are flimsy and permeable on every point of around, above and below. Neither has a natural buoyancy or stability in the elements men have chosen to put them. A tank is cursed with weight-wait on bridges, in the snow, on ice, but it is a mighty mobile fortress compared with the airplane and submarine. While every other weapon is especially vulnerable in transit, they have relative safety only when on the move, or at least that was true before the invention of search and destroy anti-weapons. The airplane's greatest vulnerability is when it is caught by surprise on the ground, and a submarine resting on the surface is helpless against naval gunfire. Hiding as quietly as possible under the surface, its presence can still be detected by sonar, which invites attack by a relatively inexpensive depth charge.

The strength of any weapon, then, is not only in its own inherent power but in the weakness of its target. Is this not also true of any game, athletic or with cards, and of salesmanship and debate? It is necessary to realize that not only every weapon but every body of men wielding them has both. Sociological realism demands that the analyst who is attempting to alter the behavior of his opponent must study his own and his enemy's balance or imbalance between function and dysfunction before undertaking an adventure which can only result in success, failure, and at times even worse, a draw.

Weapons may be classified in many ways, but in light of the paramount importance of tactics, the functional aspect will be chosen. To all soldiers, ancient or modern, the result is the important consideration, and this aspect of weapons classification emphasizes getting results. It is, furthermore, and in broad outlines, true without regard to time or place. It is also easy, perhaps too much so. A traditional classification already lies at hand, and one just as applicable to submilitary combat as to the operations of modern powers. This system divides weapons into the following categories: those of (1) fire, (2) shock, (3) mobility, and (4) protection. It was implied in the sentence next before the last that this classification might be too simple, for it suggests that an instrument might exclusively function as only one of the above four. A piece of artillery, ancient or modern, delivers shock by fire. Whether one speaks of a modern gun or a Roman onager, it must have enough forward mobility to bring its force against its target, and to get away from an enemy if defeated.

Weapons of fire are devices for getting at a distant enemy while at the same time actually or wishfully remaining safe from his strike power. Fire weapons, then, are missile projectors. They are attempts to overcome space and temporarily to reduce the pull of gravity.

A mobile weapon, as its name implies, is an instrument for moving against an enemy, especially a maneuver towards his weaker and away from his stronger aspects. It must be admitted, reluctantly, of course, that it is sometimes desirable to have great mobility away from him in case his potential seems insurmountable. All weapons and their users must have some mobility. Sitting ducks rarely win. Some weapons, such as the trained war-horse, specialize in mobility, as do his tank-like derivatives.

Protective devices often consist of armor in one form or another, and represent the prudent soldier's wish to escape harm while administering it. A brief discussion of body armor will be included later, but for now, consider that armor is a medicine to be taken in moderate doses. Prudence (and there is a stronger word) can be pushed beyond the point of diminishing returns in decking one's self with impermeables. Mobility can be lost in this way, and with it goes the priority of the Principle of the Offensive. Weight-wait is still the rule on this planet.

There is a principle of the weaponry whose discussion cannot be postponed, one which the writer has chosen to call the offense-defense cycle. Its evidence is so incontrovertible that it is strange that most civilians and a few soldiers have failed to conceptualize it. It may be briefly summarized in the following manner.

A man wishes to do another bodily harm. Nature has provided him with teeth, nails, feet, and hands, together with muscles and a will to drive these forcibly against a defender. Since that one is also equipped with some skin protection and a fairly tough skull, as well as a desire not to be hurt, the aggressor's anatomical equipment can be inadequate for his purpose. If the aggressor, foreshadowing the penetrative revolution, picks up a stone which is harder than his fist, he can make a considerable impression upon the defender, perhaps indeed reducing his resistance and diminishing his will. If the aggressor chooses a sharp stone, he can insert this into the defender and injure him to the point of death.

The defender, unless caught by surprise, is hardly willing to remain and be pommelled. He may back away, or he can fight back. Prudence enters into the aggressor's thinking. He finds it convenient either to avoid the flailing arms of the defender, or to overcome the distance between himself and the defense as fast as possible. One must not underestimate the importance of human discretion or the aggressor's fear in the development of weapons. Should the aggressor put his sharpened stone on a stick, he has a spear which not only will increase the leverage of his man-piercing tool but will enable him to stand at a safer distance from his enemy. This spear may also be thrown. Better yet, a light spear or javelin may be projected as an arrow by a spring or bow, the deadliest weapon mankind was to know from the close of the Old Stone Age until late in the renaissance. If the defender retires to a safe distance, the range of the arrow (or artillery or aviation) must be increased. Then if the defender stands in a hole, the spear must be made stronger to root him out of his rudimentary engineering work. The projectile must acquire some power of demolition. If the defender puts his fortification on his own body in the form of defensive armor, the same process must be carried through. And so goes on the circular effect. If the offense becomes powerful, the defense must reply by by vitiating the former's weapon, at least in part. The offense invents new weapons or improves old ones so that the defense's genius must devise new replies or be crushed out of existence. There is nothing old or new about this. The entire history or prehistory of weapons is summarized in this cycle. Once the offense-defense cycle has been understood, the student has mastered the first and most important principle of armory.

The operation of the offense-defense cycle seems an inevitable inherency in military invention. The crossbow seemed the ultimate weapon in the year of its invention, but it never forced a critical decision in late mediaeval warfare. The tank, likewise, seemed to be the ultimate weapon for several of our decades, but there it moves, clumsy, of poor maneuverability, obvious, noisy, and drawing fire which has demonstrated that yesterday's fine armor plate has the impermeability of tomorrow's graham crackers. The 939 page and authoritative *Jane's Weapons Systems* published in January 1971 predicts that the sophisticated weapons of the immediate future will contain anti-weapons which will seek out and destroy submerged, missile-launching submarines. In which case, the ex-ultimate submersible weapon will have no more battle survival than Nelson's *Victory*, if as much.

Pause one moment for a word of caution. No complete protection against anything offensive has ever been devised. No complete defense against a good punch in the nose has yet been invented. None of the old weapons has lost its lethality. If an unarmored French unit were to advance against the English as they did at Agincourt, it would be shot to ribbons with yard arrows. If good modern infantry were to attack the American positions before New Orleans as the British did in 1814 with no better artillery preparation than General Sir Edward Pakenham enjoyed, it, too, would be decimated by rifles and muskets now considered museum pieces. These old killers are no safer than they once were. They have simply lost their significance in modern situations. A weapon is deadly only with reference to its context of the situation. A fire arrow could still ignite a thatched roof, but a flamethrower has more significance to a situation containing concrete pillboxes.

The question is not how much a weapon can destroy, but how it can affect a decision at the critical point. What is the goal of the instrument's operator? What is the ultimate mission? Enthusiasts for a new weapon often mistake devastation for military effectiveness. Draw a veil of charity over the substitution of devastation for victory of American aviation in Viet Nam. It devastated many a rice paddy, forest, and dirt road, and was a nuisance to the North Vietnamese, but it did not defeat them. The French civilians were told not to return to St. Lo, but they did, and the Eighth Bomber Command killed so many of them that the rubble stank for months. What, though, did they do to Erwin Rommel's determination to fight on? The German *Luftwaffe* leveled vast tracts of London, but left the marshalling yards almost intact. A bombed-out London synagogue merely demonstrated that such things could be done, which had almost as much military effectiveness as J. E. B. Stuart's ride around McClellan. It is suspectible, too, that the nuclear enthusiasts are following the same path. There is no doubt about the devastating effect of nuclear warheads. Overkill is not just a word, but who will be overkilled? A very angry army in the field?

The above discussion suggested a vast range of cultural objects intended to increase human hostile transaction. It was not thought wise to separate primary and secondary transaction in an introduction, but the time has now come to get down to basics, the primary transaction of cutting, piercing, and crushing weapons, just as much the ancestors of them all as it is sure that primary influence preceded the secondary type.

As complete a summary weaponry will be made as space allows. This will require a small backtracking on the previous statement about the inadequacy of the unaided body.

The adjective "unaided" was the term chosen, not untrained. It is easy to underestimate the deadly capacity of the unarmed primate organism. True, the simple anatomical equipment of the angry or frightened man could hardly be called a weapon, certainly not an artifact, but it is possible to develop this body into an extremely able shock deliverer. The unarmed soldier trained in judo and karate is a dangerous opponent. His is one of the most efficient types of dirty in-fighting known to man. The soldiers of the Greek and Roman patrician republican armies were trained boxers and wrestlers. Such exercises with the classical Mediterraneans were, however, only suppling up for warfare, and later deteriorated into simple sporting spectacles. Many American Indian societies, in a similar manner, permitted adult males to spend most of their waking hours in such exercise, and for similar reasons.

The persistence or even perfection of hand-to-hand unarmed combat today shows that primitive war still lives. While it is true that there are no units specializing in such work, yet the modern motive is truly military, and extremely useful in jungle and street warfare, or in any other situation wherein mayhem and death must be accomplished silently. Trained, unarmed soldiers can and have disarmed those equipped with knives, broken their arms, and slain them.

About the simplest aid to the human body one can describe is the war club, and no one can tell just when it was invented, as baboons will seize natural sticks and go for the band enemy. The club increases the crushing blow of the natural fist, lengthens the arm, and provides the latter with an extra joint. The club lasted a long time, for the English peasantry, not being gentlemen and hence bereft of the sword, became expert at quarterstaves. Many people have used the device with skill. Some Polynesians used hard wood clubs edged like long swords, and it took a hardy foe to charge their fighting lines. Likewise, an almost political group of societies was found on the North Pacific Coast of the American continent—

Kwakiutl, Bella Coola, Nootka, and others—who ground stone war clubs about a foot or more long. These were fierce and able Indians practicing the rudiments of true war, and they knew where to hit. The stone war clubs—almost swords—may have been a response to the heavy cedar helmets of the region, but the Indians discovered that a blow coming up from the ground would crush the jaw of an opponent. Surely a man with a shattered mandible was inclined to foreswear his former political opinion and abjure the fray.

The highest development of the non-thrown war club was the mediaeval mace, a response to knightly armor. The wielder did not always consider his opponent's heavy helms as anvils, but directed the mace against his arms and shoulders. The mace could not penetrate chain armor, but he could make its wearer's arms and shoulders weary and bruised. After plate armor came in as a response to such bruising, the mace, either with a simple head or with a spiked ball attached to the haft with a short chain, was used as we take hammers to open nuts. The English knighthood deemed it typically unsporting of the French to consider them oversized walnuts and mace openings in their armor plate, only to insert shorter than usual swords into the interstices. Maces were efficient in persuading a fallen knight that ransom was preferable to death. The English archer, at the height of his fourteenth century glory, practiced this extraction, for he, too, carried a maul on his back. He was no gentleman, of course, and being a mercenary, enjoyed living beyond his means. The mace has survived into this day as a ceremonial emblem carried before cathedral and academic deans, and one rests in honor on the desk of the Vice President of the United States when he presides over the Senate, and in front of Mister Speaker in the British House of Commons.

The war axe, too, is only an improved war club. The stone celt, a hatchet lacking a hafting hole for the handle, was an early Neolithic invention whose chief function was forest clearing for farming. Museums have cracked skulls of the same age, however, to show that the uses of the celt were not always peaceful. They have many canoe-shaped stone axe heads, obviously copies of bronze ones, which had only a hostile use. They were introduced into Neolithic Europe by an unknown but obviously fierce people archaeologists call the Battle Axe Folk. The axe and shield were the bases of Anglo-Saxon warfare. The eastern Indians of the North American continent made excellent stone celts for forest clearing, but they were adept in using them to clear the same of other Indians, French, and English. Modern derivatives, the robber's sandbag and the policeman's sap, are not unknown to American cities.

A direct derivative of the war club is the sword, a shock weapon par excellence, and one with no other function. One is not speaking of daggers here, which are only enlarged knives with an anti-human rather than anti-material use. Of course, they are derived from peaceful knives, but the sword itself seems to be an outcome of the war club development. Indeed, it is a war club provided in some instances with a piercing point, and in all cases, save the rapier, a cutting edge as well. Several peoples who had not discovered the use of metals had war clubs which to all purposes were slashing swords. It has just been noted that the Polynesians made them of hard wood, nearly man-high, flattened, with no mean cutting edges. Some of these South Pacific islanders improved the edges with shark's teeth, ray's tails, and other objects provided by nature. Certain Middle Americans enhanced the sharpness with insets of obsidian.

Metal casting in the Bronze Age made the sword the great weapon of both infantry and cavalry up until a few decades ago. The Bronze Age probably marked the beginning of true warfare, and it certainly was a time of trouble and turmoil. The Metal Age folk had something to fight about, and did. The older bronze swords were quite short, for the smiths had not learned how to cast long weapons. It is regrettable in many ways that they ever did. A lesson which both nonliterate and civilized soldiers had a hard time learning and retaining is that it is not the edge of a shock weapon which is dangerous, but the point. Anyone who tried to train cavalry recruits a few decades back knows how hard it was to keep them from slashing. The best function of a cutting edge is to enable the assailant to withdraw his weapon from the spasmodical tissue of his penetrated enemy. A slashing blow is easily seen, dodged, or parried. It rarely hits a vital spot and therefore wounds the enemy without killing him. He may be left alive, but angry and vengeful. Any slashing blow leaves the body of the slasher without guard unless he can cover with a shield, a clumsy substitute for skill. A jab with the point is easily aimed and, if it meets its mark, leaves the target with little argument potential. As the Bronze age technicians increased their abilities in casting, swords became longer and heavier, and were transformed into cutters and crushers having all the flaws just mentioned. The reply to this was the cast metal helmet, a false reply to a false threat. Many prehistoric European Metal Age swords were so specifically designed as cutters that they developed a broad flair towards the point end. The ancient Italic people developed the folly by increasing the length and weight of their iron swords, especially overweighting the weapon near the point, which threw it out of balance. When they received a few defeats from the Celt-Iberians of Spain, who had retained the older weapon, the Romans readopted the short sword, much to the subsequent discomfiture of the Gauls. The Italians became sword thrusters, the Celts remained sword swingers, and we know who won.

The mediaeval knightly sword was derived from the old Roman long sword, *spatha*, which name survives as a suit in a deck of playing cards, or "spades." Long and straight with a simple handle and guard, it remained substantially the same for centuries. The end of the mediaeval period saw the appearance of the glaive and falchion, curved cutters about two feet long. Like their Indonesian counterpart, the bolo, they were effective as decapitators, slicers, and torturers of fallen soldiers and unarmed civilians, but never forced a decision against armed man. They were the mercenary infantryman's pride, and helped the hired killers of Charles le Temeraire, Duke of Burgundy, acquire their nickname of the decorticators, or skinners.

The rise of the renaissance mercenary infantry gave the Swiss and German hired men a long, thin sword taller than a man. These were wonderful stickers and slicers, either in the straight or wavy (*flamberge*) form. They had a serious drawback, however, as the mercenary footman swinging at the man in front of him was apt to slice one of his comrades to the rear.

There was a strong movement as the baroque period drew nigh to use simple thrusters, at first heavy ones, and then later lithe, flexible blades which did not pretend to have an edge. Late renaissance Italians so equipped invented fencing in our sense, which nation remains one of the world's masters of the art. They carried a dagger in the left hand as well as the rapier in the right, a custom widely adopted but soon relinquished. The Italians favored fancy guards and hilts at the time, necessitating more reliance on the flexibility of the wrist than of the fingers, a practice despised by the French swordsmen whose flexible fingers are remarkable. The sword, then, vanished as a military weapon for footmen and tended more and more to become a status symbol. The European nobility developed such an intense sense of personal honor that it was said that 6,000 French noblemen died in duels in the ten-year reign of King Henry IV. The last infantry actually to kill with swords were the Japanese officers, who carried their marvelous samurai swords into battle against Americans in World War II, and did very well against the wounded and prisoners.

The cavalry saber of classical shape lasts to this day as an officer's emblem, but was always a poor weapon from a mounted soldier's point of view. The weakness of a curved sword has already been mentioned, but since Europeans had taken such drubbings from the

Turks, their cavalry emulated everything Ottoman, including the flaws. The finest cavalry sword was invented by General George Patton, Jr., who was awarded the title of The First Sword of the Army. It was a long, straight-edged, pointed weapon issued to United States troopers in the Nineteen Twenties. It had brass knuckles built into the heavy cup guard, designed to smash opposition horsemen in case of a close *melee*. It was equipped with a brass snap at the top of the guard so that the trooper could stick the sword in the ground and thus dispense with carrying a pole wherewith to pitch his shelter tent. The only blood this fine weapon was to draw was during the march on Washington by veterans of World War I. President Hoover did not enjoy this confrontation, and ordered General MacArthur, then Chief of Staff, to do something about it. The latter ordered the cavalry from Fort Meyer against this political riot, and one veteran lost an ear to a trooper's slice. The last persons in western civilization to meet death by the cavalry sword were the Spanish loyalist victims of Franco's Moorish cavalry.

It is now time to speak of another weapon which developed out of the club, namely the spear, from which all shafted weapons are derived. It has been one of the world's most effective killers, and its career is not quite over. This is functionally the fingernail and arm extended and provided with an extra joint, following mankind's ancient desire to keep away from his opponent while inflicting harm upon him. The spear and its derivatives are almost the ultimate weapon for penetrating the skin of the opposition.

There has been speculation about its origin, for it is certain that its invention long antedates that warfare it has served so well. If Neandertal Man knew of the poking power of a stick with a fire-hardened point, there is no evidence that this is so. The Australian aborigines make such spears, and culturally they are not much beyond the Neanderthal Mousterian level. It is very certain that none of the Mousterian flints could have been used as lance points, but the Cro-Magnon race family which succeeded the Neanderthalers in west Europe are known to have used lances and javelins, and to have pointed them with elaborately carved heads of reindeer horn. It is thought that these were hunting and fishing tools, for after the close of the Aurignacian-Perigordian epoch, they were carefully barbed. A hunter wants the point to remain in his quarry's body, but the warrior seeks to free his spear for the next blow. This did not prevent the Cro-Magnons from spearing humans. Their spears and javelins may account for the abrupt disappearance of the Neanderthal people, the most striking ethnic change Europe was to know. The genocide of simpler natives occupying desirable real estate does not seem to be new.[3]

The first unchallenged evidence of the occupation of America by humans during the Pleistocene geological epoch was the verification of the beautifully flaked Folsom and other points which could only have been lance or javelin heads. The evidence, however indicates that these were hunting devices. The commonest post-Pleistocene surface finds in North America, though, are broad, crudely flaked Archaic lance points, but whether their function was economic or anti-human is not known. It is known, however, that in that later and short-lived Great Plains culture, the Indians under European observation used lances but little better, not only to slay bison but as weapons against men. As such, they were poor things in contrast with our knightly tradition. It could not have been otherwise, as the use of stirrups, as soon as the late Plains Indian cultures knew about them, was considered too effeminate for warriors.

Of all the warriors and soldiers without writing, few would deny that the spearmen par excellence were the AmaZulu of South Africa, or at least, that is where we find them today. Their great King Dingiswayo knew of Napoleon, and set out to follow his example. The east Africans are spearmen rather than archers, but Dingiswayo's men hurled their spears far too often. King Chaka, who succeeded to the Zulu kingship, was a wiser man. He made his troops destroy their long throwing spears, and shorten the device into the famous or infamous *assegai*, a man-jabber of great efficiency. Chaka knew that good troops love to close with their enemy, and he instilled this spirit into his men. Thus he drove southward from the region of the tropical great lakes, sweeping all other blacks before him, decimating the Dutch Boers, and eventually whipping the British regulars, for all their nineteenth century fire weapons. The British called out some of their territorial (national guard) troops, and Chaka defeated them. King Chaka's success exemplifies the principle that *men* win battles, not weapons. Chaka's successor was defeated by the British who bought Gatling guns from the Americans, exemplifying the principle that better weapons in the hands of good men are a help in defeating other good men.

The discovery of copper, bronze, and later iron brought in a new day. Museums have many beautiful Bronze Age lance heads, for that age was famous for both artistry and bloodshed. Indeed, there may be some kind of functional relationship between the long, metal-tipped spear and the drilled infantry line, and hence the dawn of tactics. One of the first pictures recovered of the Sumerians, who occupied the Tigris-Euphrates valleys "after the flood," is one of spearmen in a line led by an officer.

It is finally known that the spears used by the Greeks against

Troy were relatively light, could be used in either overhand or underhand thrust, and could be thrown upon occasion. The battle line of the classical Greek heavy infantry, however, used spears so long, and shields so heavy, that the mobility of the ranks was greatly reduced. The Romans, who laughed at and destroyed the Greek hoplites, corrected this error. The Latin heavy infantry reduced the lance to about five and one half feet, an iron head occupying the top third. The Roman legionary ordinarily considered the *pilum* a fire weapon, but he could also use it as a jabber.

The stirrup, as has been seen, made the heavy cavalry line the queen of battles for centuries, for now the mounted knight or man-at-arms could carry a lance outreaching the spears of the infantry of the times. The mounted man's lance could once be wielded, for the Bayeux tapestry shows Norman knights using it in an overhand thrust. Diminishing returns set in. Horses and armor became so heavy that the knightly lance could only be crouched under the right arm, and the Greek infantry pincushion was reinvented, but this time with formidable mobility. Why did it take so long for someone to observe the flank vulnerability of this charging line of heavy cavalry? Well, the English did at Agincourt in 1415.

And so it came to pass that the knights and their men-at-arms, so over-armored and over-armed, developed a tendency to dismount and leave their swords, shields, and lances behind. They fought in line with bills, derived from the old farming pruning hook, and other poled weapons: halberds, oxtongues, poleaxes, guisarmes, fauchards, partisans, and such cutters and thrusters hafted on long sticks. The return of the infantry as the queen of battles was foreshadowed. The Beautiful Book of Hours of John Duke of Berry shows his knights and men-at-arms practicing this kind of fighting. Bosworth Field was fought in this way, and poor Richard III was said by his political detractor, Shakespere, to have been far from his horse when he wanted him. It must be observed that the English gentlemen always thought more of their infantry than did their French opponents. A ring of armed pikemen made a haven of refuge for the weary knights upon occasion, and if these men kept their discipline, the French knighthood was loath to charge into it, and the French horses shared this reluctance.

One would have thought that the beginning of the great day of infantry gunpowder warfare would have seen the last of the pike. The reverse was true. The old fire weapons took long to clean and load, leaving the arquebusiers and matchlock men vulnerable, and a threat to no one. They had to be protected, and the response to their helplessness was a square of pikemen around them. This lightly armored infantry carried spears as long as 25 feet, longer than those of the Greek hoplites, but lighter in weight. No cavalry charged into this porcupine with sword and lance, but renaissance and baroque horsemen thought out a reply to this.

Parenthetically, some cavalry retained the lance into the nineteenth century. The Union sent one regiment of lancers against Stuart's sabermen, who greatly enjoyed the encounter. Indeed, into the valley of death some fool whose name need not be mentioned sent the British light brigade against a crescent of Russian artillery at Balaklava in 1854. The lancers rode out of the valley of death, but hardly the six hundred. "Someone had blundered," which statement constitutes one of Tennyson's more accurate observations.

But to return to the infantry scene. This mixed unit of musketeers and pikemen was a dreadful waste of manpower. Only a part of the command could be at work at any moment of the engagement. And it came to pass, or at least legend says so, that a body of French peasants on a bandit-exterminating expedition found that they had run out of gunpowder. In desperation, they jammed their knives into the barrels of their arquebuses, and a new day dawned on the French military mind. Again, according to legend, a gunsmith of Bayonne took the hint and began manufacturing knives with iron plugs especially designed to fit into a musket's barrel. Soften the enemy by fire, then plug the gun with a bayonet, and assail him with shock. The European generals saw the light, and the day of the pike was over forever.

The fire weapon was useless, though, when plugged with an iron knife, but some Frenchmen with their, to the British, sneaky ways solved the problem. They cast two iron rings to the bayonet enabling it to be slipped over rather than into the barrel. Some of Britain's King William III's best, seeing the French advance on them by fire, waited until the latter had stuffed bayonets into their weapons. Even if the British did observe the glint of the bayonets, the French came on, firing all the time.

And so here is the spear's end. The bayonet has taken terrible toll in the days of mass infantry charges. The Americans did dreadful things to one another with it in their civil war. When a senior American medical officer derided the weapon's effectiveness in World War I, saying that he had many bullet-wounded men in his hospital, but no bayonet-wounded men to treat, he gave the arm a compliment. Bayoneted men did not get to the hospital. It was an ideal weapon for trench raiding. It was used but little in World War II, but seems to have regained some popularity in jungle fighting, where silent killing is often required, and fire might injure a comrade in the not very straight lines in southeast Asian fighting.

This, indeed, is the close of more than just the spear thrust. No one in his right mind foresees the end of primary social interaction, although its importance has been yielding in bulk to that of secondary interpersonal relations. Let others discant on the problems of culture, personality, and society. The decline in the importance of piercing, cutting, and crushing weapons should likewise have been predicted, for they are vehicles of primary hostile transaction. In spite of the rise of missiles of a sophistication unbelievable to Caesar, Napoleon, or Lee, no soldier would enjoy going into combat without an artifact capable of defending him from an enemy whom he can see, touch, or hear.

FOOTNOTES AND REFERENCES

[1] Laura Thompson, *Towards a Science of Mankind*, New York, McGraw Hill Book Company, 1961.

[2] Reginald Bretnor, *Decisive Warfare*, Harrisburg, Stackpole Books, 1969, consult Chapter 1.

[3] The older terms of Neanderthal and Cro-Magnon are used here because they are more familiar than the newer and more accurate professional ones.

Chapter 7

MISSILE FIRE

The Ballistic Revolution

Prudence, cowardice, efficiency, call it what you will, but to eliminate, or harm an enemy while remaining safe one's self is an ancient hope. This ambition could have been achieved long ago had not the defender been as dedicated to the offense-defense cycle as the aggressor. This is the essence of the ballistic revolution, from the dart and dart thrower invented in the last great glacial cold to our own day when deadly missiles of intercontinental range are sobering realities. The absolute destruction of intervening space has always been the missile man's dream, limited by certain controlling factors. Perhaps the most important of these is the effective wish of the user to obtain such a weapon as measured by the amount of sacrifice he is able or willing to demand from his clientele in the search for absolute weaponry. Mankind has surely come a long way in his fight against space, from the very respectable range of an arrow to the earth orbiting missile which is now known to be in use to gather intelligence, and which could also contain nuclear warheads. Of course, space exploration may be only in the interests of pure science, but the nation which first erects a launching pad on the lunar surface or a manned space platform will have considerable effect on world politics.

Projectile weapons present certain problems for solution. The following list is not all-inclusive, and the reader is invited to suggest others. The ones cited are for convenience, and will not be discussed in detail for each military artifact.

1. *Distance*, or range, the essential struggle against gravity.
2. *Accuracy*. Weapons vary greatly in this respect. Some of them were so inaccurate that they were more weapons of morale than

of destruction, and it is hard to frighten good troops more than once with the same bogey.

3. *Rate*, or rapidity of fire. This rapidity is much to be desired, but there has been more than one retrogression in this virtue. It will be necessary to understand this preference for the inefficient over the effective.

4. *Weight*, or gravity in the pure. A heavy weapon reduces the mobility of its handlers. Large-sized armies must contain all sorts and conditions of men, the relatively weak as well as the strong. There simply are not enough champions today to accomplish the state's purpose. Closely related physically to the weight problem is that of recoil, which is one but recently solved.

5. *Expense of production.* He that owns the weapons will control the state. If the government is poor, and the soldier rich enough to possess expensive weapons, he will control the political structure, and not vice versa. Again, the size and effectiveness of a fighting force will in part depend on the costs of the weaponry. The percentage of any nation's gross national product spent on arms is not under discussion. That is another story. Nevertheless, the dawn of nationalism and its need for mass armies, and the requirement of cheap, mass-produced weapons had a twin birth.

6. *Area of impact.* One rifle shot can hardly be expected to hurt more than one man. The same can be said of an arrow. A solid cannon shot will destroy only those directly in line with its fire. Nevertheless, if the cannoneers can fire their weapon so as to enfilade their enemy, at or near his flank, its damage can be extreme. If it hits the earth before its range is expended, it can roll like a bowling ball down the ranks of many unhappy ten pins. The invention of fragmentation missiles, exploding artillery shells, old or modern mortar missiles, aviation bombs, which count their area of impact in square blocks, only foreshadowed the nuclear warhead with multiple explosive devices which counts its area of impact in parts of continents.

7. *The human factor* of which the chief consideration is training. Large armies cannot be well trained, so the direction towards automation began with the crossbow, and the end is not quite in sight. If quick training of part-time soldiers is the ideal, the brains must be built into the weapon, shifting the importance from the operator to the designer. Again, with the disappearance of the elite corps of professionals, the physical selectivity of recruits had to decline. It took a strong athlete to be a knight. Modern armies must be built around weapons which can be carried and operated by less than athletic men.

As projectiles are our present study, just plain throwing rocks at people was and is an effective way of exhibiting hostility, and such behavior shows no tendency to diminish. It is not necessary to explain that a half brick is called Irish confetti. The hand-cast stone today has been replaced by a metal one filled with efficient explosive. The hand grenade is a device well beloved of combat infantry, so cherished that soldiers empty their pockets of food to make room for grenades. The grenade was a response to the trench warfare required in the eighteenth century siege methods. It took a strong man in those times to throw the grenade of the period, but he could lob it over the parapet of the opposition and expect results. Such a grenade could be cast at oncoming bayonet men, too, with some expectation of dampening their ardor. Indeed, west European powers raised whole regiments of grenadiers which survive today in name only, as the soldiers have been actual riflemen for a couple of centuries. The old grenade simply did not work well enough. The idea was good, but the explosive was not, and the fuses worse.

The weapon was revived in World War I for largely the same reason, a response to trench warfare and the new machine gun. A man could lob a Mills grenade over his own parapet and that of the enemy which protected the machine gun crew. The latter weapon discouraged looking over one's own parapet. This little fragmentation bomb, if it came anywhere near its target, ended the careers of anyone nearby. In somewhat later times, an able infantry squad found that it could distract the attention of a machine gun crew holed up in a concrete pillbox while a soldier could introduce a modern grenade therein.

The Germans, who feared tanks through World War I, discovered that if they could get a hand grenade into the track-laying device of the vehicle, they could dispose of it at will. The German hand grenade never reached the power of their opponent's missile. Their wooden "potato mashers" are cheaper to make; training in their use is easier; they can be flung by weaker men. Their power of detonation, however, leaves much to be desired. A gas cannister flung by police at rioters can be a sickening device, and could be more so if a non-lethal gas other than of the tear type were used. Well, a hand bomb or explosive rock is still useful, and virtually anyone can make a cheap "Molotov cocktail" to hurl at persons of divergent opinion.

It did not take humanity long to discover that a rock thrown with a sling could work personal and political wonders. Somehow, the world has always warmed to David's elimination of Goliath. The Old Testament praises slingers who could "throw at a hair and not miss."

But why should stones remain hand slung? The tendency of the defense to erect walls around itself inspired Rome's "base mechanicals" to make an improvement on hand thrown rocks. Rome's favorite siege engine, the *onager* (wild ass, so-called because of its kick), was fundamentally an oversized sling-and-rock arrangement. The leather sling itself was about fourteen feet long with a pad in the middle. One end of this was made permanently fast to a long pole equipped with an open hook to receive the sling's looped free end. The pole, beam, or improved human arm had been inserted into a twist of material—rope, wet hide, thongs, we really do not know—near the front end of a wheeled wooden carriage. The torsion of this skein was winched as tight as possible, the beam worked from the upright to horizontal position, the sling loaded with a rock the size of a basketball, the whole engine given something of an aim, the trigger released, the beam swinging upright again to be stopped by a padded bar near the machine's front, and the projectile was on its way. Smaller onagers lacked the sling, and had an iron cup as a substitute for the human hand, but they had nothing like the sling weapon's range. Rome's heaviest rock-throwing artillery was the *ballista*, a somewhat different weapon, but worked on the same principle as the onager. It is said that a heavy ballista could hurl a sixty pound stone about 100 yards, which if so, compares favorably with early eighteenth century cannon. These engines could do real damage to the earth and log pallisades of the Gauls, but one doubts if they could hurt a well-built stone wall. Cast over the wall, however, they could scatter confusion among the people behind it.

But return to the spear as a fire weapon rather than one of shock. It was not highly praised as a projectile cast with the unaided hand. When thrown by a dart thrower, or as it was called in technical anthropological terminology after an Aztec word, the *atlatl*, we see something else. The atlatl is still used by the Eskimo, some north Siberians, and the Australian aborigine. It is an instrument antedating the bow and, it is said by some anthropologists taking the pains to become expert with it, is as good as a poor bow. It is fundamentally a length of material a little shorter than the human arm. A handle is on one end, while the other is provided with a ledge, or hook, or something against which the butt end of the javelin or dart could rest. The dart is laid on the atlatl, the butt end against the ledge or hook. One grasps the handle with the ball of the hand and the two lower fingers. The upper fingers and thumb go around the dart and the dart-thrower. The atlatl thus provides greater arm length and an extra joint. The operator raises both the dart and the dart-thrower over his right shoulder, leans as far back as he can, and gives all a smart, overhand whip, releasing the dart with his upper fingers as the top of the arc is reached. Once one has become proficient, he can cast a dart farther, faster, and more accurately than he ever could without the instrument. This was originally a hunting weapon, but humans can be killed with it, too.

It is known that the Cro-Magnon peoples brought this weapon with them into Europe during the last three epochs of the Palaeolithic, or Old Stone Age. It was originally a simple artifact, using the cannon bone of the cave bear but little improved. Later it developed into a sculptured work of art. The Cro-Magnon peoples are mentioned, for the hypothesis of William Edwards is that the dart-thrower enabled the agile newcomers to exterminate the slower Neanderthalers who had no projectiles. The atlatl is known to have been a fighting weapon in Southwest United States before an invader introduced the bow. It was also a war weapon among the truly military states of Middle America. It is apparently easy to play down this weapon's efficiency. It is recorded, for example, that when Captain Cook discovered Australia, some of his men teased the aborigines about their atlatl's relative efficiency compared to their own eighteenth century muskets. A friendly match was arranged, and the winners were not in His Majesty's Navy.

The arrow is really a small javelin, and the bow is a spring for propelling it. All peoples of any competence at all fastened feathers to the butt end, preferably on an angle, to increase the accuracy of the flight, and to make the projectile spin. The best material of all times for points is flaked flint because it produces more shock and bleeding than any other raw material. The Eskimo and later Plains Indians exhibited a preference for bone and horn, both of which have too clean an entry. The same Great Plains bison (and man) hunters found that the iron they received from the white traders had the same fault, too sharp and too clean. The same can be said of the Indo-Malaysian's hardened bamboo points, except for those who are usually designed to break off in the wound, and those charming people have a way of poisoning their arrowheads. The bow itself is a strong spring, or in the composite type, two springs. Much larger volumes than this one have been written on the bow, and a large monograph could be written on arrow-release alone, which literature, of course, cannot be reviewed. The weapon is now known to have existed among the hunters of the Final Palaeolithic (Capsian) epoch of North Africa. It was imported into Europe in the Mesolithic or Middle Stone Age, a fact not originally recognized because these people made their arrowheads to cut, not pierce, and archaeologists could not comprehend anyone being that stupid. The flaked flint point was known to the European Neolithic, which was a prewar, submilitary age. The Neolithic uses of the arrow were not always amicable, though, as points have been found inside the skulls of certain Swiss Lake Dwellers. It was originally a homemade artifact, but truly military people gave the job to professionals, as the surviving family name of Fletcher, arrow-shaft maker, indicates. But in any event, the bow was the killer for all times, up until now, and it changed war's direction. Fire and movement became a fact, not a wish. Mass fire now became possible, as King Harold discovered at Hastings, where he was killed by Duke William's mercenary archers.

Do not be deceived by the toy used in girl's gymnasium classes. Remember that only Ulysses was man enough to pull his bow. Strong athletes of today, not trained to the weapon, have trouble drawing the arrow of many Indian bows to the cheekbone. No American Indian culture contained really good archers, fletchers, or bowyers, but even Indians could drive an arrow clear through a bison or deer. The English archers could not only put an arrow through a man but could pierce good French armor. The modern American distance record, so far as this writer knows, was made by Jack Stewart in 1949 with a 640 yard flight. (Robin Hood could shoot a mile? Ha!) The bow used by English mercenaries at Crecy (1330) had a 100 pound pull, while the modern American sporting bow has a pull of between 50 and 60 pounds. The standard long, or "livery" bows, used at Crecy were six feet long, and the ideal arrow length was a "cloth yard," although this would certainly take a strong man to pull the butt to the jawbone.

It was expected that an iron-tipped arrow, especially the English archer's rather blunt military "pile," would kill a horse at 200 yards, and pierce mail armor at the same range. Plate armor required firing at closer range. Modern tests with a long bow have driven an arrow through a one inch oak plank at 220 yards, which is not a bad record for a rifle. A good modern sportsman can shoot seven arrows into the air before the first hits the ground, and what musket or crossbow has that rate of fire? Sir Walter Scott awesomely reported that his fictional heroes could split a previously fired arrow resting in the target, but modern sportsmen have done this time and again. Musketry achieved no such accuracy until well into the eighteenth century. An English sportsman, General Thord-Gray, in a friendly match in 1924, put 70 arrows out of 72 in a 26-inch target at 80 yards. His opponent, armed with modern pistols, failed to do as well at much closer ranges. The military ideal in the fourteenth century was to fire 12 arrows per minute at a man-sized target at 240 yards, and hit each time. If these records, mediaeval and modern, are true, and they may be duplicated any time, why was the bow given up for two less efficient weapons, the crossbow and the powder-charged tube? Has the human factor been considered, that element so overlooked in the discussion of warfare?

The crossbow was considered with such horror when it was reintroduced into Europe that a kindly pope forbade its use in warfare. King Richard I. the Lion-Hearted, a man not overgiven to respecting scruples, papal or otherwise, adopted the weapon gleefully, and was killed by the same. This volume has deprecated the crossbow in more than one paragraph, and one must ask why. Even light ones were slow firers. The crossbowman, after firing, had to rest the bow element on the ground, and if he were using the lightweight type, put his foot on an iron step, and take both hands and pull the string over the release mechanism. The heavy crossbows were equipped with a pulley or winch whereby the archer could bend the great bows by winding them up. This took some doing, and some time as well. The low bow had six times the rate of fire as the best crossbows. The latter, while having a terrific impact, were accurate only for short ranges. But it took the love of a lifetime to become an archer. Even little Indian boys were given toy bows almost as soon as they could toddle. Archers the world over considered shooting at marks their chief leisure time sport. To train a good crossbowman took only a few weeks. It took a powerful man to draw the yard arrow to the jaw, but any weak man can wind up a crossbow's winch. Of course, if one wishes to go further, if any infantry recruit or draftee, armed with a modern rifle, *does what his sergeant tells him* and does not deviate, he will hit the bull's eye consistently in a week of training, and any weakling can squeeze (not pull) a modern trigger. The old musketeers did not fire at specific targets, as the archers did, but in the general direction of the enemy.

Too little attention has been paid to this training factor. The crossbow pointed the way to mass-man armies, and it took little time to train an arquebussier or musketeer. Rising nationalism needed more soldiers, and with briefer training periods than before. From then until now, weapons developed not only because of greater fire power but also as skill-savers. Many an "old sarge" has lamented the passing of the Springfield rifle, but he spent a lifetime learning to operate the bolt, and we cannot take that much time training mass armies.

The foregoing paragraphs have obviously been leading to a discussion of powder-driven fire weapons. Now the power of an expanding gas in a tube has long been known to many culturally simple populations. The blowgun was apparently a southeast Asian invention, and one of considerable antiquity. That it is known to the Indians of the South American rain forest, the Antilles, and the Cherokee of the Great Smoky Mountains of North Carolina is a problem for the general ethnologists to solve. The weapon is fundamentally a barrel of reed or other material open at both ends. A poisoned pellet is inserted in the muzzle end, and made fairly airtight with some kind of down. The firer raised the blowgun to his lips, sights with both eyes down the barrel, and with a remarkably small amount of breath, can accurately propel the projectile an imposing distance. Yet, even if this principle had been known for centuries, it was re-invented for powder-driven firearms.

Gunpowder had long been known to the Chinese, but just who first discovered it as a propelling agent remains a mystery. Before the "knowns" of the subject are discussed, a rather surprising fact must be cited. In spite of the usual principle in the development of material culture that if a small artifact is good, a larger one is better, practical fire weapons began with very large artillery, while shoulder and handguns followed much later. The chances are that the black powder of the day was too powerful and unstable to be contained in small weapons until the technology got around to casting barrels capable of containing this still formidable explosive.

The first gun to be used in combat, so far as this writer knows, was the mediaeval *pot-de-fer*, which was hardly more than a pear-shaped iron pot with a touchhole and a neck into which an iron dart could be stuffed. This football-sized plaything was laid on the ground with its muzzle and directed somewhere in the enemy's direction, and fired. There is no record wherein this enemy was thereby injured, and at first glance, it seems to have been more dangerous to the gunner than his foe. Not long after this, some genius put two and two together and saw that a two-inch iron ball could be discharged from an iron tube closed at one end and open at the other, and the proto-cannon came into being. This weapon had no carriage. The tube was laid on the ground facing the foe, its muzzle end elevated to the desired trajectory by a heap of earth, and fire applied to the touchhole. The English brought several of these pieces afield at Crecy, but if anything was hurt by them, it was the French idea of English chivalry, which was not very high in any event.

Poor as these two specimens were, the world got the idea. Almost immediately guns of tremendous size called bombards appeared. After all, our mediaeval ancestors were well aware of barrels for beverages, and they began making fire weapons of heavy wooden staves bound by iron hoops. Changing these staves from wood to iron took but little imagination. One mentions iron staves, for the technology of the times was not capable of casting solid tubes with the required bore. The bombard cast, or because of the gas leakage, really boosted a carefully shaped stone ball as much as 25-inch diameter at the enemy wall. We do not ordinarily succeed in building 25-inch guns even now. These enormous weapons had no carriages. They had to be labored towards the enemy, their muzzles raised by wooden wedges, and their back ends rested against something solid. The bombard was fundamentally an anti-material rather than an antipersonnel weapon, but there is no record of such a siege piece actually bringing down a strong stone wall. They might have been effective against gates and weak spots. The expense in man-hours of shaping the stone balls, and their rate of fire of some three or four per day—the heat they generated required that the barrels cool for a long time between rounds—bespeak their ineffectiveness. Their operators were hired civilian mercenaries rather than soldiers, which did not endear them to the rest of the command. The death of the bombard was foreshadowed when some German learned to cast iron balls which, of course, fitted the barrel closely and hence made better use of the expanding gas. About the same time in the late fourteenth century, Teutonic genius improved the saltpeter, which led to more effective gunpowder. The new chemical tended to blow up the bombard and the bombardiers, although some such guns were in use as late as the early sixteenth century. Artillery's great problem, and the one only partly solved today, is the quality of the aforesaid powder. It was so poor for so long that removing the fouling from the barrel and the touchhole seriously slowed down the rate of fire.

The second half of the fifteenth century saw a great development in what were really cannon in the modern sense, guns with smaller bores and fairly long barrels which could take advantage of the gas expansion longer. The cast metal walls had to be thick in order to withstand the better powder. These guns threw rather than tossed much smaller balls, and with great force. The smiths had learned to cast guns in one piece, and a few smart ones cast "trunnions" right onto the barrels. The trunnions are the metal projections one sees on the cannon in old forts which, when set in carriages, enabled the gunner to elevate the gun for the trajectory desired. This improvement in casting both barrels and balls led not only to smaller bores but also great diversification in the size of guns for specialized functions. The sixteenth century saw attempts at breechloaders, too, but as the improvements in powder came faster than that of casting safe breech locks, there was a return to muzzle-loaders which maintained until the mid-nineteenth century.

The high-walled castle became obsolete, and was replaced by the many-bastioned forts with low walls and earthen curtains set way before the main defenses to absorb cannonballs. The reply of the offense to this type of engineering was to attempt to harm, not the fortification but the persons within it. This was the function of the Roman onager, but in the sixteenth century a more lethal instrument was invented, the mortar. An unknown German composed this very short cannon with a high trajectory to fire over the wall and land the projectile inside. Up until almost this day, mortars have had to have very thick walls to contain the shock. They were harmful enough, but some Netherlander suggested that they fire a hollow, not solid, ball and one filled with powder. This man, then, blest the world by inventing the bomb, or shell. The early mortarmen, though, were less than happy artillerists. First, the gunner had to stuff the powder into this heavy, short piece, and arm the touchhole. Then, with help, he would edge in the ponderous shell with some gentleness. The bomb's fuse was kept to the fore so that the gunner had to reach into the bore, light the fuse, then fire the touchhole. Consider the poor powder of the day, suppose that the fuse set off the bomb, but the propelling charge of the gun did not ignite? If the shell exploded in the gun, it would render the piece permanently useless, and probably do the same to the crew. The first solution was to realize that if the fuse were not next to the propelling charge, the latter would ignite it, and hand firing would not be necessary. Too often, though, the propelling explosion drove the fuse into the shell, causing it to explode just as it left the barrel, destroying the crew and leaving the enemy unharmed, unless he died laughing. Seventeenth century gunners, however, realized that if the fuse were loaded toward the muzzle end and away from the powder charge, the heat of the detonation would ignite it. The mortar was and is a wicked weapon.

The modern mortar developed out of the inaccurate "trench mortar" of World War I days. Neither has much resemblance to their prototype of the enormously thick walls. Its shell contains its own propelling charge, and the walls of fine alloy provided by modern technology are light. It can be carried by just a few men, or even one. This very accurate weapon's old immobility is now solved. Its extremely quick explosive makes it deadly to personnel over a wide sheet of territory. (The Japanese invented a "knee mortar," so light that it could be held against one man's leg and fired with deadly effect. It might also break that leg.)

But returning to the not very good old days, artillery is very heavy equipment, and its mobility has been a problem which only our own latest day has solved. Towards the bombard's last days, gunners tried to put it on a four-wheeled truck. Even the first great cannon with trunnions were mounted on two-wheeled carriages, but they required 20 to 40 horses to haul them. Note, too, that the muzzle of the gun in transit was away from its enemy, making the piece slow to come into action. This problem has just now been solved, a fault not very serious in large siege pieces, but a sad one in field guns if quick action against an aggressive enemy is needed. Artillery on the road has always been vulnerable to cavalry able to sweep around its friends' flank. Indeed, its slow fire in one direction made it vulnerable to aggressive infantry which had broken through to it. The latter problem was solved in Napoleon III's day.

The more devastating the cannon, the greater the weight, and the less the mobility. This problem had to be solved. Better metal casting in the reign of Elizabeth I produced a culverin weighing two tons which could fire a 30-pound shot. A better gun of the same caliber weighing but 140 pounds was invented in the reign of Charles II. That great master of artillery, King Gustavus Adolphus of Sweden, who thought cannon should be used against people instead of forts as a reply to the improved muskets, had guns which could be hauled by two horses, and when necessary, by men alone. These were 14-pounders which weighed only 500 pounds. The great soldier king invented, or caused to be invented, the canister shell, actually a can filled with musket shot which would explode in the midst of the massed infantry of the times. These guns outranged the infantry muskets, and the brilliant monarch tried what we have just accomplished, making some artillery organic to infantry units as well as a cooperating branch of service.

The mobility of artillery provides an interesting example of the offense-defense cycle. Gustavus Adolphus, as just said, liked to bring fieldpieces up front to counter the range of infantry muskets. Napoleon had the same idea, and brought his fieldpieces loaded with canister and grape up forward to ruin the opposition's infantry. By the time of the American Civil War, however, the situation was reversed. Cannons firing case and grape shells had short ranges, while footmen had increased theirs, forcing artillery so far back that it ceased to be a menace to infantry, for the time being. But, in Gustavus Adolphus fashion, the Americans solved the problem, and "light artillery" is a term of the past. The modern "recoilless" artillery rifle was originally of 75 millimeter caliber, and now calibers of 57 millimeter are standard. These can be fired from tripods one man can carry, or from a quarter-ton truck ("jeep"), or even when held by an infantryman over his shoulder. Their effect is greater than the old four-inch fieldpiece, and they have no recoil at all, albeit a dangerous blast to the rear and side. They do not have the range of mounted artillery of the same caliber, but they can go anywhere an infantry footman can walk. This, however, does not solve the problem of transporting heavy ammunition. Tractor-drawn heavy pieces were invented by the end of World War I, a fight which saw unbelievable suffering on the part of horses and mules. This efficiency has been increased so that tractors can pull even the heaviest land guns over roads at normal motorized marching speeds. The ultimate is self-propelled artillery which looks much like tanks, but is not. Guns so mounted can move as fast as tanks, though, and their muzzles are pointed towards the enemy when in transit, not away from them.

Almost everyone in the old days scoffed at the idea of rifling cannon, for only a lead ball would grip the lands, or rifling, and sufficiently large leaden balls simply could not be cast. Neither could they be transported. An attempt was made to put a lead belt around the iron cannonball which would make the proper contact. The Italian Cavelli made the first successful rifled cannon, but it fired a "bullet"-shaped projectile, not a ball, thereby dooming both the smooth bore and cannonball forever. This was a breechloader, too. Rifled cannon were just too powerful for cast-iron breeches, which problem inspired a series of experiments. The Germans, of course, began working in steel breechloaders, and thereby destroyed the political aspirations of the French Second Empire at Sedan in 1870.

There was punch in the muzzle-loaders for some time, however, and John Dahlgren invented in 1850 a powerful one of smooth bore which fired a bullet-shaped shell. This proved to be very embarassing to the Confederate coast defenses. New smooth-bored 13-inch mortars contributed to the same political outcome, doing great damage to Fort Sumter, and the beautiful colonial architecture of the city of Charleston.

Experiments with fixed artillery ammunition were conducted at about the same time. This was simply the enlargement as has been seen in the present day, hand-rifle cartridges. The propelling charge is in the metal casing, the explosive shell permanently fitting into the fore-end until the detonation separates the casing and the shell. This made for more rapid fire and easier transport.

The artillery recoil problem remained, and the first attempt to solve it lay in making a great gun's rearward energy serve instead of frustrate. The late nineteenth century Americans became badly frightened by the news that the Spanish Admiral Cervera's fleet was at sea, and ringed the east coast with forts containing "disappearing" guns. The great rifle was raised with its muzzle over the parapet by counterweights, fired, and the recoil brought it to the rear and down back into the gun pit for re-servicing. Of course, the gun was practically invisible from sea, but the airplane did away with that solution, and all other guns in fixed positions.

The first really practical solution of the problem was that 75 millimeter fieldpiece of such great political importance. The gun tube was not even set in trunnions, but mounted on a sleigh which rolled back along the carriage. The recoil forced it rearward, where the power was absorbed by pistons in tubes of nitrogen gas, which pressure returned the piece to the firing position when the original recoil was expended. Two rounds could be fired by the time the reader scans this description. But more importantly, it provided for an independent sighting system, and thus relatively accurate indirect fire, the result, its greater range, almost 8000 yards, could be exploited effectively. The 75 enabled the French to embarrass the German infantry, and the American allies as well, who had to admit that they had nothing as good. The latter made many improvements, but 75 shells would not pierce German tank armor in World War II. A gun was found which harmed German armor during the American invasion, but during the Ardennes counteroffensive only antiaircraft artillery fired point-blank could penetrate the new Royal Tiger. The German show-off piece in World War I was the Paris gun, often miscalled Big Bertha. This gun from 75 miles distance killed 256 Parisians and frightened millions more.

Military aviation was not invented as high-grade artillery, but effectually it has so become. The race since World War I has been for countermeasures. Planes in that war were so slow that they were brought down now and then by 75 millimeter gunners who would take a duck shooter's lead on them. Planes are of great speed now, but antiaircraft artillery with its own built-in radar takes the proper lead automatically, computes the speed and altitude, and fires a shell with a proximity fuse which detonates close to the aircraft without trying to hit it. Such a gun dispenses with human sight through fog or darkness, and aims and fires itself.

The largest American land artillery which can be discussed at the moment is the now obsolete 280 millimeter gun requiring two trucks to transport it. Its accurate range was about 20 miles. It was a general all-purpose heavy piece. It could fire any type of shell, although it was generally called an atomic gun, and it is assumed that other powers were doing as well. The gun is now greatly improved. Whatever happens regarding atomic bombardment by missile, virtually everyone assumes that atomic artillery will be used should a confrontation of great powers occur, and training is directed along that line.

There are, of course, many classified topics of artillery considerations which cannot be discussed by the general writer of any great power, and indeed are not known to him. Napoleon might have been wrong in saying that "God is on the side of the heaviest artillery," but it is suspected that guns of the most advanced design, manned by the best possible gunners, and existing in adequate quantity, are comforting possessions in any sociopolitical difference of opinion.

The late middle ages attempted to use a hand cannon, a crude tube fastened to a piece of wood to be tucked under the gunner's arm. This man pointed his piece somewhere in the direction of his enemy, then looked away so that he could place a coal on the touchhole. From this simple beginning to the highly sophisticated shoulder rifles of modern infantry, now virtually small machine guns, was a long way to travel, but the journey was made. The renaissance saw the introduction of the culverin, a term later confined to artillery with trunnions. This was a crude piece with an equally primitive stock which was held up near the forward end by a wooden crotch to which it was lashed. The first great improvement consisted of a "slow match," a length of chemically impregnated cord. This enabled the gunner to keep a more or less permanent source of fire to apply to the touchhole without looking around for some when needed. This two-man hand cannon was the fourteenth century's terror, but who was terrified? There were pressing problems, however, as the shortage of archers was beginning to tell, and the crossbow was improving in fire and range. The culverin began as a reply to the best of the crossbow, the arbalest. It acquired longer and longer barrels, a well-made rest which could be moved instead of being driven into the ground, and a rate of fire almost as good as the arbalest, and with greater range. Indeed, it could knock a knight out of the saddle at over 100 yards. The powder it used fouled terribly, and it had to be cleaned after each round. It fired a leaden ball which expanded and caught the gas, but contributed to the fouling.

The progress toward automation began when it was discovered that the slow match could be attached to a type of trigger mechanism, and the great matchlock which was to rule the world for so long was born. Here was the beginning of the struggle to make a weapon with its own built-in fire. The matchlock, of course, required an improved firing pan to receive the downward moving, smouldering rope, which process was still in progress at the end of the American Civil War. When some German began solving the fouling problem by cutting straight grooves in the barrel, the shoulder fire weapon was in sight. The weapon under discussion, the arquebus, was to have a long life. Lest one think that this was a magnificent improvement, let him recall that, along with the matchlock itself, the arquebussier had to carry a ramrod, a scraper, a bullet extractor to clean out misfires, cleaning rags, a supply of lead for casting bullets, and a brass mold for the same, flint and steel for re-igniting his slow match, a gun rest, extra cords for matches, and a sword in case his gun misfired just when an aggressive enemy broke through. Obviously, he needed a helper to kindle and keep a fire going to cast bullets, as well as aiding in carrying this equipment about. And still it had a faster rate of fire than its arbalest rival.

The next step was fabricating a gun containing its own fire: the Dresden "monk's gun," a clumsy thing indeed, but it attached the then popular method of making kitchen fire, a roughened bar near the touchhole and a device for drawing an iron pyrite over it. A poor thing, but the gunsmiths of Nuremberg got the idea. They began putting a roughened wheel inside the piece which could be wound up like a clock. A trigger mechanism would jam the iron pyrite against the whirring wheel, and shoot sparks into the pan. And thus the wheel lock was born. It was far too expensive to issue to infantry, and was used first as a sporting weapon. It nevertheless put cavalry back into business, for the long matchlock was too much for a trooper to handle from the saddle. This was the first pistol, and in those days pistoleer was synonymous with cavalryman. The wheel lock was shortened, the end of the fifteenth century saw it only two feet long, and it assumed a wooden stock which foreshadowed modern times. Shorter wheel locks could have been made, but the civil authority forbade their manufacture. Gangsterism and banditry are not modern inventions. The short wheel lock was called a dragon, and there are modern cavalry regiments still called dragoons.

The cavalrymen of the day had no desire to charge into the porcupine of pikes the infantry presented to them, and someone had to think of a way to break up this formation. The problem was solved by German mercenaries, the *reiters*, lightly armored in black steel, and equipped with two wheel locks apiece. They attacked slowly in 20 mounted ranks. The first rank would fire into the infantry, and wheel out of the way towards the rear. The next rank would fire, and do the same thing. By the time the original first rank was on the line, it had cleaned and reloaded. The infantry with its hedgehog of pikes over 14 feet long, with some arquebusiers in the middle of the square, was a formidable formation. The cavalry, for a change, went them one better. King Charles's cavaliers carried four wheel locks apiece. They tried this tactic on Cromwell's "roundhead" pike infantry, but there simply were not enough mounted royalists, even with the Germans who came over with Cousin Prince Rupert, to alter the course of English politics. The infantry reply to this threat was the musket, actually a long matchlock which could outrange the cavalryman's pistol. Unfortunately, it was so long that it had to be fired from a rest. The Spanish invented the musket, and simultaneously the idea that a gentleman could serve in infantry. The idea caught on, so that many of the scrapes of King Louis XIII's Three Musketeers involved that concept.

Seventeenth century soldiers saw the pistol as a fundamentally useful weapon, but one with several problems which had to be solved. One was that a light hand weapon, often carried ahorse, had to contain its own fire. Matchlocks were unbearable in pistols, and even wheel locks were seen to be too complicated. The inventor of the flintlock is not known to the present writer. Once the flintlock pistol was proven practical, the firing device was transferred to the musket. A long flintlock musket was called a *fusil*, hence the honorary name of some existing British regiments, fusileers.

The accuracy and range of muskets still did not please the Germans, who initiated an interesting example of cultural diffusion. The grooves in the musket were given a twist, and rifles became quite common on the continent by the end of the sixteenth century. The British did not trust them, and tried their smooth bores on their dissident American colonists, with unhappy results to themselves. The loyalist Colonel Johnson invented a practical breechloading rifle, but he never received a hearing. The Germans, however, had been invited into the Pennsylvania colony, and they brought their gunsmiths with them.

The frontiersmen came over the hill and admired the German rifles. These men had to hit both game and Indians in order to survive. The gun plant at Lancaster, Pennsylvania, kept improving the German flintlock rifles under frontiersman pressure, with the end that the Kentucky rifle was virtually perfected by 1727. The Kentuckians insisted that the weapon was too heavy, and its weight was reduced. Being poor men, they could not afford either the powder or lead the originals required. This five-to-six-foot rifle had its place in politics. Cressap's Rifle Company, of whom it is said that every recruit could put 19 bullets out of 20 into a one-inch target at 60 yards, was feared by the British. They picked off the British officers at Saratoga in 1777.

Most American revolutionary troops had to use smooth bore flintlocks out of necessity. The King of France sent them 23,000 Charleville models, and they had to be used. The idea of the rifle was afoot, though, but still the British did not learn, even from their hired Hessians, who were riflemen, not musketeers. General Pakenham brought good troops against Jackson at New Orleans in 1814, but they were armed with smooth bores. General Coffee's Kentuckians were armed with squirrel rifles, and the British racked up their heaviest casualty list, about 1000 British to one American. It must be recorded that the British brought one small rifle brigade afield at Waterloo, which was an object of hilarity to everyone but the French.

Rapidity of fire had always been a problem, but the technology was not adequate to solve it. An attempt at multi-barrel quick firers was unsuccessfully tried as early as the end of the fifteenth century. Actually, multi-barrels were successful on pistols before they were on rifles. The development of pistols will not be discussed at length, as their problems were basically the same as those of shoulder weapons. Recall the adage, though, that it was not the Declaration of Independence which made men equal. It was Mr. Colt. That genius saw that it was not a series of revolving barrels which was needed, but one of revolving chambers with one barrel. His product greatly discouraged the native American side of the Indian wars. In one instance, fifteen Texas Rangers defeated 80 very able Comanches in no time, killing 42 of them.

The problem of giving infantry a quick-firing device was first practically solved by the French under Napoleon III in the nineteenth century. The emperor was disturbed by the way aggressive infantry swept around and attacked his artillery, and he demanded that his ordnance expert, Montigny, do something about it. The result was the first successful multibarrel, the *mitrailleuse*. This was a hand-cranked machine which sent a firing pin into a specific hole and discharged a specific barrel in its turn. Louis Napoleon's high command was famous for mistakes, and it made two egregious ones with regard to this fine weapon. It was given to the artillery because it was invented to defend it, and it was mounted on a cannon's carriage. The French artillerymen of the time had received some severe lessons, and enjoyed staying far behind the range of rifle fire. Had they brought this gun forward to counter the German steel, breech-loading rifles, the political complexion of subsequent Europe might have been different. The other fault was the Second Empire was so spy-conscious that the mitrailleuse was kept under secrecy too long. There were too few trained gun crews to operate it when the great day came.

From then on out, the Americans have been the great inventors of machine guns. A physician, Dr. Richard Gatling, invented a far better multi-barrel than the mitrailleuse. It had ten rotating barrels, and could fire 800 rounds per minute without overheating them, as each one only fired every tenth round. The learned doctor tried to get the Union to adopt his gun, even giving a battlefield demonstration with a civilian crew, but the generals' minds were elsewhere. Gatling guns were standard equipment in the Spanish-American War, and they were used further to convince Indians that reservations were safe sites of residence. The British, as noted, bought some of these, and used them to the same purpose against the Zulu. Dr. Gatling did solve a problem which has dogged machine gunners ever since. Even the finest modern guns must be fired in bursts rather than in sustained fire. The barrels heat and spoil, eventually even those with water-cooling jackets, for that liquid is somewhat hard to come by in battle. For that reason, the United States has returned to a heavy gun built on the Gatling principle, the VAD (Vulcan Air Defense), which can fire 1000-3000 twenty-millimeter rounds per second. Ordinary machine guns are not adequate against low flying, fast aviation, and antiaircraft and ground-to-air missiles are designed to shoot at high flyers. The new multi-barrel gun with the Gatling nonheating principle under sustained fire is now under production to help solve the problem of low-flying craft.

Lowell, Hotchkiss, Gardner, Lewis, these names exhibit the American interest in machine guns, and the European powers have or do use their guns even if their fellow-Americans do not. Hiram Maxim, though, in 1885, ended the old cranking principle by making the gun eject the used round, reload, and fire by its own recoil power. America's great weaponizer, however, was John Browning, on whose principle United States machine guns are based.

Returning to pistols for a moment, the Colt "automatic" .38, later .45, is probably the American army's most beloved weapon, except for those who cannot fire it well. Just why Americans love this piece is hard to say. Recruit training with it is difficult. It is hard to clean, maintain, and repair. It is now rather obsolete, despite the tears of its experts, for mass training of today's recruits has dictated a fast-firing carbine as the "side arm" for close work, and a shoulder weapon is always more accurate than a handgun. Nevertheless, the Colt semi-automatic principle was bound to find its way into rifles, and General George Patton said that the Garand, which incorporates this pistol's principle, was the greatest military invention of all time. It is now giving way to a light, completely automatic rifle. One asks, though, does anyone really have an idea what the waste of ammunition such a shoulder "machine gun" entails in the hands of half-trained, nervous recruits? And what of the training in its use? The hand submachine gun, especially that of Colonel Thompson, has proven a lethal weapon in the hands of both soldiers and gangsters. The British and Germans, however, make cheaper if somewhat inferior weapons. As things stand now, heavy machine guns are getting heavier, proceding in the direction of quick-firing artillery, from the .50 caliber of infantry to the machine cannon of aviation. By contrast, light machine guns are obsolete, for every infantry rifleman will have one very soon. Sky sweepers for searching out airplanes can and are being used against tanks. So the problems of accuracy, rapidity of fire, and the element of human frailty have all but been eliminated. Yet there is a paradox here. Automatic warfare has given into the hands of the infantry sergeant more firepower than one of Washington's, or even Grant's, or even Lee's majors had. This should have reduced the need for human intelligence. The reverse is true. The aforesaid sergeant must know more and be a better soldier than Napoleon's, Wellington's, Washington's, Grant's, or Lee's major.

The strains of the United States national anthem remind one that the British saw the possibilities of the rocket's red glare by watching their East Indian subjects play with fireworks. The military version they developed from this toy was a 32-pound rocket with a 15-foot tail, headed by an explosive iron cone, and capable of a two-mile flight. Like our Fourth of July skyrockets, it was fired in a trough vaguely pointed toward the enemy. There is some fact in folklore, for Andrew Jackson's first defense before New Orleans were indeed cotton bales, which the invaders promptly enflamed with their rockets. Old Hickory fell back from Chalmette Plantation during the night, and entrenched on that of Beauregard in the conventional manner. The rockets had little effect on the wet, alluvial parapets. Indeed, they did not reduce Fort McHenry, whose garrison merely went underground until the British attempted a land attack, which was beaten off. The British army held with rockets, however, and used them in World War I, the tails being replaced by three vanes to hold the projectile on course.

It took some time for this good idea to develop into something practical, but that happened, giving in the end the ordinary infantry squad the firepower of the old artillery. The Americans modernized this eighteenth-century invention into the World War II 2.36-inch rocket launcher, fondly called the "bazooka," as a reply to German tanks. This was a metal tube open at both ends, made long in the interests of accuracy. A trigger activated an electric primer, sending the rocket on its way. It had no recoil, and could easily be fired over the shoulder of one soldier. The impact it had on the target was very great, and it fired a "shaped" charge concentrating the force on a very small area, it penetrated tank armor and sprayed inside the vehicle with molten metal, destroying the inmates, and firing the ammunition and gasoline. An improved American form knocked out seven Russian tanks with seven rounds in its first combat use in Korea. It is now thought that all military powers have rockets which will penetrate any known tank armor, an example of the offense-defense cycle which has shown that the tank is anything but the ultimate weapon.

Alarmed by their loss of expensively trained aviators, the Germans developed the so-called "buzz bomb," actually a small rocket-propelled airplane which caused some loss of British materials and more to their morale. This cumbersome, slow, and vulnerable rocket was replaced by the formidable V2, which sailed at 3,000 miles per hour and beyond the artillery counteroffensive of the time. This weapon dropped 2,200 pounds of TNT on target, but it was developed too late to save the Reich designed to last a thousand years. What did happen, however, was that it inspired the intercontinental shower whose threat frightens us all, plus the antimissile campaign, and no one can predict the end of this cyclical development.

Dropping unpleasantness on besiegers is as old as the invention of protective walls. The charm of this activity did not come into its own until the Wright brothers revealed their incapacity to mind their own business. Fixed military positions, immobile artillery, and forts above ground, all of these are as obsolete as the arbalest. German "block-busters" did harm to the logistic and transport complex of Great Britain, but not enough, and at tremendous expense. Anglo-American aviation ruined the technological capacity of the Third Reich, and at some cost, too. Such bombs were supposed to have terrific effect on civilian morale, but the British lived profanely through such bombardment, and so did the Germans. It is not known what effect American aviation could have had on the logistic capacity and morale of the North Vietnamese, for the weapon was never really exploited.

And what rockets and missiles lie ahead? There are prophets aplenty these days, some of whom should be stoned like those of old.

Weapons specializing in mobility will not be discussed at this place. The tank, of course, has become the modern expression of heavy cavalry-cum-artillery, but every reader is so familiar with the weapon that it will not be described. As for aviation, it is also of this generation and speaks for itself.

There is a note which runs through all of this missile discussion. Reflect on the process of artillery from the crude mediaeval *pot-de-fer*, through bombards, cannon, great guns, and aviation, which is really high-grade artillery, to intercontinental missiles. All of these are artillery, and serve the artillery function. The untold suffering and labor of men and mules is only hinted, but it was tremendous.

Where mud defeated the draft animals, or steep, boulder-studded hillsides inhibited the labor of horses and mules, strong men straining at wheel and spoke got the guns into position. If they sang that cannoneers have hairy ears, and boast what they could do to leathern breeches, all power to them. They do not labor any more (who does?), but their arm in its various form has become almost paramount. When Josef Stalin heard an American describe the infantry as the queen of battles, he replied that this may be so, but artillery is the king. Perhaps he was only reflecting the longtime Russian devotion to gunnery. Perhaps he was foresighted.

It has been a long road from hand-thrown rocks to intercontinental missiles, but mankind has travelled it.

Chapter 8

INTERPOSITION

The Engineering Revolution

The essential permeability of man is increased or decreased according to the offense-defense cycle. This will now be accented, remarking the essential vulnerability of man as basic, and that efforts to interpose something between him and his enemy's ambition is one of his greatest defensive aims. If protection were all there is to it, though, a static defense is the result, the initiative lost, and the ancient desire of missilemen to immobolize their foe, to pin him down by fire so that he may be eventually finished by other means is achieved.

This chapter deals with the fighting man's efforts to put something between him and his enemy's weapons, aided as he has been by technicians and engineers. The first phase of the present essay is to sketch the search for invulnerability for specific persons. The second will show how social groups have put protective devices between themselves and other social structures who wish them ill.

The personal protective devices are usually called armor, or to speak correctly, defensive armor, for the terms "the armory" and "the weaponry" are synonyms. Use of the word "armor" will be continued for familiarity's sake. Body armor has long been a response to the enemy's shock and fire potential. The human skin is capable of transmitting the sensation of great pain to the central nervous system, and is a poor shield against personal destruction. It is no surprise, then, to discover that the artificial shield is known to every continent save Australia. A poor protection it is, too, for shields of any size reduce mobility, increase the bearer's visibility, and draws fire. Good troops, like the older Romans, who could link their infantry shields into a so-called turtle (*testudo*) and attack behind this moving wall are not only something else but are extremely rare.

Body armor is characteristic of almost all fairly advanced societies. The able Indians of the American North Pacific Coast had wooden rod armor, and very good cedar helmets, responding to the stone war clubs, almost swords, of the region. The Polynesian wooden war clubs, which approached long swords in function, also produced an amount of wooden body armor. The armies of the Iroquois League, and they were virtually that, had specialized shock troops clad in wooden rod armor. Able textile-making people, such as the Aztec, used quilted shirts to minimize arrow fire, and they were so good that their Spanish *conquistadores* tended to drop their heavy metal armor and adopt the quilted gambesons of their foe. Body armor, however, has a problem which has been only partly solved in our own day. This is weight. Should a tank be lightly armored, and hence mobile in attack and withdrawal, or should it be virtually impermeable, slow, and fall into the waddling duck category? An armored man can also become like a dinosaur. Having found that a certain amount of protection is good, the principle of diminishing returns and violation of those of mobility and the offensive are just around the corner.

There is evidence of the above dysfunctions right at the beginning. The later prehistoric Bronze Age produced able slashing, crushing swords, and immediately an oversized, overweighted, but extremely beautiful helmet was produced. Military history dawns, to some degree, with that blend of the old Sumerian and new Semitic elements called the Chaldean. These able soldiers, who invented the phalanx with which the later Greeks became enamored, were content to wear a light bronze helmet and carry a medium-sized shield. Their successors, the Assyrians, added a linen jacket of many layers glued together. This device diffused to the Egyptians, who never really gave it up. The Assyrians also invented a leathern shirt with small overlapping plates sewn to it, which scale armor persisted in Europe until the seventeenth century.

The early prehistoric Greeks were not overburdened with armor. They did not wear their later massive helmets against Troy. Their shields were figure-eight shape, made of an unknown material. They had cuirasses of overlapping bands of bronze, seemingly in imitation of human ribs. They apparently did not wear metal shin guards, or greaves, for the schoolboy's illicit translation of "the well-greaved Greeks" is in error. The word used means bronze chiton, or shirt, not leg piece. When the heavy infantry phalanx became the classical Greek battle formation, helmets of two types appeared, both covering not only the top of the head but the face as well. Both front and back of the fighter were covered with a bronze cuirass, and the shields became very heavy, large, and round. The only people defeated by such shields, besides other Greeks, were the Persians. Those people preferably attacked as mounted archers. All the Greeks had to do was to duck behind their shields and let the arrows rain off them until the ammunition supply was exhausted. Oh yes, the Persians destroyed King Leonidas and his hoplites at Thermopylae, but this was because some smart Persian spearman noted that the Spartans were barefoot, and started jabbing their feet in a despicable barbarian manner.

The Romans also began as over-armored infantry, but they were quick learners. Their helmets became simple iron caps with cheek pieces, entirely lacking the tremendous crests of the Greeks. They abandoned the solid cuirass and returned to the overlapping metal bands for the upper body held up by suspenders of strips of iron. Their shields were slightly convex squares cut out at the four corners and decorated with the devices of the legions. The Romans were swordsmen, and not like the Greeks, pikemen, and their fighting methods were so successful against such enemies that the above armor type held for about 500 years. Their light infantry, *velites*, of slingers and troops trained to flow around the enemy flanks, wore simple metal caps and leather shirts. Their almost useless cavalry wore scale armor, and carried light shields. (Almost useless? There will come a day!) Line officers were armored not much differently, but field-grade officers affected solid metal breastplates modeled to fit their bodies, and some fancier helmets.

Rome's later barbarian enemies wore only leather caps, and carried small, round shields. This basic military costume applies to all barbarians without regard to tribe. The beginning of the ninth century, however, saw that Charlemagne's better troops had borrowed the chain mail shirt from Constantinople, but the cavalry revolution was on its way by that time.

The cataphract, or stirruped heavy cavalry arm borrowed from Byzantium, wore a hauberk or shirt of chain mail covering the body to the lower leg. There was a simple conical helmet with a nosepiece. This pattern was maintained for about 300 years, when mail stockings, slippers, and mittens were added. A mail hood replaced the solid helm. There were still some animal-haters around, so mailed caparisons had to be invented for the horses. All this, horses included, was very expensive, as the technicians had to hand-forge each ring in the chain armor. No one as yet understood the art of drawing wire. The costly equipment, plus the poverty of the state, were the functional base of feudalism, as is known.

The Battle of Lewes (1264), wherein Good Earl Simon de Montfort attempted to bring some kind of responsible government to

England, found the knighthood with only mail coifs, or hoods, resulting in some very sore heads on that day. The mounted arm began casing the head in the true helm, or iron pot with small openings for seeing and breathing. This must have caused great Crusader suffering in Palestine's heat. This helm originally rested on the head. Then the march of diminishing returns began. It ended with the head covered with a quilted fabric hood, then a light helmet (basinet), and the whole surmounted by a ponderous helm resting on the shoulders. The Middle Age closed with the basinet only, equipped with a visor which could be raised. This was the true helmet, or little helm.

Chain mail has a great disadvantage, for even if it shed sword and lance blows, and poor arrow fire, a man's shoulders and arms could be so wearied and bruised after being pommeled all day that he was almost out of service. The Germans found in plate armor the answer to this fatigue. This was eventually carried to such ridiculous extremes that it destroyed the maneuvering ability of cavalry, limiting it to straight-on charges, and wearied both men and horses in less than a day's action so that they were practically useless. It became so heavy that even the great horses of the day could not carry the knight, forcing fighting on foot in static lines.

But let us start at the beginning. An argument ensued at Benevento in 1266 between Manfred von Hohenstaufen, who was King of Naples, and the wicked if brilliant Charles of Anjou, who wanted to be. Manfred lost the field, his life, and his crown, but the point here is that his German mounted mercenaries wore plate armor. The opposition hammered and clanged the Germans most of the day to no avail. Then some bright-eyed member of the Angevin command noted that as the Teutons raised their arms to swing the sword, the plate did not protect them under the arms from potential sword jabs. "Look to their armpits, look to their armpits," he cried, and that was about all for that day. Germans learn quickly, though, and when they returned two years later under young Conradin, the last Hohenstaufen, to avenge Uncle Manfred's death, the armpit jabbing did not work. The Germans and their Spanish allies had put on mail shirts under their plate.

And so the dismal progression went, and its end is known. It must be said before this end, the knighthood had abandoned mail underwear. The horses had to be armed or barded even more, as archers tended to acquire efficiency. The fifteenth century, however, experienced a great improvement in the technology, and proof armor was for sale for those who could afford it. This meant that a suit of armor was stamped as having been fired at by a crossbow of known pull from a known distance without harm to the plate. A double proof of having the test distance reduced by half was also available. And so, the wedding of science and armaments began, a mating which seems to be increasing in felicity rather than otherwise.

The rebirth of infantry saw the footman clad in a light helmet, light breastplate, and often chain mail. Experimentation and the inductive logic had discovered the means of drawing wire, which reduced the price of mail rings to the infantry private's level.

The cavalry regained a moment of glory, as said a few pages back. It reduced its armor, now of improved steel, so that it would shed arquebus balls from a distance, and cavalry became mercenary pistoleers. This distressed not only the arquebusiers but their pikemen protectors. Heavy infantry liked to wear complete cuirasses with morions, or helmet bowls whose brims turned up in front and back. Cromwell's heavy infantry wore the round-headed helmet with a nosepiece, which inspired an unfavorable adjective on their opposition's part.

Entrepreneurs sold the frightened mass of Union draftees alleged bulletproof vests in the American Civil War which, while probably unable to shed a heavy hailstorm, may have helped the morale of the command.

Body armor returned in force in World War I, when the British reply to shrapnel was the hated "tin hat," an uncomfortable and unbecoming helmet. The French designed theirs with more chic, and the Germans modeled one after a bucket with no more style but with greater comfort and safety. The Americans improved theirs into a rounded bucket for World War II, which nearly the whole world has adopted.

The United States used a quilted nylon shirt in Korea, much like the old archer's vest, which was credited with saving many lives. It also reinvented the bowman's brigandine, a shirt with many plastic discs sewn into the pockets. Neither of these will stop a direct hit, but they are good in shedding flying debris. We cannot predict to what extent armor will return. Who knows? Maybe chivalry will return with it.

So much for the search for the invulnerability of the individual fighting man. This chapter really emphasizes a similar effort for the impenetrability of whole social systems, from small ones by private castles to those of populous cities, a never entirely successful effort.

One of mankind's favorite ways of interposing artificial materials between the enemy's will is fortification. The concept, of course, is from the Latin *fortis*, strong, and *facere*, to make, but what is to be made strong? One hardly needs repeat that any social system can be penetrated by either subtle or violent means. One deals here with the real engineering revolution. This effort almost always involves a very considerable social organization. Even the simple works of some nonliterate societies took planning and thinking into the future. It took collective work to construct even the rudimentary fortifications revealed by archaeology, the building group thereby announcing that it does not wish to be penetrated, and that it entertains the opinion that some other social system might have this in mind.

Basic to all this is the energy consumption required for erecting even simple defensive works. The builders had to be sufficiently well fed to perform this effort. The greatest works testify to a surplus of energy production by economically successful societies which could afford to devote people to build extensive fortification.

Defense by fortification is an application of the tactical Principles of Security and Utilization of the Terrain. It is, as a feature of material culture, an expression of dissatisfaction with the ability of unaided nature to provide for human wants. Taking cover both offensively and defensively is fundamental to survival, and it is not surprising to find that one of the first artificialities in so doing is digging holes in the terrestrial environment. This is almost universal. Simple entrenchment is far from dead. The Keri-Keri, a relatively simple folk in the African Sudan, for example, build their villages on precipitous hilltops and surround the bases thereof with trenches concealed by vegetation. Indeed, the captains of World War I could think of little better. Vast gun galleries in the natural stone mark such mighty fortresses as Gibraltar and Diamond Head. The current atomic dread is sending mankind once more to earth, either as political folk digging deeply to protect their vital installations, or, as just a few years ago, individual families burrowing like gophers in their own backyards. Digging pits and arranging them in checkerboards before the rudimentary works are reported for Indonesia. These are filled with sharp stakes, often poisoned, then cleverly concealed with vegetation. These traps taught the Americans during the Philippine Insurrection to approach such fortified villages with great caution. Even if the origin of these checkerboards was in animal hunting, great powers recently designed similar checkerboards of deep, concealed holes as tank traps before positions intended to be held. A tank falling nose down into such a pit was worse than dead. It died slowly by flamethrowers and similar metal-piercing chemicals. Another Indonesian trick of surrounding a position with booby traps firing strong arrows at the unwelcome was used, and will be used again. The modern booby trap, however, is of violent explosive, and as a mine has killed many a tank, both Allied and German, as well as passing infantry.

Fortification beyond individual burrowing, however, is not indicative of civilization, but does suggest a strong, authoritative social structure. The royal and noble Polynesians often palisaded their villages, the *pai* of the New Zealand Maori being the strongest. The palisaded villages of the North American Iroquois deserve some attention. The Iroquois palisade was of strong trees set upright into the ground which, considering that the villages were quite large, represented a great amount of labor for a people without metal tree-felling and digging tools. The ground plan was an elongated ovoid, but there was no gate for an entrance. In fact, the wall overlapped itself so that there was an open passage almost as long as one side of the works. The enemy was invited to enter this fool's trap and be mowed down by archery. Logs and large stones were placed in this passage in times of danger so that the attack could not rush in, but have his progress and organization disrupted and slowed, making him a better target for the archers on the firing platform of the central wall. This latter was strengthened by log braces which also helped bear up the platform. If possible, a trench was dug around the interior of the palisade into which a stream was diverted. The enemies of the Iroquois were well acquainted with fire arrows, and in times of siege the women and children dipped their birchbark vessels into this stream to extinguish fires as they occurred.

So far as I know, the Iroquois were the simplest people to reinforce their main work with a curtain. A curtain is a simpler and usually lighter circumvallation outside and beyond the main work which is meant not to be impregnable. Whether of wood, stone, barbed wire, or, as in the case of the Iroquois, scantlings of light trees, it was meant to break an enemy rush, reducing his shock power, compel him to extricate himself while being subject to fire. It was intended that his power would be withered before he could attack the main wall. This is an example of the defensive Principle of Increasing Resistance. Examples of a water curtain, or moat, are not known among a nonliterate folk, but a broad belt of terrible thorns and cactus is reported for the mud walls of the West African Ashanti. This, however, may be a diffusion from southern Morocco, where they have been surrounding Berber strong points and chiefly residences. The Berbers were a naive republic with a rudimentary civilization before waves of first, Romans, then Arabs taught them a better and more deadly way of life.

When major fortification is discussed, however, civilization properly so-called is under consideration. There must be something to defend. There must be labor, voluntary or otherwise, to erect the walls. There must be a numerous and trained force to defend the circumvallation, or all this work is in vain. Thus, heavy fortification, the hydraulic or irrigation-based civilization, the old priest-kingships of the eastern Mediterranean, Meso-America, and Peru all enter history or late prehistory in combination, for they are functional relatives of each other. Egypt of the Old Kingdom was naturally protected by terrible aridity on either side of the valley, and with the exception of minor works west of the Delta to discourage the wild Libyans of the Mediterranean desert, and some east of the mouths of the Nile built against "the detested Asiatics" (Pharaoh's words, not mine), that seemed enough. It was evidently insufficient, for the Old Kingdom decayed and was invaded, and if its dynasties had spent more effort on stone forts and less on pyramids, it might have lasted longer. The succeeding epoch of the Middle Kingdom was one of social turmoil and invasion. The Egyptians then managed to build massive forts at Pelusium against the aforesaid Asians, and at Aswan against the black Nilotes who seemed anxious to improve their own way of life. We know little of these forts except they were comparable in size to the largest mediaeval European castles. It is the present opinion that they were not battlemented or machicolated.[1]

War got down to sociopolitical earnestness somewhat later in the Near East, and the Assyrians were the most earnest of the lot. At the height of their power they built large stone castles with walls sixty-feet high, protected by flanking towers. These walls were apparently machicolated and often moated.

We now approach that glory and shame of the human race, the city, pertinent here because the early ones were fortified, and so remained until the eighteenth century of our era. From Greek (*polis, astus*) and Latin (*urbs, civis*), the city has given us such words as politics, policy, police, astute, and civil, civic, urbane, and more substantial things such as weights and measures, literacy, temple worship, drilled troops, civil government not based on kinship, commerce, metallurgy, and many other traits of precious functions, and dysfunctions we have yet to solve. These early city states had something to defend against foreign enemies and casual marauders, and needed soldiers to expand and protect their markets. The charisma of the priest-kings could persuade or force the subjects to build walls and defend them. The Tigris-Euphrates Valleys gave us civilization, city-oriented societies, and the greatest spur to military aspects thereof was the rise of Assyrian power.

While the record does not justify too firm a statement, it is suspected that this Assyrian upsurge contributed the flanking towers, battlements, and machicolations, which were transferred from their massive castles to municipal fortification. These features were either unknown or forgotten by the European ancestors since Roman days. The Romans were indifferent urban fortifiers in any event. They preferred active to passive warfare in either offense or defense, at least in their better days. We do not discount the Romulus-Remus legend about building the wall first, and then the city, especially in regal times, but Rome soon outgrew this. The city state of Rome, however, considered its real wall the shield of its iron infantry. Cities were not walled in the Roman civil wars whose object was political control, not plunder. The leaders of these armed elections wanted the Latin civilians to be prosperous. The beginning of the barbarian invasions with loot as a motive caused most important Roman towns to wall themselves. The Emperor Aurelian (270-275) caused the imperial city to be walled, although it had not been attacked for half a millenium, and would not be until a century after his death. Fright does these things to cities.

One recalls that an eighteenth century garrison, named Fort Rosalie in modern Mississippi, abused some Indians, which the warlike Natchez chose to resent in an armed manner. Fearing that the able warriors might start downriver and mar the New Orleans image as the City Care Forgot, a stout wall was built with forts defending the corners, one where the old Federal Building is now, another where the former United States mint and now jail stands. One face of the old circumvallation is still called Rampart Street, although all these fortifications have long since been pulled down. The *Vieux Carré* of the older city still has the compact form and narrow streets of a formerly walled town.

Nevertheless, either the Assyrians or a people nearby gave us a concept which has held until very recently. A strongly fortified city has never been breached by siege prior to the rise of chemical artillery. Hunger and thirst can do their work, and political chicane and treachery can do more. One of the few military geniuses of the Middle Age, the elder Simon de Montfort, could not take Toulouse, but gained entry by political means. William the Conqueror did not try to breach Saxon London, which could not have been more than one square mile in area. The crusaders despaired of taking Antioch with its well-stocked granaries. This great city had twelve miles of solid walls sixty-feet high with four hundred turrets for the defending archers, and had taken a millenium to build. It was too strong for crusader might, but not for native treachery. It was not until the fall of Constantinople in 1453 that a major city fell by storm.

At that, imperial Constantinople was defended by only nine thousand soldiers against a vast Turkish army. It was blockaded by the supposedly Christian fleet of Venice. The final breach was made by artillery designed, forged, and operated by Christian renegades for good pay.

The impregnability of a walled city should not be hard to understand. If it were a commercial venture, the citizens could afford strong walls. The citizenry itself feared penetration, and developed enough skill to man the parapets. It takes a mighty besieging army to isolate a city as large as Antioch, the siege of which caused one death by starvation among every seven in the investing Christian army. Even little Jericho fell by treason of a prostitute and divine intervention.

The rise of mediaeval towns, with stout burgers to defend the commercial walls, has had much to do with our sociopolitical development, but so have rural castles. The terms town and castle are not necessarily antithetical. When some lords permitted towns to grow around the bases of their strongholds, and later allowed the burgesses to wall them, they served themselves well. While the citizens were defending their own walls, they could not avoid delaying an attempt to penetrate the castle. The latter and its inhabitants, however, are fundamentally expressions of that rural life which developed into feudalism.

Castle building originally occurred out of the necessity of survival. One looks back on that civilization called Gallo-Roman and sees little which would offend a modern man to whom life in the country with a fine little city not too far away could be a pleasant way of life. The large farm houses, or villas, were open and accessible. There was little to fear. Population pressure, however, began working on hungry Iron Age folk and, as the Empire was decaying at its source, there was little to keep them from raiding and looting their betters. Vassalage arose because strong points of resistance were required. Land was held in military fee from a prince or overlord, and the erection of these points of resistance was part of the duty of landholding.

The centers of refuge in the West also became pivots of maneuver for the heavy cavalry patterned after the Byzantine cataphracti. The Vikings, having burned and pillaged all they could, would find their poorly organized rear harassed by the mailed horsemen, their stragglers chopped to pieces, and the retreat to their ships often became a rout. This combination of fort and horse did much to nullify the Viking and Saracen incursions by the end of the ninth century, and provided good training to meet the Magyar threat which was frittered away by this offense-defense combination a century later.

Some Vikings became Normans, however, and there never has been in Europe a people more able to organize and work others, perhaps not even excepting the Romans. The Normans stole horses and became excellent cataphracti in their own right, discovering that taxing and infeudating were more profitable than killing and looting the golden-egged goose. They settled down to stay. Like the Romans before them, the Normans were workers, and they never willingly camped without fortifying their bivouacs. First, they dug a round ditch and heaped the earth inward to form a mound. This was the *motte*, a word which still occurs in many aristocratic French family names. An elevation for arrow fire was thus provided in case of a native counterattack. If time permitted, and this particular raiding band intended to stay, a square wooden tower was erected and a palisade of pointed logs was set up around the mound. The horses could be protected therein, and the attackers could not reach the base of the towers without fighting. Of course this was not enough for the energetic Normans. The palisade could be breached, so it was replaced by a stone wall. Even when covered with wet hides, the wooden tower was vulnerable to fire arrows, so was replaced by a stone one. Thus the plan for the Norman motte-and-bailley (courtyard) castle took form early, and was satisfactory for a long time. Some of them still exist in fair condition, and Castle Hedingham, of one simple tower in England's East Anglia, could still be defended against light artillery.

The Normans had a different idea of warfare than the Romans. The now-civilized Scandinavians could not rely on an iron wall of infantry, for that they never had. They had to rely on a passive defense, and therefore made better use of the terrain than did the Romans who rarely sought the heights or cliffs since the building of The City on defensive hills.

The Normans and their copiers put their faith in one great, solid tower, the keep, of as good stone as available. This was preferably three-stories high, giving height for archers from the roof (called the platform). This was the *dominium*, or lord's dwelling, which word was later shortened to *donjon*. It had only one small door as entrance, and was set high off the ground of the bailley, and provided with a light drawbridge. This method of entrance into the donjon, which later became the point of final defense, was kept up almost to the end. The height of the door and the narrowness of the drawbridge forbade the Anglo-Normans from retreating into their own keep when Philip Augustus forced the inner ward of Chateau-Gaillard. This disaster taught Richard Lion Heart a needed lesson. This was much later, of course, but at the time under discussion, the massive keep or donjon was quite enough for passive defense. Someone once said that it took only one man at the door to defend it, and two on either side to besiege it. This, of course, is an oversimplification, but the donjon was a simple defense against simple men.

The simple castle of which we have spoken was truly feudal. The great ones in the following discussion were signs that the Old Middle Age was about to be replaced by the High Middle Age, which was a stepping stone to modern times. Wealth is the source of those tremendous walls we see at Pierrefonds. They were not built with peasant labor, nor defended by the local serfs and tenants. They were not the property of cozy little lordlings, but of great magnates and princes. Sometime about 1100 A.D. Christendom recovered from the Dark Age. There was an upsurge in production and wealth, and a great increase in knowledge and skill. Indeed, it has been suggested that mighty castles and cathedrals were make-work efforts to sop up excess production and provide employment for laborers whose secular work was not needed at the time. Castles became larger and more complex, and they required more and more economically nonproductive, professional soldiers to defend them. Although Coucy-le-Chateau was chopped into too many wards (courtyards), Violet-le-Duc estimated that it required five hundred mercenaries to man the walls. Such expense would squeeze the little lord out of the picture and point towards the centralization of political power just as surely as the small merchant has been obliterated by the modern, centralized chain stores, and for not dissimilar reasons. Many lords, disappointed in finding the Holy Land anything but one of milk and honey, simply had to give up and go home. The crusading religious orders, the Hospitallers, the Templars, the Teutonic Knights, inherited the vast Palestinian castles of the Latin Kingdom of Jerusalem by default. The siege engines became more efficient at about this time, and castles had to become so expensive that only the very powerful and wealthy could afford them.

Whatever else can be said against the Crusades, and much has been, they were a source of cultural diffusion to the West. The Arabs, and later the Turks, inherited the strong fortress-building of the East. If the Franks expected to remain, and they did, their simple castles had to be improved, and they were. The donjon became the citadel of last resort, but not the principal defense. The tactical Principle of Increasing Resistance had to be rediscovered, and it was. A massive wall was built around the entire area to become the chief line of defense. The defensive had also to become offensive, which it always must, if good. The flanking towers mentioned for the Assyrians were set up at the corners. Dead space, then as now, had to be eliminated.[2] The attackers must have no refuge from enfilading fire. They must find no security at the base of the wall where they can set up their penetrative engines with impunity. Flanking towers were seen to be inadequate, and were jutted more and more out in front of the wall. The crusaders were not defending themselves from incompetent barbarians now, nor some neighboring baron with limited siege resources. They were against that hardy old professional, the Turk, and they had to rise to his standards of warfare.

The Franks had learned to build battlements to their walls before they left Europe. They had previously learned to build wooden hoardings or platforms beyond the top of the wall. Arrows, stones, and boiling liquids could be dropped therefrom on the attackers and their protective devices hovering along the base of the wall. Palestine and Syria, however, are treeless regions, and a substitute for wooden hoardings had to be found. As sometimes happens, the substitute proved better than the original. The tops of the towers and walls became machicolated, as the Assyrians had taught the Semitic peoples, who taught the Turks, who taught the crusaders. Machicolation originally was simply building stone supports beyond the wall on which wooden platforms could be laid, but these proved ineffective. Their enemy, Salah ad-Din Yusuf ibn Ayyub, Saladin to them, kept a pet chemist who taught him how to make naphtha, which in flame is very destructive to anything wooden. The crusader castles then became entirely machicolated with stone, not wooden, galleries.

The other lesson learned in Palestine was that the light curtain in front of the main work was not enough to stop an able enemy. Thus, as had been indicated, a new era of castle building was born, eventually to pass its point of diminishing returns, as at Coucy. It had to re-simplify itself, which it did at Pierrefonds. The castle then shrank to the aesthetically unimpressive Vauban type of fortification, which strengthened the fighting world from the day of Louis XIV until the Wright brothers of Kitty Hawk spoiled it all.

The first of the great new crusading castles was Kerak-in-Moab, thrust forward as it was to gain and keep control of the Dead Sea, and built at a guess date of 1140. Like all its sisters, it magnified the Principle of Use of the Terrain by using steep cliffs on three sides. The relatively narrow front flat space was protected by a deep, sharp ditch cut into the solid stone before the curtain. This latter was no flimsy thing, but as strong a wall as the inner one, and had mighty towers all along its face. The space between the curtain and the main wall was kept narrow so that if the attackers forced the former, the intervening space was too constricted to permit them either to mass their forces against the latter, or to swing siege engines of any size between the two walls. Then, too, if they should break down the curtain, their own rubble would constitute a first-class obstacle for them. Should by chance the attackers reach the inside, they would find that it was divided into two courts, not one, with the massive donjon in the inner ward. This plan was introduced into Europe when the crusaders were finally expelled from Asia. Thus, the Principle of Increasing Resistance was architecturally almost perfected. Very important passageways were defended by portcullises. A portcullis is a huge grill of whatever material is available which can be raised or lowered from a chamber above the gate. The device had been forgotten in Europe, and was either re-invented by the Franks in the Near East, or copied from a Turkish-Arab survival.[3] Saladin eventually took the Kerak, but at great cost to himself, and largely because its Templar garrison was exhausted.

Is too much space being devoted to describing old things for modern readers? One thinks not. It is important to understand these military revolutions which changed the lives of all. The stirrup, or heavy cavalry revolution, saved for us what Roman civilization westerners did retain in the face of the barbarian invasions. This was accompanied by the engineering revolution sketched here. The Dark, the Early Middle Age, and the High Middle Age did happen, and carried us along with them. With this in mind, two great forts will be briefly mentioned: the Krak-des-Chevaliers in Palestine, and Chateau-Gaillard in Normandy, the latter showing the cultural influence of the Latin Kingdom of Jerusalem on the more immediate homeland of our ancestors.

As the Templar Kerak-in-Moab was the first enormous stronghold introducing the engineering revolution, the Hospitallers' Krak-des-Chevaliers illustrates its perfection. The enemies of the Krak were so impressed by it that they called it "The Mountain," and it is so termed to this day. Lawrence of Arabia deemed it "the most wholly admirable castle in the world." It was never taken by siege, although it endured twelve formal ones in its century and a half of military history. It was surrendered on 6 April 1271 on the basis of a lie.

How the crusading Knights Hospitaller ever mustered enough labor to build the Krak is a mystery, but the Mountain still stands, representing the apex of Franco-Burgundian skill, combining all the defensive devices known at the time, and it still looks impregnable. All of the Krak's towers and walls were machicolated. As for towers, soldiers had long known that the corners of a square tower were vulnerable to siege engines, and that a round one would shed catapulted stones unless hit directly with no angle. A battering ram would likewise be less effective on a curved surface than a flat one. The manifold towers of the Krak not only eliminated dead space but were massive stone cylinders with machicolated and battlemented tops. It was the world's first completely concentric great castle, perched on a high hill in the first place, then built in tremendous rings, the inner one higher than the outer, according to the Principle of Increasing Resistance.

The wall of the inner ward was backed by a talus of rubble stone. This offered no obstacle to the defenders, but should the attack actually breach this wall, a mass of stone would not only tumble on them but would also form an obstruction to communication in the space between the main wall and the curtain. The stones of the main wall were blocks often measuring three by one and a quarter feet so carefully shaped at the quarry that they could simply be fitted together. Those of the Krak hardly needed a binding material to hold them together to keep them strong. We often forget that real portland cement was the invention of the Middle American Indians, and that mediaeval mortar was hardly better than high-grade clay and sand. At that, the great Incan forts in Peru, Olantay Tambo and others, depended on careful quarrying and fitting rather than cement.

Krak-des-Chevaliers foretold the declining value of the keep, or donjon. Indeed, some experts say that it lacked one, but this is hardly true. The inner ward had two such connecting towers, smaller than tradition dictated. The curtain was penetrated by several little gates, permitting the defenders' exit to fight in the field according to the knightly tradition of "all day in the field, all night in the castle." These entrances were not straight through the curtain wall, but on an angle, so that if the defenders had to retire within the curtain, their left or shield side was presented to the enemy. The main gate of every castle was its weakest part, but the entrance to the Krak was by a narrow alley of several right-angle turns. It may be that this made slow work for the defenders to take out either infantry or cavalry piecemeal, but it could not be rushed by foes either mounted or afoot, as Simon de Montfort did the walls of Beziers in the so-called crusade against Albi.

The crusaders, especially the military monks and friars, pushed castles into enemy territory whenever they could: Subeiba-beyond-Jordan, Montreal, and Kerak-in-Moab. These religious soldiers built no Maginot Line, so while leaving fighting space between castles for enemy penetration, they were sited to aid each other. Krak-des-

Chevaliers could signal the news of Saladin's progress by fire every night to Jerusalem, fifty miles away.

Richard I Plantagenet might not have been the greatest soldier who ever wore armor, but he was one who could learn. He took the best of the Krak, and others, back to Europe when he had to retreat, and made some improvements. He built the greatest mediaeval stronghold in the West, Saucy Castle or Chateau-Gaillard, to reaffirm his claim to the Duchy of Normandy. It was eventually taken by King Philip Augustus of France, to whom this political aspiration was repulsive. Gaillard fell because it was not adequately garrisoned, and attempts to relieve it were weak. At that, the success of the final assault was due to a stratagem and internal treason. The second mightiest castle in Europe was Coucy-le-Chateau, which was never taken. Indeed, when the Germans retreated in World War I, they did not wish to leave this stronghold in French hands, mediaeval though it was. Their engineers placed a large amount of TNT in the ground floor of Coucy's donjon and detonated it. Instead of demolishing the works, this charge merely shot the floors of the keep into the air, cannon-fashion. The monumental castle was injured, but it still stands. But explosives have been mentioned, and the decisive shock was the penetration of the walls of Byzantium by bombards.

The boom of the gun just heard signalled the end of the city's invulnerability. In 1450, Constantinople was breached by Turkish artillery, and the old world came to an end in more ways than one. This period is called The Renaissance, or rebirth, but aside from the freedom of the minds of an elite, which is so often praised, it behooves the serious student to ask just what was reborn. Certainly one rebirth was the loss of immunity from sack and pillage of a captured city. Steps were taken to repair the strength of a town. As infantry began as the Queen of Battles, succeeded by the heavy cavalry centuries, in the Renaissance, Baroque, and Rococo Periods, engineering became at least the Prince of Battles in a very real way. Thus was ushered in the period which could be called the Age of Vauban, named for as great a soldier as ever lived. Few have had as much effect on his own and succeeding times as this infantryman turned engineer. Of course, the trends mentioned below began before his birth, but he was the culmination of them. His works and ideas died at Yorktown with the surrender of Cornwallis, the last major siege in the classical manner the world was to know.

Sebastian Le Prestre, Seigneur de Vauban, belonged to that class of the poor but proud which has given the world, and France in particular, some of its best soldiers. He belonged to that impoverished petty gentry, or minor nobility, which produced Napoleon and in our day, de Lattre de Tassigny, Le Clerc, and Ralph Monclar of Korean fame. Vauban grew up without the necessities of life, especially that one which was essential in his day of privilege, the protection and favor of a great man. He fought his way to the top by merit, intelligence, originality, and industry. He died Marshal of France, a legend in his own time, for it was said that "A city besieged by Vauban is a city captured, a city fortified or defended by him was impregnable." He secured the frontiers of France with thirty-three new strong points and modernized three hundred more. He directed fifty-three successful sieges for his king. His impeccable life and his charming, agreeable manners made this soldier a beloved man not only in his own craft but among the intellectuals. St. Simon said that he was the most honest man of his day. His king should have loved him, and so he did until the marshal did what many generals before and since have done. He gave some political advice, and was disgraced by Louis XIV. His radical idea was that taxes should be levied equally and fairly on all social classes alike, without favoritism or privilege. That was enough to make the Sun King forget the benefits received at Marshal de Vauban's hands. "Put not your trust in princes," King David sang, and he should have known.

We speak of the age of the improved cannon, and how in the offense-defense cycle Vauban, his predecessors and successors countered the threat. The first effect of the new artillery was to force the walls of the fort or town to be lowered and thickened. Their target characteristics simply had to be reduced. The machicolated walk around the walls had to be widened so that guns could be rushed to the point of the works where they were needed. This wide road atop the new was called the boulevard, indicating how the meaning of words can change. The wall itself had to be protected, as of yore, but the curtain now became the counterscarp, stronger and thicker than the main work, wide enough to have its own boulevard. The counterscarp was separated from the main wall by a deep ditch, preferable water-filled, which was an improvement on the old mediaeval moat. There were bridges over the moat from the counterscarp to the main wall, but just a few and easily destroyed ones so that if the former fell, the defense could retreat into the main area as the place of final resistance. The principal battery of the main wall, the heaviest in the fort, was designed to fire on the enemy over the counterscarp. The main walls, however, were pierced by many gun ports for both cannon and muskets to rake the attackers should they force the counterscarp and get in the ditch. The counterscarp itself was protected by an outer work called the glacis, a thick, gradually sloping wall of earth designed to absorb the solid shot of the time. Actually, the glacis was so high and wide that the fort was hardly visible from the fields around it. The tourist often drives from the Mississippi Gulf Coast to New Orleans without noticing Fort Pike and Fort McComb built to protect the sea entrances to Lake Pontchartrain. I have driven many times along the base of the strongest land fort ever built, Eben Emael, constructed between the last two world wars to act as the main defense and pivot of maneuver of the Belgian industrial city of Liege, and have never seen the fort from the highway.

The great towers of the castle had to come down, for they had become liabilities instead of sources of strength. They assumed no more height than the walls in this Vaubanist trend. They eventually became great triangular works (French *bastion*, German *bollwerk*) jutting far out from the walls. Their points divided an attacking enemy. They eliminated dead space along the wall where he could protect himself, and they reinforced each other with flanking fire, by both cannon and musketry. Indeed, they were dares for an enemy to get in between them. If the attackers had any idea of capturing the place, or surviving, they ceased trying to gain or breach the main wall. Their efforts were directed towards capturing one of the bastions, and using it as a fortress of their own. Thus the fight along the boulevard became an exciting infantry as well as artillery exercise.

We speak of the past. The forces of penetration have become so strong with the perfected artillery and aviation that no one wants to wall himself up in something an enemy can pinpoint on his map.

So now a brief word on penetration is in order. How can great fortifications be taken? Well, as in so many things military, the best attack is sociological rather than technological. A fortress was built, maintained, and defended by a social system, which makes this very structure the prime target. Treason, chicane, and lies are cheaper than men and materials in a long siege. Thirty pieces of silver are often good currency in this politico-military complex. It is surprising that so many men are for sale for so little. If a society rises to civilized levels, there always marginal men loyal to no one but themselves. There is always a class hierarchy, and the defenders of the walls may not be much loved by the surrounding peoples. If such soldiers are mercenaries and foreigners, as has so often been the case, even the castle servants who dislike them may know just enough to help the attack. And then there are the disillusioned, men who were promised so much, or saw such bright promise in the defender's cause which was not, to them, adequately fulfilled.

One of the ablest generals on the continental side was Benedict Arnold, and in his deep disillusion with what he might have called

Washingtonism, he almost succeeded in yielding the strong fort at West Point to the British. Then there was a Christian Syrian named Firous who had no reason to love his Moslem masters, and for quite a reasonable price directed the crusaders to a little known, and to the defenders, unappreciated portion of the walls of Antioch. A party of Christians scaled this by night, quietly found the city gates whose guards they killed, opened the town to their comrades who, using the Principle of Surprise, destroyed the overconfident defenders. Again, while King Philip Augustus would have eventually taken Chateau-Gaillard, he was not above saving a few lives in the process. He found it was cheaper to suborn a man who knew the castle well. This one showed the French how they could sneak up the latrine into the chapel and surprise the garrison, a very unchurchmanlike and unknightly trick. And then there is the direct lie. The castle-capital of the Hospitallers, Krak-des-Chevaliers, had been a thorn in the Moslem side for a century and a half. Sultan Beibars in 1271 introduced a forged order from the garrison's absent supreme commander. This paper purported to be a direct order to abandon the fort and fall back on Tripoli. The disciplined and not very bright commander of the garrison obeyed. Of course, the spy is a useful man. Over many years such men managed to supply the Hitlerist Germans with the details of Fort Eben Emael. The German intelligence service has always been adept in fitting small pieces of information together, and finally they had a complete picture which they handed over to their engineers. Eben Emael was duplicated in large-scale models, and meticulous practice of its investiture went on for years. The great Liege fort, then, fell easily and never performed its delaying mission.

As the fort's function is to protect human beings, the man is still the best target. As General Coats has said,[4]

> "... Fortification and other protective measures are fundamentally defensive in nature, but in themselves they do not constitute the defense. It is the activities of men employing these protective measures in conjunction with the means of creating violence that provides the defense."

If, therefore, the enemy can adequately strike the stomach of this military organism, the brain and muscle must eventually yield to him. If the attack can really blockade the place, and if its relief can effectively be prevented, no matter how adequate the logistics of the fort once were, starvation, followed by disease will reduce the number of fighting effectives within the walls. The defense's ammunition, from arrows to gunpowder, will eventually be exhausted. Jean-Baptiste-Donatien, Comte de Rochambeau, Marshal of France, knew full well that the army of Charles Cornwallis, Earl (later Marquis) Cornwallis, was starving and sickening in Yorktown, and could tell by the increasingly desultory cannon fire that the ammunition was running low. The noble count gave the equally noble earl a wonderful dinner with good French wines after the surrender. Well, food is of prime importance, but an athletic man can fight for several days when hungry. Water is something else. Many fortifications are on hilltops where cisterns are the only sources of water, and if these fail, that is a fallen strong point. The sagacious Nathanael Greene discovered that the British and loyaltists he had walled up in Fort Ninety-six, South Carolina, depended on a certain spring, which he had captured. Toiling and perspiring under the southern sun, the loyal garrison was on the point of exhaustion and surrender when a strong force from Charleston saved the loyalist day.

The desultory siege is another economical and sure avenue to victory if time permits. If one has his enemy blockaded so that he cannot be reinforced, but the attacker can be, he kills as many of the defenders as he can without risking many of his own men. A death or injury in his ranks may mean little. Any casualty in the defender's is a catastrophe. This is again directing effort against the human being, and the Turks took many a baronial castle in the Latin Kingdom of Jerusalem with such a chess game.

Major fortification, however, is the result of the engineering revolution, and if treachery, lies, some Trojan horse or other feint, and starvation fail, it takes engineers to undo their colleagues' work.

Building mobile towers which can be rolled up to the besieged wall was known to both the Assyrians and Romans. This requires fire superiority from the ground, and probably from the top of the tower as well. If the defenders have not succeeded in demolishing it, a drawbridge can be lowered to the top of the wall, and besieging infantry can pour onto it. Richard the Lion was fond of such engines, but his worthy opponent, Saladin, used flaming naphtha against them. These wooden towers had been vulnerable to fire all along, but the chemical was too much for the Lion. He tried facing them with iron, but soon ran out of the then precious metal. Actually, the tower need not touch the wall provided it is the higher of the two. Arrow or bullet fire from such a height can devastate the defenders within the circumvallation. The continentals used this successfully on several smaller British strong points in the Revolution, Fort Augusta, Georgia, being an example. Akin to the above, provided the offense has both fire superiority and a large labor force, a slanting earthen ramp can be built leading to the wall's summit.

The battering ram is too well known to need discussion. One has to have fire superiority at its point of hammering, which was not too hard in some of the older castles which had not solved the problem of dead space. The corners of the older square towers were particularly vulnerable to this treatment, which weakness was considerably reduced with the invention of the round tower. King Richard I had his towers at Chateau-Gaillard so widened at the base and built of such magnificent stone that King Philip Augustus's efforts in that direction proved useless and much less effective than his assault on the privy. Building defensive walls and towers right up to the edge of a rocky precipice also vitiates the ram's effort, as does narrowing the ditch just before the fortification. This denies the besiegers swinging room.

Mining and sapping had been known from of old. The attacker starts tunneling out of range of the defender's fire and digs beneath his wall or tower. In former days, the weight of the under-dug fortification was shored up with dry logs. These were then covered with pitch, lard, or whatever inflammables were at hand, and then set afire. As these crumbled, the weight of the fortification made it come down as well. This was a favorite method of that great castle-taker, King John I Plantagenet. Of course, the sappers were in danger as well. The defenders could hear the digging and start a counter-sap. If these met underground, as intended, there was murder in the tunnels. The Turks were adept sappers in their attack on the Latin Kingdom of Jerusalem, but as they had a limitless supply of slaves for the labor, the loss of these fellows counted but little in the Osmanli way of thinking. There is a charming story, and one hopes that it is true, that a baker in besieged Vienna heard the Turks sapping under the city wall. He informed the Christian command, and the city was saved by a counter-sap. The baker was then permitted to shape his delicious rolls in crescent shape as a reward for his acuteness.

While water moats were originally built to keep the attackers from the walls, they also served the purpose of drowning the sappers should they break through to these trenches. Some large French and English castles were built on natural or artificial islands in lakes or swamps to make mining and trenching a virtual impossibility. It is said that one Pedro Navarro improved, if he did not invent, the use of explosives under the defender's works. The Union tried this at Petersburg, and their infantry was trained to rush the supposedly destroyed Confederate works as soon as they heard the explosion. Unfortunately, the Union engineers did not dig their mines far enough forward. The explosion did not harm the Confederate works, and the destruction of the disciplined infantry who rushed into the crater should never have happened to any army. The British General Sir Horace Plumer tried to undermine the German works at Vimy Ridge in World War I, and only succeeded in producing a noisy explosion.

The Vauban Age made digging the curse of all soldiery. If the engineer became the Prince of Battles, the spade was his sceptre. Dig like a mole, the soldiers were told, and they hated it so that the martial pride of the renaissance, the Swiss mercenaries, had it inserted in their contracts that they would not be required to dig trenches. The new Vauban forts could be taken by Vauban's methods, but time and back-breaking labor were involved.

First, the enemy was encircled. The cavalry found a new role in these siege methods. Their mission was to see that the defense should not be relieved or supplied. All around the site they rode, and if successful, they kept the defense isolated. It was rather easy work, in fact, often none at all, and was a relatively safe operation. They were ill recompensed for their idleness and safety, though, for when and if the town fell, they were forbidden to enter it until the infantry and artillery were sated with the booty and beauty it contained. Riches and rage belonged to those who had earned them with the shovel.

A trench was then dug far from the range of the defense's guns, preferably in some natural shelter. There was no hurry. The offense had plenty of time, and the defender did not. A trench or trenches were then dug from this first line straight forward until the range of the defending fire was approached. Then the trenches were dug at angles to prevent enfilade. When this had gone far enough, a forty-five degree turn was taken, and the digging continued. Then another turn was taken, until the besiegers have the defense in range of the former's better cannon. This done, the first large trench was dug in the same line as the fortification. This was the first parallel. A minor earth fort was erected here by night, and protected with a dirt wall and baskets full of soil to absorb the impact of the opposition's cannon, especially around the besieger's own gun muzzles. Then the zigzag resumed again, and if need be, again and again. New parallels were built closer and closer until one of the bastions could be assailed. If attacking artillery contained mortars with high trajectory, they could add to the defender's woe by lobbing shells over his parapet into the enclosure. If the defense commander knew that his situation was hopeless, he would probably surrender, and all the commissioned personnel on both sides could enjoy a fine dinner. This was the Age of Reason, which was that of Vauban. This was the period of *La*

Guerre en Dentelles, when the lacy gentry, professional, few, and treasured, fought battles in which Cyrano de Bergerac would have been at home. The sack of the city was left to the enlisted men, of course, as part of their pay.

The joke of it all, if one can smile at the deaths of so many thousands, was that in World War I on the western front, the trench ceased being the approach to a fort, but became the fortification itself. It was a war which no one deserved to win, and there is an opinion abroad that no one did.

Safe, or apparently so, with thousands of miles of unprotected borders, beyond which dwell peaceful, friendly, and militarily weak nations, the United States since their independence have not been given to building great forts for protection from the land. (The flimsy ones against the Indians were hardly great.) Oh yes, there was one. Early in its independent history, the United States government built a mighty fort against Canadian invasion, Fort Niagara. The Canadian engineers sat silent and amused until the completion of this Gibraltar, then informed the American authorities that it was built entirely on the soil of Canadian sovereignty. The American engineers finally ran an accurate survey line and discovered that this was true. The Canadian government then graciously ceded this real estate to the United States, and both sides recognized the folly of offensive or defensive fortification against each other. The United States have indeed built many powerful coast defense forts, most of which have never come under fire. Corregidor did, but its sad story is so recent that it needs no repetition here. Several were of great strategic importance, however, although space forbids the recount of their histories. As two examples, Fort Monroe, Virginia, was of great help to the Union, and is still garrisoned, although the guns have long since been removed. Fort Fisher, commanding the sea entrance to Confederate Wilmington, North Carolina, not only made a mockery of the Union blockade but kept Lee's army supplied in the field. The fall of Fisher marked the end. A story which someone should tell in another place is that many of these great forts never heard a gun fired in anger and served only to house and starve prisoners of war. No tourist should pass by Fort Delaware, commanding the sea approach of Philadelphia, without visiting it.

Perhaps we should look to our own future. If the present trends of urban sociology are not reversed, another cycle may be in the process of turning. The walled city is ridiculous, is it, but what of the fortified suburb or subdivision? If the central or municipal authority cannot protect its citizens from turmoil, the latter may do so for themselves. We would not think of building private forts such as one sees in the family towers of Italian renaissance cities. They speak of social fragmentation. Our society is not a very cohesive, unitary one. One already sees many industrial plants surrounded by remarkable metal fences, some electrified, and some guarded by mercenaries and fierce dogs. They are not invulnerable to ammunition, but they are to people, and they suggest that a shadow of the old days may be casting itself over us modern men.

The huge city is hardly able to keep itself in water. Dependent on electricity for survival, it can have power breakdowns. Its food supply could easily be disrupted by a few trained, dedicated saboteurs. It has thousands of defenseless human beings herded together who could easily become hysterical. We bravely speak of civil defense, but cannot protect ourselves against refuse accumulation if only a few workers fail to cooperate. Could this urban population, unassimilated and perhaps unassimilable, protect itself like the citizens of the past? Evacuate the city? Is one aware of the staff work needed to move only a division of disciplined trained troops only a hundred miles, even when directed by an experienced battalion of military police? Evacuate the city quickly and safely during a missile shower? Perhaps it is more fruitful to hope for the birth of another Vauban.

FOOTNOTES AND REFERENCES

[1] Battlements are the squares of stone on top of a wall behind which archers could take cover. One even sees them on the walls of large mediaeval churches. A machicolation is a gallery atop and beyond the wall held up by stone props from which hot oil or lead could be dropped on the attackers, or from which they could be raked with arrows while crouching at its base.

[2] Dead space is an area which cannot be reached by the defender's fire: arrow, rifle, cannon, or machine gun.

[3] The last serious portcullis known to me was built on the land side of Fort Pulaski, Georgia, an antebellum defense of Savannah to protect the land side of the fort from a rush by marines. Its builder was that famous military engineer, Captain Robert E. Lee.

[4] Major General Wendell J. Coats, "Normative Conduct and Contingent Violence," paper read to the American Sociological Association, September, 1970.

Chapter 9

ENERGY USE AND SUPPLY

The Logistic Revolution

Supply is a familiar enough word to everyone. Each family, every institution, indeed, every specific person must be supplied and resupplied with consumption goods adequate for survival and efficient operation in the transactional world of men. Most readers of these pages are members of the leisure class, in a way of speaking, insofar as they do not produce the food and clothing requisite for maintenance, and one hopes, more than that. This does not mean that they are not workers. One may labor harder and longer than the producers, but the availability of the goods consumed is the responsibility of others. The civilized soldier is no exception. He makes no pretense at producing the food, weapons, clothes, and other essentials necessary for his trade. Although in wartime he may be a mighty toiler, and often in peace as well, he is a leisure-class worker *par excellence*. He is the essential nonproductive consumer. He has neither the time nor the skill to weave, till the soil, or to collect his provender in the market. He differs from readers and writers only in degree. It was different under the conditions of primitive war, but that is not under consideration now. He is now a specialist, as are most important people, those whose efforts are directed to providing the social system with more than is used.

The term "service of supply" is a term not always used with merited affection. The term "logistics" may be unfamiliar, but as Secretary Forrestal once said, it is "the process of providing what is needed, when it is needed, and where it is needed." Antoine Jomini said that "Logistics is all or almost all of the field of military activity except combat," and if this nineteenth century tactical genius said that, then the rest of us, from civilian to combat veteran, might speak respectfully of the art of logistics, for the Greek word *logistikos* means one skilled in calculation. Logistics is at the center of the material culture of warfare. First, though, some very hard theoretical considerations must be faced before going into the subject. Civilians in their peacetime safety never do. Their parliaments rarely do and, one fears, some commanders fail to consider some basic facts as they should.

The military is an action pattern supreme. Now all action is expenditure of energy against the frustrations of gravity, and its twins of space and time. Perceptive soldiers are often bitterly aware of this. The whole story of human culture from the first use of fire until now recounts the search for improvement in, control of, and use of energy. The military is not exempt. Its actions are more apparently and immediately bound by energy-space-time than many of the other activities of men. What does it mean? The meaning of meaning is action, and action is the expenditure of energy against the forces of gravity. Work is the purposeful consumption of energy, while meaningless energy waste is turbulence, a senseless thrashing about, a tale told idiots, infants, the senile, and demoralized soldiers, full of nothing but sound and fury. Meaningful action is what is wished to be reserved to one's own side. It is hoped to introduce turbulence into the enemy, for an army in panic uses up as much energy as one advancing with purpose. War properly so-called is a political system's attempts to expand its energy system by controlled violence, or through the same means of force, to keep what it has.

A very humiliating fact must be faced. Man is an inefficient energy converter. He does about a well as his friend the horse, but he does not do well enough to achieve all he wants out of this world. Eat well he may, but out of one hundred calories eaten, he can convert only about twenty percent into work and action. Ideally, as an adult, he must eat 2,600 calories per day for effective action. He fattens if he eats more than 3,000 calories daily, and he sickens if he has less than 2,000. The members of many societies do eat less than this, and are generally termed shiftless, worthless, and contemptible, and with mathematical reason.

A healthy draft horse will eat 17,000 calories per day, and deliver twenty percent thereof as work. Obviously, then, a military unit supplied by pack or draft horses will fare better than one served by human porterage. The horse eats rapidly growing, relatively cheap food, too, and if permitted, can largely support himself by grazing. The Mongol cavalry brought only grazing mares in their invasion of Europe, who also fed the horsemen with their accustomed milk diet. A coal civilization, though, is a high energy one, for one pound of coal will yield 3,500 calories, which is 500 over and above the daily needs of a man. There is no mystery, then, as to why a railroad-supplied army, other things being equal, will defeat one supplied by animals.

The favorite tactical and logistical fuel of this generation is petroleum. Diminishing returns, though, set in immediately at the opening of the well. Dr. Zimmerman and many others have warned of the possible exhaustion of the American oil fields, and were not thanked by the optimists. If one can imagine figures so high, let him consider the drain on American oil fields by two world wars, with the high consumption of large trucks and heavy tanks, both American and allied. Americans are already relying on foreign imports over thousands of sea miles from the oil fields which they do not control politically. Every logistician and strategist knows that the United States must maintain its command of the seas, or their citizens may have to learn how to walk again.

And so, to return to the well-fed soldier, who is or should be efficient. Hungry ones will eventually lose the initiative, go on the defense, lose their disease resistance, and perish. This is the core of military logistics, and must never be forgotten. The adult human can deliver as work only between 400 and 600 out of his 2,000-3,000 daily calorie intake. Or, to put it another way, an adult man can deliver between 1/1.6 and 1/07 horsepower hours as work regardless of his skill or valor. On such a thin margin does heroism rest. Also hanging on this tenuous margin are all civilizations and higher culture. It is the controlling factor of productivity, and every civilian employer should realize this. The military commander must realize that there is a point beyond which the "be a man" admonition is not relevant.

The commander can be too solicitous, of course, as Robert Lee was on one fatal occasion. George Pickett's division had a fairly hard day's march to join the Gettysburg affair, arriving in the appointed place in late afternoon. Pickett sent word to Lee that his men were fairly tired, but full of willingness to fight then and there. Lee sent back instructions to let the men rest. They were not needed that day. We know with the infallibility of hindsight that they should have been marched into the line and allowed to rest there, or at least, roused by midnight and put into position for the dawn attack which was delayed for many hours. No Confederate leader has ever lived down this delay, neither Lee, Longstreet, nor Pickett.

This is all very well, but even if it is not relevant on any particular day, eventually valor and victory rest on this margin between 1/07 and 1/1.6 horsepower hours, which is just as true for the civilians who support the effort as it is for the soldiers. Old China permitted overpopulation to make men the rivals of draft animals for food, and men had to turn into burden-bearing beasts. From an abject peasantry, through a declining civilization, to a weakened government and a debased military, China fell prey to any nation wishing to exploit it.

Considering the ineffectiveness of man as an energy converter, historic slavery was an answer only in very fertile areas which can produce an excess of food, sending the military abroad to skim off the surplus population of other people. Citizens who might otherwise be used for food production may be relieved by slaves. The Germans rediscovered this in World War II, enserfing thousands from France to eastern Russia to man field and factory, a better-trained class of slaves than Rome ever knew. The short-time survival of these slaves did not affect the conscience of the Reich. There was an unlimited reservoir of *Untermenschen* to be tapped. Servility can only postpone That Day, however, for in time an active, productive, loyally enthusiastic home work force is as essential to military operations as are trained soldiers with good weapons.

Transportation is a direct consumption of energy in the fight against gravity. Moving objects from here to there has always used up a large proportion of energy available to man. It is possible that simple societies without draft animals use up as much energy as we do in this effort, but vegetable-fed animals do better than man, and vegetable fossil-fueled machines do better than that. Liquid fossil fuels serve best in modern vehicles, although nuclear-powered ships are at sea, and doing fairly well. Men do very well, too, but they do not go as far. Beyond the line of 60-inch rainfall, which favors the tsetse fly and inhibits draft animals, the Negroes of West Africa often erected very commendable commercial kingdoms on human porterage, but that was not good enough. So, it is not a question of how far good troops can march which is the controlling factor. It is their condition upon arrival. An infantry unit marching thirty miles per day is about finished by nightfall. This was no task for good cavalry, the very best of which could double the miles and be in fair fighting condition if it consisted of good men, well-fed horses, and blest with good leadership. A truck, however, can carry men farther and faster, and a cargo plane can do even better.

It is not a lack of energy which besets us. There is plenty of sunlight, and one and a half acres receives as much of that energy daily as was expended on the Hiroshima bomb. It is not raw energy poverty but the lack of availability which thwarts us. Solar engines have been rather disappointing so far. Since Napoleon, too, and his prize to someone to rid Europe of the British sugar monopoly, the world has suffered a glut of that commodity. A truck could not exhaust the energy in a pound of white sugar during its lifetime, but who is about to split a hydrocarbon atom?

Primitive war, or submilitary combat, thought so little of the supply function that it had to remain in that category. Even at its highest, the warrior supplied his own needs. If his weapons were lost or broken, he was out of action. Even a mounted late Plains Indian's arrow quiver was soon exhausted, and there was no replacement. No packhorse carried more, though they knew how to pack an animal well. His wife made him an extra pair of moccasins, but beyond that his clothing was limited to that on his back. There was no social system with the authority to train and send in replacements to take the place of battle casualties, and there was no remount depot to replace a sick, dead, or wounded horse. We mention the Plainsmen as typical of the better submilitary fighting groups, but all were not up to their combat level. Thus, primitive war was largely confined to raiding and fun-killing, for it rarely altered the status quo. It is, by contrast, rare that the political status quo is altered by one battle in true or political war. Only campaigns can ordinarily force such decisions, and only civil states can fight them.

Not all of this indecisive bloodshed was necessary, or due entirely to lack of economic resources. Many American Indian societies could have supplied their forces better than they did. It was lack of sociological imagination, a defect in group thinking, and inability to look into the future. Although the North American continent proved to be one of unbelievable bounty, the typical Indian society was never far from starvation. Even with the tools and seeds they had, many of the land-tilling societies could have produced better surpluses than they did, and could have used them better. Consider, for example, the gentle Papago of Arizona and Sonora, who were more than typical of American Indian carelessness in supply matters. They were at least fair farmers, but they took only a little pine nut food with them into the war field. They wished to live on the country, thinking this would make them hard and increase their mobility. Thus, the warriors would divide into hunting groups in the late afternoon and scrounge around for an evening meal. Of course this made them extremely vulnerable to an alert enemy, had one been around.

If one considers that logistic revolution which helped raise human group violence out of primitive war, he finds that it is linked with other trait complexes in a homeostatic, functional relation. First, he finds that the rise of the civil state is the root of political and therefore true war. Only the state can authoritatively skim off the consumption goods over and above the survival needs of the civilian population and dispatch them to the support of the immediately nonproductive military. This is essentially what the logistic revolution is. Primitive warriors were responsible for their own supply. Their relatively powerless chiefs, hardly able to command them in an engagement, could not persuade or force anyone to abstain from eating the food at hand and to supply an expedition. Nonliterate societies rarely had enough economic success to afford such a measure.

One must note again that the prime reason for the invention, development, and continuous existence of civil society in contrast with kinship structures is the improvement and maintenance of economic security. In a very real way, the peaceful economic success of any society sets the limits of its military logistics. Economic surpluses must exist, and devoted to military ambitions. Only organized states could do this. There can be no true war without at least a high agriculture which can produce transportable supplies. This is both a cause and result of success in the inseparable concepts of economic and social organization which only the state can provide. This is one threshold between true and primitive war, that economic motive which either obviously or covertly lies back of all political action properly so-called. All city-building societies knew and practiced this. The logistic revolution, then, in plain speech, consists of that point when the fighting men representing the violent ambitions of the group are supplied by the social system instead of by themselves.

The arts and sciences of tactics and strategy, which marked the beyond-which-no-return military horizon, held a bloody laboratory. The tactical revolution is not too hard to understand, because one learned in this seminar or perished. Why it took man so long to appreciate the third triplet of Mars full grown, an adequate supply, is not so clear. Many old societies enjoyed the political revolution, either by ethnological diffusion from elsewhere, or by the necessities of a better life inspiring a parallel invention. When one considers the economic role of the state, it is hard to understand why it took so long to insure adequate goods to the field troops whose function was to expand or protect this economic endeavor, but so it was. Was it because tactical incompetence produces immediate and promptly visible death, while that of starvation is a slow one? This fact is vital, however, for war is violence, and hungry men are lethargic.

One can understand this inadequacy in small, kin-based societies, but the record is replete with truly political structures who could have and should have done better than they did. They already had adequately structured societies, whose principles they could carry over into the field of combat. Few others besides the early Romans applied these techniques to the feeding, funding, and arming of soldiers who were the state's external force potential. They surely discovered from primitive war that small units can live off the invaded country, but large ones cannot. There were many instances of how the supplies of a ravaged enemy country were soon exhausted, and in the return or retreat back home, privation killed far too many troops. Experience keeps a dear school indeed, and fools will learn in no other, but what of many famous commanders who were not fools?

The early Greek city states arrayed against Troy, for example, were structurally and functionally adequate for their times. So was Troy, the fortified enemy, whose probable reason for existence was the control of a trade route. According to the *Illiad* and *Odyssey*, however, it took ten years to reduce the city, though indeed, it never suffered this fate. It fell because the Hellenic troops suffering from war fatigue and other woes resorted to an impious stratagem. Of course the account of Homer as a war correspondent left much to be desired, yet the suspicion of logistic ineptitude will not down. The Greeks were well aware of the function of cargo ships. Their initial operation consisted of a descent from the sea, of which they kept permanent control. Why were not the troops fed by a permanent sea-borne supply line from home? The Homeric record indicates that there was an adequate productive population left behind. From the description of the continual feasting at Ithaca, the home front was not suffering from the guns-or-butter syndrome.

One cannot help but suspect that, once a base had been established by an amphibious operation, many of these ten years were occupied by the troops plowing, sowing, reaping, and harvesting their own provender. Indeed, not even a strong city such as Troy could fail to succumb to starvation in a decade. Prevented from revictualing by sea, the Trojans must have come from the walls and grown a few crops in plain sight of their enemies. Recognition of a continued state of belligerency was maintained by sporadic individual duels of champions, which upon one occasion a defeated field-grade officer's corpse was dragged around the storied walls of Troy from the victor's chariot spoke. Of course, an efficient conduct of the Trojan War would have resulted in a much shorter poem than the *Illiad*, but we of today might enjoy reading a more condensed version. These peoples had just undergone the political and tactical revolutions which they had not entirely digested. Perhaps it is asking too much that they understand the logistic one as well. In fact, even at the height of their classical glory, the Greeks never did.

The ancient Hebrews started out in no better fashion. They had been to a hard Egyptian school, and we know that even the Old Kingdom understood supply for its defensive wars. The Jewish experience described in *Exodus*, however, was not that of a civilized invasion of Canaan, but of an armed folk migration. The Hebrews were hungry indeed at first, and longed for the fleshpots of Egypt. There was a mana ration, too, when the situation became desperate. This movement, though, took most of a lifetime, even when led by the genius of Moses. The distance from the Red Sea to the land flowing with milk and honey is too small to require this time for a healthy, well-fed army, encumbered even as it was by women, the young, old, and ailing. As in the case of the Trojan War, these people must have reverted to their skill of pastoral nomads to keep fed, and this took time. For that matter, the adventurous explorers of Portuguese Prince Henry the Navigator paused along the coast of Africa to grow a crop or two, and they sailed caravels designed primarily as cargo carriers.

The Jews, though, are quick learners in things military, as recent events have disclosed. The *Book of Judges* shows that by the time of the campaign against Gibeah, which was early in their career, the tactical and logistic revolutions were better developed than their political one. It is written that "We will take ten men of an hundred, throughout the tribes of Israel, and a hundred of a thousand to fetch victual for the people [troops]." The concept of the rear area is not as young as some suppose, and this decimal system for the service of supply was rather close to the three rear-area men to the ten combat soldiers which was standard for World War I. It is clear, though, that Israelitish wars were by logistic compulsion short ones. Kings went for to war in the autumn when the harvest provided a plenty. The men were freed from the economic necessities of farming, and were perhaps spoiling for a good fight, which had to have an end contemporary with their ration supply.

The West African monarchies did not learn as rapidly as the Hebrew one. They provided excellent illustrations of the slowness of otherwise adequate political organizations to appreciate the logistic function, and to do as well as they could. Ashanti, Benin, and especially Dahomey were lands which hard work and economic organization could produce that surplus over the needs of the producers which is a *sine qua non* characteristic of the state and its force potential. Either the fairly fertile land and natural environment inspired the rise of the political state, or the basic idea was borrowed from Egypt, as some Africanists suggest. There was adequate food production, storage, and distribution under the very efficient Dahomean priest-kingship. This abundance produced a large, well organized population. Dahomey could have fielded armies large enough to accomplish any reasonable mission without depopulating the home land of productive workers. Indeed, this was done, for Snelgrave reports that the Dahomean army consisted of 3,000 regulars and 10,000 "rabble" to porter the supplies, baggage, and the captured heads the king wanted so much.

The Dahomean army was just poorly led, and slow to comprehend the principle of mission. Burton said that the supplies were always inadequate, and that even victorious armies had to return home under conditions of great privation. There was not enough water. Burton, one of the great of the early Africanists, said that the Dahomeans lost 200 soldiers by starvation and disease for every 100 slaves captured, the latter being the objects of the expedition.

The Zulu were with but little doubt the militarily most competent people of black Africa, and their logistics were understandably better than the western folk just mentioned. Each soldier, of course, carried as much with him as he could, and important officers had orderlies to carry their supplies. A force of girls was detailed to bear food and beer for the expedition, which consumed, this female logistic element departed for home. The Zulu were cattle people whose prized food was vast quantities of milk. It was on these beasts that the force depended when the girls had departed. A herd of cattle was driven about two miles on the flank to provide this dairy provender, and also in hopes that they would draw the enemy cattle to them.

Returning to the Mediterranean, one sees that the Persians thought in military terms when they emerged on that sea. According to Xenophon (bk. 10), they had well-organized supply trains, and whenever they were near the coast, they used ships to ease the burden of men and beasts. They were accustomed to setting up advanced supply depots in friendly countries in the direction of nations they intended to attack. Even though we divide the size of their reported forces by half, they still operated huge armies, which would have never arrived anywhere without an adequate logistic force.

Their target enemies, the Greeks, learned so much of civilization from the Persians, but never succumbed to their appreciation of the logistic revolution. The Hellenes even in their most brilliant period never charged a staff officer with the supply function. The aristocratic heavy infantry did not contemplate war far from home, so was content with what each soldier and perhaps his servant could carry along. It is true that the circumstances of the Plataea campaign forced them to organize a supply train. The idea of campaigning finally dawned upon them, and they tried to improve on their logistics, but it was too late. The supply function remained the weakest Greek military point, even while their potential masters were contemplating coming to Hellas to pick up some civilization, and whatever else might lay about.

The Romans excelled all the ancient world in organization, whatever they might have lacked in cultivation. They, like the Greeks, had founded a regal city state, but by the time they had become republican, their political organization was far superior to that of any of their potential foes. It would not seem to require much imagination to carry the political organization over into the logistic field, but as we have seen, few early polities were as imaginative as were the Romans.

The older Romans did not conceive of the civic and military magistracy as separate and distinct in either function or personnel. The consuls as civic magistrates for internal affairs were also the field generals. The state also had an elected director of administration called the quaestor. Now when a consul took the field in his dual role as general, his quaestor came as deputy commander and chief of the service element. As he had direction of civil funds and supplies in his peaceful role, he routinely transferred his skills to the fighting field. He organized the lines of communication and supply, which must have surprised the homeloving Greeks who could not think in such terms. The quaestor's function had to become more complex and important as the Romans achieved ideas of far-flung empire. The military Latins, who took as few chances as possible, kept accurate accounts of moneys and property. The quaestor's office was the finance element, paying the troops and supervising all expenditures. Even in republican times, the quaestor, as with us, had his own area in camp for his supply dumps and officers (Polybius I, 52; VI 31-35; X, 19, and Livy XVIII, 29; XXX, 37-38).

Even as early as the first century B.C., a modern, to us, civil administrative corps emerged. This clerical bureaucracy, because of long experience and familiarity with army regulations and procedures, and was largely untouchable. The quaestor was an elective official, and he had to rely on these long-term administrative functionaries to tell him what to do, and how. The Roman republican senators could have served as examples for some others of later times. Realizing that military operations were within the range of possibility, they built up stores and sent them directly to the theater of operations, if this were close by, and set quaestors in charge of them.

No social system, of course, is perfect, but in the realization of weakness and attempts to correct them lie the most important root of sociopolitical change. Roman wars ceased to be close by. Distant theaters required more complex organization, and because of this, there is seen one more feature in that theme, "ancient Rome and modern America," which some historians discuss. The Punic Wars created that industrial-military establishment which so many decry and so few understand.

The Scipios found themselves fighting in Spain while Hannibal was trying to find a passage into Italy. Supplies in Iberia were running out, and threatened with failure due to logistic poverty, the generals invented the requisition. The senators, receiving this charge, and aware of the danger, devised another modernism. The republican treasury could not meet the requisition, so the legislators advertised among the prosperous business class, offering excellent profits, guaranteeing them exemption from military service, and insurance against loss at the hands of the elements or the public enemy. These generous terms caused the invention of another modern phenomenon, the profiteer and the shady contractor. Livy reports (XXV, 3-4) that as early as 212 B.C., false bills of lading were made out for nonexistent supplies, supposedly laden in unseaworthy ships belonging to the contractors which were subsequently wrecked. Many of these entrepreneurs were tried and sentenced to banishment.

No American should sneer too much at this, nor think that his affairs could not change for the better. It has been said that more American soldiers died of tainted beef in President McKinley's Hispanic adventure than were laid low by Spanish bullets. It is unconstitutional, of course, to banish a native-born American citizen, but the penal code had other sanctions.

Those masters of organization, the Byzantines, could be expected to do even better than their Italic colleagues when the banners of empire shifted from the Tiber eastward. Soldiers were few, professional, expensive, and treasured, so right from the beginning Eastern Romans organized staff sections concerned with supply, administration, medicine, and finance which have not been equaled until this day. They founded the first hospital troops, a mounted corps paid with a generous bounty for every seriously wounded man they recovered and brought to the rear.

All of this came to naught, as is known only too well. Mediaeval logistic folly was reflected by the quite useless suffering and loss to civilization by the failure of the crusades. With the loss of the East, and eventually of Constantinople itself, the world was changed forever, and few scholars think for the better. If, as it is said, Venice is now sinking beneath the waters, there might be such a thing as sin, and it might be visited upon the children unto many generations. The Serene Republic cheated outrageously in supplying the crusades. It looted Constantinople. In case you have seen the magnificent bronze horses, you know that. They stole the body of St. Mark the Apostle from Alexandria and built a fine church around it. Had they known of such things, they would have made fortunes out of selling hot dogs and hamburgers to the Childrens' Crusade. They were among those "who profess and call themselves Christians," but it is hard to tell why.

The large land armies of the baroque and rococo periods demanded something better than the mediaeval or even renaissance practices. Cardinal Richelieu invented the ministry of war, copied by everyone else, and from henceforth it took troop financing out of the hands of little company commanders. Richelieu also created *intendants* to administer civil districts, who assumed supervision of the troops in their areas. The government then proceeded to set up stores and markets from which the troops bought their own rations. If Armand du Plessis, Cardinal Duc de Richelieus, is remembered for nothing else, his picture should be in every PX and post commissary.

The American Civil War, as it is most generally called, became the great military laboratory for all subsequent operations. All staff college graduates know that Gettysburg is the most studied battle in history, illustrating as it does the costs of tactical errors on both sides. More than this, the war was the logistic schoolmaster for the future. Battles were no longer to be tidy little local affairs, and campaigns could no longer be studied with only one map at hand. From henceforth supply lines must be hundreds of miles, and more. If the logistic revolution had already been partially conceptualized, the American interstate war gave it a boost which can never be recalled. The supplying of the troops from thousands of miles overseas was initiated. Great Britain owned Bermuda and the Bahamas, which no Federal fleet dared attack without confronting the Royal Navy in open war. Fast blockade-runners with steam auxilliaries were built and manned out of England, making the cumbersome, wind-borne Union blockading fleet ridiculous. Lincoln needed his inadequate battle fleet elsewhere, and the Union paid bitterly for the neglect of its navy, winner though it eventually was.

One such cost was the blows struck by the Confederacy against the North by a small, brand-new and, for then, modern southern navy. The destruction of the Union's merchant marine was so complete that it never recovered for a century, if indeed, it ever has. The war opened with American clippers out of Boston and Baltimore ruling the mercantile seas. The ably commanded *CSS Alabama*,

Georgia, and *Shenandoah* took care of that situation. After its victory, the imagination of the Union turned inward, caring more about winning the west than recapturing its position as a maritime power. It delivered the task of developing the era of commercial steamships to the British, who served the Americans well and cheaply, and made them commercially and logistically vulnerable to the goodwill of others. Thoroughly frightened, and painfully aware of her dependence on the United States, Great Britain even built troop transports for their American cousins. The luxury liners *Queen Mary* and *Queen Elizabeth* never pretended to be strictly commercial vessels. They always sailed under the blue ensign of the Royal Naval Reserve, and never flew the red flag of the merchant marine. They could not pay off even when sailing with complete passenger lists, but each of them could transport an infantry division with all of its equipment and service elements, so fast, indeed, that they defied the submarines of the day.

But returning to the original laboratory, there could be no such thing as the destruction of Lee as long as Fort Fisher, North Carolina, protected the harbor entrance to Wilmington, even after the fall of Fort Sumter and Charleston. The intervening space had to be wrested from Confederate control by Sherman. Meat by the tons was shipped by wagon from the cattle ranches of Florida, and Sherman also cut off that line by occupying Georgia. Lee knew that his fate was sealed, even if President Davis did not.

The Civil War, then, was the last struggle of a nation depending on vegetable energy against a high-energy state. Here was the first hint that the factory would lead to big business, which begot big government, and settled for keeps that transportation would be listed somewhere in the royal family of battles. The northern factories were almost as good as the English. The railroad was finally a success. Morse telegraphy enormously improved the transmission of information within the communications zone. The South had some railroads, but not nearly enough to serve her military ambitions. Hers remained a water-borne economy, and her Mississippian lifeline had to be cut. European theorists have said that the Confederate Army of the Tennessee was the best one which ever wore shoe leather. After the useless death by bleeding of the genius Albert Sidney Johnston, it was probably the worst led as well. Jefferson Davis, though himself a westerner, conceived the military's role as protecting the sacred soil of Virginia instead of the great breadbasket, and refused to lend the western army Lee or even Beauregard for even a brief period. The Confederate government was at least wise enough to make the armed camp of Vicksburg the strongest fortification built before that date. Even if the northern-born Confederate General John Clifford Pemberton not made a serious strategic error, Grant would have starved him into surrender, which is indeed what happened.

A dying attempt at logistic survival was made by Sterling Price in an effort to reach the food bin of Iowa, but he was defeated at the battle of Westport, actually on the Swope Park golf course in Kansas City. Price repeated Lee's mistake at Gettysburg, with even more disastrous results.

The Confederate collapse spelled the end of wagon-born transport for large campaigns. Railroads provided not only forward transport but lateral supply as well. From then on, the enemy's railroad system was a prime tactical and strategic target. Foch tried his best to break through the German lateral lines in World War I. Very few remember, but Woodrow Wilson sent William Graves and two U.S. infantry regiments to guard the Trans-Siberian Railroad after the Tsarist collapse in Siberia. We do not wish to revive controversy about Wilson's orders to General Graves, but the Americans were evacuated from Vladivostok on April Fools' Day, 1918.

The death of the wagon train was set in our laboratory war. The North had the railroads and the men who knew how to build, operate, and maintain them. As in World War I, supplies and replacements could be taken over long distances to depots, then sent forward by wagon to the supply centers for each echelon. Grant had his trains behind him. He knew that the Valley of the Shenandoah must be devastated to the famishment of the local crows, and ordered Sheridan to do just that. Jubal Early and Thomas Jackson were not reinforced as they should have been, but the Army of Northern Virginia could not spare the troops. Sherman's mission in Georgia was similar, and strangely enough, Confederate descendents are inclined to forgive Lincoln, who was responsible for both devastations, and Grant who ordered the destruction of western Virginia. The hatred is reserved for Sheridan, who later ordered Custer to do some rather dreadful things to the Indians, and to Sherman, who was a South-lover all his life, and who would not even free his wife's slaves.

Every competent tactician and strategist knows that the Union armies were never able to force a decision on the Confederates by force of arms. There was plenty of fight left in the Army of the Tennessee when Sherman finally brought it to bay in North Carolina. The Union general so admired it that he practically gave the world back to it and its commander, "Old Joe" Johnston, to the immense disapproval of the Washington government. Lee had a small but professional army at Appomatox which begged him to fight on. But Lee knew, and so did Johnston, and so did Beauregard and Hampton. Logistics won this laboratory war for the side so strong that it should have finished the matter in a few months. The Union, and Grant in particular, invented the war of attrition, which means destroying your enemy's men and materials faster than he can replace them, even if you suffer similar losses yourself, having an immense reservoir of both which your opposition lacks. The United States learned this lesson well, perhaps over-learned it, for it relied on this bloody method in World War I and in Viet Nam. It worked for years in the latter war. Had the then President of the United States seen fit to press his advantage, he could have avoided great loss of life on both sides, his own reputation, and his country's bad image.

It took millenia of mankind's experience with bloodshed to teach the basic principles of tactics, which change not, it must be said that it took even longer to arrive at some unchanging doctrine of logistics. Is this because death and defeat in the field are quick, while starvation is a slow process has already been asked. Is it because the logistic revolution is a continuing one, that the increase of practical, material technology and invention are faster than the generalizing, reflective, and thought processes of mankind? If so, this is no more than the operation of the hypothesis of the cultural lag, which all sociologists learned from William Fielding Ogburn. Indeed, it cannot be said that we have arrived at the desired immutable theory of logistics even yet, but here follow six rather broad generalizations which will merit considerable thought. The first statement is that of the author. The next three are those of Colonel Stockbridge Barker, and are italicized to indicate direct quotation. The last is likewise of the author's arrangement.[1]

The first proposition to be enunciated is a true principle, indeed, is a truism. It is one which is immutable, inexorable, and changeless.

1. *The Principle of Maximization of Energy Use and Increased Vulnerability.* Every nation must realize that, as it must seek every means to maximize the efficiency of its energy utilization as function, it must suffer the dysfunctions of increased complexity of its mechanisms, and their expanding inherency to breakdown and vulnerability to enemy penetration.

The range of all human endeavor, aided or unaided, lies between so many calories of intake, which yield only so many in work output. To reduce the energy consumption is to diminish the work potential. A machine attempts to maximize the human or animal capability, but in doing so, it introduces its own weakness into the situation. A cargo truck transfers a vast amount of transport capability from human shoulders to an unfeeling machine, but it increases rather than diminishes the inexorability of the rule that the work output cannot exceed the energy intake. Indeed, it introduces a factor of immediacy which man or beast may not have.

A truck or tank can run only so many miles per gallon of fuel, which is definite, predictable, and inexorable. A hungry man or animal may be persuaded or compelled to go a few miles farther even under conditions of privation, but an empty fuel tank is not amenable to persuasion, cajoling, or threatening. It is hard to imagine anything more vulnerable and helpless than a tank or truck with an empty gasoline tank and its ammunition running low unless it be a grounded airplane.

A human, although a carniverous primate, has quite an omniverous dietary range. A cavalry or artillery horse can graze the country and survive to the next day's fighting. An airplane, tank, or truck can consume only one source of energy, a refined fossil fuel which is expensive even in the most ideal conditions of civilian peace. A mechanized unit cannot live off the country for its fuel.

A complex army is vulnerable to penetration at any point of the industry, transport, or distribution of its energy supply. Distilled petroleum comes from only a very few of the earth's subsurfaces, all of which are subject to exhaustion and sabotage. Its refinement is complex, expensive, and requires a vast capital investment. The same may be said of its storage and transport. It is very vulnerable to aerial bombardment at every stage, as were the Ploesti fields in Rumania on which so much of the Hitlerist war effort depended. A long supply line providing petroleum products to an army is difficult to guard unless its nation controls the air space and the seas, and is alerted to sabotage.

A high-energy civilization with an elaborate road-bound transport has a high standard of consumption, but even its rear area and civilian homeland is extremely vulnerable. Let the reader ask himself what would happen to the United States if some morning all service stations would be closed, permanently. It almost happened in German-occupied France, and if one does not realize that there are those in the world with this in mind, he dangerously underestimates an enemy's imagination, dedication, and industriousness.

Again, as a nation moves towards the maximization of its energy use, the more complex the consuming machines become. Even the finest internal combustion engine with an adequate supply of fuel is immobilized if any one of its very numerous moving parts fail, or if its lubricants are quantitatively or qualitatively inadequate. No nation, then, is permanently safe in peace or war if its spare parts industry is inadequate or permeable.

There can be no argument about the comparative lethality of a high-energy rifle or machine gun over a low-energy spear or bayonet. Modern fire weapons, though, are complex and are subject to mechanical stoppage, excessive wear, and consume tremendous amounts of ammunition. A low-energy equipped unit can fight on after a fashion if equipped only with spears and bayonets. A high-energy unit's combat effectiveness ceases with its ammunition supply, which every able enemy attempts to disrupt.

2. *The Principle of Weaponry—A nation must have in being a modern weapons system before engaging in military operations.* This is a minimum requirement, and the possession thereof does not guarantee victory.

This situation should be carefully thought out by any nation considering its defense or offense by force of arms, but the principle is often observed too often in the breach, with consequent loss of life, wealth, and freedom. The question as to the identity of potential enemies as well as their possible logistic capabilities must be posed and answered. The United States have a long history of permitting obsolescence in their weapons systems in peacetimes, sometimes accompanied by certain threatening gestures in their foreign policy. Thus, while all military powers had smokeless powder-charged, non-recoil artillery in 1898, the Americans held to gun types the obsolescence of which had been established at Gettysburg. And so in the month of July of the subject year, American artillery was charged with softening the well-prepared Spanish position on San Juan Hill. Great billows of smoke, the same clouds which diminished the effectiveness of both sides at Gettysburg, prevented the American gunners from correcting their fire. They provided the Spanish with aiming targets, which they used with telling effect. Again, the War Department had only enough modern infantry rifles to supply the few regular regiments. Only old single-shot .45 rifles were available for the volunteer units, who were in the majority, and there was no smokeless ammunition with which to arm them. The exact position of the firing and skirmish lines were immediately revealed to the Spanish, who were quite capable of taking advantage of this knowledge. The American forces won, of course, but with unforgiveable losses, the guilt for which lay squarely on the citizens of the United States.

After electing a president on the platform, "He kept us out of war," the American nation promptly entered World War I with so few weapons that they had to borrow field artillery from the French, and Enfield rifles from the British. They recovered from this logistic poverty, of course, and paid their allies back a thousandfold, but what if these same friends had not screened the Americans until their assembly lines caught up with their warlike words?

This nation entered World War II in a similar state of logistic unpreparedness, with the same allies providing a not very good screen until the assembly lines caught up. The present writer felt very foolish in front of his men when he tried to train mortar squads with a third-base bag borrowed from the baseball field and rechristened "base plate," while a piece of discarded stove pipe was renamed "barrel." If the shades of Ethelred the Unready and Benjamin Franklin, who said something about the kind of school experience keeps, were amused, no one else was. How would you classify, Dr. Franklin, a military establishment who in just a few years after V-Day, and with the same president still in office, entered the Korean adventure with outmoded World War II weapons in poor condition? The tuition in this school was months of humiliation and defeat.

This chapter is not a proper forum either to attack or defend the American presidential imperium. Let Senator Gale McGee of the Foreign Relations Committee call attention to the modern collapse of our older concepts of space-time. He said in 1972, "the Founding Fathers knew nothing but the declared wars in the strife of Europe. They knew nothing about nuclear capabilities and the wiping out of the time factor in decision making as a consequence; and they knew precious little, I submit further, about the responsibilities of world leadership. . . ."

Senator McGee continues, "Nuclear capability has torn the calendar to shreds and has nearly invalidated the 24-hour clock . . . it required 15 years, at the end of the 18th Century to mount a striking squadron against the Barbary Pirates, 20 to cause Tripoli to sue for peace . . . after Bull Run, the North consumed two full years in assembling the kind of Army which could hand President Lincoln a major victory. The capture of Vicksburg on July 4, 1863; one more year before Sherman could boast, 'Atlanta is ours and fairly won!'"

Coming into this century, the United States was somewhat aware of the possibilities of a confrontation, began a halfhearted rearming almost ten years before Pearl Harbor on 7 December 1941, but it was not until June 1944 that it could mount an invasion of Hitlerist Europe. We merely comment on what logistic feebleness has produced, and let others predict what the future may hold.

3. *The Principle of Production—A nation must be capable of producing the materials of war at a rate equal to the combat rate of consumption.* This, too, is a minimum requirement, and beautifully observed in the breach by Hitler who only belatedly put his factories where his mouth was. He had used up or worn out his modern equipment in a relatively unopposed march through Poland.

He was blest with somnolent enemies who elected to have a *Sitzkrieg* to allow him to indulge in a crash production program rather than attacking him while he was relatively helpless.

The Soviet Union, being an authoritarian pretorian state, can devote almost all of its industrial potential to munitions. It can build up a peacetime stockpile to cover the initial supply shock. It does not have to wait until its industry can organize and take over the daily requirements.

4. The Principle of Distribution — A nation must be capable of distributing to its military forces the necessary supplies and equipment at a rate equal to the combat rate of consumption. Production alone will not win. Benedict Arnold, while still a continental officer, was on a mission to Washington at Valley Forge. He reported in his autobiography that he saw large stores consigned to the same place dumped, abandoned, and rotting by the roadside.

The Germans almost destroyed by submarine warfare the American ability to deliver gasoline to its own and allied armies. It was stated in a staff conference of the Commanding General, Eastern Base Section, ETO, in February 1943 that there were but twelve tank ships left in the North Atlantic. The German navy sank 3,000 ships and fourteen million tons of supplies during World War II. The convoy which suffered the most left the Straits of Brooklyn on Thanksgiving Day of 1942, taking 42 ships out, and bringing 21 into Liverpool. In the same war, the United States could not resupply its garrison on Bataan, and suffered tragic loss. The Japanese suffered the same fate in the same war, so both sides have had experience.

5. The Principle of Shortage and Waste — Every nation must realize that shortage in needed supplies is inevitable, and that its troops are fundamentally wasteful.

The standard economic theory of a few years back said that a general overproduction of goods for peaceful consumption has never existed, and probably never will. This assumes that never in the past and probably never in the future can a peaceful population receive everything in consumption goods it would like to have, and be willing to make reasonable sacrifices to obtain. No commander, likewise, ever had everything he reasonably considered necessary for the efficient performance of his mission. Even if he is admirably supplied by the home front, yet there may be oversupply of some items and a serious shortage in others. Reduction of this persistent menace requires skilled, dedicated, and informed staff officers to estimate needs correctly, and to see that the supplies are delivered where needed.

An example of adequate supplies being at the wrong place at the right time is the failure of General Patton in his first assault on the Siegfried Line. He had punched through these fortifications almost without opposition when his tanks ground to a stop for lack of fuel. He cannibalized everything he could find, including the Air Force's fuel tanks, but still he had to withdraw. The next time he forced the line it cost his own and the enemy's forces very great and very useless casualties. The public knows this story very well, but it should be told that the gasoline supply at the beach head was adequate, and so was the transport to bring it forward. The public should be told that the theft of fuel by the logistic troops was enormous, first a jerrycan here and there, then a truckload, and then whole convoys disappeared into the Franco-Belgian blackmarket. Furthermore, some headquarters higher than Patton's deliberately refused him the gasoline needed for his victory. The reason for this denial was controversial at the time, and one supposes that it still is.

The analogous, or almost paradoxical principle is that even in times of stress, logistic economies leave much to be desired unless the most stringent discipline is applied, and it rarely is. War is a wasteful operation. Even at best, it is extreme action, and in such conditions, equipment gets broken, is lost, or suffers from poor maintenance. One can observe, however, that poor men rarely waste supplies, but the allied troops in World War II considered themselves rich men. "There is always more where that came from" was the attitude. Theft has been mentioned, and it is sad to say that very little discipline was applied to the thieves. One of the articles of war plainly said that whoever steals supplies in time of war shall suffer death, or whatever the court-martial shall direct. The death penalty was never invoked against wholesale theft. Courts-martial were few, and their decrees were mild. The story of pilferage and theft should be written, but not by this author who was very familiar with it.

Theft and normal wear and tear aside, soldiers will throw away equipment not needed at the moment. The Salisbury Plain was covered with good, woolen blankets thrown away by British troops during their training exercises. The soldiers could not be burdened or bothered. The Normandy invasion took place in summer, and the American troops threw away their fine blankets by the thousands. Misty and cool though the weather was, they believed in lightening their burdens. Then when the Ardennes campaign came, the combat troops suffered bitterly for lack of blankets. Their remarks regarding the logistic command were as critical as they were unjust.

6. *The Principle of Continuing Civilian Support* — War in all its forms, and in the supply function particularly, rests on the morale of the citizens.

The British civilian productive element in World War II was superb. The guns-or-butter choices were likewise well made by the Germans, for both sides knew what the price of defeat would be. No American civilians have actually suffered since the southerners underwent their defeat, and the northerners experienced no shortages at all. The civilians endured some inconveniences in World War II, but hardly more. The Korean and southeast Asian adventures caused no one to go without hamburgers-all-the-way. Regardless of social problems at home, civilians must realize that until war as a means of settling international politico-economic disputes is foresworn, the stockpiles adequate for emergencies will not exist at the outbreak unless they make them so. They must consider that the alternatives are reverses, defeat, loss of strategic territory, all of which may or may not be temporary. A foreign policy of roll-over-at-anybody's-demand is a situation which they, not the military, must consider.

Other than in nations-at-arms, civilian resistance to the logistic buildup in times of peace must be expected. If the civilian population cannot be convinced, or perhaps reminded, that they own the government, and that it acts in their name, the civilian attitude towards peacetime logistic backlogs will be negative.

In conclusion, as war becomes more complicated, the requirements of the logistic phase will be more damaging and complex. The foregoing general principles will not operate less severely, but more so. While everyone deplores this, no one has found an answer to the problem that a larger and larger percentage of troops will perform logistic rather than combat functions. From no one being detailed to logistic work among subpolitical, pre-Columbian Americans, the percentage rose to three out of every ten United States soldiers in World War I France being engaged in supply or administrative roles. The enormous improvements in technology between Wilson's war and that of Franklin Roosevelt raised this from the above figure to nine out of every ten soldiers being assigned rear-area work. In spite of borrowing the best managerial principles from civilian industry, this nine to one ratio has not been decreased, nor will it soon be in light of the progression and complication of military technology. No one knows what the demands on manpower the future may bring, but one almost hesitatingly suggests that American women power has not really been tapped for non-dangerous tasks. War without danger? Who will be exempt from peril next time? The dedication and skill of women in administrative work surely equals that of men.

Many sociologists look upon administration as the weak link in

American civilian life. This may be, and the increase of man-hour-dollars requirements of the administration and instruction in the universities where these gentlemen teach is not particularly promising. Yet, the military bureaucracy has not grown disproportionately to that of civilian industry and government. There is reason to think that remarkable advances have been made, and cause one to wonder if they have been enough.

Repetitive though this may be, we cannot think of tactical victory today without placing it on the shoulders of logistic success. The Principle of the Offensive, along with initiative, can be vitiated by logistic insufficiency. An army suffering from lack may be thrown on the defensive, and as has been often said, the defensive cannot win. All European states planned to go on the offensive in 1914, but after the first shock, it was seen that both sides lost initiative because of logistic poverty. Neither side could succeed, so trench fighting stabilized the war into one of position and attrition. All that either side could try for was to maintain the daily needs of combat, and both or all sides did it only fairly well. Nobody stockpiled enough materials to seize the offensive. This was done only when the Germans were convinced that the United States could send limitless supplies and replacements abroad, which ability they originally doubted.

The Principle of Mass and Sufficient Numbers always has depended on supply. Modern large scale, multi-front war cannot be waged without an intense knowledge of logistics. It seems to many observers that the quality of logistic commanders and their staffs is excellent in all major powers, but that of the subordinate troops, especially in maintenance, leaves much to be desired. All fronts are worldwide ones today, to the extent that some military theorists see strategy and logistics downgrading the importance of battlefield tactics. One might claim that tactics shrank to the minor type in both World Wars, that very few British flyers won the Battle for Britain, and that only a few British and American divisions actually achieved tactical victories in World War II. Aside from the occasional Communist conventional offensives, none of which succeeded tactically, Viet Nam was usually the operation of companies, and occasionally of battalions.

Man is a classifying animal, and generally it is well that he is. He could not have become the philosopher, the scientist, or even a reasonably successful, socially transacting human being if this were not so. We cultivate and refurbish this innate tendency in our very young children. We say to them, "These two objects are both small and brown, but this is a cookie, and therefore edible, but that is a stone and you must not swallow it." Nevertheless, ever since man discovered his classifying ability, he has yielded to a temptation to overuse it. He longs to stuff his environment into tidy, watertight compartments. Every competent scientist, taxonomist, or even a reflective layman knows that this will not do. Many types of even natural phenomena run into each other, overlap each other's boundaries, and the materials with which behavioral scientists and social philosophers are especially cursed with these continua. Behavioral science systems of classification are usually averages, or as the sociologist Leopold von Wiese said, are ideal-typical abstractions. Now all great captains and all the greater statesmen know that politics, logistics, strategy, and tactics cannot be separated, but operate as four functions of a vast, systematic whole. Ever since the end of primitive war, it has been just as vain to say which is the more important as to ask a man on his way home from his work which is the more important to him, his eyes or his ears. Failure to recognize this can result only in social, economic, political, and usually personal humiliation.

Consider the following example of the blending of politics, strategy, and tactics. Although his genocidal treatment of Jews had drawn only breast-beating and chest-thumping from the United States government, it made the political decision to fight Hitler just about as soon as he absorbed and rationalized the French economy. Having a fairly friendly and fairly secure base in Great Britain, several year's of logistic buildup were absolutely necessary for the projected invasion. Then the decision to invade from the northwest instead of through the "soft underbelly of Europe" was made politically, with perhaps strategic overtones. Once German intelligence had discovered this, a faulty strategic decision was made by that great captain, Field Marshal von Rundstedt. Erwin Rommel had reasoned the more clearly, but Rundstedt was the superior. The latter persisted in thinking, or hoping, that the invasion would come across the North Sea from Britain's East Anglian coast to the gentle beaches of the Low Countries. His great compatriot, von Clausewitz, had said that strategy is the art of waging war on a map, but the field marshal did not study his charts enough. He knew that if the invasion was to be towards the beaches of Belgium and the Netherlands, he could contain it while he still had numerical superiority, and inhibit any effort to build a land supply base.

Unfortunately, for him, the Anglo-American staffs followed his reasoning. Being competent strategists, they knew that they had to invade and control a peninsula, either Brittany or Normandy. They knew that they had to run across such a neck of land so that they could protect their flanks from superior forces by the sea, and hold off any frontal counterattack with relatively few men until they were logistically capable of resuming the offensive. This tactical and victorious thrust from one coast of Normandy to the other was accomplished by First Army under Omar Bradley. Later, Third Army under George Patton could safely land and deploy behind this shield.

In those days, a field army consumed 35,000 tons of supplies per day. This required a tremendous logistic buildup in the protected zone, the Cotentin Peninsula of Normandy. The American effort was successful under the intelligent and vigorous commanding general of the Advanced Section, Communications Zone. That campaign produced some great names—Bradley, Patton, and others— but if the logistician Ewart Plank of the Advanced Section had failed, even in part, the Anglo-Americans would have been driven into the sea, and some of the above great names would never have acquired their luster. Normandy was a success because politics, strategy, tactics, and logistics cooperated as a functioning whole system.

The map-reading capacity of American politicians was defective in the Viet Nam adventure, and history is already looking on them with a lackluster eye. The American people, accepting a political decision, threw untold tons of material into this venture, and lost thousands of good men without achieving a victory. The generals were politically forbidden to secure their left flank, which was subject to constant attack, and for the same political reasons they could not inhibit the transport of enemy supplies and replacements along highways officially declared to be neutral. This was a strategic blunder which no amount of logistic support and tactical competence could ever overcome. It should have ended in disaster instead of humiliation had the Americans' enemy been led by a good, second-class general instead of Giap.

Much of the foregoing has been the story of expanding logistic functional efficiency. That increasing complexity had accompanied this technological success has been accepted by thinking men as a dysfunctional price to be paid for winning. The question now proposed is, has this hypercomplication been accompanied by an increasing permeability and vulnerability? Indeed it has, every step of the way, if for no other reason than that such expansion necessarily means that more and more people become involved in the logistic process, who know more and more about the situation, leaving more and more loose ends of information which an able enemy can pick up and use to his own advantage.

Hitlerist Germany was well aware of this. It made plans to thwart the American effort as the tones from Washington became more warlike. Scores of able saboteurs were trained and introduced into the United States, and it is remarkable that they were not more successful than they were. The Germans wisely abandoned this plan, and permitted the Americans to go to the expense of fabricating these supplies, then relied on submarine warfare to see that they did not arrive in Europe. There was some brilliant espionage and counterespionage work on both sides. If the reader can persuade his local cinema to show the film *The House on Ninety-second Street*, he will learn a great deal.

That all modern major wars are in part civil wars cannot be overemphasized. It must not be assumed, therefore, that all members of an actual or potential government will sympathize with the official position. Parliamentary democracies are particularly subject to penetration. Clement Vallandigham, a northern politician, was so helpful to the Confederate cause that he was arrested and deposited behind the lines of his real friends. Neither the presidency nor the supreme court were as delicate in those days concerning the rights of dissenters as they later became.

The author is not going to yield to the temptation to cite the figures he has about the number of American workmen engaged in highly sensitive war material plants and offices. If they are accessible to me, you, too, with some industry can discover them. It is also known that the United States services of security have constantly improved their personnel and methods. Nevertheless, it is impossible to investigate with any real thoroughness the backgrounds and records of the many thousands having access to highly classified information, and who may or may not be enemy agents. At the present moment, it is to be suspected that the most successful tool of foreign industrial espionage is the individual working alone in a particular plant or office. He is trained not only in penetrating the secrecy barrier but in protecting his own security. He is extremely hard to detect, and even harder to convict when he is unmasked. He does not know any members of his friends' apparatus save his immediate contact, and then only by code name. Somehow valuable information does get through, and this clever fellow may be the source of much of it.

Indeed, one might ask about the very top of the military-industrial complex. Is it permeable? Are there potential or actual enemy sympathizers in the management, in banking? It is common knowledge, of course, that Lenin's trip from exile back into Russia to engineer the Bolshevist revolution was arranged and financed by a powerful New York financial firm.

A concluding fact of grave seriousness must be squarely faced. Warring states before the close of the renaissance recognized the concept of neutrality only when they had to. The rise and acceptance of the maxim of international law provided the neutrals with clear-cut rights and duties. Great wars of serious ideological and economic importance have since World War I been pushing us back to the ancient doctrine of "who is not for us is against us." All major wars, and most minor ones as well, have been global wars for some time instead of tidy little bouts between two nations. This is generally accepted as a truism, but few have identified the real cause thereof, and the factor which enables this to be so. The readers of these pages have already done so. It is the logistic success of major powers raised to the highest political power.

One wishes that those responsible for naming modern wars would improve their arithmetic. The American Revolution sparked the real World War I. Great Britain paid for the neglect of its navy, and the French supplied the continentals almost at will. The revolting colonies were agricultural and mercantile, their munitions factories grossly inadequate for the task at hand. The English general (and dramatist) John Burgoyne's defeat at the hands of Horatio Gates at Saratoga encouraged the French to come to the American logistic support. Indeed, the Bourbon West Indies squadron under Count de Grasse delivered a disgraceful defeat to the British Admiral Graves in the waters around Yorktown. A French army under the able Count de Rochambeau, later marshal of France, and later the guillotine's victim, landed unopposed eventually to crush the equally able Lord Cornwallis. The American Revolution was far from just a family affair. Spain was in it from the beginning. The great Governor Galves pinned down a strong British force at Baton Rouge, which Cornwallis sorely needed. Indeed, the War for Independence sparked a global war which did not end until Napoleon's evacuation to St. Helena. Almost every nation of any importance, and some without much, such as the Kingdom of the Two Sicilies, had their fingers in this economic pie.

The American Civil War did not actually break forth as World War II, but had a potential barely suppressed. Economics and supplies lay at the center of the danger. England's Lancashire textile mills had no wish to be cut off from southern cotton by a Union and tariff-minded victory. Great Britain built and largely manned warships such as the *Alabama* for the Confederacy, and supervised the blockade-running, as we have already remarked. It was touch and go between the United States government and that of Great Britain after the *Trent* affair. Lincoln threatened Canada, with apparent

Confederate approval, and Britain strengthened its border garrison. The Confederates were planning to annex Spanish Cuba in event of their own victory. The Confederate States also had ambitions regarding the natural resources of Mexico, a fact known to the French Emperor Napoleon III, who moved an army and a puppet ruler into that nation as a counterstroke. His own war being finished, Lincoln threatened the French with a combined army of Union and Confederate veterans, and surely aided Juarez in his liberating efforts.

The point in question is that for many years great industrial nations have been able to supply themselves and others with armaments over vast distances. This is logistic war in which direct strategic and tactical confrontation need not enter, at least for the time being. Distant brush wars are ideal for trying out new equipment for flaws, and for embarrassing an enemy with which one does not prefer to fight openly, at least for now. The Spanish Civil War, North and South Viet Nam, Israel and the Arab states, where next?

A chapter on logistics could have a built-in tendency to overpraise the supply role. Let us pause for just one word of warning. An adequately supplied army, even a large one, cannot win on this virtue alone. The satrap Datis, at the command of the Persian Emperor Darius, landed vast stores in 490 B.C. on the plain of Marathon, and was whipped to ribbons by the superior generalship of the Athenian Miltiades. A general or a nation can rely too much on logistic superiority in contrast with good soldiering. George B. McClellan was so meticulous in his logistic preparations that he has gone down in history with a name worse than he probably deserved! Having overwhelmed the Germans, who had been softened by others, twice in a century by logistic superiority, the Americans tend to think that their assembly lines can win any conflict. The Detroit type of warfare did not win over a third-class satellite in Viet Nam, even before China and Russia took over Hanoi's logistic battle. Hitler's army was barely competent to defeat Poland, but The Leader was convinced that his stockpile was adequate for an attack on Russia. Russians in the past have been logistically smug. They sent troops in summer uniforms and without adequate ammunition from subtropical Crimea to fight in the cold of the northern front, and the men joined the Bolsheviks in droves. Stalin, likewise, was overconfident of his factories in World War II, and had to be supplied massively by the United States over the costly and deadly Murmansk Run. Let no one be deceived. No war since First Manasses can be fought without adequate factories. Factories, though, can only implement victory. Men start wars. Men fight wars. Men win or lose, and it is men who suffer.

ENERGY USE AND SUPPLY

And so the section on the material culture of war ends with this partial story of the great mothering service of supply. Why should the infantry claim to be the Queen of Battles, when its function is not feminine at all? Logistics is the great mother. She feeds and clothes her children. She provides them with new toys. She wipes away their tears when wounded or ailing, and mourns over their graves. She replaces them with younger brothers. It behooves the combat services to cease thinking of her as a barely tolerated, camp-following slut, and consider her the matriarch on whose efficiency their activity depends. If she is not the Queen of Battles, she may well become the Empress of Global War.

FOOTNOTES AND REFERENCES

[1] Stockbridge H. Barker, "Blueprint for Victory," *Army Logistician*, July-August, 1972. Logistic principles are cited with the permission of *The Army Logistician*.

PART III
MILITARY PRACTITIONERS

INTRODUCTION TO MILITARY PRACTITIONERS

No tool, no matter how fine a one, can be more efficient than the men who design, direct, and use it. In each artifact there is an element of inductive experiment, or science, but a certain amount of art still remains in it. This is not only true so far as the art and science of warfare are concerned but especially so, and in some ways peculiar to that culture complex. To repeat the position that warfare is a sociological phenomenon, is one of nonmaterial rather than material culture. It is futile to say that the weaponry is unimportant in quality, quantity, or function. It is not as vital to victory as the men who handle it, though, and this is a professional rather than a civilian doctrine. Now a body of military men, large or small, may be considered a tool in the hands of the commander, be he adequate or otherwise. This forces a delving deeper into the search for the truly military personnel, to the practitioners of true warfare.

The key word in the last sentence refers to persons, and a person is by definition a biological individual to which innumerable conditioned responses have been added. This speaks of human beings, and if a commander considers his men mere things, someone will be sorry. This eventually regretful fellow might be just that captain of the host. A tool is inert and inactive when the artisan is not using it. A musical instrument lies silent away from the hands of the artist. Neither of these is characteristic of the soldier. He is active and vocal in peace as in war, in garrison as well as in combat. A tool, a weapon, an instrument may be thrown away when no longer useful, or destroyed when obsolete and broken. It is a very unwise policy which treats veterans in this way. Yes, warrior, soldier, or units thereof, fine or otherwise, are weapons in the hands of the commander, skillful or inept, but men and commands thereof are people, and people can be hurt. Each human is a specific person with traits peculiar to himself. He has goals, aspirations, and vulnerabilities outside his military establishment. He is idiosyncratic. To paraphrase the oft-quoted motto of Clyde Kluckhohn: Every soldier is like all other soldiers. Every soldier is like some other soldiers. Every soldier is like no other soldier. A wise commander will never forget this. The staff personnel officer may requisition so many "bodies" of certain specifications from the human resource pool, but what his general gets is so many people.

Chapter 10

THE SOLDIER

A Man of Discipline, Training, and Organization

The basic concept of true, or politico-tactical warfare includes that of the role and status of the soldier. The reader is asked to recall the discussion of primitive war, and he will see that the differences between the warrior and the soldier are sociological ones. Simple as they are, once they were conceptualized set into a pattern, a revolution of such magnitude was produced that the world has never been the same since, nor can it be, barring a holocaust which would evaporate civilization.

There is nothing arcane and mysterious about all this. Most of the difference between warriors and soldiers lies in the five simple sociological traits, namely, (1) division of labor in the group enterprise, (2) training, (3) command, (4) discipline, and (5) organization. None of these is a separate concept, for they all assume the existence of the others in the production of the soldier.

As for division of labor, the practice of war cannot go far beyond that used in the arts of peace. Complexity in the technological, political, and military realms usually has a parallel development. This relationship is not absolute, however, as long, bitter wars, successful or unsuccessful, have taught the subsystems that must cooperate better in the future. It is certain for example, that the loose collection of Cherokee villages, populated by men who did very much as they chose, once paid attention to "chiefs" only when it pleased them, were urged by war to undertake a more efficient social organization. Harried and defeated by white settlers, this aggregate became a powerful priest-kingship, and very quickly, too. The Cherokee became soldiers instead of warriors in short order. For the most part, however, the arts of peace are the schoolmasters of military structure. War is a cooperative enterprise operating under meticulous division of labor, and this is a virtue rarely acquired by warriors.

The soldier, in contrast with the warrior, is a man acquainted with troop specialization. Granted that loving cooperation between infantry, cavalry, artillery, engineers, and aviation is not easily enforced even in this day, The Principle of the Combined Employment of All Forces, and hence victory, depends on it. The logistic element must be dependable in the performance of its supply function.

The soldier is also a trained man. This is not saying that the warrior is not. As a matter of record, it is doubtful if any military man spends as much time year in and year out in training as the stateless Indians of Southeast United States, or of the Great Plains. These men devoted far more time to athletics and sports which they considered hardening exercises for war than any soldier, indeed than they did in economic production, and their women permitted it. Valiant men of this type trained themselves, which is a far cry from heeding the suggestions and criticisms of a sergeant. They were taught the arts of weapons use, stalking and spying, and other actions, by their fathers or parental surrogates, who were inside their own kinship. Their primary loyalties and emotional attachments were therefore to the kin, and not to an overall system. The soldier originally may have been taught many militarily useful crafts by his father, uncle, or older brother as a spare-time occupation, but he was taught warfare by a man outside his kin, probably a stranger, engaged in a full-time trade.

We are speaking, of course, of the familial educational process inherent in all human societies. This can be excellently, indifferently, or incompetently performed among our own civilian selves, from the family, through kindergarten, to the university graduate school. The conditioning, enculturization, and socialization of the family is almost ineradicable in later life. It therefore seems wise to isolate young recruits into training centers to learn new skills, but especially to form new fraternal squad families. Some research has been done into the success of this stick-and-carrot training. It would seem to be highly successful for some young conscripts, providing youths from the poorly structured families of today with their first strong father figures and sense of community. These ex-boys leave the service better men than when they entered. By contrast, many cannot adapt to this life, and are given unrewarding busy-work, or allowed to malinger, or are otherwise rejected by despairing or incompetent instructors. These leave the service even lesser men then when they came in. The Soviet Union also puts political commissars among such troops to guarantee inculcation of the approved attitudes towards social living, punishing latent and manifest dissidents. Other powers, holding to a more democratic system of sanctions, apparently do not succeed as well.

Training young officers is something else. In the bad old days, the fathers of the supernumerary sons of the British aristocracy bought these lads commissions like so much merchandise. They were sent to "good" (socially acceptable) regiments by influential fathers with adequate uniforms and allowances, and no training at all. This was provided by their sergeants major. These striplings did well in Wellington's Peninsular campaign, and held and died in their dancing pumps at Waterloo. By contrast, they were sent to command loyalist (Tory) recruits in the American Revolution, and contributed much to the British failure by their arrogance. In contrast with this haphazard manner, the vast sums spent by the American people on West Point, university reserve officers training corps, summer reserve training, needs a thorough reinspection in light of the expense/success ratio. But at that, civilian education is in no position to snub the military.

A soldier is a man under command. This is a key concept, for if a warrior accepts subordination, he is either a real soldier or about to become one. Warriors are individualists for all the skill and dedication they may possess. A soldier is under command except when he is engaged in recreation, and often then as well. No two simple privates can be on duty in the same place without one of them being in charge. One has heard some amusing arguments between the two old sergeants as to which is in command, and the senior always is unless specifically removed by higher authority. Oh yes, one has been entertained by hearing two second lieutenants arguing about which can order the other to do something disagreeable, and having a field-grade officer suggest that arguing rank among second lieutenants is like arguing virtue among prostitutes, but one man *is* senior, and *is* in command.

The soldier is a disciplined fighting man, and in this lies one of his greatest contrasts with the warrior. We have noted that the warrior is an individualist. The soldier is group-oriented. There were far more warriors than soldiers in pre-Columbian America north of the Rio Grande, which is one great reason why the Europeans took the Indians' land so easily.

How different they were from the men of the tower, those mercenaries to whom King John and others gave the defense of their large castles. Almost any person does well in anything when winning, when the situation seems charming, but what if defeat seems probable? The men of the tower fought to hold the outer ward if the barbican and gate fell, and retreated into the inner ward. If defeated there, they found their way into the donjon, there to fight up the tower step-by-step, perhaps to die to a man on the final platform? What of the men in the days of the square-rigged fighting ship? What if the enemy had out-gunned you and had succeeded in boarding? Would the crew fight with cutlass, pike, and pistol until they had to surrender the quarterdeck? Victory has been wrenched out of the jaws of defeat by such men. Remember that his leaky old *Bonhomme Richard* had been battered into a sinking mass by the time the British captain asked for surrender, but Jones and his crew grappled and boarded, and defeated the opposition man to man. Warriors, by contrast, buckle in heart and body when things look bad. Hilaire Belloc spoke on this matter.[1]

> "Every member wishes to separate himself from the band when it is in danger. Indeed, the wish to decamp is always strongest at just that point, the tactically critical point, when the group is in the greatest danger. The prime object of discipline and training is to prevent this."

What is the meaning of this word, one so repugnant to many of the self-oriented? Frederick the Great defined the concept as the art of making the soldier fear his officers more than the enemy. This is one of the most shortsighted of all the great Prussian's *bon mots*. Discipline is not necessarily the technique of killing people and getting killed, either by the enemy or one's officers. Killing is the motive of warriors, but in wars of maneuver, few people actually get killed. The Chinese warlords of the early part of this century knew this. So did the master tactician Vegetius. So did all the captains during the War in Lace period. Discipline is not the art of killing, but the one of winning. Discipline is skill in seeing that the group's work gets done, and if this means the subordination of one man to another, so be it. Military discipline, one surely sees, does not differ too much from that of commercial and industrial society. It appears whenever there is intense division of labor, where it is necessary to coordinate the activities of primary and secondary groups into one functioning whole. It is only more severe in a military situation because the defection of one man, or a small unit, can bring disaster upon the many.

Discipline, then, is the technique of persuading the individual person to subordinate his wishes, goals, and indeed his safety and survival to those of the group. In any structure characterized by minute division of labor, it is rare that the worker or other subordinate can see the picture as a whole, but the teamwork nature of the enterprise cannot be endangered. Military discipline differs only in a matter of degree, for it is the enforcement of intense in-group identification. There can be no doubt but this is one reason why the soldier does not appear until the rise of the state, for this institution's prime reason for existence is the coordination of economic endeavor. There is too little division of labor in premetallurgical societies. Too many if not all pre-commercial cultures are confined to consumption of homemade goods. Self- or kin-reliance rarely produces enough division of labor, and hence social stratification in the arts of peace to inspire much in the practice of war. The warrior is too much a member of the general population. He fights people who are too much like himself socially and culturally. He is insufficiently involved economically, and ideologically not at all. Of course, when confronted by the expansion of civilization, he can acquire both economic and ideological involvement, namely the defense of his own space and culture. The Apaches Geronimo and Cochise did very well, and Crazy Horse defeated Custer *in one battle*. The soldier is not a member of the general population. He is a specialist. Every man can drive a nail, but carpenters do better. Any man can punch another in the nose, but trained boxers do better. Soldiers accomplish their mission through disciplined group endeavor. Warriors do not. And so, one cannot speak separately of military and other discipline apart from organization. This means mutual protection and cohesion. It is in this that the safety of the group and the individual person lies. Military organization is the cause and effect of military discipline.

Any discussion of discipline is one of personality formation or reformation. It is one of conditioning and reconditioning the reflexes of the subject. It is training in the permanent or temporary suppression of natural or acquired traits, tendencies, wants, and wishes which impede the group effort, and furthering those which are thereunto useful. It is indeed an extension of the infantile socialization of making a child want to do what it has to do. This is easier in a garrison state such as that of the South African Zulu, where from infancy boys were taught that the military provided the only avenue to goal satisfaction and social recognition. It is harder in modern America where the modal personality is shaped along lines of individual success. A wise commander must be well aware of the dominant culture and preferred personality of his men, issuing his orders along such lines. When it is necessary to do otherwise, and the time will come when it is, this must be done with such skill, understanding, and sympathy that his unpleasant orders cannot be considered tyrranical. The commander must want to live, too.

Just to what extent the individual person should be subjected to the group constitutes a delicate question on the part of commanders. An effective fighting man must have some freedom, as this book occasionally comments on the failure of armed slaves. Effective discipline is something which comes from within, and in the very end, the only kind on which the commander can rely is the self-discipline of his soldiers. The amount of cohesion and subordination depends on the situation, the kind of actions fought, and the weaponry to accomplish the mission. There is a fine balance here, and all too often a war begins with a concept of discipline successful in the past, but which the stern laboratory of battle reveals as outmoded. Sometimes a commander can learn in time to avoid disaster.

One consideration which stands out is that a command which has more "chiefs" than "Indians" is hard to discipline. Officers by the nature of their work are and must be more individualistic than other soldiers. A recent case in point is the record of the United States Army Air Force before it became a separate service. Combat flying was originally performed exclusively by officers, the enlisted personnel remaining on the ground for the grubby work of servicing the planes. Then, as World War II had to be fought, the large bombers carried enlisted men as well as officers, airborne soldiers of high-chevroned rank. Far too often a great plane was manned by "buddies," the only real rank aloft was that of rates of pay and little decorations on the costume. Far too seldom such planes returned to the base. There must be subordination in war, and this requires some social distance. Buddies cannot command buddies and expect that obedience on which survival depends. Bloody and flaming death in The Bright Blue Yonder finally taught a grim lesson.

There is an old story to be read here. Even though the cohesion of classical Greek units existed due to their strong public spirit and sense of ethnic unity, nevertheless, Hellenic forces were horrible examples of the lack of discipline to be found in armies of equals, or almost equals, possessing their own armaments. Athenian discipline was almost nonexistent under the old patrician republic. A commander could only prefer charges for insubordination *after* the war was over, and the legislature was very loathe to punish one of its own kind for exercising the dominant egalitarian attitude and behavior of the national character. Whenever you wonder why Greek polities did not last longer than they did, remember this fact. As for the stern Spartans, they were but little better than the Athenians. Their insubordination brought disaster upon them more than once, for example at Mantinea. Athens eventually corrected this flaw by organizing an army of mercenary professionals, but it was a lesson learned too late. This treatise frequently emphasizes the family feeling of successful military units. The Athenian phalanx consisted entirely of "fathers" and no "sons," and everybody considered himself the personal and professional equal of the general. The units were too large, and only the Spartans could break them down into more intimate subunits.

The Romans, by contrast, provide evidence that the best discipline is self-discipline. Their old patrician military republic had a citizens army, too, but the Roman had a better appreciation of unit cohesion. Furthermore, almost from the start the legion was subdivided into subsidiary units wherein the association and command could be more intimate. Every Roman officer, even a lowly centurion, could expect his orders to be obeyed. No classical Greek officer could say this, not even the general.

The claim is made in some quarters that the decline of Rome was due to one in the old Roman discipline. This is not quite fair. Rome's collapse, whatever its other causes, was one in internal and political capacity. The despotic Leviathan polity seemed good to Augustus, but it proved a failure in the end. Generals constantly trying to become emperors themselves produced such diminishing political equilibrium that the standards of training and discipline could not help but be lowered. Later and very able emperors, such as Aurelian, Carus, Claudius II, and Probus, tried to restore this old Roman virtue by harsh punishments, but it was too late.

The reader then may well ask, if Roman group discipline ensured such good results, why was it that the egalitarian Germans stopped them at the line of the Rhine? Most Germans were surely tribal warriors instead of soldiers of a polity. The answer is plain. The Romans were stopped by the extension of their lines of communications and supply, not by Germanic valor. The Germans rarely defeated the Romans in battle, and when they did, it was usually due to the stupidity of such a commander as Varus. As has happened since, and may happen again, the Germans fighting as guerrillas wore the Romans down far from the latter's bases. Neither were all the Germans political and military incompetents, particularly the Chatti. (If one knows the operation of Grimm's law of phonetic change, he will see that the modern word for Chatti is Hessians.) Tacitus said (*Germania*, 30), the italics being mine, of the Hessian naive republic:

> "They elect magistrates and listen to the man elected; know their place in the ranks and recognize opportunities; reserve their attack; have time for everything; entrench at night, distrust

luck, but rely on courage; and—rarest thing of all, which only Roman discipline has permitted to attain—depend on the initiative of the general rather than on that of the soldier. Their whole strength lies in the infantry, whom they load with iron tools and baggage, in addition to their arms. *Other Germans may be seen going to battle, but the Chatti go to war."*

What Roman civilization as was spared for us depended on the perfection of that heavy cavalry against which the barbarian could not stand, either as a footman or light horseman. Yet, as a base for disaster, the feudal cataphract never really got the tribesman out of his bones. He was always in part a warrior. He often deserted the campaign in a huff, and took his vassals with him. Added to this were the requirements of the heavy cavalry line. The shock assault was almost entirely delivered by units composed of what we today would call commissioned officers. This is the repetition of the old Athenian folly, is it not? Too many sons and not enough fathers. Indeed, the knightly title of "Sir," and that of the head, "Sire," both mean father.

True, the discipline of apprentice knights was as severe as the world has seen. A five-year-old upper-class boy was sent as a page into the castle of a great noble, ripped from the bosom of a supposedly loving family, and taught obedience. He not only became a servant but suffered blows from the cook for not scouring pots and pans to that culinary serf's liking. The page was required to serve at table in something like a busboy's capacity. Indeed, Edward the Black Prince served King John of France, who was his prisoner, as if the great Prince of Wales were only a menial before a king, any king. (We have lost this lesson, have we not? Might be worth trying again.) Then through the extremely severe training in arms, he became a bachelor, and then an esquire and, if finally successful, a knight. Once having acquired the golden spurs, this soldier was then an aristocrat, and by theory, the equal of everyone in the brotherhood of chivalry. Far too often he behaved in just this way. He owned his own horse and expensive armor, so was not subordinate to the Service of Supply. Again, the heavy cavalry charge was by necessity the exploit of skilled, rich men, and as soon as the trumpet sounded for it, the knight was on his own. A cavalry line can be kept in order when forming, and at the walk, but once the trot has been achieved, and the extended gallop is entered, control vanishes. The knight's very work and weapons, then, made him an individualist.

We have seen that only the finest infantry could stand up to this charge. The knight originally had no such opposition. He swept the foot element before him like chaff, but good infantry did come on the scene. The feudal cavalry, however, learned too late to save the Latin Kingdom of Jerusalem. They had found no opposition in the poor infantry which originally faced them. The Arab light cavalry provided them only with fun. The Arabs could not learn. The first Turks, however, did learn from their crashing first defeats at knightly hands. They developed superb infantry, men who could stand and dare heavy cavalry to strike home. A recent historian says of them that "The Turkish army was...a perfect example of stringent discipline, of a rigorous and even fanatic unity of purpose, of the concentration of supreme tactical power in the sole person of the Sultan."[2] The Near East was lost, perhaps forever, to western civilization, which was probably a first-class calamity.

The United States may have this lesson to learn all over again. A very large proportion of today's enlisted men, or rather involuntary conscripts, sometimes surpass their officers in education, cultivation, and sometimes in income as well. Much can be said for and against an officer class, but with the democratization of the American officer corps went the ability to treat arrogantly young soldiers whose every phase of life has taught them to judge for themselves.

A similar story may be read from the modern weaponry. A sergeant in a modern armored unit controls equipment costing more than that of one of Washington's regiments, having very close to the same firepower, and requiring several times the technical knowledge. The picture of Marquis de Lafayette riding up and down the ranks of the Pennsylvania Line and lashing soldiers with his riding crop would be somewhat out of place in this day. The dispersion needed if and when atomic artillery now in the possession of the two great powers is used will require even more self-reliance in small units.

An African ethnologist could recount several examples of superb discipline among his subjects. The fact that Negro Africa was particularly incompetent except where strong kingships arose, and there both discipline and performance were excellent. African kings were notoriously contemptuous of human life, demanding holocausts of their own subjects for decapitation, so it is not surprising that the Kabaka (king) of Uganda inflicted bloody punishment on his defeated army. He did not lead the troops himself, giving this task to a professional general. This worthy was invariably executed after a defeat, a practice no doubt providing dedication and efficiency.

The Zulu King Chaka might be called the harshest disciplinarian of all times, and he swept the other Negroes, the Boers, and several English battalions before him. He said that all cowards should die, and even if there had been none in the battle, the officers appointed a few. A soldier returning from the fray without his *assegai* (short spear) was killed as a matter of course. Units of young recruits and individuals were taught implicit obedience by ordering them to kill a lion without weapons, either as groups or alone. A veteran *impi* (regiment) was ordered to slaughter a unit which retreated or was defeated. A soldier could be ordered to kill an innocent son or brother just as a loyalty test. Zulu discipline nevertheless did come from within the personality. Men delighted in dying for Chaka. Suffering in his service was the only worthwhile avenue to honor. Chaka, like Patton and other great captains, was as lavish with praise and reward as he was with punishment. It is a petty commander who can conceive of the stick without the carrot.[3]

Battle discipline is something anyone can understand, but the more complicated the society and polity to be served, the longer time needed for training, and the interminable waiting required before commanders and their staffs can coordinate the complex troops organization into battle effectiveness, the longer the period of "hurry-up-and-wait" which all soldiers resent. The longer the training period, the worst this is, especially as it cannot be expected that all units will arrive at combat readiness at the same time. This is a disease particularly afflicting mass-man armies, indoctrinated or over-indoctrinated with an ideological enthusiasm which is bound to be eroded by long periods of doing nothing worthwhile under conditions of field or semi-field discomfort. Idleness, even when pretended to be something else, damages the morale of all troops except elite professionals. Such life is short on excitement and long on boredom. It is during this period that discipline is almost as important as in combat. Morale declines and unit cohesiveness is lost, which are difficult to regain when needed, and almost never can be by the commander under whom they occur. This man must be moved before the unit actually becomes operational. It is at such times that great command skill must be exercised, an ability always under short supply.

This is a period of make-work, or busy-work details, of training which does not train, all of which normal troops see through easily. A commander must worry not only in exercising his control over his men but over his junior officers as well, for this "eyewash" work and control is more apparent to them than it is to the troops. Many men who will submit to subordination when it is necessary resent it when it is not. This is not a new problem. It is so old that one would think that the command element could have solved the question of at least two thousand years of known history, but it has not. Tacitus (*Annales*, I, 20) records that a Roman infantry unit early in the reign of Augustus mutinied because its officers doubled the weight of their packs on a practice march on the pretext of increasing hardihood. It was the scourge of both armies in the American Civil War, and might account for the widespread use of illegal narcotics on the Union side. One late Roman event should constitute a lesson to superior commanders. The good Emperor Probus attempted a makework exercise on one idle unit by ordering it to clear a swamp, hardly a proud infantryman's work. Without plan or plot, the troops rose and killed Probus. Remember, Sir, that Probus was a good emperor, a good soldier, and an able commander. The wish to slay a commander of busy-work is always latent, even if it has been some time since it has become overt. Is there any old soldier unto whom these presents may come who will deny the temptation?

Instilling discipline, then, is the art of making soldiers out of those who want to be such and, which is more difficult, out of those who do not want to be. Dedication to a common cause makes this task easier, as among revolutionary soldiers, or the militant Christianity of the three crusading orders, The Order of the Hospital of St. John, The Order of the Temple, and The Teutonic Knights.[4] Fortunately, some of the concept spread among the other crusaders, but not enough and not in time. Disciplinary training in a way rests upon the ambivalent character of primate psychology. There must be rank status in any serious group endeavor, in war especially. All higher primates dislike equality, and feel safe in structured groups, *providing actual abuse is avoided*. The hateful, aggressive features of primate nature must be directed to the common enemy, and restrained within the we-group. By contrast, the very cooperative character of primates must be accentuated and improved within ingroup relations. The nature of discipline depends on the culture and modal personality of the times, the mission, the number of combatants, and the dominant weaponry. These in turn will vary with the changes in the nonmilitary features of the social system, particularly in the technology. Abrupt changes in the social order will produce a voluminous literature of the how-to-do-it nature. Changes in military sociology and technique are no exception.[5]

The next proposition is that the soldier is a fighting man who operates in, for, and through an organization, and the warrior is not. Warriors in stoneworking cultures have too little organization in ordinary life to carry over into pre-combat, combat, and post-combat situations. Organization in war is something else, for "Organization, mutual protection, and cohesion are, were, and shall be vital issues. They are the cause and effect of discipline; they are the fighting man's greatest source of safety."[6]

Organization is part of the military horizon. It is one of the *sine qua non* requirements of true, in contrast with primitive war. Specialization in weapons and troop function is impossible without it. While the great tactical Principle of Correct Formations and the Combined Employment of All Forces cannot operate without it, it is implicit in all the others. There is no more mystery about why military organization succeeds over its lack than why supermarkets have displaced the local, independent grocer in this century. Civilians and soldiers endure it because efficiency requires organization, and the more complex the division of labor in any walk of life, the more organization is required. The more intense the organization, too, the more need for administration, that "army paper work" which is the bane of all field soldiers. It exists because it is indispensible. True, as with all bureaucratic organization, there is such a thing as diminishing returns. It is doubtful if any one man can comprehend what is called "The Pentagon," even the Chairman of the Joint Chiefs of Staff. It has more than one latent dysfunction, we agree, including the loss of contact and communication of the general with his soldiers. There are so many channels between him and them that they are not his any more. Be all this as it may, given similar valor, organized military men win over those who lack it. Prince (Bonnie) Charles Edward Stuart, the Young Pretender, was above organization at the Battle of Culloden, but the equally youthful Duke of Brunswick was not, and we know what happened there.

It is written in Herodotus (I, 103-104) that when the Medes first invaded the Assyrian Empire, they were roundly defeated and expelled. Their king, Cyaraxes, though, was a man who could learn from his enemy and his own mistakes. "It was he who first divided the troops of Asia according to arms, and organized them into separate companies, spearmen, archers, and horsemen; until then they had been mixed together." This ethnological diffusion sent the Medes on their way into history, and they took their Persian kinsmen with them.

A persistent theme of this work is that there is a close connection between the patterns and structure of a society in peace, and the same in its war practice. These patterns seem to operate in an almost functional dependence, for changes in the one are apt to produce changes in the other. Defect in peaceful sociological coherence likewise produces military incapacity. The Thracians, say the old writers, could easily have threatened Greece, but their intense localistic attitudes prevented them. They once had as many as fifty "tribes," or so it is said, and Strabo knew of as many as twenty-two in his time. Herodotus (v. 3) called them the most powerful people in the world, and repeated the opinion that they would have been invincible if they had been able to effect internal unity. They did not, and "herein therefore consists their weakness."

The allied field of tactical organization has been revealed very indifferently in the classical reports. Perhaps this is due to the small size of most submilitary war parties, for in many ways, organization is a function of size. Forbes reports that the Dahomean polity of west Africa could muster fifty thousand men without difficulty at the height of its power, so its army was divided into three echelons.[7] The first division consisted of three thousand females of great alleged ferocity, but whose military effectiveness is open to much doubt. The second consisted of the residents of the capital, including the palace guard. The third consisted of the militia of the able, adult members of the population. The older eyewitnesses were astounded at the regularity of the Dahomean formations with their units, officers, and standards.[8] Yet in other pages we have remarked that even a victorious army almost starved on its way home, so we can be a bit conservative about accepting these reports of excellence.

We know that the Dahomean state was well organized and efficiently administered, and we accept the foregoing ethnographic report on their military effectiveness, but they would undoubtedly have been defeated by that master, King Chaka and his Zulus of east Africa. When that prince came to power, he immediately set about organizing the chaotic Zulu mass, using the traditional age-groups of "circumcision gilds" as a base. These were the boys who had gone through the puberty rituals together, and already had some sense of unity. These were seldom large enough to serve his purposes, so he altered them into regiments. The need of organization is apparent when one considers that Chaka kept a force of 100,000 men under arms, one half of which was on constant call, and the others serving as a reserve. The South African regiment (*impi*, or *yimpi*) was about the size of a modern infantry battalion. The essential tables of organization had been worked out in northern Mthethwaland before the great drive into the south of Africa where we now find them. Chaka had been inspired by his royal predecessor, King Dingiswayo, who knew of Napoleon and tried to imitate him. In any event, King Chaka could probably have swept the classical Greeks before him on his organizing ability alone, for he did just that with the well-armed Boer unit who opposed him, and more than one British regular army unit who tried to help the latter. Both the Dahomeans and Zulu, then, were soldiers and not warriors, even though neither was literate. They both were fighters for established polities, however, and they were not alone in Negro Africa.

Passing to our own tradition, one would wish for more information regarding the Egyptians than is available. It is known that they had separate companies of archers and slingers to provide firepower, and heavy and light infantry for shock and mobility. They did not know the horse until the New Empire, and then used him to form an elite corps of charioteers. We are all but ignorant of their military administration, but as this Leviathan state was over-administered in everything else, we can be sure that the army did not escape bureaucracy. It is known that some men were called "scribes of the army," and that they held senior rank. It is fairly clear that these scribes had logistic responsibility.

The Indo-European-speaking folk entered the written record more as warriors than soldiers. Homer composed magnificent poetry concerning about as poor an army as one could imagine. The "bronze-shirted Greeks" had just emerged into naive pastoral monarchies, and their military organization was as simple as could be, with equally simple results. Homer describes the army as a collection of champions with their followers, and these great men did just about as they pleased. The *Illiad* is a needlessly long poem about an inexcusably long war.

The Greeks learned better, but not too much better. The organization of the Athenian army was simple, one largely based on wealth. The very richest citizens formed a virtually useless light cavalry, they having abandoned the chariot of Homer's day generations before Hellenic greatness. The basis of the fighting army was the phalanx of hoplites, heavily armed infantry of the well-to-do, athletic, politically powerful, and manly, almost completely armored pikemen who have not been excelled as such to this day. A pity they could not have learned from experience as well as they did from philosophers. The poorer and ill-respected free citizens formed a light infantry which the Athenians never learned how to handle. They had the privilege of acting as esquires for the noble hoplites, and occasionally as archers. They could not have been completely poverty-ridden, for they had the leisure to practice and serve without pay. The majority of the population were the disenfranchised and slaves who did the disagreeable noncombat work every army has. There was a corps of slingers enlisted entirely from allies, the Rhodians being the best. The social and military organization was identical. The army was the legislature-in-arms which, after the abolition of the kingship, did not trust each other enough to have a permanent general. The battle was led by a polemarch drawn by lot instead of knowledge, and this poor soul tried to control without intermediate echelons or channels of command. He lost his troops the moment the terrible clash of shields and pikes was effected. As this walking wall of metal won over the Persians, it learned little from them.

The Persians might have won that war, and would have had their army been composed of public spirited freemen instead of such a terrible example of mass-man soldiers that the device should never have been tried again. We must discount most of Herodotus's remarks about the size of the Persian army. After all, 4,000,000 men under one commander marching as a unit in one campaign! No modern army with every means of advanced transport has equalled that figure. The infantry organization was superior to the Athenian, though, for it relied on an elite guard in the center, "The Immortals," so-called because they were always kept up to strength. Should a member fall, he was immediately replaced from a waiting list of those considering such a promotion an honor. Other troops were organized into divisions of 10,000 each, and so on down the decimal system to squads of ten men.

The Persian wars did teach the Athenians something about the high command. A kind of Department of the Army was formed of ten elected generals, and any man who wished to achieve political influence tried to be nominated to this committee. A field commander was chosen from this board at the outbreak of war, and each of the others had some subordinate command function. The record shows confusion and overlapping as to what they were supposed to do. The actual battle was still performed by the phalanx of hoplites, the ideal number being 10,000, with a rigidity which cost Athens dearly. The battle line was normally four files deep, the best being in the first line, with the next rank, and sometimes the third, trying to reach the enemy with pikes over the shoulders of the others. The ranks have been known to be sixteen files deep, which considering that, aside from immediate replacements for the fallen, the chief function of the rear lines was to push the front ones. This prickly wall of metalled human flesh was irresistible to anyone foolish enough to accept its charge, and was almost impenetrable on the defense. There was still no intermediate command, so the general lost control as soon as the battle was joined.

The garrison state of Sparta, inferior to the Athenians in literacy and gracious living, was superior in things military. The basic Spartan unit was the *mora* of 400 hoplites under a field-grade officer with the same title. Each mora consisted of ten companies called *lochoi* under a *logachos*, which is still the modern Greek word for a captain. It seems, too, that the lochos was divided into platoons or sections. Drill was performed by sections, and so was marching, the soldiers merely following their noncommissioned officer. The Spartan phalanx was likewise formed by sections, so had better pre-combat maneuverability than the Athenian type. Once the clash was joined, however, control was likewise lost. The phalanx was too inflexible a unit.

King Philip of Macedon did not see this weakness, but his son Alexander did, and in part rectified it. His phalanx contained a unit of lighter infantry which served as a connection with the heavy cavalry, which he may have invented. The fact remains, however, that the Greeks, Macedonians included, were not very good organizers in their civil lives or in the army. None of them ever saw the value of a combat reserve. Something better was long overdue, something with more maneuverability of constituent units, something the general could control and command from a headquarters, and not simply as a spectator rejoicing or lamenting over the behavior of his own battle line. Why could not the Greeks have conceived of a headquarters which could have taken the worry over details from the commander, or did he worry much? Rome did all of these things, and hit the Greeks, too, with the result that a large proportion of the civilized world speaks some form of Latin, and only Greeks speak Greek.

The regal, republican, and imperial western Roman military is sufficiently discussed elsewhere. The late Roman and Byzantine organization, which should have contained the germ of something better, was largely founded on Emperor Justinian's concept of the *tagma* as the basic administrative and tactical unit. The tagma was the older *numerus*, or in Byzantine Greek, *arithmos*, whose strength was 1,000 men. This was divided into platoons of one hundred each, and this into squads of ten. By the time of that great military genius, the Emperor Maurice, the army shrunk so that he stabilized the tagma at 300. Considering the ability of this man, it is surprising that he did not see the need of intermediate peacetime commands between the general and the tagmai, although he did for war. He organized a type of regiment consisting of three tagmai, and these formed into a kind of division of three regiments each. This strangely unimaginative organization was maintained in Europe until the American and French Revolutions. The old prerevolutionary European armies were tactically indivisible, too, and why men of known ability did not see that a general needs help, or why a commander of Maurice's stature did not comprehend that generals and subgenerals need experience in handling large numbers of men in peace is hard to understand. The Americans paid a bitter price for this in their civil war, and just as much in World War I.[9]

How Byzantine heavy cavalry usage and equipment diffused into west Europe, and contributed to a social revolution, and how the barbarians who thought they were Roman officers organized their tenants as infantry and beat off even wilder barbarians to save a remnant of civilization for us all, is told in other pages. Nevertheless, if one speaks frankly, the feudal system once it achieved something of its final form, was organizational retrogression in the direction of the warrior. Of course it is out of the question to speak of feudalism as a whole, as folk differed from folk, and indeed, one manor from another, but one can say that mediaeval society was well organized at the bottom, the socio-economic goal being local defense, but was confused, feeble, and chaotic at the top. In this, it was something new in the world. It was almost as if some pacifically minded master planner had designed a regime of international peace. The greatest and most successful military adventures were accomplished not by feudalities but by volunteers outside the preferred social system. William's invasion of England is in point, a war wherein the minority of the combatants owed the Duke of Normandy any feudal due at all. Actually, most successful mediaeval wars were won by the weapons of mercenary free companies, units strictly structured within, and with virtually no organization between the general and the specific company. A mercenary division was unthinkable to the men of the times. There were no mercenary regiments or brigades. There was nothing a modern soldier could call a staff, and the despised army paper work was hard to accomplish by illiterates scribbling on parchment. Thousands of combatants died of neglect, too, because of this lack of logistic administration. Read even an amateurish history of the crusades. Many desirable social, economic, and cultural ideas died aborning because the feudal upper-class simply was unable, and with certain notable exceptions, incapable of organizing anyone besides their own serfs. The world might have been richer and safer if the crusaders had won.

There was a light, however, in the East, if one can call Genghis Khan a light, who could have taught westerners a lesson if he had gotten far enough. One can only call this man a phenomenon, and if he burst upon the world in our own mediaeval period without affecting it much, this was probably a blessing. Any man who caused the deaths of 5,000,000 humans cannot be called an entire failure. And speaking of genius and leadership, this man persuaded, or kicked, a loose, localistic collection of warrior societies into becoming soldiers, and not in a generation but in a few years. Genghis and his Mongols illustrate the importance of organization almost more than any other people. The Mongols were no more than ordinary Turko-Tatar pastoral nomads, indulging in the pettiest of sub-tactical raiding. Genghis rose to power by two means, luck and organization. Actually, luck rarely favors any man for long. Often what the vanquished think is the victor's luck is his power of organization and his foresightedness in preparing for any emergency. Genghis really owed his success to the second factor, his enormous capacity for organization and his tireless vitality in seeing that his wishes were carried out. He rose from a petty chief to a world power, and he did it by absorbing other petty chiefs and putting their fighting forces under simple but effective tables of organization. He was one of the first commanders to appreciate the value of a communications system. He figured that no man can command the attention of more than ten men at a time. He gave his commands only to ten generals, and they to their ten ranking subordinates, and so on down the decimal system to squads of ten with their leaders. (Is there something of old Persia in this?) Genghis, however, illustrated the comfortable doctrine that he who attempts to eat the world bursts. One hopes that this still holds true.

We must, however, return to our own mediaeval period, especially towards its end when there was a conscious or unconscious drive towards nationalism and national armies. Joan of Arc, or her marshal Dunois, had a lasting effect on the French. Of course this phenomenon would have evolved in the world anyhow, for England was on its way towards a national army. The French just had a few year's edge on England, for driving out the hated "Goddamns" suggested to King Charles VII (1422-1461) the need for a national instead of feudal force. The States General urged this king to move towards a regular establishment, to which he gladly agreed. In 1444 he issued a decree which virtually brought this about. The scandalous behavior of his mercenaries impelled this reform. The French crown first seized the right to appoint all of the captains of the "free companies," and forbade anyone else raising a private company. Second, he formed a permanent, professional, paid force answerable only to himself. He formed fifteen *Compagnies des Ordonance du Roi*, which he alone commanded. Probably fearing a rise of too much power in any one of them, he limited each ordinance company to one hundred "lances." A lance consisted of one paid man-at-arms, his esquire armed like his master in knightly fashion, a groom who was lightly armed, and three archers, in other words, six men whom the king considered enlisted men rather than gentry.

These men were nationally recruited, and not by feudal barons under contract as in contemporary England. This, as we shall see, bolstered the power of the great English lords rather than destroying it. One could have expected an uproar from the French baronage, they being the most feudalized in all Europe, and naturally this row occurred. But consciously or otherwise, Charles took the sting out of his penetration of the barons' military monopoly by giving employment to their younger sons, who were eating them out of castle and home anyhow. "Good riddance, my lad! Just you go and be one of the king's men-at-arms," and many a poor seigneur felt relieved by this. The commons liked this new organization of the lance, for as archers they could be set on the road of upper social mobility. Charles VII is accounted a stupid, weak king by his enemies, but he succeeded where his English cousin failed. He improved discipline by making each feudal noble responsible to him for the acts of his vassals, just as much as hired captains had been. One sees here, then, the reappearance of the Roman channels of command and responsibiility, and the wise if inelegant doctrine, "If the fish stinks, the head of the fish stinks; and if the head of the fish stinks, the fish stinks."

Charles VII, seeing the success of the Maid at the relief of Orleans, was the first west European leader to recognize artillerymen as soldiers instead of hired laborers, a type of engineer who was only a toiler and no gentleman, and French artillery has been excellent ever since. He proclaimed a permanent artillery department under a Master of Artillery.

While a regular army in the modern sense had to wait until Louis XIV, the experiment of Charles VII inspired the English to move in the direction of military nationalism. The idea was carried by England to America, where began the now almost-finished struggle between the Federal government and the states. Germany finally went all the way after World War I, for before and during that conflict, they felt like American southerners. The regular and imperial army was the smallest of the forces which Kaiser William II could order into France. Even at that time, most German soldiers took oath to the heads of their states, the King of Bavaria, of Saxony, and so on, and touched their regimental rather than imperial flags when they did so. The nationalist movement was furthered more when Charles VIII moved his French forces into Italy, and one might say that the drift ended with the nationalization of our own National Guard.

It is apparent, then, that the company, commanded by a captain who, when it increased in size, was assisted by "petty captains" or lieutenants, is the oldest post-Roman military organization. It was, and still is, the basic tactical and administrative unit in any army. Handling large numbers of troops demands organization above this level. The first intermediate command was the regiment (Latin, *regimen*, a rule, a system, an order).

While regiments in the modern sense were first decreed for French cavalry sometime in the mid-sixteenth century, it is quite clear that the real foundation for the unit was Spanish. The Spanish wars against the Moors were, of course, fought with feudal levies, by any number of independent lords and their retainers who took orders only from the king, when it suited them. As expelling the English started France towards nationalizing its armed force, war with the Moors suggested the same to Ferdinand and Isabella, who were behind no one in power-hunger. This regal pair then set up a royal, not feudal, force on their French frontier. They copied the French in constructing this force out of ordinance companies, but they divided them into three parts, the *tercios*, or thirds. The tercio was to last a long time. The Spanish needed to copy no one in the fabrification and use of swords. The first tercio, then, was composed of swordsmen. Then, seeing the great success of the Swiss push of pikes, the second one was of pikemen. Firepower was obtained by the last tercio composed of crossbowmen and handgunners. The ordinance company then declined in size to about 100 men, a force far too small to constitute an adequate border patrol. An army, though, was too large and cumbersome for this duty. What was needed was a little column, not a great one like an army. Now it may be that the original word for the "little column" is Italian, the *colunela*, which was commanded by the senior captain present for duty, the *cabo* (head) *de colunela*, but the idea was Spanish. In their language, a little column is a *colon*, and its commander a *colonel*. As these were crown troops, the Spanish corrupted the spelling and pronunciation into *coronelía*, commanded by a *coronel*. Following the French who taught the Americans so much, we have kept the old spelling for this officer, but altered the pronunciation so that it does not resemble the written word.

In spite of the success Cromwell had with the unit, the English have never liked the regiment. The one which they brought to the colonies, however, emerged from the Revolution as the old American regiment of ten companies with no subcommander between them and the colonel. As with the Germans and the French, the regiment became the emotional focus of the American soldier. Either because of the growing tactical popularity of the battalion, and therefore accidentally, or by bureaucratic design to scrape away this loyalty and make of both officer and soldier impersonal units who could be shifted about at will, the United States high command began denigrating the regiment at the end of World War I. First its band was taken away and assigned to a division, which was supposed to become the emotional center. The regimental flags were next taken away, and finally in the reforms of 1957, the regiment was eliminated as a tactical unit. The Pentagon apparently thought that it had gone too far, and has tried to revive the old pride by conferring the flags on honorary regiments of loosely grouped battalions and squadrons, and with some little success.

Napoleon divided the regiment into three battalions in order that the responsibility of its commander be shared with field-grade officers closer to the companies. Actually, this is the old mediaeval "battle" which was the senior tactical unit until the invention of the regiment. The new unit was nothing like as large as the old battle, so was called a little battle, or battalion. Even after the Americans adopted the battalion, they followed the French in retaining all administration in regiment. There are American field manuals no older than many readers of these pages which read, in effect, that the company is a tactical and administrative unit, the battalion is a tactical but not an administrative one, while the regiment is both a tactical and administrative unit. This seems strange today, although since present day battalions are as large as some old regiments, they have great administrative and staff problems. The British, perhaps due to their colonialism, have long considered the battalion as the core of the army. They always speak of a front as being so many battalions wide. A vague regimental headquarters was kept at home, but should a serious problem arise, it was not sent there, but to brigade. The home battalion received and trained recruits, while the second was sent to the colonies. These British and American super-battalions are commanded by a lieutenant colonel. The "old," meaning blue-clad, American army had two "strange beasts," one lieutenant colonel supposedly the regimental executive officer, but actually of such small importance that the office was often left unfilled, and one warrant officer who was bandmaster. Now commanding lieutenant colonels and administrative warrant officers are swarming all over the command.

Sentiment and tradition are very necessary for the control of the common worker, civilian or military. Useful as sentiment is as a means of social control, the high command in either civilian or warlike enterprise are bound by the norms of success and efficiency. King Francis I of France tried to turn the Battle of Pavia (1525) into a mediaeval jousting show, and lost his freedom. His great Chevalier Bayard lost his life. Organization is stronger if reinforced by tradition, but war is a deadly game. Military organization must be altered to fit the times and their needs. Thus, it happened that a force larger than a regiment but smaller than a division was needed, so the brigade consisting of from two to three regiments was invented and put under a brigadier general. The Americans liked this unit, as it fulfilled a command need in the post-Civil War Indian-fighting campaigns. Thus, in the lull of the second decade of this century, the American infantry "square" division consisted of three rifle brigades and one of artillery, with the service units, of course. A cavalry division consisted of two rifle brigades and one field artillery regiment. The requirements of World War II reduced the size of the division into the "triangular" type, and the brigade was abolished except for nondivisional engineers. The American adventures in Viet Nam have tended to bring back the brigade.

The division, as a French invention, taught the world during that people's global schoolmastership in things military. Actually, the American Revolution suggested to the royal French that permanent divisions consisting of two or more brigades had great strike power, but it was the French revolutionary General Carnot who invented the modern infantry division, while Napoleon grouped his horse regiments into cavalry divisions. The division, commanded in this country by a major general, has proved its worth. Assuming that it is being fed supplies by civilian or military logistical organization, the division is the smallest unit which can live and fight entirely with its own resources. The armies of old had units which combined all arms. We have seen that the ordinance companies did the same. All of this violated the principle of specialization and efficiency of labor, so the various armies and logistic units were made separate. The division, then, is a revival of the old self-reliance. Originally consisting of two or more rifle brigades with artillery, engineers, and logistic support, it is difficult to outline its organization today. There are infantry, armored, and that strategic threat, the airborne division in some armed forces. The Soviet Union is the only power with artillery divisions, but the Russians have always loved that arm. Each type of division in each nation differs in strength and organization, and this is far from static. It would be useless to include here a table or organization for an American infantry division. There are retired officers who have seen three arrangements, and a fourth, the pentomic division, is under consideration.

Even the huge division — it can consist of between twelve and twenty thousand men — is not large enough for the modern mass-man wars. The corps, commanded by a lieutenant general, consisting of at least two divisions, has proven useful, but World War II was fought by "field armies" consisting of two or more corps, and commanded by a general. The American assault on Germany in that war was by three field armies in a line, called an army group, while on its left was the British Twenty-second Army Group consisting of two field armies in a line. The field army is a superior peacetime administrative unit, but America's more recent Asian adventures have provided no fronts wide enough to use them tactically. The American Civil War was fought by field armies, of course, and the names, the Army of the Potomac, of Northern Virginia, of the Tennessee, of the West, are part of our heritage.

Phalanxes, maniples, cohorts, legions, tagmai, numeri, battles, companies, battalions, regiments, brigades, divisions, field armies, and groups of armies! This chapter said that it intended to contrast the soldier with the warrior, and surely it has done that. Can one imagine a primitive war, or submilitary combat, organized into such secondary groups? Certainly the administration of all these is a function of literacy, and writing and record keeping came in with the political state. Social organization has come a long way, from city state to leviathan, from family businesses to corporations and cartels, from the fighting band to the group of armies, and none of it entirely without pain. Now what does the society want? Call a rose by any name, and it still has thorns.

Submilitary combat may be considered a type of recreation, as fun by persons bored or otherwise frustrated. It must be entertaining, for millions of men have indulged in it without compulsion from time immemorial. Short, successful wars by naive polities were probably considered amusing, too, but what of true, political war? Yes, Professor Durkheim, all social organization is in part repressive of the organism. Each of us knows this. There is a seed of rebellion in everyone. The root of mutiny exists in all our peaceful organization, from the loving family and on up higher. Organization always comes at some price of individual freedom, and some latent rebellion against it surface in most of us at some time in our lives.

Why, we must ask, do men submit to the organization and discipline of true war? Well, warriors do not, and herein they differ from soldiers, and it is the latter who have survived. Why, indeed, do men submit to the organization and discipline of our economic and political life? Well, some do not, and become alienated therefrom. Some drop out upon the green, which is reversion to primitivity. Why not let them alone, the noncriminal at least? The economy can afford their simple wants, even if parasitism is one of biology's dirtiest words.

It is vain to say that soldiers, producers, and citizens conform because their superordinates compel them. One can always quit. Any man can always die rather than submit. Relatively few do this, or desert, either. They accept disciplined organization in all walks of life because they have been persuaded that the goals desired are obtainable in no other way, and the military structure differs from the peaceful only in the degree of severity.

This chapter has dealt with soldiers in general. Next follows a consideration of two types of hardcore professionals. First, there are the mercenaries, troops whose action is against the external relations set. Then there are the pretorians, soldiers whose activities are directed to the internal relations set. But before all, there must be a recounting of the leaders of these men, good, bad, or indifferent, and the indifferent are the worst.

FOOTNOTES AND REFERENCES

[1] Hilaire Belloc, *Poitiers*, London, 1913, p. 112.

[2] Aziz Suryal Atiya, *The Crusade of Nicopolis*, London, 1934, p. 71.

[3] W. S. Ferguson, "The Zulus and the Spartans: A Comparison of Their Military Systems," *Harvard African Studies, Varia Africana* II, Cambridge, Harvard University Press, 1918, passim.

[4] Discipline among the Knights Templar was extreme. Even the highest of them could be severely flogged for violations of the rule, small things which would merit only a reprimand among their civilian contemporaries, the Cistercian monks. Sir Walter Scott, whose knowledge of mediaeval civilization was virtually nil, and whose understanding of the military monks was even less, cites three flogging offenses on one page in the novel *Ivanhoe*. The hateful Templar, Sir Brian de Boisguilbert, came into the lists to do battle to the death with the hero, with a resplendent white plume in his helmet. The first whipping session would be because he permitted himself the knightly title of "Sir." Templars were only called "Brother." Second, they were forbidden to wear feathers or any other ornament on their helms. Third, he engaged in a forbidden, formal, private duel. It is well that Ivanhoe slew Brother Brian before his superior in the Order got him.

[5] There were, of course, many such changes producing the renaissance, then later baroque and rococo wars. The following manuals exist in American microfilm, and are well worth study by both tactician and sociologist.

James Acheson, *The Military Garden, or Instrvctions for All Yovng Sovldiers and Svch Who Are Disposed to Learne, and Have Knovvlledge of the Militarie Discipline*, date and publisher unknown.

Robert Barret, *The Theorie and Praktike of Modern VVares*, printed by R. Fields for VV. Ponsonby, London, 1598.

William Barriffe, *Military Discipline: or the Yong Artillery Man*, printed for R. Mab by R. O. Fulton, London, 1639.

Gerrat Barry, *A Discourse of Military Discipline*, by the vvidovv of J. Mommart, Bruxells, 1634.

⁶ Harry Holbert Turney-High, *Primitive War: Its Practice and Concepts*, Columbia, South Carolina, University of South Carolina Press, second edition, 1971, p. 45.

⁷ Frederick A. Forbes, *Dahomey and Dahomeans*, London, Longmans, Brown, Green and Longmans, 1851, Vol. I, p. 14.

⁸ William Snelgrave, *A New Account of Some Parts of Guinea and the Slave Trade*, London, J. J. and P. Knapton, 1734, cited in Herskovits, *Dahomey*, Vol. II, p. 80.

⁹ It is known that the Emperor Maurice wrote many military manuals, the most famous being the *Strategon*, a voluminous how-to-do-it book dealing with everything, from how to be a successful general to how to train a squad. It is widely quoted by military theorists, but is almost unavailable in the United States. A French book based on it, and reported to be excellent, is F. Aussaresses, *L'Armée byzantine à la fin du VIème siècle d'apres la Strategon de l'Empereur Maurice*, Paris, 1909, can be had in the larger technical libraries in this country.

Chapter 11

THE CAPTAINS OF THE HOST

The Problems of Leadership

It is a commonplace that the caliber of the leader of soldiers often spells the difference between victory and defeat. We can only present an introductory outline here, for whole books can, have been, and should be written on the qualities of good officers.

Since the forerunner of the academic profession, Socrates, liked to teach with a negative approach, we will begin by illustrating what not to do. One would like to expand this to book size, mentioning the Generals Braddock, Burgoyne, Clinton, and Howe, who wore red coats on this continent, and such masters of ineptitude in the Civil War as Braxton Bragg on the one side, and Ambrose Burnside on the other, but economy of space will afford only this one bad example drawn from antiquity in order to offend no one. Varus, though, was one of the best in the history of failure.

His was the story of a political pet, one of the founders of a long tradition. He was not an officer and a gentleman. The Latin language never had a term even vaguely translating this concept. Varus was only an aristocrat and a general. So, as in many subsequent instances, it was not what you know, but whom you know, and our subject knew Augustus Caesar, master of most of the world known to western man of that time. Varus was typical of the then Roman upper-upper-class. He was a man of superb literary taste, a connoisseur of the intellectual and artistic, loving legal knowledge and forensic debate, profligate of life, and given to extracting bribes. As the French army before World War II loved the fleshpots of Indo-China, Varus enjoyed his service as proconsul of Syria where, it was said, courage in men and virtue in women had for centuries been unknown. This was his training for ruling the tough, independent, woman-respecting Germans. He tried to introduce some of his ideas on recreation to the Teutons, and his officers were worse than he was, which suggested even greater license to the brutal soldiery. Augustus withdrew from Germany a capable, suspicious, and able general, his unloved kinsman, Tiberius Claudius Nero. This man became the capable, cautious, suspicious and able Emperor Tiberius. Varus took command in A.D. 9.

The lessons that Varus has to teach junior officers follow these lines. Follow him and Custer in getting yourself hated by your subjects. Give them real or supposed reason to think themselves your moral superiors. Your name will thus ring throughout history but, in case of your probable defeat, try to destroy any pity your conqueror might show you. Refuse to learn about your enemy, but permit him to know you very well. Allow your foe to choose the battlefield where the terrain will practically guarantee your defeat. Give him the initiative by all means, and never recover it yourself. Despise your enemy's ability. Die in your attempt, for you might be promoted upstairs into obscurity.

The situation at the end of the first decade Anno Domini was something like this. Roman arms had conquered and pacified about half of what we call Germany today. Many Teuton chiefs collaborated and enjoyed Romanization, but there was one whom oppression infuriated. His name was Hermann, but since a Latinist could not pronounce this rude word, let us call him Arminius. He was joint chief with his brother of the hard Cherusci, but his sibling fled to Rome, became a citizen, and changed his name to Flavius.

Arminius had once been given Roman citizenship, too, in an attempt emasculate the Germans as Rome had the Britons, but he rejected it. He was no primitive warrior. He served in the Roman army at the height of its efficiency. He knew the superiority of its organization, training, discipline, its ability to stand under stress, and the uses of its superb equipment and armament. He knew that his less well-armed tribesmen and allies could not meet the legionaries in the Roman line clash of heavy infantry. He was fanning revolt, and he knew that he could win only by outwitting Varus, which proved to be no great task. He knew he must strike soon lest his fellow-chiefs and allies grow lukewarm, and he knew that his enemy could not afford to allow this revolt to develop.

And so Publius Quintilius Varus, Proconsul of the Germanies, assumed command and set off from his headquarters in mid-Westphalia to teach the Cherusci and allies the folly of speaking anything but Augustan Latin. The only tactical principle he observed was that of sufficient numbers. He had three legions of heavy infantry which, even excluding men on detachment, had to be about 14,000 of the finest. He had between eight and nine hundred Roman cavalry, and about the same number of provincial allies. He relaxed Roman discipline by bringing along a huge wagon train and droves of camp followers. There are no trustworthy figures on how many troops Arminius had, but even with qualitative inferiority, he probably had numerical superiority. Our authority is the historian Caius Cornelius Tacitus, himself a Roman aristocrat who respected the Germans.

This was a season of torrential autumn rains, and even the plains became soggy enough to weary the heavily armed Romans. Arminius, though, had no idea of fighting on any plain. He kept drawing Varus towards the Teutoberg Forest, an area with which the Romans were totally unfamiliar. Why did not the Latin cavalry leader, Numonius Vala, scout forward and send back information about the terrain? Varus could at least have advanced his numerous light infantry as a screen, but no! These were largely Germans themselves, and at the whistle of the first missile they decided that this was no war of theirs, and decamped. Why did not Vala make some effort to act as a rear guard?

The ground became more and more broken, and less favorable for legionary tactics. The storms had felled numerous trees, which the engineers had to clear away. Soon it became apparent that not all the trees were laid low by the weather. Arminius had chosen his battleground, the Teutoberg, in what was recently the Principality of Lippe, and is now in West Germany. The forest is a branch of the great Hyrcanian one, and mighty trees on the hilltops and sides were perfect cover for an enemy. The bases of the hills were a perfect quagmire, the River Lippe and its creeks having overflown what banks they had. The terrain was also broken by large stones and small hillocks. The column, already attenuated, kept crashing into the engineers who were trying to build some kind of a causeway. The legionaries not only could not form their favorite front but they could keep no Roman march order.

Varus now saw that he had to abandon his wagon train. This irritated the infantry, whose morale was already low. The legionaries broke ranks to find their personal belongings, and either did not hear or obey their officers' orders to reform. Then Arminius struck their flank. A hailstorm of German darts broke them up more than they already were. Arminius with his personal bodyguard then attacked the cavalry, already knee-to-belly deep in the morass. What horses survived this mire bucked their riders into the mud, and plunged into the legionaries who were trying to form. Some troopers, with their commander, escaped and fled. The Germans caught and destroyed them to a man.

Varus then decided to retreat towards the nearest Roman garrison on the Lippe, but he was surrounded by now. The Germans charged him, and he was wounded in this attack. He suspected that Arminius wanted him personally, as Crazy Horse desired Custer, and Varus committed suicide belatedly, if one thinks of Roman military honor. The Latin second in command fell dead, and the third ranking man surrendered, hoping for quarter. He became a human sacrifice.

Roman discipline recovered itself to some extent, and the infantry managed to form some kind of a line. The infuriated Germans assailed it by fire and movement. The legionaries could not keep their famous compact formation, and the Germans broke through in several places. And then the slaughter began. Those who survived were bound and sent under the yoke of servitude, but survival in slavery was not to be theirs. They were tied to the altars of the Teutonic gods, and killed in cold-blood.

Teutoberg Forest was one of the most decisive battles in history. Rome settled for the Rhine-Danube frontier as its extreme boundary, and the Germans were not latinized like the Gauls. Their partial romanization was accomplished by the Roman Church, aided in part by some violent conversions by the Frankish emperor. Yet time after mediaeval-renaissance time, one or another of their princes called himself the Holy Roman Emperor. Of course, it was Crassus who established the fact that a superb Roman army could be defeated, and this by a Parthian general who wore feminine makeup, but Varus reinforced the tradition admirably. Neither the Romans nor the English who succeeded them often produced a very bad general, but when they put their minds to it, both really succeeded.

Calling people fish heads is well enough, especially when safe in some staff or academic office. We may call some of the victims scapegoats, men who were offered up as sacrifice for their superiors' mistakes, or because they were politically unacceptable. One could write a fair-sized book on them, including Horatio Gates, whose victory at Saratoga virtually made the American Revolution a success, but who lost on the political front. There would be James Longstreet who provided Confederate buffs a scapegoat for Lee's tactical error at Gettysburg, but who was so right all along. There would be General William Mitchell who was disgraced for foreseeing the role of the air arm with great successful detail. King Leopold III was castigated by Winston Churchill and the French premier for the unpardonable sin of not sacrificing his army to cover the British retreat on Dunkirk, of which he had not been forewarned. Space, again, permits the mention of only one, but perhaps the very best. If you call the next subject a fish head, you must have a very lively barracuda in mind.

John Bell Hood was made the scapegoat for the Confederate loss of, first Atlanta, then of all Georgia. Most Confederate sympathizers, then and now, have put the blame on him, and it took a neutral, the British analyst Alfred Burne, to begin the tardy redemption of this gallant man's name.[1]

On 5 May 1864, a blue-clad army of 110,000 under the colorful William Tecumseh Sherman invaded Georgia to strike and destroy Joseph Eggleston Johnston's 80,000 Confederate force. The well-led Union drove the good but overly cautious, uninspiring Johnston within ten miles of the key city of Atlanta. Seriously blooded, defeated, ill-armed, and demoralized, the troops had lost confidence in "Old Joe," who was relieved, and Hood put in his stead. Note that Hood had no part in planning either the campaign or the battle. He arrived when they were not only in progress but virtually lost. That he was able to salvage as much as he did out of what he had inherited is one of the great feats in the history of leadership. We will speak of personality at some length in a few pages, but note this. He was bold, dashing, and perhaps too uncautious. He had lost an arm at Gettysburg, and a leg at Chickamauga, but strapped to the saddle, he could and did lead. Burne says that "Among the many and remarkable generals whom the Civil War brought into prominence, in some respects the most remarkable of them all was General John B. Hood." A Colonel Snow, quoted by Burne, described his thirty-three-year-old general as "one of those whom no disaster or physical ailment—not even the partial dismemberment of his body—nor any amount of external trouble, annoyance, or ill-will can crush."

He sparked a discredited, defeated army, sick with failure, into a fighting force. Though greatly outnumbered and with poor equipment, he seized the initiative from Sherman, and this was no mean feat in itself. He maneuvered Sherman almost back to the point where he started. He instilled fear and overcaution in the great Sherman to the extent that he never won a truly decisive victory over Hood. The latter reverted to the doctrine that the best defense is a vigorous offense, which has been abused by more than one injudicious leader. He knew that his only way of escaping attrition was to strike, and at once. He was a master of the Principle of Surprise, and time after time threw Sherman's subordinates into confusion. While Johnston might have defeated Sherman at Cassville on 19 May, he did not take the trouble, but the blue army had no such opponent this time. Hood knew how to judge the critical point, and he hit with all he had with devastating effect. He proved himself one of the masters of fighting on interior lines, and kept Sherman guessing where the next blow would fall. He knew that he must defeat his enemy in detail, separating columns and attacking them, for he had no chance in an overall confrontation of lines. Hood never forgot the Principle of Mobility. He concentrated Wheeler's cavalry, while Sherman dispersed his horse on distant railroad demolition, and so was blind.

Why, then, did Hood lose, if he did? First, losses were blunting his weapon more than they did Sherman's. His first subordinate, William Hardee, was jealous because, although Hood's senior, Richmond has given the latter command. Hardee fought with a dragging foot. Hood made brilliant plans, and moved with despatch to execute them. One of his Union enemies, General Dodge, who by chance rather than design came up to reinforce the critical point, said that Hood's counterattack at Atlanta was "one of the best planned and best executed attacks," and another Union general, Chamberlain, said "Upon what a slight chance hung the fate of Sherman's army that day." And Hood had been decisively beaten by Thomas at Nashville, but he learned, so let us face it. Hood was not decisively defeated during the Atlanta campaign, as he could have been. He was relieved and damned for not performing a miracle. Sherman respected John Bell Hood, and so should we.

The task now lies ahead to analyze the fact and reason of command, and to see how leaders like Varus and Hood became the men they were. This would be a lifetime task were it carried to its full fruition, but a beginning can be made.

The great French sociologist, Emile Durkheim, taught that authority is the very core of social system, and that every such equilibrium must have its moral code. Discipline is the chief source and maintenance device of such a normative system. He said that social doctrines "that celebrate the beneficences of unrestricted liberties are apologies for a diseased state, for it is through the practice of moral rules we develop the capacity to govern and regulate ourselves, which is the whole reality of liberty."

None of us involved here is an authoritarian, one who venerates authority for its own sake. Social control is respectable only for its utility, and only insofar as it is useful in suppressing the Id-harbored rebellion which is in us all. One must hope that the current moral confusion and lack of consensus is only a temporary discouragement. If a revolution against the present authority-moral structure is in progress, and many think this is true, then eventually this "diseased state" must pass. If a permanent and complete collapse of civilization is to be avoided, the goals of authority and its substantiating moral code will be redefined and enforced, although the redefinition might not be to the liking of many of us. Anomie, to use Durkheim's word for normlessness, for not knowing what to do, of indecision as to what is "right" and what is "wrong," is characteristic of inefficiency and unproductivity in social systems, and of neurosis in persons. If the old authoritative structure has passed the point of diminishing returns, if it no longer interprets life as it *must* be lived, not as it *ought* to be lived, it will be changed, painlessly, one hopes, so that it does conform to reality, or what the effective majority thinks is real. Norms—manners, morals, and laws—are ready made answers to potential crises, and as such are meant to prevent and resolve them. If they do not, crisis is king and anomie is queen over a neurotic society.

If there are men to be led, some must be leaders. A point can be made, too, that the military situation is only a particularly stringent one. Leadership and followership are inherent in every social situation, and this includes the higher infrahuman primates as well as man. This lies back of Leopold von Wiese's refusal to consider two transacting humans as a group. There not only can be absolute equality in a pair of friends but there often is. Absolute equality vanishes if the relationship consists of three personalities. The structure, the rank status, the tendency to lead appears even in a simple, informal friendship group. It is unfair to the great German to say that of course Professor von Wiese *was* a German, and a count at that, and that commanding and obeying goes clear to the backbone of the Teutonic national character. Discount the opinion of Professor Doctor Leopold, Graf von Wiese und Halmbach, if you so desire, but look around and see for yourself. Even among the three, one will be the originator of action even in recreational activities, and two will follow, or either consciously or unconsciously, the two will combine to exploit the one. This conscious or unconscious "natural" leadership is all that primitive war had, but it was sufficient to humiliate the United States Army at its worst-led on more than one occasion.

Natural leadership of the above type is not enough. We have already seen that superordination-subordination is a necessary fact in any permanent group, from a smoothly running family to a massive corporation. On the face of things, it would seem that a military unit should seek out and use these so-called natural leaders. Sometimes a command does, but more often it does not, and wisely. A leader in horseplay and fun may not do well in serious work. In the early days of Russian communism, the popular election of foremen in industry and officers in the army proved a failure. The severity of what we would call company punishment in the present Soviet Army would not be tolerated in any western nation. The Red Army may be one of comrades, but it is not one of "buddies." It would seem that natural leadership can be very successful in primary transaction, say on a small shop or squad level, but as industry, government, and the military tend to become rationalized bureaucracies, something must be added. The bureaucratic norms of the maximization of efficiency have little to do with friendship, admiration, or sympathy for repeated mistakes.

We must now ask if there is a personality difference between commanders and soldiers, or should there be. All analysts, civilian and military, emphasize the importance of the leader's personality in achieving success in the groups' goals. What, then, does this often abused word mean? Reams of paper have been consumed in controversy over a definition, and since the psychologists have not satisfied each other, it would be folly for us to try to settle the matter here. They all know what they are talking about, though, and really so do we. In any event, the quality of the commander's personality may spell the difference between success and defeat. There are modern ways of estimating personality, the Rohrschach protocol being the simplest. Since performance failure is becoming more and more dangerous, it would seem that candidates for commissions, and surely for higher rank, should be given this cheap, easy, and painless "ink blot" test. This has become standard procedure in many corporations and, for that matter, for entrance into some monasteries. It is a little thing to ask of an army.

We may then ask if the successful commanders have similar personalities? Now it well may be true that the military profession attracts extroverts, those people whose mental life is largely external to themselves, in contrast with introverts, with their richer internal life. Yet if the general is primarily a "do-er," a man of action, he had better have a good general staff to do his thinking for him.

The answer to the above question must be vague. The British analyst, Burne, quotes Colonel Stone who knew him that William Tecumseh Sherman was "tall, angular, with flashing eyes and rapid speech. He was quick-eyed, ingenious, nervously active in mind and body, sleeplessly alert on every occasion, with a clear idea of what he wanted and an unyielding determination to have it." Some of these objectives apply to any successful commander. Many of them are foreign to the icon-like image of Lee. The mercurial terms are applicable to George Patton, but not to Omar Bradley. Reading of Washington, Wellington, Lee, and Sherman, one sees a stubborn determination to win, but a power of self-criticism, a flexibility of mind which could say, "Well, that did not work. Let us try something else," as the Iron Duke said several times in the Peninsular Campaign.

In the preface of their classic on culture and personality, Kluckhohn and Murray classified the forces which determine much of the personality as (1) constitutional, (2) group membership, (3) role, and (4) the situational determinants. We might take a passing glance at each.

The constitutional determinants refer to the quality of the organism. This, of course, does not mean mere bulk, although the profession of arms has always favored the large and athletic. These men impress their subordinates without even trying, but if this is all they have, they will be revealed as strawmen, and their troops will lose confidence in them. Both Napoleon and his opponent Wellington were rather small men, but their troops trusted and followed them. Lee Christmas, the famous or infamous mercenary of the first part of this century, was slight and had very poor vision, but whoever hired this American had a way of winning. Rather than bulk size, physical and mental vitality seem to count the more. Physical health, though, not only impresses men but it aids in that clarity of thought which can affect the outcome of battle.

The unpleasant subject of illness must be touched on briefly. This is something our common clay shares, some escaping it more, some less. Whatever micro-organism afflicts emperors, marshals, and generals is no concern of ours. It becomes our affair on the day of battle which changed the fate of our fathers, and hence our own. Thus, was Napoleon suffering from piles at Waterloo? Two excellent biographies published within the year have taken opposite views. The affirmative makes a good case, saying that the emperor withdrew to treat himself every half hour or so. The other denies this with some vigor. In any event, it was not the old Napoleon who fought Wellington that day, and his marshals knew it. Something distracted him. His responses were slow, his decisions delayed, and he left too much to his subordinates. Again, did the courtly Robert E. Lee eat something noxious on his way to Pennsylvania? Did he have diarrhea at Gettysburg?[2] In any event, it was not the old Lee when he needed most to be. He was as aggressive and formidable in appearance as before. He was known to be in fine fighting form at Chancellorsville just two months before. He had suffered a severe heart attack in March 1863, and was plagued by angina for the rest of his life. He was terribly fatigued when he entered the Gettysburg affair and could hardly dismount from his saddle at its end.

Mental health is even more important than that of the lower colon. Perhaps there is a touch of madness in all the very great. Was Alexander the Great an alcoholic? It would so seem, and he might have changed the world more than he did except for his premature death attributed to his orgiastic style of life. Then consider

Frederick the Great. No child psychologist or psychiatrist would expect a normal adulthood for him, reared without love, rejected by a father, and subjected to a discipline appropriate to a contemporary Prussian line soldier. When the courtiers remonstrated with his father, they were told, "I am rearing a soldier." Well, King Frederick William I did that, and one of the greatest, but he produced a neurotic homosexual as well, and his title passed on to a very ordinary nephew, King Frederick William II. There are situational and group pressure determinants here, but health is health, and the House of Hohenzollern could have used the genes of the great one.

For an example of plain, useless sadistic madness, it would be hard to excel that of Banastre Tarleton who, in his small way, changed the course of history, just a little. The simple German farmers, in what is now Lexington County, South Carolina, were either loyalist or indifferent during the American Revolution. King George II had just given them thousands of acres of farmland, and they were not hostile to the British Crown. A visit by Tarleton changed their politics. The brilliant cavalryman hanged from their own windows all the leading citizens of Cayce, now a Columbia suburb.

Depression may be even more deadly. Napoleon was given to such fits. He had one on the day of Borodino, and sulked in his tent most of the day. He had not expected the resistance which cost him so much. He had several such episodes on his trip out of Russia, and then he ran away from his troops and let them suffer as they might. He had previously deserted his army in Asia Minor when things got bad. Napoleon was a good winner, and who is not, but a poor loser. He had some depression at Waterloo which, according to Wellington, he could have won. He ran away from his beaten troops again.

Let us look at an American winner who also suffered from depression. Happiness eluded Ulysses Simpson Grant, and surely he deserved more than he had ever had. He was accused of drunkenness time and again. He once fell off the seat of a wagon, and lay on the ground in an alcoholic stupor for all the troops to see. He was not like his extrovert enemy, James Longstreet, who loved to get roaring drunk at group carouses, and sing grand opera from atop a table. Grant was a solitary drinker, but one cannot help think that the charge of alcoholism was unjust. A heavy drinker, yes, and one inclined to drown his frustrations in whiskey. His depression was very marked towards the end of the war. His last field command, the Army of the Potomac, had once been as fine a fighting force as the world had seen. His own style of fighting and that of his predecessor and nominal commander, George Meade, had caused too many casualties, and his replacements gave Grant reason to be depressed. He was, and he settled down to a war of attrition without brilliance. He knew he could not lose playing that game.

Personalities can either change under stress, or the exigencies of the situation may reveal aspects which were always there. Even with the pre-professional pictures we have of him, this fact is illustrated in the life of William Tecumseh Sherman. We have four pictures of him. The first is of the last president of the Louisiana Military Institute, now Louisiana State University. As a very young person in Baton Rouge, I inquired about him of his surviving contemporaries, especially Generals Magruder and McGrath. After the old gentlemen stopped sputtering about the march through Georgia, they agreed that Sherman was a quiet, agreeable, and pleasant man. He was probably mildly introvert, as would be said today.

All this is contrary to the second profile of the neurotic, insecure, manic Sherman of the Kentucky campaign. He thought his command was inadequately small, and belabored Washington for more troops than were thought necessary for his mission. He was just plain frightened of his enemy, and obviously of himself as well. His contemporaries said that this resulted in a "nervous breakdown," and he certainly had to be temporarily relieved of command. Joining Grant in the lower valley, he appeared indecisive, unsure, and given to inaction.

William Sherman, though, found himself, and it may well be that success, or the possibilities of success, or the self-recognition of one's talents to win, is the best therapeutic for anxiety and insecurity. Eyewitnesses describe the third Sherman, the aggressive victor at Atlanta, as a man of resilient personality. He appeared cheerful at all times, even in adversity. He was never downcast when he failed. His soldiers loved him, calling him "Uncle Billy."

An opinion might be held that Uncle Billy Sherman was a man at war with himself, a dedicated, honest man whose profession asked too much of a kindly teacher of youth. Of course, the martinet Thomas (Stonewall) Jackson and later, Robert Lee, were professors, but they escaped the trauma. Neither of them knew the gentle, leisurely life of Zachary Taylor's campus at Baton Rouge, the low-keyed living of South Louisiana with its good food, good drink, and good conversation. Sherman was a lover of the South and southerners. His wife was a slave owner. He was, though, a duty-driven man. This may account for his disabling inner conflict during the Kentucky phase of his career. Having overcome his anxiety by a few successes, one may think that the cheerful Uncle Billy was a mask. One recalls that the root of our term "personality" is the Latin *persona*, which means a mask.

The chances are that William Sherman was not cut out to be the modern Attila, but that he was. He admitted to many millions of dollars worth of destruction in Georgia which had no military objective or value. The details of his burning of Columbia not only refute his later claim to innocence in the matter but exhibit evidence of vengefulness. From being a man who apparently wanted to be loved, especially by southerners, his became the most hated name in the latters' region.

The last phase of Sherman's public life finds him transferred to command of the Indian wars in the Far West. The brave soldier remained, for he almost got killed in the campaign. Uncle Billy, though, had been killed before, and the General Sherman we find at this time was described as bitter, sour, unsmiling, cantankerous, and needlessly cruel to the Indians. Sherman's career has been given more space here than that assigned to any other military leader for a very practical reason. Relatives and associates of veterans of long and savage wars should realize that their personalities might be permanently changed. The Veterans Administration hospitals have been full of men suffering the extremes of war-produced mental illness.

Stupidity, though, is not mental illness, and many authorities believe an hereditary factor is involved, but just how much is not known. How stupid men achieve high command is a matter of political sociology, and a government and society which promotes them should gain sympathy from no one. If you enjoy reading about them, Charles Fair has provided a devastating catalog.[3] One can savor his dedication page, "To the Memory of Ambrose Burnside—One of the Greatest in a Tradition Still Very Much Alive."

Whenever a great man emerges from the commonalty, biographers will consistently invoke heredity, which is a constitutional determinant. Since the question will surely come up, it must be asked if military talent runs in families, to which question no affirmative-negative answer can be given. If talent means unusual intelligence, few except the most sectarian environmentalists will deny that it is in part hereditary. It is sure that a silk purse cannot be made out of a sow's ear, but such ears are very functional for sows, and many silk purses are neither functional nor ornamental. Far too little is known about the genetics of human talent to be dogmatic in this generation. As for aptitude and temperament, let the experts settle their argument.

It is well to skip the first chapter of a biography which describes a great man's ancestors, for historians begin snooping around his heels waiting only for his death to provide him with a near-divine origin. Now there are such things as genes, and sober scholars are more inclined to say today that ability is in part genetic than they once were, but it must be asked, ability to do what? Certainly not to do just one thing well. Now each human being has sixteen great-grandparents, and each one of these persons had sixteen great-grandparents, so along which line does this remarkable ability run, especially in societies which have a preference for exogamy (marriage outside the kin), as does ours? It is better to look for postnatal conditioning to find "inherited" military, musical, or scientific accomplishments.

Can it be emphatically denied that military, and other, talent runs in families, and to this question, the answer must be a cautious negative. If a culture group tends to marry only with its peers, there may be a genetic factor, but even then one must account for families, being culture-carrying devices, exerting pressures on children to conform to certain standards. Should we not attribute both group pressures as well as a possible inherited factor for the endogamous (marriage inside the kin) Prussian officer corps?

Students agreeing with the conviction sincerely hope that the either-or, black-or-white, dichotomy will some day vanish into the museum of past errors. A man, any person, is a whole thing, and the causative factors of his personality are many-faceted. Heredity and environment are not mutually exclusive concepts. Following the pressures of the present American intellectual establishment, we hear in every juvenile court session "that is all the fault of society." The English have never been quite so sure, and there was a finality for certain bloodlines in their doctrine of "Hanged at Tyburn, burnt at Smithfield, and beheaded at the Tower." Perhaps the East African King of Uganda improved the strain of professional generals by executing each defeated one, perhaps not. At least he created a vacancy in grade, which was appreciated by the juniors.

Whatever else warfare is, it is solving a crisis for the in-group and creating one for the other-group, for we must revert to group analysis wherein we may feel more sure. The seriousness of combat requires intense identification of the members with the group. The leader, from that of a squad to the commander of a field army is himself a member of that group, and much more. Such a group, primary or secondary, promotes its cohesiveness by making its commander a symbol, nay, emblem of its existence. The greater the danger, the more the very survival of the group is challenged, and the greater this symbolization must be. General Coats has said:[4] "In a military crisis the threat of violence becomes overwhelming in the absence of group identification and activity to abate or reduce the threat. It is the function of the leader to focus the attention of the group upon himself, and through himself as the representative of the group, to give direction and Unity to the efforts of all."

And later he says, "The role of the leader has two fundamental facets: Group solidarity, and coordinated operations. As a symbol representative of his unit, the military commander in his actions and orders mediates between the perspectives of each individual soldier and the force as a whole. A strong leader represents the group to the individual. The loyalty and faith which the members feel for the group are in large measure sentimentalized in the symbols of leadership. For his part, the military leader justifies and strengthens the bonds which hold the force together through the skill with which he employs them to conduct effective military operations."

Observed from another aspect, all group endeavors can be reduced to role playing. History is replete with examples of leaders who were cast above their ability, and collapsed under roles which were too much for them. Why did George Pickett accompany his troops halfway up the hill at Gettysburg, then turn back and seek safety in the rear area? All of his brigadiers were killed on this fatal march, and all of his field-grade officers were brought down, but Pickett of Pickett's Charge escaped unscathed. By contrast, if men make roles, sometimes roles make men, and some very ordinary personalities have tried to live up to an exalted role. A politician of unsavory record, Chester Arthur tried to be a good president of the United States when the assassination of President Garfield cast him in this role. Edward was such a playboy that it would be hard to tolerate him in today's Buckingham Palace society. Cast upon the throne, though, by Victoria's belated death, he tried as King Edward VII to succeed, and recaptured much of the respect his previous licentious life had lost.

Indeed, not only the person within the group but the group itself has roles to play in which it may or may not succeed. The military itself is a subculture within the overall culture of a larger social system. As such, it has its specialized roles to play, whether well, indifferently, or poorly. The psychiatrist Henry Murray and the anthropologist Clyde Kluckhohn have said,[5] "... Likewise, it can be said that every group (social system), in order to develop, maintain, express, and reproduce itself, must perform a number of *social* roles, such as recruitment and training of new members, hierarchical organization of functions, elimination of incorrigible members, defense against attack by rival groups ... and so forth. Finally, both persons and social systems [each taken as a consensus of intentions] are desirous of improvement, of living up to their ideals, of deserving recognition and prestige. In the personality it is the governing ego system which assumes responsibility for the integration of *individual* roles and the actualization of plans. In the group it is the leader or government . . . that assumes responsibility for the structuring of *social* roles and the carrying out of policies [domestic and foreign]."

Every successful personality, of course, performs many roles. Indeed, a summary of them is deemed a person's social position, and it is also a shorthand description of his personality.

It is rare that the commander can know and control all the variables needed for victory, no matter how careful and skilled he and his staff may be. There exist in all large operations human, geographic, weather, and other inexactitudes which will forever keep warfare from being an exact, or surely a precise, science. The military term of "the fog of war" has grown up around the uncertainties, a miasma which has plagued us since the beginning of armed force. This fog seems to favor one side at one time, and the opposition upon other occasions. If one wishes to call this luck, he might as well.

A feature of the personalities of great leaders might or might not be a matter of luck, but it must be mentioned. Some leaders are able, apparently with great ease and not always consciously, to project their personalities on their followers, to identify with them and evoke a reciprocal identification which suggests a type of infallibility even in the face of occasional defeat. What is this spiritual essence called charisma? It is an emotional response, of course, so the rationalized armies of today may have to bid it farewell. This may not be so, and if true, it is folly to underrate its effect on the followership. Alexander the Great had it. Augustus had it before the Roman world wearied of him. Joan of Arc had it, and her opponent the Duke of Bedford did not. It surrounded Lee like an aura, but did not descend on Grant.

Part of the charismatic character is surely a greater than usual belief in one's own powers, a self-confidence almost approaching divine infallibility. If the leadership believes this as much as the followership, there may be a touch of madness here. If the leader does not believe in his charisma, he is an exploiting cynic. Were the great masters of the twentieth century—Hitler, Stalin, Roosevelt, and Mussolini, charismatic rulers all—of this type of believers? One is sure that Napoleon believed in his destiny, and with some reason, but he was defeated by Kutuzov, and "that old dowager" would have laughed at charisma. Eisenhower did not have it, nor his senior subordinate Omar Bradley, but George Patton did, and the mystery that was Patton has not even yet begun to be dispelled. His opponent Erwin Rommel had it, for he was a man among millions. Clausewitz recognized its existence and called it "an inner light which leads to the truth."

Whether fortunate enough to be a charismatic leader or not, one sure way to the respect of the troops is to expect high performance from them, and to give them reason to expect the same from him. All great commanders have been strict disciplinarians, but they have identified with their troops while expecting marvels from them. The senior French commander in the American revolution was a stern disciplinarian in the eighteenth century European fashion, but the soldiers called him Papa Rochambeau. Genial, just a little obese, he had their interest in mind, they knew, and he never sacrificed them uselessly.

Theodore Dodge wrote of the great captains of antiquity,[6] "All maintained discipline at an equal standard. All fired their soldiers to bear privations in the field, and bore it with them. All equally won their hearts. All obtained this control over men by scrupulous care of their armies' welfare, courage equal to the test, readiness to participate in the heat and labor of the day, personal magnetism, justice in rewards and punishments, friendliness in personal intercourse and power of convincing men."

Love, of course, is a great ingredient in interhuman relations, but it is not the prime one. The troops loved George Brinton McClellan, and followed him gladly, but he is generally accounted a failure as a general. His ultimate successor, Ulysses Grant, inspired little affection, but his troops elected him President of the United States.

Respect and confidence won by success are more valuable than love. Does the commander know what he is doing? Does he cover every contingency and, most important of all, does he win? Even mercenaries with no political involvement in the cause will fight like tigers for such a man. King Frederick the Great urged his generals to acquire the love of their men, while he himself endured their flaming hatred. The Prussian soldiers hated their aristocratic officers, but had confidence in their training, dedication, and leadership. Officers and men joined in hating the king, but all ranks knew that he was not a spurious pretender. He knew his craft, and could be expected to exercise it. He did not inspire the love of his civilian subjects, either, for they named the devil for him. He was *The Old Fritz*. The troops did not love George Patton, the newspapers to the contrary. "Our blood and his guts," they said, but they did what he asked, and with a verve. As for me, I will take Grant and leave McClellan to you. As an ex-cavalryman, I will take the irascible Nathan Bedford Forrest and give you J. E. B. Stuart.

In spite of Bunker (Breed's) Hill, and several engagements of similar quality, it should be apparent that the role and status of the officer is or ought to be professional. Guerrillas Marion, Sumter,

Morgan, Ashby, and Guevara achieved some success, but the blood seminar has taught that there should be prerequisite courses before enrollment in the same. The difference between an amateur and a professional must be faced. What are the professional men in contrast with other workers? The language student will at once perceive that "amateur" contains the root for love, that such a man follows a calling for love instead of for pay. A skeptic might add that the professional is good enough to warrant pay, while the amateur is not. Winston Churchill was a painter for love, but who would buy one of his pictures as a work of art and not as a political artifact, or who would hang one painted by Hitler, a man who wanted to be a professional artist? Very well, consider for a moment that the professional is paid for his labors.

This attitude would exclude most of the patrician line soldiers of Athens and older Rome. Love and duty were their motives, for the state did not pay the seniors. These gentlemen lived better than the common kind did, but this would have been their right had they not donned armor at all, which was also true of the mediaeval military aristocracy. Expert enough to draw pay? George Washington received no pay during the Revolution. (He sent Congress a tremendous expense account when the war was over, though.) Was he an amateur?

Washington, of course, represents an exception, and perhaps a compromise might be made. If professional status did not also include eating, the society would have too few able servants. Granted that a professional man must receive compensation for his work, no matter how great this may be, pay must be secondary to service to the clientele. The career military officer is clearly in the professional class in this respect, for service, dedication, and self-sacrifice must come first if he is worth any pay at all.

Any standard dictionary definition virtually equates the professional and the intellectual classes, as indeed it should. Perhaps it would be more accurate to say that it is the leisure class which is meant, of which the intellectual is only a subcategory. The term should not include the idle, as some think. It is well to think of the leisure class a nonproductive laborers, meaning that they do not produce material consumption goods and services. Few materially productive workers equal the hours of arduous toil of the dedicated physician, trial lawyer, or academic research man. These men are fed, clothed, and housed by the labor of others because the overall society believes that their professional services are worth the outlay. Considered from this aspect, the career soldier of all ranks is a professional man.

There is an obvious, and perhaps temporary, animus directed

towards the military by certain members of the intellectual class, some of it reasonable, but for the most part, it is emotional. Yet all the professional *scholars* who voice such opinions have heard of Socrates, whose fame as a member of the class will probably outlive theirs. The sage began his six years compulsory service in the hoplite line of heavy infantry beginning at eighteen. As evidence that he gloried in his status as an active-duty soldier after his compulsory duty was over, he served as a volunteer in the Battle of Megara, and was present at the siege of Potidaea. Indeed, it was during the latter engagement that he was first seized by that supernatural *daimon* to whom he attributed his philosophical inspiration. He stood in a rigid trance for hours, and even overnight, and the troops gathered around to hear what he might say. His philosophical calling, then, dated from Potidaea, but he was well into middle age when he fought voluntarily in the long Athenian-Spartan war.

And then there was Napoleon whose achievements as an intellectual were qualitatively superior and of longer beneficent effects for his people than were his military feats. His reformed system of weights and measures are in point, for the scientist who devised it did so at his command. It was one of his young artillery officers who discovered the Rosetta Stone, and delivered it to the expert, Champollion, instead of throwing it away or keeping it for a souvenir. Since then, we have been able to transcribe the Egyptian hieroglyphs. It is incorrect to allege that he merely delegated the codification of the Franco-Roman law into the *Code Napoléon.* The First Consul was a lawyer's son, and he took an active part in framing what many juridical scholars say is the best code of law in the world. More civilized people are governed by it, anyway, than are served by the Anglo-American Common Law.

A profession is also based upon a knowledge, an *expertise*, which can be transmitted by instruction. One hardly needs belabor the point that the military is such an occupation. Herein is the great difference between a pure science and a pure art. Any science, if it be a science—natural, physical, behavioral—can be conveyed by instruction. An art, however, rests upon that undefinable grace called talent. A fairly competent painter or pianist can be produced by instruction, but a great one cannot be. Something must be added. A man can spend his life reading prayer books on his knees and theology in his study, and never become a saint. Another man can memorize the entire legal library and remain only a high-grade law clerk, but fail as a court room pleader or judge. The medical sciences are indeed based on biology, but the greater practitioner is vested with an art. And so it is with the military. Instruction and constant post-school study can make a very competent commander, or useful assistant in a staff office, but never a great captain of the host.

And last, one should add that a profession is a full-time occupation. It must take the whole of a man, his all, leaving little time for hobbies, and perhaps too little for recreation. This requirement therefore removes the officers of the patrician military republics. These gentlemen had other fish to fry, and often did them to a turn. What, then, shall we say of the citizen soldier whose loyalty and skill have served every nation in emergency? So many have demonstrated both field and staff competence, if the war is long enough so that the incompetents can be weeded. There is a very delicate relationship here, one which must be raised, but which cannot be solved here. If a professional officers' corps exists, and it does, the citizen officer must be included as a member of the club if he is to function competently.

The rise of a professional officer corps in the modern sense ought to surprise no one. The increased need of training, experience, and *expertise* in the civil government has clearly expanded the authority and power of a permanent corps of bureaucrats at the expense of officials designated by the electorate. This is the rationalization of government, which must and usually does go on regardless of whom the public likes or dislikes. The rationalization and professionalization of war and warfare are only functions of this general political trend caused by increasing complexity in the technological and economic structure. It is not as new as some might think. The yielding of the citizen nation-at-arms type of armed force to the full-time professional happened in later Rome and Byzantium. The officers commanding during the War in Lace period considered themselves professionals. An officer corps based on intense peacetime training was glimpsed by Louis XIV, and became an obsession with Frederick the Great, who considered it the foundation of the safety of the Prussian state. Great Britain, France, and Russia have known the phenomenon for years. It is only the United States which has lagged. Janowitz may be correct when he said that professionalism in the modern sense hardly appeared before 1800, although we may be sure that Cornwallis, Rawdon, and Rochambeau who fought in the American Revolution, considered themselves members of a professional officers' corps?[7]

Wendell Coats says that the officers' corps is a professional group characterized by three fundamentals: 1. *expertise*, responsibility, and corporatness.[8] Let us ask ourselves if the political scientist Samuel Huntington is not correct in saying that this is true of all professions.[9]

The possibility, nay, the desirability of reinstituting professional military class raises the spectre of militarism. This is a dread word, infected with more emotional value judgments than need be. Thank Alfred Vagts for giving a definition of the term,[10] "Militarism thus is not the opposite of pacifism; its counterpart is civilianism. Love of war, bellicosity, is the counterpart of the love of peace...." but militarism is more, and something less, than the love of war. It covers every system of thinking and valuing and every complex of feelings which rank military institutions and ways above the ways of civilian life, carrying military mentality and modes of acting and decision into the civilian sphere.

There have been times when, through their great power and prestige, the dominant military class, or even caste, has penetrated and controlled the civilian sphere. The serious situation, however, is the penetration and domination of the civil state. The patrician military republics were militaristic insofar as there was no real differentiation of the roles of the citizen and the soldier. The Prussian state was a militaristic one, and it left a long-time mark on the West. The takeover of the French Republic and the installation of De Gaulle as the powerful chief of state was accomplished by military means, but the nation did not become militaristic. De Gaulle turned on his military benefactors in a very savage way and prevented this.

The question must now be posed, are militaristic states more prone to foreign war and aggression than civilianistic ones, and the answer is not as clear as might be supposed. Surely Sweden under the later Vasa kings was warlike, and Prussian Frederick was no man of peace. In contrast, we quote the same section in Vagts, who says, "Generally speaking militarism flourishes more in peacetime than in war. In wartime, however, the pursuit of ends not identical with the winning of victory is militaristic; enterprises for sheer glory of the reputation of leaders, which reduces the fighting strength of armies and wreck them from within, come under that head."

Militarism is usually considered a dirty word, but what of the penetration and political domination by other occupational classes? Military domination served us well at one time, rescuing our civilization from hordes of barbarians, of which the Huns were only the worst. The upper agricultural classes ruled England for a long time, and perhaps squirearchy is a bad word. The mercantile-industrial-financial class invaded and often controlled our own government and, in this capacity, provided us with a magnificent standard of consumption. Is capitalism a dirty word? Some think so. The Trade Union Congress periodically takes over the government of Great Britain, but why go abroad? Using their tremendous wealth,

American trade unions can keep legislation against extreme violence and civil disorder from getting out of Congressional committee files. Even the Supreme Court ruled that the relatively innocuous Hatch Act did not really mean to forbid group mayhem in pursuit of the legitimate aims of the unions. Now is trade unionism a dirty word? Some think so. No one has coined a very dirty word about our academic selves, but it might be done some day. The intellectuals ruled both India and China, but few consider the terms brahmin and mandarin besmirched. The political ambitions of the modern intellectuals are called government by expert, and so far only the mild reproach of braintrusters and whizz-kids have been applied to them. The religious branch of intellectualism has acquired a dirty word, that is, clericalism, but the Church ruled Europe fairly well at a time when it needed it. The Prince Bishop of Liege was the first western sovereign to proclaim that every man was equally bound by the supremacy of the law, and his city of Huy was the first municipality to be freed from the control of feudality. We have outlived all this, and no one wants to see it return.

None of these words is written in rebuke. They are meant to show that the military class is not alone in political ambition. A social system gives power to occupational category which can best allay its fears or serve its desires, and none has abjured the use of armed forces.

FOOTNOTES AND REFERENCES

[1] Alfred H. Burne, *op. cit.*, see Chapter 13.

[2] George R. Steward, *Pickett's Charge: A Microhistory of the Final Attack at Gettysburg*, Greenwich, Connecticut, Fawcett Publications, Inc., 1963. A page number will not be given, for every reader should digest this brief book for its fair description of the personalities of both Confederate and Union leaders.

[3] Charles Fair, *From the Jaws of Victory*, New York, Simon, 1971 (permission of Simon and Schuster, Inc.).

[4] Wendell C. Coats, *Armed Force as Power*, New York, Exposition Press, 1966, p. 52f. (Permission of Wendell C. Coats.)

[5] Kluckhohn and Murray, *op. cit.*, p. 18.

[6] Theodore A. Dodge, *Great Captains*, Boston, Houghton Mifflin, 1889, p. 100.

[7] Morris Janowitz, *The Professional Soldier*, Glencoe, The Free Press, 1956, p. 6 (permission of The Free Press).

[8] Coats, *op. cit.*, p. 52f.

[9] Samuel P. Huntington, *The Soldier and the State*, Cambridge, Belknap Press of Harvard Press, 1957.

[10] Alfred Vagts, *A History of Militarism*, New York, W.W. Norton and Company, 1937, and revised edition, Meridian Books, 1959, p. 13ff. (Permission of Alfred Vagts.)

Chapter 12

THE MERCENARIES

Professionalism and Its Clients

The previous chapter closed on the note of professionalism. It might be well, then, to carry this theme to two logical conclusions: the mercenaries discussed the present chapter, and the pretorians to be outlined in the next one.

The evil value judgment invoked by the very term "mercenary" makes definition just a bit difficult. Mercenary soldier is a role and status of easy definition, but the obloquy lies in the adjective, not the noun. In the first place, the mercenary soldier is a trained, disciplined, professional purveyor and receiver of violence. Gladiators of old, though, fell into that category. Some were killed or injured in the practice of their craft. If they were successful, they became pampered pets. The servile gladiator was bought and sold. This brings up a second consideration. He was not a volunteer. The mercenary soldier is, and his organizations are often called "free companies." The third and perhaps key characteristic of these merchants of force is their financial preoccupation. Members of a state's regular or citizen military components are not mercenaries even if they are paid because they are citizens of the polity they serve.

The mercantile implication of the troops in question must, therefor, contain that of noncitizenship. They owe no "natural" fealty or legal obligation to their paymasters. The Greek officers of the Byzantine Emperor were paid 20,000 per year in our gold dollars, but they were not mercenaries, for they were subjects of the Divine and Sacred Emperor, Equal of the Apostles. The latter's Varangian Guard were mercenaries, because they were Teutons. The French Foreign Legionaires were and are mercenaries, for parsimoniously paid, fed, and housed as they are, they are not *supposed* to be Frenchmen. One can hardly call two of our early American Colonial heroes mercenaries either, for although in their past they had both been hirelings, they lived as they could here, like any other colonist, and were as much citizens as anybody else. One refers to Captains John Smith and Myles Standish.

The requirement of "nationality" should not be stressed too much, for while the concept of "stranger" is old and universal, that of "foreigner" is as young as the rise of nationalist states. Captains Gower, Fluellen, Macmorris, and Jamy in Shakespere's *King Henry V*, while more or less of the same budding "nation" as that king, owed him no feudal service, and were not invading France under any lord to whom their fealty was a matter of legal course. They were hired, free English, Welsh, Irish, and good ones, it seems. By contrast, the English knights and lords in·the play were not mercenaries, for they were legally bound to serve.

Fourth, it is perhaps well to note that mercenaries are not emotionally or ideologically involved in the wars they fight. Thus, the continental leaders, Marquis de Lafayette, Count Pulaski, and the Barons de Kalb and von Steuben were not foreign mercenaries. These men were deeply involved emotionally and ideologically, we were hundreds of Americans who fought in the Spanish republican army against Francisco Franco's royalist insurrection. The Ten Thousand Greeks in Xenophon's *Anabasis* were true mercenaries, for whether Cyrus or Darius should be Persian emperor was none of their concern. Mercenaries often become emotionally and ideologically involved later, as combat tends to make either converts or deserters, but such was not their original motivation.

In general, it seems that the basic cause of mercenarism is a gap between the offensive or defensive goals of a state and the qualitative or quantitative military potential of its own manhood. There must also exist recruit reservoirs external to such political systems, such as warlike people like Germans, Irish, or Scots, whose fertility exceeds their homeland's capacity to provide the desired means of subsistence. Thus, as early as 1470, Switzerland was overpopulated by young men of tremendous skill, valor, and need of work which their own country could not provide. The Swiss of the day were not exporters of chocolate, watches, and secret bank numbers. They exported as good infantry as the world has ever seen. They were not, as now, receivers and entertainers of tourists. They were the tourists, and very well armed ones indeed.

As distasteful as the phenomenon might seem to some Americans, or to almost any other fairly patriotic people, the mercenary has a long tradition. The record is far from clear, but it might well be that he is as old as both true war and the institution of the state. The primordial polities of the eastern Mediterranean depended on the noble companionate of the little kings to maintain order within, and to fight the aggressive and defensive wars against both rival states and the swarms of primitive warriors with which they were well supplied. Actually, this situation did very well for the little bucolic Indo-European states of both the Greek and Italic peninsulas, but such states have a way of either growing or disappearing. Certainly the basic Greek populations were never very warlike, perhaps because of the adequacy of the patrician military republics which developed out of the armed companionate of the priest-kings. In the Fertile Crescent, though, the polity began as a despotism, and the early irrigation states very soon had foreign ambitions which exceeded the dependable military manpower of their own subjects.

One of the first lessons which one is presented in this whole story is that despotisms, or Leviathan states, do not make for warlike general civil population, benevolent and paternal as they may be, there is too much social distance between the governed and the governors to form a patriotic climate. These divine irrigation monarchies might have been as able and efficient as imaginable, but compulsion in economic production is a poor school for soldiers at any time or place. The overweening sacredness of the priest-kingships provided no effective military inspiration, either. It seems that the divine monarch cannot have it both ways, then or now. If such states had the slightest idea of expanding, or keeping their own borders inviolate, they could only hire professional appliers of force. The mercenary army, then, might be a function of highly organized, charismatic states, for it appears almost whenever that type of social system arises. One may suspect that the more complex the organization, the less willing and less able the citizens might be to bear the military burden.

The record of the early Leviathans of Mesopotamia is not very clear until the rise of the militant Assyrians. The relation of the officer corps of these despotisms and the common soldier is dealt with elsewhere. The story of Egypt is better recorded.

Egypt was ruled by a bureaucratic administration headed by a very sacred personage. Her internal relations were maintained by the sanctity of the god-king, and usually very well when bolstered by pretorians. Militarily, Egypt was protected by nature. Both flanks were contained by the great African desert. It required but a small garrison to keep the Suez region from incursion by hungry Asians. The southern frontier of the Nile cataracts was not too hard to hold. Later this was held by a mercenary garrison of dark skinned Nubians. Whatever effective army the Egyptians of the Old Kingdom had was more engaged in keeping this divine work camp down than in any foreign adventure. This should not have been an impossible task, for the irrigation despotism invented the old "way up and way down" economy of food energy distribution, the gathering in of vast amounts of eatables during good years, and its expenditure in tremendous public works in times of need.

Egypt was eventually invaded successfully, and the Old Kingdom was brought to an end. The Hyksos, a mysterious people of probable Semitic speech, conquered the Two Lands. (Josephus, the Jewish historian, thought they were Israelites. *Contra Apionem*, i, 14) It is almost sure, however, that these steppe nomads had collected a few Asian mercenaries on their way. Indeed, it has been suggested that the term *habiri* (Hebrew) might mean mercenary soldier, although this seems farfetched. The Hyksos and their strong men set up the Middle Kingdom, or rule of the shepherd kings, a feudalism of short duration. If the descendents of their hired men were put to work making bricks without straw, this is not too hard to understand. Mercenaries have been stranded without friends since.

The revival of Egyptian strength, called the New Empire, saw the new Pharaohs with definite foreign ambitions. One reads of the Battle of Armageddon, and thrills to it, but Pharaoh Rameses III failed in Palestine. His timing was wrong; he was too late. The Middle East of the time was characterized by an Indo-European folk migration which Rameses could not have foreseen. Pressed back into its traditional borders, Egypt was more and more ruled by incompetent and weak kings. Ordinarily the old traditional Egyptian bureaucratic machinery would have carried her through, but a new element had been added to obstruct the priestly scribes. The Egyptian army by this time was composed almost entirely of non-Egyptian mercenaries from west of the Nile.

The ancient Egyptian Leviathan was a perfect base for a mercenary-based state. The population was not warlike. The Egyptian people were oppressed with a death wish, or death fear, as exhibited by the surviving monuments. They were governed by a too-sacred government. These facts may not contain a universal lesson, but there are some other homilies to be read. This all-things-to-all-men type of government could hardly evoke public spirit or patriotism. It could, though, be headed by a king quite capable of dreaming of projects which could only be implemented by a military which he would not find in his own subjects. The god-king could not identify with his people, nor they with anyone so remote and sacred. There is a lesson to be learned here about political charisma. A common person might die for his god-state, but a vibrant polity needs masculine men, not dedicated corpses. Old Egypt would not have survived without a pool of fierce non-Egyptians willing to trade blood for rations. There was at hand a warlike reservoir, willing to keep down the Pharaonic slave camp in pretorian service, or to guard frontiers of those too engrossed elsewhere to protect themselves. Libya, the desert west of the fertile Nile Valley, was full of very hungry, very bellicose social systems unable to unite themselves into a firm polity, yet admiring the fleshpots of Egypt. Here was an area suffering from intense population pressure, and so joyously fecund as to constitute an inexhaustible flesh pool. Immigration into and death in Egypt's armed services was a comparative blessing to living in the fragmented, unproductive social systems of Libya. The belated effort to set up the New Empire was largely attempted with their arms, and might have succeeded earlier. The point here is that this adventure was undertaken with Libyan mercenaries who had many virtues, but being Egyptian was not one. Indeed, profiting by subsequent pharaonic weakness, the Libyans set up their own dynasty, after the fashion of mercenaries. The desert men exhibited their great physical endurance in this take-over, but their modal personality betrayed them. They could not unite and operate a civilized state without direction, without someone else performing the administrative tasks, so their rule was short-lived.

The old nation recovered some vitality and independence under the XXVI Dynasty, and found the invading Greeks something with which to contend. The Pharaohs of this dynasty did not fight the Greeks, but made peace with them. Pharaoh Psammeticus was taught by an oracle that "men of bronze" would rescue him from his troubles, and they did. The early, and later Greeks, were ideal mercenaries. It would be many a century before any people could successfully attack their line of heavy infantry, or resist the steam roller attack of the hoplites.

It was too late for even Greek mercenaries to save Egypt. Her last burst of shabby independence was due to a revolt of her Nubian mercenaries guarding the southern borders of the kingdom. It is known that these black men were called Nubians, but it is very doubtful if they were Negroes in the modern sense. That race type was not to break from its narrow west African homeland to overrun a continent until about the time of Roman Augustus. Black the Nubians were, however, and this garrison simply marched north and took over. It was a dynasty of but two pharaohs, father and son, who attempted too much. They challenged the power of Persia, and Cambyses invaded Egypt largely to exercise his troops, and the independence of Egyptians, as Egyptians, was apparently lost forever. The Greeks, however, were launched on their career.

Lest one lose track of pre-Columbian America, things also happened here. As in Hellas, the divine, irrigation despotisms of Middle America were incapable of forming strong, centralized states until it was too late. The Book of Chilam Balam of Chumayel records that the sacred princes did form the League of Mayapan, but, as in Athens, the prince of Chichen Itza played a fast game with his allies. Seeking to become the overall lord without his colleagues' consent, he invited in the half-wild Nahua-speaking Toltecs as mercenaries. Having won the war, the mercenary tribesmen liked their new home and remained, not as hirelings but as lords, and why should they not? So the great Mayan civilization had really become a subject of archaeology even before the Spaniards came. Have we not read such a story a few paragraphs back? Are there not striking similarities in all these despotisms, so divine that they can religiously overawe the commonalty into making such great sacrifices in food production, taxation, and labor in public works, and in the process take the pith from the people? The sacrosanct character of the charismatic monarchy is strong medicine. It is a wonderful substitute for force in the internal relationship, but what if violence appears from outside which does not subscribe to the godlike nature of the government? The noble companionate in Hellas, in Mesopotamia, and in Polynesia was quite adequate for the short wars of naive polities, for these were men dedicated to violence, and were almost as sacred as the priest-king himself. But what if an external enemy appears on the boundaries in great force? What if the divine king has foreign ambitions which require numbers and willingness to continue the conflict indefinitely? To whom can he turn when the noble companionate is dead or suffering from war fatigue, and his armed peasants tremble at the twang of an enemy bowstring? This prince has no other direction in which to turn. His problem is not whether or not to use mercenaries. He is concerned about their adequacy in numbers, quality, and trustworthiness.

The military changes in the Roman social system from tribe to empire have been discussed elsewhere. The service of foreign mercenaries in the troops of the Purple is recounted in the proper place. We have also seen how feudalism saved much of Roman civilization for us, its heirs. We have seen man and baron stand to die or win in repelling the barbarous hordes of Huns, Teutons, Saracens, Vikings, and others. The rise of that military society called feudalism is not pertinent here, nor are the struggles of prince against prince, crusaders against Moslem and Greek, or Holy Roman emperor against his reluctant vassals. There were some mercenaries in most of these fights, but what lies before us now is the decay of mediaeval society, the reappearance of the mercenary as a real, telling force, and his rise during renaissance days to a monopoly of arms, at least in Italy.

In fact, the mercenary had a real place in all mediaeval wars as soon as the feudal system was firmly established. First, there was the knight errant whom romanticists do not call a mercenary, but that is what he was. There are few things certain in the sociology of stratification, but one is surely the high fertility of a military aristocracy. It was the middle, mercantile classes which discovered birth control, not the gentry and nobility. There were titles and estates to pass on for as many generations as possible, and as both were held on condition of military service to an overlord, such feudal warfare consumed sons. Indeed, the Hundred Years War, followed by the War of the Roses, so utterly depopulated the English military aristocracy that there are virtually no titles or peerages in the present House of Lords of real knightly, aristocratic background. Where is the great Chandos, and does de Bohun sit in the upper chamber? Hardly, for they are dead. In normal times, then, there were younger sons who by their birth had to be trained and knighted, but their services were not needed if peace was obtained locally. Their sires and older brothers had too little to feed their hungry mouths, and those of their squires and horses. There was nothing for these young men to do but seek service as "free lances" under some lord or prince, as hired knights errant, or noble mercenaries, if you will. The phenomenon lasted until that flower of dying feudalism, Geoffrey Chaucer, could extol the virtues of his knight. It is true that the poet outlined many wars wherein the knight of the *Prologue* had served his own king in feudal due, but he was in every armed argument in the world in his forty-some years of service. He could have been nothing else but a mercenary lance, though Chaucer calls him "a verray parfit, gentil knight." He also seems to have been a master in veterans' talk, interminably recounting his travels and exploits after the manner of his kind.

One of the greatest generals of the Middle Age was John Plantagenet, King of England. His name is encountered often in this work as the master of mediaeval warfare at its best. He nevertheless laid the seeds of its destruction. John had some experience with his own baronage at Runnymede, a lesson in feudalism which he did not forget. Once his humiliation at the hands of the baronial, oligarchical republic was over, his disgust at it lived with him until he died. John became the greatest of castle-builders of them all, and as an engineer, a mighty destroyer of them, too. All the English municipalities were loyal to him with the exception of London, so he was already provided with many pivots of maneuver in the walled towns. The burgers were quite capable of defending their own circumvallations, and this they did for the king. He needed an increased line of defense against his rebels and their French allies. He built castle after castle, but he did not depend on the local untrained peasantry to garrison them. He scoured the continent, hiring mercenaries for this purpose, and they served him well. This might surprise us, but what we are inclined to forget is that patriotism in the later nationalistic sense was unknown in those days. Men swore allegiance to their immediate lords, not the nation.

Actually, one should have surmised this. The defense of a small country castle could have been entrusted to the lord, his tenants, and a few men-at-arms. This was not true of the great ones. One could not expect the walls to be defended by the heavy feudal cavalry, the mainstay of mediaeval warfare. The castle was a place of refuge for them, and a pivot of maneuver. Of course, the knights and men-at-arms did their duty in case of siege, but static defense was not their role. Neither their training nor equipment was designed to defend the walls and gates. This was increasingly the role of professional archers, pikemen, and halberdiers who were more and more hired professionals, and not vassals of the lord of the house. And who did the hard work of the siege of such places? Not knights with sword and shield and lance. The Saracens used slaves for sapper work, and it cost them many. The Christians had no slaves.

And as for life in the open field, military men know what is not generally mentioned. Mediaevalism was not brought down with one flight of English arrows at Agincourt. Chivalry, or the reliance on the feudal cavalry, had been sickening long before. The need for more infantry fire power had been appreciated for some time, and its realization found bowmen and crossbowmen inflicting dreadful casualties among the horses and horsemen. And so, from the Battle of Poitiers onward, the knights and men-at-arms customarily dismounted to fight on foot, not as true infantry, but as dismounted cavalry in their full armor. Who invented the legend that the knight in his heavy armor, which surely had passed the point of diminishing returns in body protection, had to be hoisted into the saddle with a derrick? Esquires were taught to vault into the saddle from the ground, clad in armor which surely must have weighed more than 150 pounds. Fighting ahorse, then afoot, then ahorse again in the same day required this.

In any event, the last years of the Hundred Years War showed an increase in the use of mercenaries. One would have thought that this marked an increase in the national wealth of England, but the reverse was true. The Black Death had reduced the realm to poverty. The answer is that England, and other powers, were gradually becoming centralized states at the expense of feudal independence. Edward the Black Prince, far from being the rose of chivalry, openly spoke of the divine right of kings, thus foreshadowing a renaissance concept, and one inimical to feudalism. This centralization of power meant that of funds, too, which meant the ability to hire mercenaries of whatever tongue, masterless men without a feudal lord.

Whatever the dysfunctions and loss of life the Hundred Years War entailed, it set England on the way to nationhood in the modern sense. The aforesaid Black Prince's father, Edward III, had some claim to the French throne, but we cannot discuss the morality of the war here. Edward, however, knew that England was poor, and that France and its King John were rich. He must have known in his heart of hearts that, given equal transport and other logistic support, France had to win. Edward also knew that the English enthusiasm of the tenant for his lord, and the lord for the crown were things of the past. As this feeling was far from dead, or even ill, in France, he knew that he could not match the feudal power of John Capet, whose crown he coveted. His solution of the problem of gap between his ambitions and feudal resources was not to order the lords and their commonalty into the field, but to contact with the former to hire whatever of their vassals who would fight for king and almost country for a fixed rate of pay. The great Plantagenet had already conducted a military laboratory against the Scots, and found the value of infantry firepower. The English long bow, so-called because it was a Welsh invention, had devastated the Stuart king's ranks. So off to France started Edward III Plantagenet with his cavalry levy bound to him by feudal dues, and somewhere between six and seven thousand mercenary mounted men-at-arms, together with 10,000 hired contract archers, and between three and four thousand hired among the Welsh who, then as now, had little love for anything English.

We cannot discuss this campaign of bumbling on both sides, but we all know that the French were roundly defeated at Crecy, largely due to the precision of the English mercenary archers. The French had their firepower, too, some 6,000 Genoese mercenary crossbowmen. The burgers of Paris had volunteered for this duty, but were scorned as baseborn hucksters. And so on the great day, the Genoese with their clumsy weapons were shot to ribbons by the English archers, who not only could fire three arrows at them while they were winding up their little winches, but who outranged them as well. This infuriated the Duc d'Alencon in command of the French van. This noble knight, instead of blaming his national reliance on this weapon of exaggerated potential, spitefully rode his heavy cavalry into his Genoese ranks and butchered them.

Certainly the English kings by the end of the thirteenth century were progressing towards a national army, whether they knew it or not. Their ambitions in France strained the patience of the baronage to supply heavy cavalry, and the militia of all free men inherited by the Normans from the Anglo-Saxons were loathe to provide infantry for longtime service abroad. The law of contract was increasingly revived in England's progress towards commercial mercantilism, and this legal drift obviously affected the practice of war.

Edward II surely relied on mercenary contractors, even foreigners such as Sir Walter Manny, to provide him with troops of all ranks and arms. This service was purely for pay at stated times, usually a year. Being mercenaries, feudal homage was not required of these men. We know that in 1316 a knight-banneret was paid four shillings a day, a simple knight two shillings, while mounted men-at-arms and squires drew one shilling per diem. Enlisted pay was one shilling for centenars (commanders of a hundred), while mounted archers, armored infantry on foot, and hobilars (mounted infantry) were paid at sixpence per day. Foot archers and walking Welsh infantry got two pence per diem. This pay seems small, but we know that in 1346 eggs cost one English penny for two dozen, chickens sold at two for a penny. Booty, too, was over and above this, and lucky the contract mercenary who could capture a nobleman able to pay a fortune for his ransom.

All the royal Edwards probably saw this mercenary pool as the foundation of a national army which would free them from the feudal nobility. This is eventually what happened, but not right away. The magnates closest to this people pool were those very lords. They themselves became the contractors, and the position of the middleman has always been a lucky one. Then, thought they, if contract soldiers are good for the king, they are good for us, too. The baronage was also discontented with its feudal resources of men, and began amassing contract mercenaries to man the castle walls, to operate the new artillery, to serve as heavy infantry in the baronial feuds, and to act as just plain status symbols, strutting about in their livery.

Thus, the manifest function of a contract royal army obedient to the king alone was accompanied by the latent dysfunction of baronial contract armies. A duke or an earl with a sizeable private army did not become more amenable to royal discipline than he had been. It is recorded, too, that these new nobles, should one of them think he had a weak case before the increasingly important royal judges, usually brought as large a retinue of his liverymen to court as he could. If the judge could not be bribed, perhaps he could be overawed.

An interesting point is that the late mediaeval mercenaries of north Europe, frankly commercial fighters, patterned their organization after that of the merchant and craft gilds of the day. Indeed, they were craft gilds, electing their own officers for terms of office as did their peaceful counterparts. The behavior of these "free companies" contributed much to the bad name the term "mercenary" has to this day.

Now if we may call Louis XI the last mediaeval French king, we must deem his son, Charles VIII, the first renaissance sovereign of that land. Charles of France thought he had a claim to the Kingdom of Naples because of his kinship with the defunct House of Anjou, and in 1494 began his invasion of Italy. Louis XI, that knight-hater, had vainly tried to form a French national infantry, but his son had a great fear of arming the French common man. Charles showed that the Middle Age was over by taking with him 40,000 hired foot, the best of which were 10,000 Swiss and German mercenaries. The pike was the traditional weapon of these men, who by the number of 6,000 in light armor formed the front ranks of the battle square. The center was composed of 4,000 armed with the new *hakenbusche*, or arquebus. This was actually a light cannon, you will recall, with a stock, equipped with a hook to go over a stick to absorb the recoil. It is recorded that the invaded Italians admired the order of these Teutons because of their great size, their gaudy uniforms, and their marching in step to the sound of the drum, a strange thing in that day. In contrast with them, the French infantry was a sociological mess. If they were a poor sort, the Italian mercenaries who opposed them were worse.

Guiccardini, an Italian contemporary, said of them,[1] "...many of the men at armes are either peasantes or populares, subjects of another Prince, and depending wholly on their Captaines...; they have neither by nature nor by accident, any extraordinary spurre or provocation to serve well. The Captaines are very rarely vassales of him that entertaines them; they have for the most part diverse interestes, purposes and ends; full of envy and hatreds. And being bound to no terme fixed for their payes, and absolute commanders over their companies, they often beguile the service with lesse numbers than they are payed for; and sometimes not contented with honest conditions, they put their patrones upon every occasion to raunsome, at their pleasure they will passe from the service of one, and enter into the paye of another, ambition, covetousnesse, or other particular interestes, making them not onely inconstant, but also unfaithful. There was also seen no lesse difference between the footemen of Italie, and those that served under king Charles, for that the Italians fought not in squadrons set and ordered, but in troupes, dispersed in the field, and oftentymes retyring to the advantages of hilles and ditches. But the Swyzzers . . . used to fight with bandes ordered, and distinct in numbers certaine; and never forsaking their ranckes, they used to stand against their enemies as a wall; firm and almost invincible, so farre forth as they fought in a plaine or place large enough to stretch out their battel; even with the same discipline and orders, but not with the like courage and vertue, did fight the footemen of the french and Gascoynes."

Mediaeval civilization was ending in Italy before it sickened elsewhere, if indeed it ever took hold on the peninsula as it did among northerners. Barring the Norman feudalities of south Italy, the old Mediterranean idea of the city state had been kept alive. It was not necessary to teach mercantile capitalism to the region which invented it. The Italian states had always been businessman polities, overshadowed for a while by the Empire. It was they who kept law and order alive when the Purple was rent. Then as now, they had an oversized merchant class. Keep this in mind when we encounter the rise of Italian fascism. Mediaeval and renaissance Italy was cut up into small states, each with resources too limited to wage war when they became infected with post-Roman military ambitions. The oversized middle class which should have fought these wars held to one mediaeval tradition: fight one battle and go home. The hinterland was populated by the Italian peasant who had survived Caesars and barbarian invasions, and was too wise to take any lord seriously, too prudent to fight often, or very hard. Neither the burgers nor peasants had been thoroughly feudalized, so there was a lack of heavy cavalry in an era dominated by that arm. Cities do not produce the mailed gentleman. The towns, then, had too much survival of Roman luxury, and the countryside was peopled by a peasantry for centuries too interested in self-preservation. These are poor sources of a military spirit. The citizens could and did man their own walls well and bravely, but were unreliable on the offensive. And war is a strange thing. It must have an aggressor to exist at all. Political aggression there was aplenty, the Guelphs and the Ghibellines constantly seeking politico-economic advantage over their rivals. All of this was the mercenary's special dish of tea.

Thus, as first Mediterranean Europe, and later all of it, marched away from the Middle Age with its military ethic of the armored gentleman, and towards that of mercantile free enterprise, warfare had to conform. It has a way of paralleling the arts and organization of peace. This happens because it must. Thus, from the Italian thirteenth century to the middle of the fifteenth, a type of skilled, professional craftsman rose to fulfill a felt need. This was the age of the *condotta*, or band, commanded by a *condottiere*, or captain. Such bands could be of any size, but they were often over a thousand. The *condottieri* became not only professional, hired soldiers but that class always beloved of the gods, monopolists. The feudal wars of the north were waning or over, leaving that burden of all polities, the unemployed veteran, in great plenty. It did not take these men long to discover that Italy was in turmoil and willing to pay well for their services. They did not even have that nuisance to all professional soldiers, involvement with the civilian population, to say nothing of courting their approval. They were hirelings of a little absolutist, or would-be absolutist prince.

The apparent founder of the renaissance Italian mercenary structure was, of course, a foreigner, one Montreal d'Albarno, who founded the Grand Company. This Provencal was a realist, and understood that an armed mob would accomplish little. He organized his men into a clear-cut, formal structure, subjected them to hard, careful, and constant training and discipline in the internal relations set, and paid them not only with good coin but with absolute permissiveness towards the civilian population, enemy or friendly. He knew that the day of chivalry was over, and with about 7,000 heavy cavalry and 1,500 elite infantry, a mediaeval cooperation which was always hard to beat, D'Albarno terrorized Italy. The enlisted personnel was largely German, commanded by a Frenchman, another combination hard to beat. Rienzi, the self-appointed Tribune of the Roman People, finally caught up with him without his support and executed him. His successor, Conrad Lando, left no better reputation. And lest the English become too ethnocentric on this point, the White Company, founded by Sir John Hawkwood out of veterans unemployed by the Peace of Bretigny in 1360, made the English language unpalatable to the Italians for a long time.

These condottieri were far from armed amateurs. The captains were not only men of vigor but were obviously more intelligent than their employers. It was a poor day when they could not lead these semi-literate princes around by the nose and extract political as well as financial rewards from them. Not being bound by the knightly code of the "faith of a gentleman," they could do to their hirer just about what they pleased. Indeed, towards the end of the great period of the condotta, a peasant named Muzio Attendolo Sforza, organized a very successful band. His son, Francesco Sforza, inherited this company, and with it imprisoned and probably murdered the lawful lord of Milan, and became quite the patron of renaissance art.

Late mediaeval and renaissance Italian politics, then, depended on free bands of mercenary cavalry. Although the dawn of infantry as the queen of battles should have been obvious, the captains adopted it slowly. They had little use for footmen, and used them mainly for siege operations. Despite the pride of the French and American engineers in their elite corps, their Italian progenitors left such a bad name that it took a long time for engineers to be accepted as soldiers, officers, and gentlemen.

The captains were businessmen in the pure, acting in a land which invented the European phenomenon. These free enterprisers believed in keen competition among themselves but, as in subsequent days, would band together against the common enemy, the consumer. As the craft gilds before them invented featherbedding and the slowdown of production, they took over these concepts with the seemingly modern ring. They knew that their employers were militarily illiterate, and constantly misadvised them to keep wars going which could have been composed. A striking victory was the last thing they wanted, and they rarely exploited one when it fell into their laps. Who likes unemployment? Machiavelli looked on them as obstacles to the rise of patriotic, national armies of citizens, and inveighed against them, largely in vain. Professionals do have a way of out-competing amateurs in almost everything. Nationalism and national armies did arise, but with no help from the condottieri.

Baseborn as they often were, these professionals were literate, and studied the military manuals available to them. Their favorite was that of Vegetius, who was the mentor of the later Roman empire. They founded and maintained schools to hone the efficiency of their men, and conducted exercises or laboratories in the field to test new ideas and to discover improvements. They loved and protected their soldiers whom they recruited and trained at their own very considerable expense. A soldier, then, was a skilled craftsman whom they could ill afford to lose in battle. Of course, there are industrial accidents. Management always has these, but a captain reckless with his men's blood would suffer a labor turnover he could not afford at all. The captains had to put on a good show, as any contractor must if he intends to be retained, but their goal was not their employers' success. A long war and a merry was their maxim. If an employer ran out of cash, they would quit in the middle of a battle, and such strikes were often fatal.

We have noted that the Italian mercenary captains read books appropriate to their trade, but apparently wrote few. Our conclusion on them, then, is based on the literate detractors. These men said that such heavy cavalry soldiers were not gentlemen, but they never said they were. They did not identify with either the prince who hired them or with his population, and hence their rapacity went unchecked. They unblushingly changed sides for pay. They fought their opposition in Vegetian battles of maneuvre, providing a spectacular day's work with as few casualties on either side as possible. They were tied to their enemies by professional bonds more than to their patrons, so they had no ambition to hurt their opposition very much. Today's enemy might be tomorrow's ally, or even one's commanding officer.

They invented the humane treatment of prisoners. Prisoners of war were rarely killed, for one cannot ransom a corpse. They abjured prisoner torture, for such behavior would enrage the other captain, and, due to the fortunes of war, who was victorious today might be himself a prisoner in the not distant future. And thus the international law of mercy had a strange birth.

The beginning of the end of condottiere rule was foreshadowed by the founding of a semi-mercenary, half-patriot band by Count Alberigo of Barbiano out of his own subjects towards the end of the thirteenth century. The career of national armies could have been foretold by that event.

The fate of national armies rose and wavered, but there were breaks which again favored mercenaries. Turn your mind again to the British in America attempting to fight a limited war while their revolutionary opposition had total war in mind. The prime minister, Lord North, had warned his king that he could not fight a French-Spanish combination in the eastern hemisphere, and a first-class colonial war in the western one. King George III then made an effort to hire mercenaries, asking his kinsman, the Landgrave of Hesse-Cassel, to provide him with 17,000 troops. Other German states gave 12,000, although all were called "Hessians" by the continentals. The term of recruitment of these Germans is not perfectly clear even in this day. Not all of these were mercenaries, no matter how commercial their prince was. As regulars, they went where they were sent, and did as they were told, after the manner of their kind. Many officers and men were straight-out hirelings, and their subsequent desertion rate was high. The lamentation of these German "enlisted" men was often loud. Considering that their transports were no better than the typical slaver in the African trade, it is a wonder that they served at all. One might add, however, that the German desertion rate never equalled that of the continental Americans. It is clear that whole regiments of elite troops were sent under terms not known to me. Indeed, military historians maintain that the Jäger were the best units in the British army. In any event, the hired German troops constituted about one third of the British forces in America.

High school history books tend to discount the military effectiveness of the Germans. They take pride in Washington's clever spoiling Von Rahl's cozy Christmas party at Trenton. Dysentry and wounds had reduced Rahl to three effective officers, less than 2,000 soldiers on that day to oppose 10,000 continentals. Such historians overlook the drubbing the "Hessians" gave the continentals at Long Island, White Plains, Newport, and Charleston. Had George III and Lord North really wanted to win, they should have fired their high-society generals and put hardcore professional Von Knyphausen in high command. In any event, some 11,000 Germans remained in America after the peace, where they and their descendants made a reputation for industry, frugality, and civic virtue.

With due respect to the horrors of Andersonville and Libby prisons, Confederate prisoners of war were subject to deliberate neglect by Lincoln's own order. Offered freedom, enlisted pay, and a promise not to be used against their own people, thousands of these men enlisted in the Union cavalry to fend off the Indian incursions the Civil War encouraged. Lincoln could not afford to send his good but numerically inadequate troops out west. These ex-Confederates were mercenaries in that they were trained, fought for pay, and in a cause they did not consider their own. Thousands of Confederates with no homes worth returning to, and also many Unionists who had learned the soldier's trade were available to European powers after Appomattox. However, barring the Franco-Prussian War, peace settled over Europe. At that, Napoleon III would have done well to have enlisted Confederate cavalry under the disgusted Nathan Bedford Forrest. Sedan might not have been such a fiasco. A fair number of ex-Confederates did take service under the Khedive of Egypt. On the whole, however, Hitler's experiment of enlisting thousands of captured Russians to serve against the Anglo-American invasion of France might be something of a warning. They surrendered in such droves that it was logistically impossible to feed, house, or even keep them in fairly hygienic conditions. There may be a factor of national temperament here, though, which has been overlooked.

Some Americans served as mercenaries in twentieth century Central America, often determining the direction of "revolutions," but after World War I, the United States began offering these soldiers of fortune loss of American citizenship. This brought the movement to an end. It is doubtful if the hundreds of Americans who fought in the Spanish Civil War can be called mercenaries, for they could not have been paid beyond subsistence.

The greatest use of foreign mercenaries in the twentieth century was by France in her wars of colonial expansion. These men were largely unemployed Germans, and their half-Teutonized Foreign Legion French was heard in almost every North African bazaar until quite recently. The discipline they received was severe, but not unjust. France was suffering from war fatigue, contraception, and lack of public interest in the colonies. Legionaires were worked at road building, and other works of "peaceful penetration" few born Frenchmen would tolerate. Most of them remained faithful to their soldier's oath even after Hitlerist Germany occupied France, retiring deep into Africa with Generals de Lattre de Tassigny and Le Clerc. They served France well in southeast Asia, dying on the Plain of Jars and at Dien Bien Phu. Nevertheless, the corps was peremptorily punished by De Gaulle whom it had helped put in power.

The ethical winds which characterize the mid-twentieth century would lead one to think that the mercenary as a military phenomenon is as obsolete as the pitched battle with pikes. Actually, he is very much a part of the modern scene. One straw in the wind could have been detected at the close of World War II. The prisoner of war cages were prematurely emptied, and thousands of battle-trained Germans, disillusioned with Hitler, hating the Russians with venom, unemployed in a war-ruined country, and having faith in little but their own military skills, would have been happy to serve as a mercenary *Freikorps* under the United States flag. Their officers saw the Russians with stretched lines of communication, logistically exhausted, their best troops decimated, and therefore extremely vulnerable. Many wanted to do something about it, and the *Stars and Stripes*, PX privileges, and GI chow suited them just fine. The time was not right. Perhaps it was all for the best, but such units might have done well in Korea.

The existence of 45,000 mercenaries made up of Cambodians, Laotians, Montagnards, and deserters from the North Vietnamese regulars and the Viet Cong organized into Civilian Irregular Defense Groups shows that the American ethical thinking may have shifted. Recruited and trained by the magnificent soldiers of the United States Special Service (Green Berets), their combat record has been excellent, especially in constructing and garrisoning holding positions.

Look at another continent, and see almost all of Africa in turmoil with no creditable black army south of the Sahara. Add a host of foreign soldiers disillusioned with the policy of their home governments, or just bored, and see that the mercenary has flowed into the interstecies he has always occupied, the gap between the politico-military ambitions of new rulers and the martial manpower resources available to them. Modern Africa has been a fertile field for mercenary endeavors, and it is regrettable that space is not allowed to recount their deeds and misdeeds. There was the Englishman Michael Hoare who crushed a rebellion for Moise Tchombe in the Congo with his Five Commando. There was the debonair Frenchman, Robert Denard, with his *Affreux*. It was said that the Englishman John Peters would raise an efficient ground or air force for any African chief who could pay well. The Belgian Jean Schramme had a good record of rebellion-smashing. Carl Schmidt, the German "mercenary's mercenary," was a man with whom to reckon. Many things have been said for and against their forces, but one of them probably contains more truth than many would like to contemplate. It is very probable that had all the foreign mercenaries in Africa united and had the conditions of civilization in Negro Africa remained the same, they could have controlled any succession state in the black continent, and not unthinkably all of them. There is usually a reservoir of unemployed fighting men at the end of major wars. Can they be recruited, Sir John Hawkwood?

The status of the Cuban armies in Africa is not clear. Are they mercenaries, as the American press often alleges? Who pays them, their host country or their own, or both? Volunteers they are, but they are dedicated to a cause and Russian trained. Are they like the army of Rochambeau in the American Revolution, who were not mercenaries?

This chapter makes no value judgment for or against the mercenaries. Like the subject of the pretorians to follow, they have their place in the founding of this world. If anyone thinks that their role is over, he had better take another view.

There are alternatives to a mercenary army, but not too many for an expanding Leviathan. The despotism can decide not to expand, and reduce its standards of living. This means going on the permanent defensive, which may or may not be possible in an age of missileship. A gap between the political and economic ambitions of the state and those of the people constitutes the real danger. Does the existence or nonexistence of this hiatus spell the real difference between the citizen and the subject? Well, subjects may live very well and permissively and, aside from the mounting tribute exacted from the productive element, suffer little mistreatment. If the citizen retires or is forced out of most of the political process, it would only be rational for him to withdraw from the ultimate reason for the polity's existence, and to demand being protected in war as in all things else. Marshal Soult, who founded the French Foreign Legion, revealed a reservoir, if any one wants to organize, train, and equip it. These men are spoiling for a fight, any fight, that could be provided. A deep war fatigue and allergy to combat settled over the youth of much of the world, making it a dubious prop for either defensive or offensive ambitions. There exists, Gentlemen, a hardcore, numerically small mercenary potential, but it could be magnificently armed and trained. Nevertheless, mercenarism has taught us a few lessons in the past which we ought not need to relearn.

FOOTNOTES AND REFERENCES

[1] Guiccardini, Francesco, *History of Italy*, Book I, translation of Fenton, London, 1599, cited in Oliver Lyman Spaulding, Hoffman Nickerson, and John Womack Wright, *Warfare: A Study of Military Methods from the Earliest Times*, Harcourt, Brace and Company, New York, 1925, p. 417.

Chapter 13

THE PRETORIANS

The Defenders of Statism

Any discussion of organized civil government will eventually point to a specialized corps of troops which has been correctly called pretorian. Such soldiers have one primary function, and they are rarely called upon to perform another. They protect the government from its own people, and often from its rebellious soldiery as well. If there is a serious gap between the state's goals and those of its people, it is the pretorian role to fill this hiatus.

In the examples of pretorianism to follow, the Roman condition was chosen for extended treatment because of its general familiarity, its adequate documentation, and its warning to all states progressing into Leviathanism. Rome was not even the first state to make extensive use of pretorian troops. Surely the old hydraulic despotisms of Mesopotamia and Egypt made maximum pressure of the charisma, the divinity of those priest-kingships, to keep the mass of the population quietly at work, and just as surely this was not enough. Civilization and oriental despotism had twin births. Charisma or no charisma, the arm of these irrigation civilizations was the pretorian soldier. Instead of being something new in the world, the pretorian is man's oldest regular military establishment. He may be the last, too, for if the intelligence of man ever solves the problem of international war, that of a social consensus riven by ever increasing division of economic labor, or perhaps an increasing percentage unable or unwilling to meet the demands of the new technology, the shadow of one armed man remains of all old things. It is that of the ultimate political scientist, the prefect of the pretorian guard.

The command of the Roman *praefectus praetorio*, as we all know, gave the name to the subject phenomenon wherever found. From the simple commander of the palace guard to the most powerful appointed official the world has yet to see, the progress of the prefect of the pretorian cohort is one of the most instructive careers one could find. The death of the senatorial republic under Julius Caesar already found the city full of dispossessed farmers who came more and more to town without hope of employment, but more and more able to create a clamor. Discharged veterans of the civil wars roamed the streets, men of violence without hope. The head of the government was an obvious usurper, and it took a long time for the *princeps* to be acknowledged universally as a constitutional emperor. Even from Tiberius on, the senate lost power with almost each passing generation. The throne not only gathered old powers into its own hands but the expanding command of the known world created new ones. And so began the rise of this prefect and his command.

Almost nowhere does one see the term "pretorian" used with anything but distaste. The greatest Anglo-American military analysts only speak of the office with loathing and contempt. It is said that the pretorians and their prefects were emperor-killers, and many of them were. So, too, were the field troops who more than once elected their own commanders to the purple and marched on the city to slay the incumbent. And yet there must be an element of the counter-myth here. How could the empire last so long, ruled as it so often was by the pretorian prefect? No one seems to mention the long list of devoted public servants loyal to the Antonine emperors. The pretorians and their commanders were often scoundrels of the deepest dye but, good or bad, they became commanders of the city troops, then of the field armies, then prime ministers and assistant emperors, then supreme chief justices from whose court there was no appeal.

They did indeed murder Emperor Caligula in 41 A.D., took bloody revenge on the assassins of Emperor Domitian in 97 A.D., set up Pertinax then murdered him, and auctioned off the purple to Didius Julianus in their own camp. They killed Emperors Elagabalus in 222, Balbinus and Maximus in 238. The office of emperor was not an elective one, except rather fictitiously on the part of the senate. The citizenry and troops could not get rid of him by party primaries and general elections. Even discounting myths, though, the emperors just mentioned were criminal by the standards of their own times. On the other side of the picture, one starts reading the list of pretorian prefects slain by their rivals, by paranoid emperors like Commodus, or by the latter's ex-slave favorite Cleander, or by their own troops. One begins by being horrified, but ends with being bored with the regularity of their deaths. Yet somehow this massive empire lasted for many centuries, and largely through the efforts of the pretorian prefect. One suspects that, in the man-bites-dog style of reporting, many historians and all Hollywood emphasize the careers of Emperors Nero and Caligula and their prefects. (Why have they never picked up Elagabalus whose private and public life would have the "adults only" sign in the foyer?) They never stage the lives of Emperors Vespasian, Titus, Marcus Aurelius, and Hadrian, or even simple, efficient Galba, and each had industrious, able pretorian prefects whose names are known to less than a hundred scholars.

Whoever wrote the contra-pretorian myth included the charge that the guards were only "tin" soldiers living luxuriously in Rome and avoiding battle. Yet the cohort died to a man with Emperor Maxentius at the Battle of Milvian Bridge. Many prefects had been distinguished field generals themselves, Perennis surely murdered his way to the prefecture, but he had been a great field commander before. As supreme judge, he tried and ordered the execution of the Christian senator Apollonius, but almost eyewitness St. Eusebius in his *Ecclesiastical History* describes him as a just and able administrator, and so does contemporary historian Dio Cassius. As in any successful myth, there has to be a grain of bitter truth, but there must have been something besides evil in the prefecture.

In any event, as early as the late republic, a general had a bodyguard called the pretorian cohort. And it came to pass after the managed death of Julius Caesar, no constitutional ruler in any case, his less than constitutional party leaders, C. Julius Caesar Octavianus, later called Augustus, in company with Marcus Antonius, pursued and defeated the senatorial army under Marcus Brutus and Caius Cassius at Philippi in 42 B.C. The campaign over, Antony and Octavian found themselves with 8000 of their veterans who refused to be discharged. There was nothing to do but to divide these up between them and make them bodyguards, which both men needed.

Octavian, eventually sole ruler and deemed Augustus, knew what he had to do. Taking his "old boys" and increasing their number to nine cohorts, he set up a guard for the city and suburbs, which should have been done long before. We know the story of his great peace, the *Pax Augusta*. There was little for the army to do but act as a scattered constabulary in the provinces, and keep the frontiers with a reduced number of legions. The pattern began to jell, for Tiberius succeeded Augustus, and a great administrator he was until either from boredom or senility he retired from the city and hard work to live on the Isle of Capri, where the description of his amusements still must be written in Latin. His pretorian prefect, Sejanus, had to take on more and more of the administration lest it relapse into senatorial hands, and that was unthinkable. The idea dawned on Sejanus, with his command of from three to five cohorts, that he might as well be emperor in name as in fact, so he joined a senatorial plot headed by one Piso to depose Tiberius. News got to Capri somehow, though, and the old serpent proved himself far from dead. The senate met to depose him, but guess who sat in the chair to preside? Tiberius, of course, with a host of loyal troops. It was too soon, and what happened to Sejanus should not happen even to a pretorian.

The die was cast, however, for Emperor Caius (Little Boots) Caligula, the successor of Tiberius and one of the more unsavory characters in Roman history, entered the arena's grandstand to enjoy a pleasant afternoon of bloodshed. The city and the state were sick of him, but somehow this did not penetrate his head. Walking to his seat, he made a lewd sign at Prefect Chaerea standing at his post of guard, indicating that the latter was a homosexual. The colonel chopped him down then and there, and the pattern was set. The senate met to restore the republic, but they knew it was too late. Chaerea Praefectus Praetorio and his merry men hunted the palace seeking some member of the Julian family whom they could make a puppet emperor, and found poor Uncle Claudius, who only wanted to be a comparative linguist and amateur anthropologist. Given the option of becoming either a Caesar or a corpse, Claudius thought there was only one real choice, and he proved far from a puppet or an inadequate ruler.

The strength of the pretorian guard varied from time to time. Augustus probably had ten cohorts of as many as 1000 men each, which Tiberius seems to have reduced to about half. Caligula had twelve cohorts, and Vitellius raised the corps to sixteen. The strength settled to about ten cohorts, and there it remained until the abdication of Diocletian, who himself had done much to reduce the military power of the prefect. During the time that they were the props of the empire, they enlisted only Italians. Unlike their imitators, the janissaries, the corps declined when it could not find enough warlike Italians to fill the ranks and had to admit Germans, Macedonians, Spaniards, and such foreigners. The prefect himself had to be a Roman.

The corps was always of heavy infantry. If it needed cavalry for special occasions, such troops were attached to it and were never organic to the corps. There was one weakness in the army as reorganized by Augustus which that executive genius should have considered. He maintained the corps primarily as home and personal guard, which no doubt led the later pretorians to be considered battle-shy parade troops. He should have formed a much larger pretorian guard of hardened veterans near Rome, or in some other centers of the empire, which could have acted as a central mobile reserve to be shunted where needed. The Turkish sultan with his police troops, the janissaries, did not make this mistake.

None of this Roman pretorianism was intended. Legally, the emperor was at first only a military commander-in-chief, as the names *imperator* or *princeps* indicate, to whom civil jurisdiction was "temporarily" granted due to the seriousness of the times. Just as legally, the prefect of the pretorian guard was only the channel through whom the emperor spoke to the city and the army. Channels have usurped power since, of course, but this is not the way it was intended. And so the process continued, and it may be that even without usurpation of power, all this was inherent in the supreme military police office if the corps was as large as it was, and kept in one place. Surely as early as Emperor Domitian, his prefect Aelian could say that his rank was the highest of all, and certainly by the time of Commodus, the office was actually that of vice-emperor, and "almost royal."

The danger of too large a guard is suggested above, but actually there were never enough pretorians to do the job. Keeping such a turbulent city quiet was work enough. Disciplining the home garrison of line troops, if any, was also quite enough. From their numbers, the continual parade and ceremonial duties of a palace guard took many away, for the emperors did not follow the simplicity of Augustus once their power was secure. Dio Cassius, no lover of the corps, said that they were overworked. Then when the prefect had to be the supreme court, chief of general staff of the army, and chief of administration of a sprawling empire as well, that man had to be overworked if he were any good at all.

The prefect was by custom if not in written law a man of equestrian rank, or of hereditary middle class status, as we would say, and never an aristocrat. Later ones were made senators *ex officio*, not as an honor but so that they could try senators. Equestrian Perennis was criticized for trying Senator St. Apollonius. Many could have made themselves emperors, but this writer recalls only three who did: M. Opellius Macrinus in 217, M. Annius Flavianus in 276, and M. Aurelius Carus in 282.

Roman pretorianism had lessons to teach future generations. One is the homily read in many of our paragraphs, that historical myths must be taken with some salt. It is not the evil men do which dies with them. It is more apt to be the good which is interred with their bones. There is no present effort to whitewash the Roman pretorian guard and its prefect. Everything, or almost everything reported against them, was probably true. Nevertheless, if that orderly government we call Roman justice existed from Augustus, or at least from the Severi to Constantine, it was largely through their efforts.

If they were corrupt, the reason lies in Lord Acton's off-quoted dictum, that power corrupts, and absolute power tends to corrupt absolutely. This and similar works make a point of distinction between authority and power. Authority is ritualized, publicly recognized, overtly legal ability of certain persons to persuade or compel other persons to do their will. The recipients of this aggressive action might not like it, but they admit its existence and legality. Power is this ability to initiate less than pleasant action no matter how it is achieved. While it might through tradition become legalized in future generations, it never begins that way. All of us have felt its weight. We all know what it is, and none of us likes it. We succumb because we must, and in this submission we become *particeps criminis*, accessories before, during, and after the fact of crime. Granted that the Roman senate was powerless to stop the undesirable features of pretorianism, though this was not always true, the Roman citizens were not. They, however, were too busy enjoying the guaranteed food ration, the free admittance to the circus, and the free bathhouse built for them by Emperor Caracalla, the most lavish the world has ever seen. The pretorians, however, did not hurt the individual citizen. They only hurt his principles. All the citizen had to do was to cheer *Ave Caesar* at the right time, and at the right person, and avoid subversive association with such persons as the Bishop of Rome and his fellow travellers. The public has thrown its waves of naked bodies against pretorians since, and died, but the pretorians died with them. The Emperor Caligula once said that he wished the public had only one head so he could cut it off with one blow. Considering the public with which Little Boots had to deal, he could have been right.

The progress from small nation to great empire is sometimes rapid, and legislation, for reasons often cited and not all of them are valid, is always slow. The people and their legislators are often stunned with this speed, some of which is inherent in the situation, and some of it is deliberately manipulated to keep objection off balance. The law, constitutional law especially, is deliberate, and it should be. It should also be realistic. New roles, new jobs to be done, and new crises appear, and someone must rise to meet them, law or no law. Ambitious men, or dedicated men, or both, will step in to accomplish the apparently necessary, and once in are loath to step out. Let the people and their constitutional legislators cry in their watered wine all they want. They did not act when they should have, and other men did. Power always flows into the chinks where authority is weak or where nonexistent but needed.

Much of all this was done in the name of conservatism. Augustus said that he was no innovator but a restorer, a protector, a conserver of the old ways and virtues, and the pretorians were right behind him. It could have been that both were in part sincere. Legislative and constitutional changes were being made rapidly, all in the name of the good, old, virtuous Roman ways, and all so fast that threshholds were passed, making returns to the supposedly noble past impossible. The Roman people were and are notoriously conservative. They did not like new offices, new titles, new officials. If new jobs had to be done, they preferred giving new functions to old offices. The old men never meant to give legislative power to the chief of the palace police, even though many of the laws the later prefects decreed were necessary. The original writers of the United States Constitution did not intend to make the Supreme Court the ultimate arbiter of the law, either, and the people complained not. And so it would be well if Americans cease using terms of disapprobation about the seizure of power and update their own constitution by constitutional means. Whose fault was it in Rome, if fault it was? Look to the standards of the legions, for on them were the large letters SPQR, *Senatus Populusque Romanus.* The Senate and the Roman People, and you will find the answer.

So let old Rome die. The walls of the New Rome, Constantinople, were to know the weight of the Turkish janissaries. The world had never known quite such a pretorian force before, and was not to know another until the rise of Hitlerist units, and the able Russian counterpart. The janissary corps was militarily more efficient, protected its masters better, and had a longer history than its modern imitators. It is much too soon to comment on the Soviet police troops except to observe their great loyalty and efficiency.

The actual date of the founding of the Turkish janissaries is not known, and the corps may have evolved rather slowly. It is known to have existed in its traditional form from 1330 until its last master, Sultan Mahmoud II, ordered all other troops and the population to fall upon and slaughter it in 1826. The sultan was by then the Sick Man of Europe, his empire obsolete, and his pretorians more so, but he signed his death warrant along with theirs. This was the most powerful pretorian corps ever to exist. The counter-myth says that they were killers of commanders and kings if their pay was not forthcoming, but the fact remains that they were the most famous corps in the Ottoman army. The success of the sultans was the victory of the janissaries. The glory of the Ottoman Empire was their glory. They were the Ottoman Empire which took its name from its founder, Osman or Otman.

The founding sultans did not trust a Turkish army. They knew that the assemblage of feudal levies which carried them into Anatolia would never conquer the world. They knew the weakness of such knighthoods and their vassals, to fight when they cared to and to disperse when bored. They knew, too, that their army of light horse could not defeat the heavy crusader cavalry, man for man and horse for horse. They also found out that the light skirmishing feudal horsemen could not meet the heavy infantry of the Eastern Empire. They needed a stable, warlike, disciplined, and dependable infantry, and they knew that they could not make this out of Turkish materials yet. The sultan, just which one is not really known, needed a new (*yeni*) army (*asker*), and the germ of the *Yeniceri*, janissary, was sprouted. It is seen, then, that a common western opinion that the janissaries were the invention of the Constantinople sultanate is in error. Sultan Mehmed II brought as many as 12,000 janissaries against the walls of the city in 1451-1481.

Perhaps the Holy Roman and other great sovereigns lacked success because they did not have the cynicism and complete disregard for the conquered enjoyed by the Turkish leaders from at least Orkhan, the half-legendary founder of the janissaries, onward. It was not only a new army, but a new idea. The Turkish Empire was won and maintained by non-Turks, and not mercenaries, either. Recruitment into the corps was the most unique the world has ever seen. What sovereign would not be envious of a military unit completely and unconditionally detribalized with no allegiance or even memory of family or other relationships and loyalties, with no culture whatsoever except that learned in military kindergarten? What if this corps from infancy had been socialized into a faith that the merest whim of the sovereign was religious law, and that death in his service was a sure guarantee of everlasting bliss? In a way, the armies of the Inca of Peru, and they were successful, had these virtues, but the sultan added one more. The janissaries even differed in obvious racial characteristics from the other soldiers of the empire, so that such troops could not appeal to them in terms of brotherhood or shared nationality. The Sultan or the Aga of the Janissaries could safely order them to fall upon and butcher Turkish units who were rebellious, or almost rebellious, or seemingly lax in the performance of disagreeable or hazardous duty.

It is said that the early janissaries were recruited from the young men of the conquered who were forcibly converted to Islam and trained as the soldiers of their people's enemy. The Turks, once they had overcome a population, thought of a better plan than this. They instituted the *devsirme*, the regular periodic tax in human flesh.

Turkish officials would systematically remove a percentage of the strong and handsome youths from age 5 to 20, and take them to the janissary barracks. This was a custom which had the force of law. Indeed, it was eventually made into law, and the imperial rescript (*firman*) went all the way, and demanded and got the younger and hence more trustworthy. About 1000 infants between the years of five and seven were eventually recruited with force into the janissary schools every year, at an age when the tree is inclined as the twig is bent. One wonders if Pavlov ever heard of this. Parents might weep and wail, or even marry off their five-year-old sons, as the janissaries were restricted to the unmarried. The firman promised the harshest measures to villages and parents who obstructed the imperial wish, and when the Grand Turk said harsh, he meant just that. The sultanate anticipated Malthus, for it knew that the population tendencies of Greeks, Macedonians, Albanians, Serbs, Bulgars, Bosnians, Herzegovinians, and others, would keep its elite corps up to strength. The devsirme was enforced with complete vigor until the end of the seventeenth century, and then fell into laxness. Ahmed III ordered it enforced savagely in 1703, but his officials paid little attention to him. The empire was in retreat by then, and the corps was outmoded. The ordinary Turks had become excellent infantry. The general population was apathetic when Sultan Mahmoud II ordered his 140,000 janissaries, garrisoned so widely that they could not help each other, to be butchered by the other troops.

One sees here, of course, roles other than purely pretorian ones assigned to janissaries. They were an elite corps of combat troops, but they were still highly paid and pampered pretorians at bottom. Their schools were stern academies whose "outside activities" consisted of killing people. Perhaps the sultan erred in one way by allowing the more brilliant of the young janissaries to be trained in civil administration. Of course this permitted those so favored to become rich, but they had from childhood been conditioned to obey their military superior, not their chief of bureaucracy. In this way the Aga of the Janissaries always knew just which civilian officer thought ill of them, or constituted a menace to their power, or was plotting against either them or the sultan, or stood in the way of the imperial national policy which was often janissary dominated. This official did not live long. Many prime ministers, or grand vizirs, were strangled to death in the Palace of the Seraglio. But why stop at vizirs? One wishes he had at his disposal the list of sultans liquidated by the janissaries. We only know that they were several. It would be interesting, too, if the list dominated the sultans and vizirs who, like Caligula and Elagabalus in Rome, needed killing.

There was an inherent weakness in the law of succession to the sultanate shared by many an oriental monarchy. Western ones were governed by the law of primogeniture, the absolute right of the oldest legitimate son to the succession. Oh, one knows that this was an ideal broken more than once, but such was the law. Now excessive polygyny could have been entertaining to the patriarch, but it was a nuisance to his successors. Every son of a father is equally legitimate according to Koranic law, even if born of a slave woman. The Turkish sultan, therefore, provided his people with a superabundance of royal princes, and the oldest one might not be the ablest, nor the one favored by, guess who? The senior officers of the janissaries had far too much power in deciding the name of the next sultan. The heir apparent might spend too much of his energies ingratiating himself with them, and once upon the throne have too many debts to pay these fierce, intelligent men. The sultan was blest, though, in their clear-cut devotion to the glory of the empire. Of this he could be assured. He could also thank them for the consistent murderings of half-brothers who might be tempted to raise a rebellious army.

Every sovereign who has in mind the rearing of a corps of Pavlovian monsters to help him on his road to power had better see just what he could be nourishing in his bosom. The janissaries became not only an exclusive military class; they were a caste. As such, their greatest loyalty was to themselves and their own corps. The Roman pretorian cohort weakened the day it admitted non-Italians to its ranks. The Turkish counterpart withered when it began accepting Turks. Perhaps severe techniques of social distance between the despot, his force element, and the rest of the people are needed, but the Turkish sultanate went too far. The Turkish master of Constantinople, though, had one advantage which its Byzantine despot and his Italian predecessor never enjoyed. While the succession to the sultanate itself was not clear, the divine right of the House of Osman was. The janissaries never wavered from this. They might kill, depose, and dominate this sultan or that prime minister, but their devotion to the imperial family never faltered. They never set up a separate ruling house, as the Mameluke pretorians did in Egypt.

There is no need to describe the Arab invasion of Egypt, bright jewel of the Byzantine emperors. The Arabization of the Nile was so complete that today the liturgical language of the Christian remnant of the Coptic Church, founded by St. Mark the Evangelist, is Arabic. That the Arabs themselves were in turn overwhelmed by their Turkish coreligionists is well known, including their cries into their minted tea that they were persecuted by them. A *de facto* independent Turkish state was set up in Egypt, and its sultan needed pretorians as no one before him. He built up a corps from bought Circassian and Turkish slaves, and repeated the old cycle. These devoted warriors were not only some of the most magnificent mounted troops the world was to know but became the bitterest and ablest enemies the crusaders ever had. So much for their valor, but as elsewhere, the Turkish quasi-sovereign of Egypt could trust virtually none of his subjects. More and more he put his mamelukes into government administration, and the old die was cast again. The mameluke agas killed whatever sultan or khedive displeased them, enthroned whomsoever they pleased, and deposed him if unsatisfactory. Tiring of this play, their chief assumed the throne himself, and the Mameluke Empire of Egypt became as such a government, ruling unwarlike Copts and dissident Arabs. Egypt became the plaything of nineteenth century Britain and France, who unseated the Turkish khedivate after World War I and made its last representative a supposedly independent king. This puppet was overthrown by an Arab colonels' junta after World War II, which succession state is being watched very carefully at the moment of writing.

Let us consider one or more imitator of the Grand Turk who was greater than any Egyptian Moslem. Tsar Peter the Great had a serious problem which he resolved with great ferocity when needed, and sometimes when it was not. His ambition was to weld an antique collection of feudalities into a modern (in the baroque sense of his time) bureaucratic despotism. He saw that the loosely knit empire he had inherited would be the prey of almost any west European power which would choose to carve it up, the Germans on his west being particularly in his mind. Russia had from time to time lost territory and population to what had become her hereditary enemy, the Turks to the south. Peter had reason to admire Turkish organization and methods, the use of janissaries in particular.

The recasting of a ponderous, reactionary nation in one generation was a monumental task, but Peter was a monumental man. The opposition to his reforms was tremendous, for he had to strike first at Russia's heart, the Orthodox Church which fought him when it dared. He rewarded its conservative hierarchs by abolishing the patriarchate of Moscow and replacing it with the Holy Governing Synod, a group of laymen appointed by and answerable only to himself. The confessional, then, became an intelligence tool of the crown, and for this reason was one of the first czarist institutions to be decimated by the Bolshevist revolution, quite aside from the Marxist doctrine that it was the opiate of the people. Obviously some of the nobles favored Peter's reforms, but far from the majority. There are cases of feudal lords voluntarily giving up their privileges, but they are few. Peter had opposition from within his own family. His mother was the last half-haremized Tsaritsa of All the Russias. The later ladies were modern czarinas. Peter's own son and heir, Alexei, was bitterly opposed to the new ways and fled for refuge to Italy. Alexei was betrayed into returning to Russia, and was murdered, perhaps by Peter himself. Peter Romanov knew that not only his new bureaucratic despotism but his own life as well were in danger. He looked southward towards the janissaries, and found them good.

Peter then formed an elite body of musketeer pretorians, the *strieltzi* or *strelitz*. This corps had a bloody if glorious history in eliminating Peter's opposition. They were undoubtedly the best soldiers who ever served a tsar, and may well be the best in Russian tradition. Their own history was brief, as Peter's successors knew the Turkish story, too, and abolished the corps lest they become its servants.

The later Romanov pretorian cavalry, the Asian Kazaks, were a worthy successor to the strieltzi, and the Soviet corps of police troops continue the Romanov tradition in no mean way.

Let us take a look at the papal Swiss Guards. They look very splendid in their uniforms designed by Michael Angelo, but let no one be deceived. They are a close-knit, hard-trained, superbly armed, and dedicated corps, surpassed by no troops in the world except in size. It is the affair of the Roman Curia to decide whether or not they are needed, but no one knows the Roman mob as it does. One needs no more than to stand in St. Peter's Square when the pope appears on his balcony to bless his people. The wildness of enthusiasm is impressive to a social psychologist. Roman mobs have also screamed in favor of Caesar, and against him, too. What if the irrational enthusiasm were directed against a locally unpopular pope, and the mob should burst into the Vatican with murderous intent? This has not happened? The old popes sometimes could get into the Tomb of Hadrian, long since called the Castle of St. Angelo, but could their successor? An organized, well-directed, and large force of, shall we say guerrillas, could overwhelm the apostolic pretorians, but that seems to be the honorable fate of Swiss guards.

We are not called upon to take sides in the political and ideological struggles of a foreign nation. If one can become emotional about a loyal body of pretorian mercenaries who stood their ground and died to a man for a cause not their own, he must stand before the moving monument of the Lion of Lucerne and mourn. If he has a soldier's respect for himself and his profession, he cannot but swell with pride in viewing the dying lion in stone, and say, "We had, we have, and we will have men like that."

No man of taste disparages the fine dinners of Paris, but on two occasions they contributed to the sadder part of the French Revolution. One remembers, of course, that de Launay, commander of the Bastille, was far away smacking his lips when his old fortress was overwhelmed. It was no loss, garrisoned by old soldiers, and kept exclusively to imprison the upper class. The Royal Swiss Guards were something else. The officers of this splendid if small corps were away having dinner, too, when the Parisian mob successfully swarmed into the Palace of the Tuileries. The Swiss were upon that occasion commanded only by sergeants who held their fire too long, doubtful if they had the authority to harm the subjects of their host country. They died to every individual on that day.

The French Revolution did produce the largest and finest fulltime pretorian body in the modern world, The Republican Guard. Out of the dubious material of the revolutionary National Guard, the government created the fine troops one sees in Paris today. No one knew the Parisian mob as well as did the revolutionary leaders. They had been part of it. The tourist may admire the dragoons on picturesque, ceremonial duty guarding the Opera on gala nights, and be deceived. These are not parade troops. The government, in effect, maintains a small army of police troops to perform but one role, the ancient pretorian one, one of protecting the government against its not always loving citizenry.

Now the army is the force element of the state. There is not the one without the other, so far. What if there should be a reversal of roles? This happens sometimes. A military *junta* is a social phenomenon wherein the senior member's of a nation's armed forces actually takes over and becomes the government either by force or a sufficient threat of force. This does not mean a "garrison state," or a "police state," which are other forms of political control. The term junta (Spanish, *council*) means that the armed forces take control of what was once a supposedly constitutional government. The military junta rarely makes a claim of legitimacy other than the righteousness of the reforms the generals, colonels, and their troops say are needed. The colonels usually say that as soon as the Augean stables are cleaned, they will return to their garrisons and their constitutional role of protecting the fatherland. This is pretorianism in the pure, the naked and bald rule by the army. In a way, but no more than that, this was the bald fact just discussed. The old palace guard more than once said who the emperor and top officials should be in both Rome and Turkey, but if they chose to rule, it was covertly and through a puppet. Rule by a junta is, by contrast, direct, overt rule.

This form of pretorianism could be one of the sources of the phenomenon's bad name, and very dispassionately one must admit that much, but not all, of this is deserved. In the first place, the civil governments in states subject to junta revolutions are very weak. Almost all of them claim to be democracies, but are often in fact unimaginative tools of a ruling class so exploitive, so determined to permit no more than enough of a nation's economic product to seep down to the majority of the population that they dare make no more than a token appeal to the popular vote. Such nations maintain an inordinately large military establishment in light of either a defense against foreign aggression or as an offensive weapon to enforce the national ambition against a neighbor. Such armaments and personnel have but one role, the one described in the first paragraph of this chapter, the protection of the government against its own people, but with this addition — the entire army and navy may exist for this simple reason, not just an elite guard.

The United States Federal government cannot be said to have pretorian troops as such, the constitutional fiction that the police power is reserved to the states being maintained to this day. In case a state government, or subdivision thereof, fails to enforce federal law, the precedent has recently been established of sending federal combat troops into such states to do just that. The United States government dislikes the concept and practice of martial law with reference to its own citizens and, contrary to popular belief, has exercised this privilege only twice in its history. Both federal and state governments lean to the legal concept of military aid to civil authorities; in which case civilian magistrates retain jurisdiction instead of having it lapse to military government and provost courts.

The pretorian, or security function in the United States, is primarily the responsibility of the state governors. The National Guard is still under their control in peace time. If there is some possibility of conflict with federal troops in enforcing a locally unpopular national law, President Eisenhower established the precedent of federalizing the state guard units at the outbreak of trouble. The organization, training, and equipment of national guard divisions is identical with that of the federal regular army. Should, however, the state national guard be federalized and sent to a foreign theatre, state governors have the right to organize, equip, uniform, and train part-time citizen soldiers as militia under their own control.

Great Britain does not employ pretorian troops at home, save the rather ceremonial Brigade of Guards and the yeomen one sees on duty at the Tower of London. She had a very unhappy experience with the Royal Irish Constabulary (Black and Tans) after World

War I. Her Sikh mercenaries were exemplary if harsh while the British Empire still existed in Asia. The mounted constabularies in Canada and Australia are famous. The organization and equipment of Russian pretorian troops is not known to this author.

Communist China has a large corps of Public Security Forces. In 1967, this force was organized into divisions of 8,200 men each, consisting of a staff and headquarters, one signal company, one guard company, one reconnaissance company, one artillery battalion of twelve 122mm howitzers, and three rifle regiments. A public security regiment consists of 2,350 men, staff and headquarters, one reconnaissance company, one signal company, one guard company, one battery of four 76mm artillery, and three rifle battalions. A public security battalion consists of staff and headquarters, one heavy machine gun company of nine guns, one mortar company of nine 82mm mortars, and three rifle companies of 100 men each.

Chinese pretorian troops are not considered part of the army, although they are uniformed as such, and are under the control of the military regional commanders for operational purposes. While they also have responsibility for border defense, the Chinese consider them the chief internal political enforcement agency of the Communist state. They are directly under the Minister of Public Safety, which fact makes this official equal to the modern Roman prefect, and someone with whom to reckon.

As for conclusions regarding pretorianism, the first and obvious one is that it is a serious and delicate problem. Even after millenial experience with the phenomenon, it must be admitted that as many questions as answers obtrude themselves upon our concern. It is nevertheless our obligation to make an attempt to profit by the experience of the past, and to offer some tentative opinions.

The first consideration is so obvious that one might think it a truism, but is it? A state had best put its house in order, examine its cultural lags, its obsolete vested interests, and see if it fulfills its pretended role — to serve its clientele so that it is loved and respected by the effective majority. Second, if a state is to survive, it must wish to live. This is true of all social institutions. As for the complex ones called bureaucracies, including industrial, religious, or even charitable ones, the record of any of them offering to disband bcause its old role is obsolete or because its mission has been fulfilled is extremely rare. The state in particular must survive, population growth and sociopolitical evolution having gone as far as they have, or most of us will die with it. It is not only certain that the state must want to survive, it must act that way, and let this wish be adequately understood by its constituent groups. If this means the use of force, then both qualitatively and quantitatively the use of illicit, organized violence must be met with legal, organized violence.

Force itself is a weak reed upon which to lean. One need not invoke a value judgment of tyranny. This position has often been validated. The means of adequate force will never be available in the long run to maintain a hated modern state. Force is therefore a temporary thing. If used overlong, the state can well become the slave of the appliers of force, which is pretorianism in its worse sense. One must recall, too, that the pretorian is a human. He can make judgments on justice, too, and if his sympathies for those he must control are invoked, he can let his chief of state down on some critical day. This has happened. Thus, as the revolutionary mob stormed the Winter Palace in what was then St. Petersburg in 1918, the government belatedly called out the feared and hated pretorian Cossack cavalry. The mob shrank from contact with these deep Asians, for they knew the capabilities of their long, steel-tipped whips. As they rode forth to protect their master, however, the Cossacks winked at the mob and let it through, and were slaughtered for their friendliness. This should be a lesson for pretorians forever, for the Soviet Republic to this day persecutes the Kazak tribes.

The pretorian guard, as must have been apparent in the foregoing pages, is the servant of only one kind of state. The nation-at-arms does not need it. The patrician military republics would not tolerate it. There is too much consensus within simple democratic republics and rudimentary naive monarchies to need this weapon. Pretorianism is a function of complex, bureaucratic despotisms, or near-despotisms here called Leviathan states. There is no value judgment in these terms, for the Greek *despotes* once meant no more than "master," or even "mister." The despotic state exists if it is superordinate to all other authority, if it takes precedence over all other social institutions, and can dictate to them their terms of membership, behavior, and existence. This may be all for the good, of course, for the bureaucracy won out in government, business, education, and elsewhere because it was more efficient, more productive than its predecessors. Some forerunners were not forcibly gobbled up by the despotic Leviathan. They often defaulted in the performance of their announced services, and some agency had to pick up their roles. All of the above is the primary subject material of general political science, but the student of pretorianism also has a stake in it.

It would be well, for instance, if mature students should admit that the state is often a liar. Now the state has many jobs to do, and the whole truth can hardly be told every voter or the operation might fail. The bureaucratic state is in a worse moral situation than any other kind. An industrial, educational, and especially political bureaucracy must have cold, practical efficiency as the prime ethic. The morals demanded from its clients and servants, by contrast, are those of emotion, dedication, loyalty, patriotism and, if need be, self-sacrifice. And so it often occurs that when part of the real truth is leaked to the public, it is time to alert the pretorian barracks. This is likewise true in the bureaucratic army. If all the discussion in the general staff meeting were published to the troops, there would not be enough military police to conduct them into battle.

It may well be that through the operation of the law of diminishing returns, the day of the great state is coming to an end, that it has tried to undertake too many functions, amass and digest too much information. It may be that there has been so much division of labor and specialization that even with massive police action it cannot integrate and button up the competing and often conflicting subgroups of its society. These are things to consider, but also for considerations is that no American, African, or Asian polity has found a way to solve its social problems other than an even greater drift towards Leviathan, with only the computer as a solution to complexity. Even a pretorian corps as large as the janissaries did not, and probably could not keep things connected forever.

What then, is the role of pretorians, assuming that some states must have them? Experience teaches that they should be used only for the suppression of serious disorder and not for ordinary criminality. We quoted Dio Cassius's opinion that the pretorians were overworked at the height of their Roman power. True, the pretorian prefect was ambitious to become assistant emperor with legislative, judicial, and administrative power, but he was also pushed into this position. One should remember that when *de jure* authority weakens, *de facto* power will flow into the interstices, and what is *de facto* in one generation can become *de jure* in succeeding ones. Then some Livy, Suetonius, or Tacitus starts crying on paper about tyranny.

There can be no doubt about the quality of pretorian troops. They must be the best, and not the unemployed, otherwise unemployable, or the sweepings from the army. The above statement refers to officers as well as men. Pretorians must be under able commanders, and wise ones as well. Power is strong medicine at best, so when a corps is given the authority to dominate not only the civilian population but the military as well, it must be of the highest quality. The prefect, or provost, and his men cannot expect to be loved. They must in any event be respected and, at worst, feared by those to whom fright is the only appeal.

The pretorian guard, as inferred above, must be military, serving under martial order, training, and discipline. There have been times when they had to take their place in the infantry line in defense of the state. Pretorians, too, have from time to time been needed to protect the state from rebellious elements of its own combat army. In such cases, they must not be lacking in morale, training, arms, and discipline.

The pretorians, however, are specialized troops. In the last analysis, of course, the safety of a nation in internal affairs as well as external rests on the bayonets of the regular army. This is a matter of the last, not the first, expedient. No matter how excellent line troops may be, they do not make good pretorians. The use of airborne infantry from Fort Campbell, Kentucky, by President Eisenhower to subdue the lacerated feeling of Arkansas, when he had an idle regular army military police battalion at Fort Gordon, Georgia, betrayed an appalling lack of insight. Pretorians are trained to receive insult without replying, to be targets for occasional missiles without firing, and to act with violence only when ordered to do so by their own officers. Considering the Roman, Turkish, and French experience, it seems evident that veterans from the regular combat forces make the best pretorians. These men need highly specialized training after their regular service, however, and this takes time.

There is in the above a problem of social distance. The pretorians in their off-duty hours must be kept aloof from the regular troops and the civilian population. They must be fine fellows, handsome fellows, but under no circumstances "good fellows." Let the regular troops fraternize with the civilian population, and with each other, but there must be no intimacy with pretorians. What if serious disorder should break out among just those persons with whom the pretorians are at the moment fraternizing? What then, of their authority? What of it, too, if an unruly soldier or civilian should spy a comrade of his in the pretorian line advancing the riot to quell? This is not a problem of easy solution, but it can be solved. During the late British control of much of the world, one never saw a pretorian Sikh sitting at a cafe. One should never see a pretorian "under the influence," even if out of uniform. One should never see an off-duty pretorian with a known doxy on his arm. If pretorians are to correct evil, they must avoid the very appearance thereof.

Pretorians must be responsible to the highest command only, and the Roman emperor rightly kept them under his own jurisdiction. They may be given temporary duty under subordinate commanders and officials when crisis demands, but they must never be directly subject to them. Such a subordinate commander is too apt to fritter away pretorian effort on minor violations which he or his troops could control. There are never enough pretorians, so they should not be bothered with civilian jaywalking or keeping other soldiers' buttons burnished. Their authority, too, is naked force, and this is a dangerous arm in the hands of a man too involved in the local situation. He could use this weapon to work off local dislikes, grudges, and vengeance.

Professionalism is the key to successful pretorianism. These men should be hardcore, permanent, full-time, highly trained and harshly disciplined professionals. Since more is expected of them than ordinary troops, they should have special privileges and high pay, but this is true of professionalism in all occupations. It is highly advisable, too, that they should, like the janissaries, be strangers to the local population. No one denies that many American state national guard regiments have enviable combat records. No one says, either, that their record as the governors' pretorians has been without success. Part-time soldiers are inclined to use too little force when needed, or too much when not necessary, thereby acquiring an enduring hatred for themselves and their chiefs of state. The national guard or state militia are at bottom home town boys. They and their relatives are too involved emotionally in the disorders they are required to quell. At the worst, too many American adjutants general commanding the guard are elective officers, and civil disorder, rebellion, and disastrous natural calamity make poor platforms on which to run for reelection.

The foregoing suggestion of too much or too little force raises the question of the amount of pretorian violence to be used. The theoretical answer is simple, even if the application requires some discretion and intelligence. The amount of force to be used is just enough and no more than needed to accomplish the mission. It must be adequate, or the disorder will worsen. It is better to let a mob have its way in looting and destruction than to stop it partly. This encourages it to greater and more unacceptable behavior at best, or the slaughter of the police at worst. A commander should not send out a boy to do a man's work, nor a man to do a boy's. He should not send troops at all if he does not mean to use them. No one has ever disproved Machiavelli's advice that it is better to hurt a few on Monday than to be dilatory and indecisive and be forced to kill a thousand on Friday. Nevertheless, if at all possible, force must be used with such discretion that hatred for the pretorians, and for the government itself, does not become a tradition. Those in power, pretorians included, must remember that the present disorders will probably pass. Their bad reputation may not. Never inflict a wound which cannot be licked and cured. Pretorians must strive to acquire a reputation for service as well as force. They may be the only source of protection and aid in disasters and other social collapse, and the subject population needs to turn to them for help.

The question now arises as to how great should a nation's force resources be? It should equal the force potential of its internal enemies. If this means a large proportion of the effective majority of the citizens, that government is doomed anyway, and its masters had better follow the example of many others and transfer as large a fund as possible to Swiss banks.

A discussion of pretorianism is agreeable to neither the writer nor the reader. Its consideration is a duty on both parts; however, if we keep faith with our military and civic responsibility. So this essay may close with a paraphrase of another of Machiavelli's bits of advice: I would not say these things to you if men and the governors of men were as they should be. Seeing, however, that neither is as it should be, you must look upon them as they are, and think and act accordingly.

PART IV

AN EPILOGUE

Chapter 14

CIVILIANS AND NONCOMBATANTS

The Popular Substratum

Preceding chapters have traced structures and methods from the simplest to the most complex. The time has now come for an epilogue for what has gone before. Untold volumes have been written about the reasons for this war and that, but this book has avoided entering that discussion, save for this final chapter. We can no longer avoid mentioning the essential, the core cause of war and warfare, and there is one.

The civilian lies at the very center of the war complex of massive, complicated political systems. The state exists to serve and protect him, and it had better keep this in mind. No matter how secretive or even cynical the masters of the polity may be in their war planning, in the very end the civilian can veto and nullify such schemes. The German population virtually did just that at the end of World War I, lending some credence to the army's contention that it had not been defeated, had not been driven out of France, but had been betrayed at home. We know the results of such sentiments. The British public was not very enthusiastic about that war. Many disliked the armed forces.[1] The role of the civilian in the Tsarist military collapse is too well-known to require comment. The Confederate women, by contrast, were tenacious and willing to fight on after the war chiefs realized that the cause was lost. The French army in southeast Asia was defeated, not alone by General Giap but by the home people as well. And surely the civilian population vetoed the continuation of the American adventure in the same area. They had no guns or butter decisions to make. Their standard of consumption was the highest in their history. The armed forces had not been defeated. It is unfair to say that funds were diverted from domestic problems to the war effort. Never had such sums been disbursed to the domestic disadvantaged as in the Great Society. The propaganda campaigns of World War I and II were not repeated. Despite the fact that the Vietnamese national character contains some less than loveable aspects, no effort was made to capitalize on them.

The man-at-arms is only the force potential of his social system, be that a tiny, kin-based, unallied hamlet in the bush, or a vast empire. The real activating one of force anywhere is the population, unless one is speaking of one of those short-lived systems dominated by military aristocracies. The soldier is only the attorney-at-arms in quest of the goals sought by the people, or the princes they tolerate. The blood he sheds is on our hands, too. He could not operate without you and me because we provide him with the supplies and moral support he needs. You may debate this proposition, you may deny it, you may take pride in it, or you may be ashamed, but you had better give it consideration.

There is a principle of Common Law which says that a thief cannot confer a title to property. The fact that the stealer comes with weapons, singly or with a few cronies, does not alone legitimize him. He can acquire a legal title if he comes in a nationalized mass, though, for the Law of Nations, and popular will before it was codified, recognizes the right of conquest. Every one of you is living on land gained by the bloodshed of former owners, or by some chicane called purchase. And now you want to call quits, and quite correctly plead that warfare is killing and maiming people and taking what was theirs. If calling this immoral assuages your conscience, or refurbishes your superego, go right ahead, but do keep on eating. If, though, the doctrine of social homeostasis is true, if there is an inherent drive towards consistency in sociocultural complexes as there is in the physical cosmos, it just well may be that the sins of the fathers shall be visited upon the children of more than the third and fourth generation. Call this Mosaic harshness if you will, but deny it only if you dare, for much of this visitation has already occurred, and more may be in prospect.

That is why this discourse ends with a consideration of the populace, of the popular, and let the professional soldier fend for himself for a moment, but only for that length of time. He cannot get along without us. Backing and reinforcing his efforts are ourselves, his own nonfighting population, and in front of him is his real target, the unarmed people of the enemy. It is they who sit atop wealth needed for our expanding standard of consumption, and it is they who must manipulate this economic land for our benefit, or get out of the way. Unfortunately, and we hope temporarily, there stand his fighting force acting as a shield. This must be penetrated, defeated, and if need be, obliterated. Of course, others have similar ambitions about our own goods and property, and we have fended them off, sometimes but not always. War is violent action or the threat thereof by one social system against another. The offensive seeks to penetrate its opponent, to erode the popularity of his struggle, and to weaken the nonfighting willingness to support its armed forces. All war is popular, offensively or defensively, for it must fail if it is not.

Civilized, political war is either an overt or covert assault on, or defense of, an economic system. The civilian is at the core of any economic system. He is the producer, the manipulator of the environment in the interests of energy production. He is the essential consumer, and he hates retrogression in his consumption habits. The armed man is only a shield for his civilian population, or a lance directed against the soldiery protecting the resources of another system. If this economic man who operates behind the front, and for whom the front exists can be breached, all the fierce tenacity of his armies will come to naught.

The social position of noncombatant and civilian is an achieved status and not one inherent in nature. This is true of many of the "human rights" of which so many pages have been written. These are not the irrevocable gifts of "Nature and Nature's God," so happily assumed to be such by the inheritors of the American and French Revolutions. If I, as the author of these pages, have a "right" to compose them in relative security, it is because my fellow citizens by custom and law have conferred it upon me. For anyone to say that such has been accorded to me by natural right is to betray a complete lack of comprehension of cosmic and organic evolution.

There were indeed peoples and cultures so gentle that they found man-killing repugnant. Such populations were very small, isolated, and so beset by subsistence anxiety that they could hardly lift a hand to defend themselves, to say nothing of assailing other groups. If they, too, were beset by biological, frustration-begotten rage, their gentleness was a culturally acquired characteristic just as much as the ferocity of the society just over that range of mountains. Both the sweet cooperation of the Eskimo and Havasupai and the armed aggression of the Yaqui and Navaho were cultural inventions, and not the gifts or curses of nature.

If one comprehends that all political war is in part psychological, and some fail in this comprehension, he will see that fundamentally, the civilian is always a target for hurt, harm, or wooing away from his devotion to his own side. Modern war's prime target is the minds of the armed opposition, but fundamentally the civilian who maintains this armed force must be included. Doubt must be instilled among the productive people who support the army. The righteousness of the foe's cause must be challenged right within his own ranks. The possibility of his ultimate victory must be questioned, and the myth of his eventual defeat must be fostered, whether or not this is well-grounded.

Psychological warfare is the combat of alienation, especially when directed against civilians. Guerrilla warfare is ideal for this kind of manipulation. The guerrilla never seems to be defeated. Actually, he is beaten time and again. His successes are self-advertising. Their evidence is overt, patent, bloody, and it is easy for them to claim an invincibility they do not possess. The same may be said for the terrorists. Successful arson speaks for itself.

The status of the noncombatant civilian was not recognized in either the old primitive war or early conventional war. It took centuries of ethical development to arrive at this politico-military concept and to have it generally respected. A suggestion was made that perhaps this hard-won immunity could be lost, and now more than an inference must be stated. Why should we not be foresighted enough to admit that this exemption from military damage has already been lost? Total war offers immunity to no one. The status of the noncombatant, meaning the unarmed multitude of an enemy state, persists in a way, but that of the civilian is almost as obsolete as the boot-to-boot cavalry charge. An able army will use its enemy's terrified civilians as weapons if it can. It will cause a retreating army's tactical and logistical roads to be clogged with refugees, and will go to great pains to do this. For this and other reasons, retrograde movement entails just as much staff planning and command ability as the advance. One can also suspect that this unarmed, defenseless, noncombatant mass could become the first objective of organized nuclear force rather than the armed, uniformed services of the defending social system. Is this not really what "first strike" means?

The end of the civilian status was foreshadowed when warfare became a matter of secondary rather than primary transaction. As long as the swordsman, the lancer, the archer, the musketeer could see his victim, he could select that man or this unit as his chosen target. The civilian status had some validity then. Indeed, it was legally perfected in those days of the simple musket and cannon. Its loss was predictable by the invention of the first long-range gun, foretold on the sand dunes of Kitty Hawk, and confirmed in the nuclear laboratory. The oft-disregarded code of mediaeval chivalry protected the civilian. That of the *Guerre en Dentelles* enhanced it. Anti-guerrilla warfare from the air, though, spares no one in a suspect village. Chairman Mao said that the guerrilla needs a friendly peasant population in which he can swim like a fish. Well, in order to poach a fish, it may be necessary to boil the water. Napalm will do that.

Weapons fired by men who cannot see their target, but rely on the mathematics of fire tables or computers did not themselves spell the end of the noncombatant, but they did of the civilian. There is no retraction here of this writer's repeated warning not to confuse war with the means of waging it. War is a state of mind, a legal condition, a matter of social organization, and weapons only implement all these. Missiles of almost unbelievable lethality, whether delivered by guns, aviation, or rocketry, are militarily only high-grade artillery, and artillery is only sophisticated rock-throwing and sling-shottery. Firepower is firepower, and has existed ever since this talented primate could pick up something to hurl. The military ends are the same. Only the means of attaining them have improved. Any other attitude is a civilian one. Yet, perhaps this civilian, or ex-civilian, is entitled to an attitude.

One of the roots of the thermonuclear war potential are in primitive war. One of the essences of that concept is the failure to distinguish between civilian and the the armed men. It is not the quality of the weaponry which separates primitive from civilized war. It is a series of concepts, of sociological inventions. Many modern rockets are now aimed over the heads of the enemy armed forces, who might live even safer lives in the field. And why should the ever-increasing logistic capacity of an enemy be spared, asks the foe, even though his factories, mines, and fields are manned by the unarmed? The effectiveness of the fighting man in the field depends on the productive capacity and morale of his civilian backing. Why, then, should not these be destroyed?

If civilization means a society dominated by an industrial or mercantile city with all its amenities, are we entering a phase of post-civilization? Did not the word "civilian" originally mean a dweller in a *civis*, a city, and not a suburban sprawl? How can the central city now be protected against weapons which can travel with accuracy across the seas?

Modern total war has an unsolved problem with its own soldiers. It is bureaucratic war, and manned by half-trained conscripts who will be the principal survivors after the small regular army is killed off. Its greatest weapon is the myth taught to partly trained conscripts and officers that the enemy, military and civilian, consists exclusively of villains of the deepest die. Such people and their property are worthy of little sympathy, and are given little. The myth also says that the allies are suffering, grateful heroes. When this myth is punctured, woe to all civilians within reach.

The type of war almost designed to change allies into foes, and to produce turmoil in the polity is what Bretnor calls indecisive war. This is prolonged war, wasteful in both manpower and supplies, wherein no decision is reached either from inability, or in America's case in southeast Asia, as a matter of policy. Harassed by confrontationists within the home structure, and inadequate news of victory abroad, the American people did not exhibit the maturity required of a global power. The Roman Empire was usually engaged in a no-win-no-lose war somewhere, in Britain, Germany, the Balkans, the Middle East, in North Africa. The British Empire in its health was seldom free from at least one. The histories of China and India knew indecisive war very well without the civilian morale coming apart. One thing is clear today. The leaders must tell the civilian population the reasons for such a war. There is a detail which must be covered before those who fight and pay for such wars can be instructed. The leaders must themselves understand.

At least some recognition of the status of the civilian appears to be very old. Pre-urban folk may have made no distinction between the armed defender of a social system and his kin, but highly organized agriculture and urban technology changed this somewhat. Early civilized folk recognized the existence of the civilian enemy as a pool of slave power. Much of Rome's foreign adventures were very profitable. The great public works we still admire were built by enemy ex-civilians, the contractors figuring the deaths required along with the stone. Even the great Greek Stoic philosopher Epictetus became a scullery slave in Rome.

The development of the status of civilian produced that of the military governor. When the conquering state realized that the enemy civilian was more valuable alive than dead, a die was cast. The spread of Roman rule over others invariably included the concept of the military governor whose duty was to organize the subject population for the benefit of the Latin state. There is no point in emphasizing that many of these proconsuls and procurators enriched themselves in the process. Carpetbagging is older than carpetbags.

Surely since the publication of *The Law of War and Peace* by Hugo Grotius (1583-1645), there has been such a thing as international law guaranteeing the conquered civilian the right to his life, property, and reasonable freedom as long as he behaves himself. Treaties and conventions followed, so that the corpus of international law regarding civilians is a well-established code. (Remember, though, that there are some powerful, modern military states who have never signed the Geneva Convention.) There have been many violations. On the other hand, it is remarkable that the international law has been observed as well as it has, for the power over a defenseless people is heady medicine. Authority and power should be confined to mature personalities, but there are not enough of such men to go around in wartime.

The Americans learned a lesson from their own history book. Unionist General Benjamin Butler was an able man, perhaps the most efficient governor Louisiana has had since the death of Galvez. His treatment of the conquered civilians, though, gave him the soubriquet of the Hero of the Battle of Three Forks and Lord knows how many Knives and Spoons. His impolitic behavior disgusted Lincoln, who relieved him. The United States government, preparing for World War II, founded the military government branch of the provost function designed to keep French, Belgian, and German civilians happy, or at least efficient, in the rear of its advancing armies. The prevention of pestilence, starvation, turbulence, terrorism, and guerrillism in the rear areas was a definite objective, and was so stated. This copy of the lacy war taught other military nations a lesson they could imitate with profit. Civilians can be cowed into submission by tanks, but they cannot be wooed by them, and there might come a day when the armor might reveal a chink.

The sack of Jerusalem by Emperor Titus, and the horrors inflicted on renaissance Rome by the Lutheran troops of Holy Roman Emperor Charles have taught us an unpalatable lesson. An external social system today looks at its rival as a whole, not as a collection of scoundrels and fine people. A victor has no means of sorting out the people who like him, especially at first, and particularly when a combat situation has heightened emotions. It may be unjust. It may not be accurate, but in a combat situation, the parts are responsible for the whole. Sherman did not have time to discover the crypto-Unionists in Atlanta and Columbia, and there were many. He burned both cities. His troops burned the Ursuline convent in Columbia, even though the superior appealed to him as a good Catholic not to do that thing. Sherman apologized for this.

Woodrow Wilson invented, or refurbished a myth which should be questioned right now. He said at the time that we were not at war with the German people, but only with a tyrannical government. As a successful political scientist, he had to know the falsity of this position. Whether we like it or not, any out-group is going to hold each one of us responsible for the deeds of our in-group. And is there not some basic justice in this? A government is a social institution, and no matter how much charisma it may claim, it is no more than that. Every social institution has only one major goal, the service of its constituent clientele. Achile Loria and other fascist philosophers may claim that the individual lives but a short time, while the state is all but eternal. The other end of the political spectrum finds Karl Marx saying that the individual is only a flash in the dark, and that the social class is long lived. Well, if flashes get together, they can cause quite a fire. The fact is that we are indeed not only responsible for our government but our subsystems as well. A certain part of the population can successfully be enslaved, enserfed, and peonized, but not the effective majority. Louis XIV is alleged to have said, *"L'état, c'est moi*, [The state, it is I] ," but you can look in the mirror and repeat the Sun King's words. It will do you little good on That Day to say, I am only a citizen, a civilian, a noncombatant. Harry Truman made his atomic shower to fall on the just and the unjust of Hiroshima and Nagasaki. The parts are responsible for the whole just as the head may be charged with the deeds of the hands.

Most students now think that General Yamashita was a decent person. When he took command at Manilla, his army and navy were out of control. Victorious armies can be merciful, but a beaten one never has been. The atrocities committed against defenseless Philippine civilians need not be reviewed here, but it is a rule of law, custom, and perhaps justice as well that authority can be delegated, but responsibility cannot be. The one responsible for the sack of the Shenandoah and the burning of Georgia was not a Grant or a Sherman, but Lincoln and the people who elected and reelected him. If there was abuse of civilians at My Lai, the responsibility lay not on the heads of little men like Calley and Medina but on those of presidents, cabinet secretaries, and generals whose names you know, and on yours, too. You never insisted that *they* be punished. In any event, The People of the United States arraigned General Yamashita before the bar, and hanged him.

We walk a two-way street. If the fingers and toes are responsible for the thoughts of the head, the brain is to blame for the misdeeds of the digits. A government cannot exist without willing workers. Pretorians in a police state may for a while rule over an unwilling mass, but a sullen, malingering lump of labor will thwart them in the end. Such a state must fall, and with it the prefect of the pretorian guard.

It must be mentioned at least, for it is true, that the peoples from which soldiers are drawn vary in the warlike spirit, and any state contemplating either an offensive or defensive war does pay some attention to this. Furthermore, a once military population can become peaceful and placid, while a harmless, nonaggressive one can change rapidly into a war machine. These may be rule-of-thumb observations, but they have some validity. We wish we knew the "whys" of the phenomenon better than we do.

Many professional analysts and observing laymen see certain regularities in the behavior of various folk which are probably the results of early childhood pressures and later institutional controls. The term "modal personality" has been applied to these regularities. Now the very term "modal" is a statistical one, representing averages, not identities. Surely the master statisticians agree that modes, medians, or any other attempts to describe a central tendency, are not studies in depth. They are hitters of high spots. Neither this nor any similar work says that all personalities in a social system are the same. The modal personality is what impresses the visitor upon his arrival in a strange culture. After he has lived there for a while he sees about the same range of personalities he knew at home. Certain emphases, however, remain which may strike him as exotic.

Nevertheless, certain biological "givens" which a child inherits are pressured to conform to what the group thinks useful to it. Personality and society are rather reciprocal concepts, for the interaction between the person and the socio-cultural environment is hardly debatable today. Now assume that the biological givens of the warlike Apache, Comanche, or Navaho children, and those of the bland, not distant Hopi, Zuni, and other pueblo-building folk, are fundamentally the same—and this is an assumption—infants of the former groups are pressured into glorifying fighting and are rewarded for conformity, while those of the pueblo folk are pressed into cooperative works of peaceful labor without which the group could not survive. The children of some societies are bombarded by folklore which glorifies the warrior. The young of others are molded by peaceful lore.

The modal personality of a folk is determined by the roles its members must play. Pressures exist either to succeed in war roles or in peaceful ones, and the person is rewarded when the self and others recognize successful performance. How can these be resisted? And now if there are those who cannot fulfill such roles, either through congenital inability or something in the early conditioning, they may be forced to become "dropouts" like the Plains berdaches. These men would not or could not go to war, so they dressed as women and performed female roles. Or to speak more harshly, nonconforming persons can be expelled, isolated, or killed. The bulk of the population may be dispersed but narrowly from this mode of personality, or it may have a wide deviation. If the dispersion is not wide, one will have either a very peaceful or very warlike people. Of course this spirit may vary from time to time, but it is this book's position that a government which wishes to wage war without the backing of a warlike general population is foolish. There are substitutes for this, but how effective they are in the long run is subject to some question.

It likewise seems that a social system, or subsystem within one, which has strong ideological convictions is given to self-sacrifice, altruism, and intense cooperativeness in war. Ideological dedication is not characteristic of the successful, but of those who would like to be, and those who have some hope of so becoming. The utterly depressed are sodden, seek only momentary survival, and are not terribly disappointed if this fails. They may be undernourished both physically and mentally, are nonresistant to indignity, and do not make even good armed slaves, or good slaves of any kind. Such people have little consciousness of the past, little hope for the future, and are not always aware that their present is miserable. The overfed, however, make poor soldiers. The ideologically dedicated have another time focus. They compose myths of a past which may be far from the historic truth, and will endure a hard present so that their descendants may have a good one. Their leaders can convince them that their opposition is utterly evil, justifying any cruelty against them, including extermination. If a sociopolitical ideology is worth the paper it is written on, it must make some pretension to infallibility, for that is the only concept for which dying is worthwhile. It makes little difference if the inspiring ideology is "true," or contains no more than half-truth. Indeed, perhaps it is better even that the successful and better informed recognize that it is ridiculous, for complete credence might lull them into a false sense of security.

The following term has been mentioned before, but it must be reconsidered with reference to the civilian's part in war. There is a possibility of serious sickness in the state. This has been called war fatigue, and it can constitute a real danger. Frustration due to conditions in either the internal or external relations system may cause or accentuate aggression. Failure in aggressive action, may result in deeper frustration. A short war and a merry could cleanse the social system of its internal dissatisfaction, provide recreation to those who find the bright face of danger appealing, and a glorious and socially approved death to some. There might be some economic advantage, too, for booty has an ancient appeal to both the warrior, his commanders, and his rulers. The danger here is that the more complicated the social system, culminating in the superstate, the longer wars stretch out in time, the more remote become the objectives for which they were undertaken, and the greater the casualties, deprivation, and frustration. Winning a short war is fun to many.

Even losing one, if it is not too devastating, can provide that martyr's crown which humanity loves so well. Such loss permits both men and social systems to project their own personal and political inadequacies on a victorious enemy. The higher primates, human or otherwise, enjoys novelty and abhors boredom. A long war is a bore, even when apparently slowly winning, and fatigue is almost inevitable.

The moral results of war fatigue are rarely mentioned, and never predicted. Either through the inspiration of the enemy or that of their governors, the citizens can be whipped to a level of self-sacrifice, devotion, and idealism which simply cannot be maintained. Either in victory or defeat, the human mass tends to revert to its normal moral level, and generally somewhat below it. Abraham Lincoln's almost holy war ended with the Grant administration, the Tweed ring, the robber barons of Wall Street. Woodrow Wilson's idealistic war to end war resulted in the Harding administration, the Tea Pot Dome, the rise of gang warfare, the millionaire bootlegger, and an unabashed decade of hedonism. The people wanted to forget it all. So did the English; so did the French. The Germans had the martyr's crown, and blamed these dubious laurels on everybody else.

And so we stand on the long beach of history and look down on the footprints. Some of them are glorious. Why deny that? Some of them represent profit, too, and that is undeniable. But who made those horrible marks in the sand? Many, or the most of them were made by us civilians, no matter which side we took. We cannot rationalize away those made by military boots, for we made or paid for the shoes.

FOOTNOTES AND REFERENCES

[1] John Williams, *The Other Battle Ground, the Home Fronts Britain and Germany, 1914-1918*, Chicago, Regnery, 1972.

SELECTED BIBLIOGRAPHY

Works Cited in the Text, or Recommended for Further Reading

Abel, Charles W., *Savage Life in New Guinea*, London, London Missionary Society, 1902.

Adcock, Frank E., *The Greek and Macedonian Art of War*, Berkeley, University of California Press, 1957.

———, *The Roman Art of War Under the Republic*, Cambridge, Harvard University Press, 1940.

Aginsky, Bernard Willard, *Kinship Systems and the Form of Marriage*, Menasha, American Anthropological Association, Memoir 45, 1935.

Air Force ROTC, *World Military Systems, OR 200*, Vol. III, Air University, 1964.

Aron, Raymond, *The Century of Total War*, Garden City, Doubleday and Company, 1954.

Atiya, Aziz Suryal, *The Crusade of Nicopolis*, London, 1934, Cited in Spaulding, Nickerson, and Wright, *op. cit.*

Aussaresses, F., *L'Armée byzantin à la fin du VIème siècle apres la Strategon de l'Empereur Maurice*, Paris, 1909.

Baldwin, Hanson, *Great Mistakes of the War*, New York, Harper and Brothers, 1950.

Bariffe, *Military Discipline: or the Yong Artillery Man*, London, printed for R. Mab by R. O. Fulton, 1639. (microfilm)

Barker, Stockbridge H., "Blueprint for Victory," *Army Logistician*, July-August, 1972.

Barret, Robert, *The Theorie and Praktike of Moderne VVars*, London, Printed by R. Fields for VV Ponsonby, 1958. (microfilm)

Barry, Gerrat, *A Discourse of Military Discipline*, by the vvidow of J. Mommart, Bruxells, 1634. (microfilm)

Belloc, Hilaire, *Poitier*, London, 1913. Cited in Spaulding, Nickerson, and Wright, *op. cit.*

Bretnor, Reginald, *Decisive War: A Study of Military Theory*, Harrisburg, Stackpole Books, 1969.

Burne, Lieutenant Colonel Alfred H., *The Art of War on Land*, with a Foreword by Major General J. N. Kennedy, Harrisburg, Stackpole Books, 1966.

Buettner-Janusch, John, *Origins of Man*, New York, John Wiley and Sons, Inc., 1966.

Callahan, North, *Royal Raiders: The Tories of the American Revolution*, Indianapolis, The Bobbs-Merrill Company, Inc., 1963.

Calvocoressi, Peter, and Wint, Guy, *Total War: The Story of World War II*, New York, Pantheon Books, 1972.

Carthy, J. D., and Ebling, F. J., *The Natural History of Aggression*, New York, Academic Press, 1964.

Churchill, Winston S., *The Second World War*, 6 vols., Boston, Houghton Mifflin, 1948-1954, Vol. I.

Clausewitz, Carl von, *Principles of War*, translated and edited by Hans Gaizke, Harrisburg, The Stackpole Company, Eleventh Printing, 1960.

Coats, Major General Wendell J., *Armed Force as Power*, New York, Exposition Press, 1966.

Creasy, Edward Shepherd, and Murray, Robert H., *Decisive Battles of the World*. Harrisburg, Military Service Publishing Company, 1943.

Dart, Raymond, "The Predatory Transition from Ape to Man," *International Anthropological and Linguistic Review*, Vol. 1. pp. 201-219.

DuPicq, Ardent, *Battle Studies: Ancient and Modern Battles*, trans. John N. Greely and Robert C. Cotton, New York, Macmillan Company, 1921.

Downs, James F., "Thoughts on Cavalry, Guerrilla Warfare and the Fall of Empires," Reprint, *Kroeber Anthropological Society*, Berkeley, Fall, 1960.

Dodge, Theodore A., *Great Captains*, Boston, Houghton Mifflin, 1889.

Durkheim, Émile, *The Rules of Sociological Method*, trans. S. A. Solvay and J. H. Mueller, ed. G. E. C. Cottin, Glencoe, Free Press, 1938.

Eccles, Henry E., *Logistics in the National Defense*, Harrisburg, Stackpole Company, 1959.

Fair, Charles, *From the Jaws of Victory: A History of Military Stupidity from Crassus to Westmoreland*, New York, Simon, 1971.
Ferguson, W. S., "The Zulus and the Spartans: A Comparison of Their Military Systems," *Harvard African Studies, Varia Africana*, Cambridge, Harvard University Press, 1918.
Frederick the Great, *Instructions for His Generals*, translated by Brigadier General Thomas R. Phillips, Harrisburg, The Stackpole Company, 1960.
Fried, Morton, Harris, Marvin, and Murphy, Robert, *War: The Anthropology of Armed Conflict and Aggression*, Garden City, The Natural History Press, 1968.
Forbes, Frederick A., *Dahomey and Dahomeans*, London, Longmans, Brown, Green and Longmans, cited in Herskovitz, *Dahomey*.
Fuller, J. F. C., *Armament and History*, New York, Charles Scribner's Sons, 1945.

Guiccardini, Francesco, *History of Italy*, *Book I*, translation of Fenton, London, cited in Spaulding, Nickerson, and Wright, *Warfare*.

Harlow, Harry F., "Basic Social Capacity of Primates," *Human Biology*, Vol. 31, 1959.
Herodotus, *The Struggle for Greece*, trans. Kenneth Cavander, with an Introduction by H. N. Porter, Greenwich, Fawcett Publications, 1962.
Herskovits, Melville J., *Dahomey: An Ancient West African Kingdom*, 2 vols., New York, Augustin, 1938.
Horn, Stanley F., *The Army of Tennessee*, Norman, University of Oklahoma Press, 1953.
Huntington, Samuel F., ed., *Changing Patterns of Military Politics*, New York, The Free Press of Glencoe, Inc., 1961.
———, *The Soldier and the State*, Cambridge, Belknap Press of Harvard Press, 1947.

Janowitz, Morris, *The Professional Soldier*, Glencoe, The Free Press, 1956.
Jomini, Antoine, *Jomini and His Summary of the Art of War, A Condensed Version*, Brigadier General J. D. Hittle, ed., Harrisburg, Stackpole Books, Fourth Printing, 1965.

Kingston-McCloughry, E. J., *The Direction of War*, New York, Frederick A. Praeger, 1955

Kinter, Colonel William R., and Scott, Harriet Fast, *The Nuclear Revolution in Soviet Military Affairs*, Norman, The University of Oklahoma Press, 1969.

Kluckhohn, Clyde, and Murray, Henry A., with the collaboration of Schneider, David M., *Personality in Nature, Society, and Culture*, Second Edition, Revised and Enlarged, New York, Alfred A. Knopf, 1953.

Liddel Hart, Sir Basil, *History of the Second World War*, New York, G. P. Putnam's Sons, 1970.

_____, *The Soviet Army 1946 to Present*, Harcourt, Brace and Company, 1956.

_____, *Thoughts on War*, London, Faber and Faber, Ltd., 1944.

Linebarger, Paul M. A. *Psychological Warfare*, Washington, Infantry Journal Press, 1948.

Long, E. B., with Long, Barbara, *The Civil War Day by Day: An Almanac 1861-1865*, with a foreword by Bruce Catton, Garden City, Doubleday and Company, Inc., 1971.

Machiavelli, Nicolo, *The Art of War*, 9th revised edition of the Ellis Farnsworth translation, Indianapolis, Bobbs-Merrill, 1965.

Mallin, Jay, ed., *The Strategy for Conquest: Communist Documents on Guerrilla Warfare*, Coral Gables, University of Miami Press, 1970.

Mao Tze-Tung, *Primer on Guerrilla Warfare*, New York, The New York Times Company, 1961.

Murdock, George Peter, *Social Structure*, New York, The Macmillan Company, 1949,

Norman, A., Vesey, B., and Pottinger, Don, *Warrior to Soldier, 449-1660*, London, Weidenfeldt and Nicholson, 1966.

Norman, James, ed., *The Evolution of Man's Capacity for Culture*, Detroit, Wayne State University Press, 1959.

Oman, Charles, *A History of the Art of War in the Middle Ages: 378-1485 A.D.* 2 vols., Boston, Houghton Mifflin Company, 1924.

Pfeiffer, John E., *The Emergence of Man*, Third Edition, New York, Harper and Row, Publishers, 1978.

Snelgrave, William, *A New Account of Some Parts of Guinea and the Slave Trade*, London, J. J. and P. Knapton, 1734, cited in Herskovits, *op cit.*

Spaulding, Oliver Lyman, Jr., Nickerson, Hoffman, and Wright, John Womack, *Warfare: A Study of Military Methods from the Earliest Times*, New York, Harcourt, Brace and Company, 1925.

Steward, George B., *Pickett's Charge: A Microhistory of the Final Attack at Gettysburg*, Greenwich, Connecticut, Fawcett Publications, Inc., 1963.

Sun-Tzu, *The Art of War*, translated by Samuel B. Griffith, Oxford, Clarendon Press, 1963.

Tacitus, Caius Cornelius, *Annales*.

_____, *Germania*.

Tactics and Techniques of Cavalry, 6th edition, Washington and Harrisburg, Military Service Publishing Company, 1935.

Turney-High, Harry Holbert, *Man and System: Foundations for the Study of Human Relations*, New York, Appleton-Century-Crofts, 1968.

_____, *Primitive War, Its Practice and Concepts*, Second Edition, with a foreword by David Rapoport, Columbia, University of South Carolina Press, 1971.

Thompson, Laura, *Towards a Science of Mankind*, New York, McGraw Hill Book Company, 1961.

Vagts, Alfred, *A History of Militarism*, New York, W. W. Norton and Company, 1937, and revised edition, Meridian Books, 1959.

Vegetius Renatus, Flavius, *L'Art de Chevallerie*, traduction du *Re Militari de Végèce*, par Jean de Meun, Paris, Firmin, Didot et Compagnie, 1897.

_____, *The Military Institutions of the Romans*, translated by Lieutenant John Clarke, Harrisburg, The Military Service Company, 1960.

Weigley, Russell F., *The American Way of War: A History of United States Military Strategy and Policy*, New York, Macmillan Publishing Company, 1973.

Williams, John, *The Other Battle Ground: The Home Fronts, Great Britain and Germany, 1914-1918*, Chicago, Regnery, 1972.

Yarborough, Brigadier General William F., "Special Warriors of the U. S. Army," *Airman*, November, 1961.

INDEX

Abstractions, tools and weapons, 22
Action patterns, 193
Aggression, origins of group, 22
Aginsky, Bernard Willard, 29
Alamein, Battle of, 59; Montgomery, 62
Alexander the Great, tactical principles, 54; organization, 240; alcoholism, 259; charisma, 264
Anatomy, Human, basis of tactics, 50; paramount nature, 129; weakness, 130; unaided, 138; energy converter, 195
Anglo-Saxons, 15
Archers, Archery (see Bow, Arrow), Crecy, 280
Armies, Regular, 117; despotisms first, 291
Arminius (Hermann), Teutoberg Forest, 251
Armor, 168; Greek heavy, 105, 169; Roman light, 109; mediaeval, 112; weakness, 135; chain and plate, 139, 168; helmet, 140; plate, 171
Artillery, vulnerability, 134, 157; shock power, 135; onager, 150; ballista, 150; *pot-de-feu* proto-cannon, 152; bombard, 154, 183; cannon, 155; early breech loaders, 155; mortar, 156, 158; mobility, 156; culverin, 157; recoil, 157; tractor drawn, 158; rifling, 158; breech loaders, 158; Dahlgren, 158; 75 mm, 159; aviation, 159, 317; atomic, 159, 317; function, 166; as soldiers, 243
Assyrian, mail, 169; castles, 175
Athens, military republic, 81; failure, 84
Attrition, 260; and Grant, 106
Augustus Caesar, 250, 297; charisma, 264; pretorian guard, 293
Authority, compared to power, 296
Aviation, 166; vulnerability, 134
Axe, War, club derivative, 139

Balaklava, Battle of, 145
Balance-Imbalance, function and dysfunction, 134
Barker, Stockbridge, 106
Base, Strategic, 50
Battle, part of war, 47
Battlements, Egyptian, 180
Bayonet, 119, 145
Belloc, Hilaire, 228
Berserk, Amok, tension release, 37
Booby Trap, Indonesian, 173
Borodino, Battle of, 121
Bradley, Omar, 215, 258
Bragg, Braxton, 70, 93
Bretnor, Reginald, on strategy, 48; 53, 62, 96, 102, 104, 132, 318
Bronze Age, swords, true warfare, 140; lance, 143; swords and helmet, 169
Bureaucracy, Bureaucratic, Roman military, 110; norms, 257; professional, 268; efficiency, 307, 317
Burne, Alfred, strategy and tactics compared, 47; interior and exterior lines, 50; on Sherman, 65, 256; on Hood, 254
Burnside, Ambrose, 122
Butler, Benjamin, 319
Byzantine, logistics, 202

Calorie Consumption, 193
Campaigns, military horizon and, 34
Cannibalism, 22; Melanesian, 38
Cannon, William, 18
Carnivores, 21, 26
Castles, obsolescence, 155; Assyrian, 175; mediaeval, 177; Norman, 178; donjon, 178; Chateau-Gaillard, 178, 181, 183, 186; Pierrefonds, 179, 180; Coucy-le-Chateau, 179, 180; crusader improvement, 179; Kerak-in-Moab, 180; portcullis, 181; Krak-des-Chevaliers, 181, 186; round towers, 182; Subeiba-beyond-Jordan, 182

330

Cavalry, Roman, 109; mediaeval, heavy, 111, 232; decline, 113; saber, 141; wheel lock, 160; cataphract mail, 170; renaissance, 172; Norman, 178; heavy, 232, 241
Centurions, Roman, 109
Charisma, priest-kingship, 175; military leaders, 264; monarchies, 275
Charles VII, King of France, 242
Chemical Warfare, Fire, Saladin and, 180, 187
China, military dictatorship, 88; overpopulation, 195; Public Security Forces, 305
Christmas, Lee, 258
Cities, fortification, 175; New Orleans, 176; impregnability, 176; modern vulnerable, 191; city state, Italian, 283; urban sprawl, 317
Civil Government (Polity, Politics, State), and true war, 27, 73; erosion of family, and, 30; and the military horizon, 75; state and, 75; origins and definition, 76; early city states, 80; residuary nature, 85; Leviathan, 86; imperium, 86, 89; totalitarian, 100; revival of Leviathan, 113; logistics, discipline, 229; military organization, 247; pretorian defense, 291; survival, 305
Civil War, logistics, 203; modern war, 216, 217
Civilians, total war, 94; psychological warfare, 101; balance of terror, 102; penetrability, 132; responsibility, 314; and noncombatants, 315; status, 316; treated as whole, 319
Civilization, characteristics, 79, 317; fortification, 174; early cities, 175; coal, 193
Clausewitz, Carl von, on strategy, 47, 214; on geography, 59; origin of war, 63; critical point, 65; on mass, 69; on pursuit, 70; charisma, 265
Coats, Wendell C., 47; origin of war, 63; defense, 186; leadership, 263; professionalism, 269
Combat, defined, 47; decision making character, 53; principles, 53
Combined Employment of All Forces, Principle of, 64
Command, 227
Commerce, state origins, 77; revival of royal absolutism, 115
Common Man, renaissance, 116

Community, invention of, 28; defined, 32
Concentration of Force, Principle of, primitive warriors, 44; explained, 65
Concerted Effort, Principle of, primitive warriors, 44; explained, 64
Cornwallis, Lord Charles, 217
Confederate Government, 204
Correct Formations, Principle of, primitive warriors; explained, 69
Crecy, Battle of, 280
Crisis, 18, 256, 296
Critical Point, importance, 57; shock and, 61
Cro-Magnon Man, 23; Neanderthal extermination, spears, 142; dart thrower, 151
Crusades, 179; logistics, 202; discipline, 235; failure, 241
Culture, thresholds, 33; universal, specialties, alternatives, 19; materialnonmaterial, 127; human weakness, 130
Curtain, Iroquois; Ashanti, 174; crusader, 180, 182
Curzon of Keddleston, Marquess, 84

Dark Age, Roman Survival, 113
Davis, Jefferson, 204
Defense, 168
Defensive, Principle of, 63; mobility loss, 131
Despotisms, bureaucratic, 84; nonwarlike civilians, 274; Middle American, 277; pretorianism, 306
Diminishing Returns, Law of, 20; bureaucracy, 90; Roman superstate, 111; defense, 131; armor, 169; morale, 256; great state, 307
Discipline, 227, 235; Durkheim on, 255
Division of Labor, 225, 228, 236
Dodge, Theodore, 265
Durkheim, Émile, repression, 75; authority, 255; anomie, 256

Economic Motivation, true war and, 40, 197; Roman, 110
Economy of Force, Principle of, 69
Edward the Black Prince, 280
Edward III, King of England, 280
Egyptian, fortification, 175; organization, 238; defenses, 274
Eisenhower, Dwight D., failure to pursue, 70; federalized National Guard, 87; at the Elbe, 97; Arkansas trouble, 308
Energy Resources, state, 84

Equilibrium (see Homeostasis), 18; human and infrahuman, 28; imbalance of power, 104
Eskimo, 19; subsistence anxiety, 41; archery, 151
Exploitation of Victory, Principle of, primitive warriors, 44; explained, 69

Falchion and Glaive, 141
Family, extended, 21; nuclear, 22, 29f; primate, 27; fighting unit, 29f; squad and company, 30, 226
Feudalism, rise of, 82, 112, 177, 241, 242, 278, 280
Fighting and combat compared, 47
Fire and Movement, Principle of, primitive warriors, 43; explained, 64; Roman, 109
Firearms, renaissance, 116; shock, 135, 153f; hand culverin, 160; arbalest, 160; matchlock, 160; arquebus, 160; wheel lock, 161; pistol, 161; musket, 161; flintlock, 162; rifle, 162; multibarrel, 163; mitrailleuse, 163; Gatling, 163; Maxim, 164; carbine, 164; Thompson, 164
Firepower, shock, 135, 317
Force, ritualized violence, 53, 133; weakness, 306
Fortification (see Castles), 172; entrenchment, 173; Vauban type, 184; improved cannon, response, 184; attack on, 183; Eben Emael, 186; siege, 187; Niagara, 190; Corregidor, 190; Monroe, 190; Fisher, North Carolina, 190; Delaware, 190
Frederick the Great, surprise, 51; discipline, 228; personality, 259; love, 265
French, 15
Fuller, J. F. C., tactical principles, 54
Function, Functional, manifest and latent dysfunction, 20; universality, 133

Gage, Thomas, 120
Garthoff, Raymond L., on Soviet doctrine, 49
Gates, Horatio, scapegoat, 253
Genghis Khan, organization, 241
German, troops in America, 100, 286; tanks, 149; Pennsylvania gunsmiths, 162; plate armor, 171; slave labor, 195; sabotage, 215; ancient discipline, 231; national army, 243; Teutoberg Forest, battle, 250
Gifting, prestige and, 41
Grant, Ulysses Simpson, objective, 62; total war, 94; mass-man, 121; Vicksburg, 205; Shenandoah Valley, 205; depression, 259; affection for, 265
Grasse, Comte de, Yorktown, 98, 217
Great Britain, in America, 103; troop carrying liners, 204
Greeks, 15; Trojan War, 80; logistics, 198; nation-at-arms, fighting methods, 105; spears, 143; armor, 169; classical logistics, 200; organization, 238; mercenaries, 276
Grenade, 149
Groups, primary and secondary, 19; survival, 74
Guerrillas, 316
Guicciardini, Francesco, 284
Guilt, in-group slaying and, 22; warfare and, 36
Gunpowder, 155
Gustavus Adolphus, King of Sweden, artillery, 157

Hadrian, Emperor, 111
Hastings (Senlac), Battle of, 113
Hebrews, ancient logistics, 199
Helm, Helmet, Bronze Age, 169; mediaeval, 171
Herodotus, 236
Hessians, ancient, 23
High Middle Age, 179; Franco-Burgundian revolution, 181
Hitler, Adolf, total war, 94; Polish invasion, 95; propaganda, 100; Russian prisoners, 287
Hobbes, Thomas, on war, 47; Leviathan, 86
Holism, 17
Homeostasis (see Equilibrium), 18, 314; violence and, 37; normative system, 74; aging, 133
Hondschoote, Battle of, 120
Hood, John Bell, Atlanta campaign, 50; Battle of Ezra Church, 54, 65; scapegoat, 254
Hoplites, Greek, 105, 238
Horizons, Thresholds, 26; military, 33; organization, 236
Howe, William Viscount, failure to pursue Washington, 70
Hunting, man-hunting, 21, 23, 26; and primitive war, 27
Hyksos, 275

INDEX

Iberall, A. S., abstract thought, aggression, 22
Incest Tabu, 29
Indian, American, 15; Plains *coup*, 22, 39; Iroquois League and Natchez, true war, 27, Flathead, 37; Crazy Dog fraternity, 37; military aristocracy, 39; food raiding, 41; Plains police societies, 76; Cherokee priest-kings, 79, 225; Incan Empire, 87; North Pacific Coast war clubs, 138; Great Plains lances, 143; Plains archery, 151; blowguns, 153; Iroquois armor, 169; Aztec armor, 169; Iroquois palisades, 174; portland cement, 182; Incan forts, 182; logistics, 196; training, 226
Infantry, Greek heavy, 105, 144, 169; Roman heavy, 109, 144, 168; baroque and rococo, 117; eighteenth century, 134; mediaeval, 144; 233; renaissance rebirth, 172; Turkish, 298
Initiative, paramount character, 57
Institutions, defined, 32; Roman lack of integration, 111
Intellectual Class, 99
Intelligence, Estimate, 68
Intelligence, Principle of, primitive warriors and, 43; and hunting, 59
Integrity of Tactical Units, Principle of, 66
Interaction-Transaction, 19; tools and, 22; tactics and, 53; tactical units, 67; warfare as, 127; modern secondary, 130
International Law, Grotius, 116; conquest, 314; civilian status, 318
Intervention, foreign in revolutions, 98
Irrigation, origins of state, 76; pretorians, 291

Jackson, Andrew, 60, 165
Jackson, Thomas (Stonewall), surprise, 57
Japan, failure to exploit, 93
Joan of Arc, 115, 242; charisma, 264
John I, King of England, 278
Johnson, Lyndon, psychological warfare, 101
Jomini, Antoine Henry, surprise, 57; logistics, 192

Kataphract, Cataphract, see heavy cavalry
Kinship, and war, 27, 28; affinal and consanguineal, 30; clans, moieties, 31; King Servius Tullius and Roman military, 109

Kluckhohn, Clyde, and Murray, Henry, 264
Kutuzov, Michael, 121

Law, paramount character, 74
Law of Nations (see International Law) state of war legitimate, 53
Leadership, 256
Lee, Robert Edward, Gettysburg, 56, 60, 65, 93, 194; terrain, 59; personality, 258; illness, 258; charisma, 264
Legion, changes in Roman, 108, 110
Leisure Class, soldiers as, 267
Leopold III, King of the Belgians, scapegoat, 253
Liddell Hart, Sir Basil, 96
Limited War, causes, 92; Confederacy, 93; Viet Nam, 93; mediaeval, 114
Lincoln, Abraham, Leviathan and, 89; responsibility for atrocities, 320
Linton, Ralph, 19
Literacy, and true war, 27
Logistics, and the military horizon, 33; revolution, 197; theory and principles, 206
Longstreet, James, Gettysburg, 65, 93, 194, 253; 260
Loyalty, Class, 98

MacArthur, Douglas, unlimited war, 93
Macedon, 107
Machicolations, Egyptian and Assyrian, 175; crusader castles, 180
Machine Gun, vulnerability, 134; Zulu defeat, 143; mitrailleuse, 163; Gatling, 163; submachine gun, 164
Mail, 169; disadvantage, 171; Korea, 172
Marriage, a sociological invention, 28, 29
Mass-man Armies, Persian, 107; modern, 120, 122; training, 153, 234
Maurice, Emperor, organization, 240
McClellan, George Brinton, 265
Meade, George Gordon, 56, 59, 70
Melanesian Warfare, prisoner torture, 37
Mercenaries, defined, 272; renaissance, 115; Swiss, 273; early states, 274; Libyan, 276; Toltec, 277; knights errant, 278; Hundred Year's War, 279; Crecy, 280; fourteenth century pay, 281; condottiere, 284; Germans in American Revolution, 286; Confederate, 287; American, 287; French Foreign Legion, 288; U. S.

334   THE MILITARY

in southeast Asia, 288; Europeans in Africa, 289
Militarism, 269
Military Crest, 59
Military Governor, rise of, 318; American, 319
Military Religious Orders, Hospitallers, Templars, Teutonic Knights, 179; Templar castle, Kerak-in-Moab, 181; Hospitaller castle, Krak des Chevaliers, 182
Militia, Greek and Roman, 108
Mobility, Principle of, primitive warriors and, 43; 60
Mobility, weapons, 135
Montgomery, Bernard Law, objective, 62
Murdock, George Peter, 29
Musket, War in Lace, 117
Myth, 317

Napoleon, objective, 62; observance of security, 63; critical point, 65; planning, 67; upward mobility, 121; the paramount human, 129; sugar monopoly, 195; battalions, 245; illness, 258; depression, 259; an intellectual, 267
Nation-at-Arms, 104
National Army, English, 423, 281; American, 243; German, 243; rise of, 286
Neanderthal Man, 21; speech and, 23; extermination of, 142
Negro, 16; porterage, 195; West African logistics, 199; kingships, 233; Dahomean organization, 237
Neutrals, 50, 217
Nickerson, Hoffman, 120
Noncombatants, and civilians, 315; status, 316
Normandy Campaign, 215
Normans, 178
Norms, manners, morals, law, 256

Objective, Principle, of submilitary combat and, 42, 56; 62
Offense-Defense Cycle, 135, 157, 166, 168
Officers, 118; training, 227; American, 233; Prussian, 265; professionalism, 266
Ogburn, William Fielding, cultural lag, 85, 127, 206
Organization, survival, 229; military, 235; Medes and Persians, 236; French, Charles VII, 242; companies, 243; regiments, 243; battalions, 245; brigades, 245; divisions, 246; field armies, 246; personal freedom, 247

Pakenham, Sir Edward, 119, 163
Patton, George, 128; sword, 142; Third Army, 215; personality, 258; charisma, 265
Pekin Man, 21
Persian, mounted archers, 170; logistics, 200, 218; Medes, 236; organization, 239
Personality, 223, 229, 257; charisma, 264; modal, 321
Peter the Great, Tsar of Russia, 301
Petroleum, 194
Phalanx, Greek, 105, 238; Chaldean, 169
Pickett, George, 194, 263
Plans, Principle of, primitive warriors lack, simplicity, 67
Plank, Ewart C., 215
Polity, see Civil Government
Polynesian, war club, 138, 140; armor, 169
Power, compared to authority, 296
Pretorians, first troops, 79; Roman state, 111; Roman, 292; Turkish janissaries, 297; mamelukes, 301; Russian strieltzi, 302; Cossack cavalry, 302, 306; papal Swiss Guards, 302; French Swiss Guards, 302; French Republican Guards, 302; Latin American, 303; U.S. National Guard, 304; English Brigade of Guards, Yeomen of the Guard, 304; Irish Constabulary, 304; Sikhs, 305; Canadian mounted police, 305; Chinese Security Forces, 305; role, 307; quality, 307; social distance, 308
Priest-Kingship, state origins, 78; Greek and Roman, 108; fortification, 175; Cherokee, 225
Primates, Primatology, 20; families, 27; anatomy and tactics, 52; rage and offensive, 56; groups, 73; rank status, 235
Prisoners, Confederate, 101. Fort Delaware, 190, 287; humane treatment, 286
Professionalism, Roman, 109; baroque and rococo, 117; Italian condottieri, 284, pretorian, 309
Projectiles, problems, 143; grenade, 149; slingers, 149; onager, 150; ballista, 150; dart thrower-atlatl, 150; arrow-bow, 151; arrow record,

152; crossbow, 153; blowgun, 153; bombard, 154; cannon, 155; shell-bomb, 156; canister, 157; bullet-shaped shell, 158; fixed shells, 158; rocket, 165
Propaganda, 99, 101
Primitive War, defined, 26
Protection, weapons, 135; incomplete, 137
Psychological Warfare, 99, 315

Railroads, logistic, 205
Rapoport, David, 104
Renaissance, warfare, 115, 183
Republics, diversity, 81; mediaeval military, 82; death of English kings, 83
Reserve, von Arnim and Haig at Ypres, 69; Eisenhower and von Rundstet, 69
Revenge Motive, 39
Revolutions, sociological, 27; political, 73; wars, 97. American and French, 97; Russian, 97; cavalry, 111; penetrative, 131; engineering, 172; logistic, 192, 197; Germans in the American, 286
Richard Lion Heart, 178, 183, 187
Richelieu, Armand du Plessis, Cardinal de, logistics, 203
Rites of Passage, combat as, 40
Rochambeau, Comte de, Yorktown, 98, 187, 219, 165
Rome, senatorial republic, 81; success, 84; Caesardom, 88; internal decay, 91; origins, 107; military history, 108; regal, 108; short sword, 141; armor, 170; unwalled, 176; logistics, 201; discipline, 231; makework, 235; Greek War, 240; pretorian prefect, 291; popular conservatism, 297; military governor, 318
Rommel, Erwin, 214; charisma, 265
Rundstedt, Marshal von, invasion, 60; faulty decision, 214
Russo-German War, 48, 218

Sacrifice, Human, economic motive, 42
Scarcity, 102
Security, Principle of, primitive warriors, 44; explained, 63; Roman, 108
Senatorial (Patrician) Military Republic, succeeds kings, 82; Greek, 105; Greek and Roman, 108
Sexual Reproduction, and primate aggressive-defensive groups, 28

Sherman, William Tecumseh, Atlanta campaign, 50, 65, 255; total war in South Carolina, 94; Georgia, 205; personality, 257; burning of Columbia, 319
Shield, 168
Situation, Estimate of, steps to determine, 68
Slavery, energy use, 195; pool, 318
Smuts, Jan Christian, 18; systems, 64
Socrates, as a soldier, 267
Social Climbing, warfare and, 38; gifting as, 41; renaissance, 116
Social Science, warfare as, 127
Soldiers, different from warriors, 225
Soviet Union, Stalinism, 88; leadership, 257
Spain, organization, 244
Spaulding, Oliver Lyman, tactical principles, 55
Spear, club development, 142; Cro-Magnon, 142; American Pleistocene, 143; mediaeval lance, 144; baroque pike, 144
Spencer, Herbert, number of wars, 75; despotism, 86
Speech, origin, 23
Staff, bureaucratic, 67
State, see Civil Government
Stalin, Josef, German invasion, 96; Fifth Column, 98; artillery, 167; logistics, 218
Stirrup, 112, 144
Strategy, defined, 34, 47; Normandy invasion, 214
Submilitary Combat, tactics and, 24
Sufficient Numbers (Mass), Principle of, 69
Sumerians, early states, 77; drilled troops, 143; Chaldean, 169
Sumner, William Graham, normative system, 74
Sun Tzu, deception, 57
Superstates, 84
Surprise, Principle of, primitive warriors and, 42, 57
Swiss, mercenaries, 273
Sword, club derivative, 140
Symbol, Symbolization, 21
System, 17

Tacitus, Caius Cornelius, Hessians, 231; makework, 235; Teutoberg Forest battle, 252
Tactics, as social science, 23, 53; principles of, 24, 56; military horizon and, 35; changelessness of, 35; anatomical base of, 50

Tank, vulnerability, 134
Terrain, Principle of Utilization of, 59
Teutoberg Forest, Battle of, 252
Thermopylae, Battle of, 60
Thompson, Laura, 131
Tiberius, Emperor, pretorian guard, 293
Tools and Weapons, abstract thought and, 22
Total War, 94; blitzkrieg, 95
Training, military horizon and, 34; poor, 120; archery, 153; 226, 234
Transportation, 195; American Union, 204
Treason, Chicane, as siege method, 185
Trench Warfare, 190

Unarmed Soldier, as fighter, 138
United States, decision in World War II, 48; rise of Leviathan, 89; total war, 94; World War I, 59; brigandine in Korea, 172; Spanish War logistics, 202
Unlimited War, 94

Varus, Publius Quintilius, Battle of Teutoberg Forest, 250
Vauban (Sebastian Le Prestre), Marshal de, 117, 180; siege methods, 119, 185; age of, 183; character, 183
Vegetius, tactical principles, 54; terrain, 59
Viet Nam, 215
Vikings, see Normans, 177
Violence, 22; aggressive-defensive potential, 27; as tension release, 36; as battle, 53; permeability, 133; pretorian, 309
Vulnerability, security, 63; universal, 132, basic, 168; modern increasing, 215

War, contrasted with warfare, 18, 46; twin birth with state, 73; limited, 92; unlimited, 94; total, 94; revival, 115, 316; blitzkrieg, 95; Phoney, 96; indecisive, 96, 318; civil and revolutionary, 97; psychological, 99, 315; Greek limited, 107; Roman unlimited, 108; baroque limited, 117; in Lace, 117; democratic, 121; modern unlimited and total, 121
War Club, 138
Warfare, 19; contrasted with war, 46
War Fatigue, psychological warfare, 101; Roman, 111; renaissance, 116, 322
Washington, George, personality, 258
Weapons, Neolithic invention of, 22; secondary to humans, 130; penetrability, 132; classification, 135; offense-defense cycle, 136
Wellington, Duke of, Peninsular campaign, 70; personality, 258
Wiese, Leopold von, 256
Wilson, Woodrow, indecisive war, 96; Siberian campaign, 205; World War I, 208; myth of civilian, 319
Wittfogel, Karl, state origins, 77; hydraulic civilizations, 78; Oriental despotism, 86
World War, mobility loss in World War I, 60; World War II airforce, 230

Yorktown Campaign, 187; 217
Yamashita, General, Manilla, 320

Zulu, AmaZulu, 27; war machine, 80; spearmen, 143; logistics, 200; discipline, 229, 233, organization, 237